JEWS IN THE SOVIET UNION

The USSR, 1953–1967

International USSR Border
Borders of the Soviet Republics
Bering Sea
60°N
100°E
120°E
OCEAN
140°E
Magadan
SIBERIA
RUSSIA
Sea of Okhotsk
OCIALIST REPUBLICS
PACIFIC OCEAN
JEWISH AUTONOMOUS REGION
Birobidzhan
Khabarovsk
140°W
Lake Baikal
Irkutsk
Vladivostok
40°N
Sea of Japan
MONGOLIA
KOREA
160°W
CHINA
0
500 Miles
0
600 Kilometers
LUCIDITY INFORMATION DESIGN, LLC

THE EUGENE SHVIDLER PROJECT FOR THE HISTORY OF THE JEWS OF THE SOVIET UNION

JEWS IN THE SOVIET UNION

A HISTORY

GENERAL EDITORS: GENNADY ESTRAIKH AND DAVID ENGEL

Volume 1:
Revolution, Civil War, and Consolidation, 1917–1930
Elissa Bemporad

Volume 2:
Dictatorship and Terror, 1930–1939
Deborah Yalen and Arkady Zeltser

Volume 3:
War, Conquest, and Catastrophe, 1939–1945
Oleg Budnitskii, David Engel, Gennady Estraikh, and Anna Shternshis

Volume 4:
Post-War Hopes and Continued Terror, 1945–1953
Anna Shternshis

Volume 5:
After Stalin, 1953–1967
Gennady Estraikh

Volume 6:
The Final Years, 1967–1991
Zvi Gitelman

JEWS IN THE SOVIET UNION
A HISTORY

AFTER STALIN
1953–1967

Volume 5

GENNADY ESTRAIKH

NEW YORK UNIVERSITY PRESS
New York

NEW YORK UNIVERSITY PRESS
New York
www.nyupress.org

Please contact the Library of Congress for Cataloging-in-Publication data.
ISBN: 9781479819461 (hardback)
ISBN: 9781479819492 (library ebook)
ISBN: 9781479819485 (consumer ebook)

New York University Press books are printed on acid-free paper, and their binding materials are chosen for strength and durability. We strive to use environmentally responsible suppliers and materials to the greatest extent possible in publishing our books.

Manufactured in the United States of America

10 9 8 7 6 5 4 3 2 1

Also available as an ebook

With deep gratitude to Eugene Shvidler,
whose generosity made possible the research and
preparation of this NYU study.

CONTENTS

FOREWORD TO
JEWS IN THE SOVIET UNION: A HISTORY

DAVID ENGEL AND GENNADY ESTRAIKH

This volume is part of a six-volume comprehensive history of Jews and Jewish life in the Soviet Union, from the establishment of the Russian Soviet Republic in late 1917 through to the Union's formal dissolution on 8 December 1991. The project was launched in 2015 under the auspices of New York University's Global Network for Advanced Research in Jewish Studies, thanks to a major gift from Eugene Shvidler. It has been carried out by an international team of scholars—authors, consultants, archivists, and librarians—based in North America, Israel, and Europe, including several former Soviet states.

The scholars have worked to fill a major need in the study of both Soviet and Jewish history. The prominence of Jews among Soviet elites during certain intervals in the USSR's seven decades, along with pressures to remove them from elite ranks during others, has long been noted as a significant factor in Soviet politics, but the extent of such prominence, pressure, and significance has yet to be explored in detail. Similarly, the Jews of the Soviet Union, though numbering about 20 percent of the world's Jewish population for most of the twentieth century and ranking second or third among Jewish communities defined by geopolitical boundaries, have yet to be incorporated significantly into a broader Jewish historical narrative.

Reasons for both phenomena can be found in the very histories from which Soviet Jews have been largely absent. For Soviet ideologues and policymakers, the Jews of their country resisted easy categorization. From a Marxist point of view, their status was confusing. Were they a fully-fledged nation? If so, how were Soviet Jews connected to Jews elsewhere in the world, including Palestine, later Israel? Without a clear ideological lens through which to regard them, certain aspects of their situation in the USSR could not be readily explained. How, for example, to account simultaneously for their prominent role in many domains of Soviet life, most notably during the 1920s and 1930s, on the one hand, and for the unofficial but universally evident restrictions imposed, increasingly from the late 1940s, on their educational choices and career paths, on the other? How did it happen that Jews, many of whom had once been enthusiastic supporters of the Soviet way, sought to leave the country in growing numbers during its final three decades? Why were Jews allowed, at various times and with varying degrees of willingness or reluctance, to emigrate, whereas the vast majority of Soviet citizens were not afforded a similar possibility? The state's guardians preferred to leave such questions in repose. As a result, historians living in the Soviet Union (and, after 1945, in the Soviet-dominated countries of eastern Europe as well) were strongly discouraged from taking up such an ideologically treacherous subject.

For historians of the Jews, Soviet Jewry presented a different set of anomalies. The Soviet state purported to act in accordance with a unique set of principles that, its leaders and advocates promised, would offer Jews greater physical safety, material security, and psychological peace of mind than would any alternative set of principles guiding other contemporary states or political movements, including those associated with liberal democracy and with Zionism. The principles' uniqueness made the USSR seem an outlier in the political history of modern Jewry. Moreover, in the highly charged atmosphere of the Cold War, those principles became associated with forces hostile to the countries in which most historians of the Jews resided. Consequently, the handful of Western scholars who displayed sustained interest in Soviet Jewish history tended to investigate the negative, tragic aspects of that history that eventually impelled many Jews to want to depart the country, leaving more quotidian, less dramatic, less controversial, and more successful parts of the story largely in the dark.

Lack of sources for studying those parts of the story compounded the problem. As long as the Soviet Union existed, it severely restricted Western scholars' access to relevant documents in Soviet libraries and archives.

Only after its demise did scholars begin to grasp the breadth and depth of the materials they had once been unable to consult. During the three decades that have passed since then, many of those materials have been brought to light. Moreover, the passage of time has been both long enough to offer researchers sufficient distance for evaluating this massive documentary record and short enough to allow them still to benefit from the living memories of the large number of Jews who directly experienced the Soviet regime. Those memories have been and continue to be tapped by several large-scale oral history projects. Thus a critical mass of new source material appears to have made possible a synthesis of the Soviet Jewish past with a degree of accuracy, inclusion, understanding, and refinement unachievable even a generation ago. That is the outcome the current project has sought.

The project's findings suggest that the results of the Soviet Union's approach to matters of Jewish concern and the attitudes of different parts of the heterogeneous Soviet Jewish population toward the Soviet Union were mixed. At first many Jews were great supporters of the new regime that replaced the oppressive tsars. Yet it was not long before Soviet Jews faced the dismantling of their religious life. Some aspects of Jewish culture were suppressed, while others were promoted. For some Jews, these features of life under the Soviets were profoundly distressing, for others less so. Some found ways to maintain certain religious and cultural practices despite official disapproval. At the same time, the regime pursued policies that helped some Jews achieve Soviet-style prosperity and reach the highest levels of Soviet society, though often simultaneously heightening tensions between Jews and some of their non-Jewish neighbors. After 1941 the Soviet Union fought the Nazis and sheltered Jews who had escaped to the East, with Soviet Jews playing a significant role in the war effort. Shortly thereafter, however, the regime intensified its own repression of the sharpened Jewish consciousness that World War II had aroused. Even under those conditions, Soviet Jews developed multiple mechanisms for excelling in this difficult environment and for preserving a Jewish identity. Some Jews became dissidents, campaigning for the right to emigrate and contributing to the Soviet regime's eventual downfall. Other Jews strove to prosper within the Soviet system, despite difficult circumstances. Some of them were more successful than others.

Accordingly, the authors of the six volumes have tried to present the multiple, changing situations in which Soviet Jews found themselves over seven decades and more as much as possible through the eyes of all the various actors in those situations, Jewish and non-Jewish alike. In doing so, their aim has been to help readers understand how the various ways in which different groups of Jews adjusted to the policies and practices of the Soviet regime at different times could make sense to their members and how the changing policies that the regime adopted at different times could make sense to the regime itself in changing contexts. They have not sought to take sides in the debates of the times they explore, to evaluate the actions or attitudes of the participants, or to identify heroes and villains. Instead they have endeavored to fathom and to represent an intricate, multifaceted history as fully and fairly as available documents and available space allow.

EDITORS' NOTE

In this book, places are referred to by the official names that were in force at the time under discussion: hence, for instance, Kuibyshev, not Samara; Leningrad, not St. Petersburg; Frunze, not Bishkek. Individuals' names are rendered as the individuals were accustomed to Romanize them. Absent evidence of preference, names are transliterated according to the language in which the person wrote most frequently. Languages using Cyrillic alphabets are generally transliterated according to Library of Congress standards, except for omission of diacritics and of some hard and soft signs. Yiddish is transliterated according to the system adopted by the YIVO Institute for Jewish Research, Hebrew according to an internal scheme that aims for a reasonable balance between the most common orthographically and phonetically based systems currently in use.

INTRODUCTION

The Soviet epoch had its beginning on the night of 6–7 November 1917, when the Vladimir Lenin–led Bolsheviks, who soon rebranded themselves as Communists, took power in Russia. The revolution, known as the October Revolution according to the Julian calendar used in Russia before 1918, drastically changed the course of history in that part of the world and, directly or indirectly, across the globe. The epoch came to its end seventy-four years later, in December 1991, when the Soviet Union, the colossal polity born of the 1917 revolution, ceased to exist.

The period covered in this book starts in 1953, almost exactly in the middle of the Soviet epoch, and ends in 1967. The choice of the bracketing years is not random—the period is bookended at one end by the death of the brutal dictator Joseph Stalin and at the other end by the Six-Day War in the Middle East. Both history-changing events deeply affected Soviet Jews, who numbered over two million and comprised at that point the second-largest, after the American, Jewish population in the world. The period under discussion became a prelude to the years when contemplation of, or practical steps toward, emigration to Israel or elsewhere began to play an increasing role in various aspects of their lives.

The Soviet Union, or in its full name the Union of Soviet Socialist Republics (USSR), was built as a multinational country, containing fifteen (until 1956 sixteen) union republics, each with a titular ethnic group, or "nation" in Soviet terminology: Russian, Ukrainian, Belorussian, Lithuanian, Georgian, Uzbek, and so on. The territory of the USSR covered a sixth of the earth's surface and was divided into eleven time zones.

Geographically and culturally, the republics were conventionally grouped into: Slavic—Russia, Ukraine, and Belorussia (renamed Belarus in 1991); Baltic—Lithuania, Latvia, and Estonia; Caucasian—Georgia, Azerbaijan, and Armenia; Central Asian—Uzbekistan, Kazakhstan, Tajikistan, Turkmenia (Turkmenistan), and Kirgizia (Kyrgyzstan); and the "ungrouped" republic of Moldavia (Moldova).

The vast Asian part of the Russian republic, east of the Ural Mountains, is known as Siberia. While it had been widely used by the czarist and later Soviet regimes as a place for incarcerating and exiling political or criminal prisoners, many areas with a relatively moderate climate enjoyed agricultural and industrial development. Small Jewish communities appeared in the area in the nineteenth century, and many more Jews settled there during the Soviet period.

Moscow, the capital of both the USSR and the Russian republic, often figures in publications as a metonym for the Soviet regime. Another widely used metonym is "the Kremlin," the fifteenth-century-built fortified complex in the center of Moscow that housed the central offices of the Soviet state apparatus and, until 1953, apartments for the regime's top figures. As a symbol of the post-Stalinist change, the Kremlin, or at least some of its areas, became open to the public in 1955. The "Iron Curtain" has also been overused as a term describing the geopolitical divide of the Cold War.

Some of the union republics contained ethnic territories with a lower, officially *autonomous*, status: republics or regions of various denominations. The status of the ethnic territory effectively determined the status of the corresponding ethnic group and its culture. The union republics were entitled to have many paraphernalia of an independent state, such as a parliament, called Supreme Soviet, a full system of education in the national language, an academy of sciences with its research centers, and even a version of the legal system. Two of the republics, Ukraine and Belorussia, were members of the United Nations. The ethnic groups with territories of a lower status or those without a specific attachment to the territorial patchwork had fewer entitlements.

Soviet Jews had a token ethnic territory at one of the lowest levels: the Jewish Autonomous Region, with the administrative center in the town of Birobidzhan, situated in the Far East of Siberia on the border with China. In fact, however, the vast majority of the Jews had nothing to do with the

Siberian "titular territory" and lived in the European part of the country. While the Soviet territorial patchwork reflected, with some precision, the historical settlement of ethnic groups, the Jewish Autonomous Region had been established ex nihilo by an arbitrary decision of the government.

Nikita Khrushchev, the first secretary (leader) of the Communist Party of the Soviet Union from 1953 and also chairman of the Council of Ministers (prime minister) from 1958, was the figure, rather ungainly in appearance and manner, who embodied almost the entire period under discussion. His ousting in October 1964 generally did not engender an immediate turn in Soviet policy toward the Jews, which came after the June 1967 war in the Middle East, beyond the time frame of this book. Previously Stalin's faithful lieutenant, Khrushchev, who was reform-minded and not particularly cruel by nature, presided over the process of shedding the most objectionable aspects of the regime. Nonetheless, whereas the practice of mass repressions had disappeared, in place remained the system of constant oversight and control that permeated Soviet society. The secret police in its 1954 reincarnation as the Committee for State Security, known by its abbreviated Russian name KGB, continued to act as the ubiquitous apparatus of surveillance and repressive power.

With Khrushchev at the helm, the country became more open to the world. Economic and social reforms of the 1950s and 1960s had improved the lives of Soviet people. This was a "liberal" period, at least on the Soviet scale, despite the fact that the fundamentals of the regime remained the same: the undemocratic rule of the Communist Party's apparatus with a facade of *soviets*, or councils, of all levels, from local to central, effectively appointed rather than elected. Every organization—from trade unions to associations of stamp collectors—and every publication remained under tight control of the Party and KGB overseers, leaving no legally permitted space for civil society initiatives.

A poorly educated person and a devoted adherent of Marxism-Leninism, Khrushchev, like many Soviet—and not only Soviet—zealots of the time, sincerely believed that mankind was destined to build Communism, a prosperous egalitarian society populated by conscientious and driven people. Moreover, the belief of that time was that Communism was not just a blueprint for future generations. Rather, the first phase of Communism, namely the construction of its material-technical basis, could be reached very soon, as early as the 1980s. The positive dynamic of the Soviet economy in the 1950s (the GDP grew twice as fast as in the USA) and its achievements in space technology (the first Sputnik in 1957 and the first man in space in 1961) gave a boost to the dream, which, however, as early as the 1960s proved to be a pipe dream.

Meanwhile, the Kremlin strategists decided that it was necessary to remove remnants of various forms of human thinking and activity that hindered the process of constructing the ideal world. People with proclivities to individualism, profiteering, loafing, nationalism, and religiosity were targeted by propaganda or even legal actions. The state had never lost completely the taste for achieving ends by using repressive means, which also affected many Jewish citizens.

Many books have been written in various languages and genres about, on the one hand, problems and obstacles that Jews faced in the Soviet Union and, on the other hand, remarkable cultural, academic, industrial, military, and government careers made by thousands of them in these same years. The climate of what is known as the Cold War—the ideological confrontation between the camps led by the United States and the Soviet Union—could not leave unaffected the corpus of writings on Soviet Jewish history. In recent years, however, declassified archives, in the former Soviet Union and the West, have opened new avenues for research. This does not mean, of course, that attempts to understand how Jews lived in the post-Stalinist Soviet Union do not encounter difficulties.

First, there is the issue of finding the right focus or, better, foci, especially as there was no typical "Soviet Jew." Economic, cultural, social, historical, and linguistic peculiarities divided various segments of the Jewish population. This meant, in particular, that they could rather differently understand what was beneficial or detrimental for them. Unfortunately, the paper trail left by, or about, a Moscow intellectual eclipses, as a rule, what a historian can find about a teacher or an engineer, and even more so about a watchmaker who continued to live in a former shtetl in Ukraine, Belorussia, or Moldavia. As a result, it is hard to avoid an imbalance between describing "town" and "gown."

Second, many published and unpublished materials are of questionable reliability, because of the bias or insufficient competence of those who committed them to paper or narrated them for recording. Let alone that it is hard to find *any* sources on numerous aspects of life that in other societies would be reflected in what was almost absent in the Soviet Union of the 1950s and 1960s, namely the Jewish press and archives of Jewish organizations. General Soviet archives, notably KGB documents, shed light on many unknown aspects of Soviet Jewish history. Foreign newspapers and journals, declassified diplomatic and intelligence documents, and archives of foreign Jewish organizations help to fill some voids.

Third, there is the issue of objectivity. The author of this book, born in the city of Zaporizhzhia, Ukraine, is himself a product of Soviet upbringing and, generally, life in Ukraine and later in Moscow. No doubt, that experience, including personal acquaintance with some of the "dramatis personae," helped immensely in writing the book. At the same time, it also could, inadvertently, leave a trace in how the author described and analyzed them and the entire period in Soviet Jewish history.

1

THE THAW

The Death of Stalin

On 5 March 1953, Captain David Stavitsky, feeling angry and frustrated, sat down to write a letter to Joseph Stalin. Similar to what happened in many other places, David's wife, Raisa, a physician, had been fired from her job a few days earlier. Her hospital administrators had invented a lame excuse, acting on their own initiative or on directives received from their superiors. This was a time when Jewish doctors were perceived as a dangerous—and at the same time strikingly visible—liability in the entire Soviet state healthcare system. Jews comprised less than two percent of the post–World War II population, yet made up a fifth of the medical profession and close to a quarter of those in medical research and higher education.[1] In some locales they dominated the profession numerically. Thus, a 1946 report on healthcare in Kishinev (Chişinău), the capital of the Moldavian republic, identified 69 percent of the doctors employed in the city's medical institutions as Jewish.[2]

David, an officer during the war, had been studying at a military academy in Moscow. A devoted, battle-tested patriot and a card-carrying Communist, he grew up and matured in an atmosphere of proclaimed internationalism that did not make him feel that the state took a negative attitude toward his or anyone else's Jewish origin. Hence he decided it was his duty to report lawlessness in malfunctioning units of the state apparatus. It simply could not occur to him that Stalin had himself approved and orchestrated the persecutions that, for the first time in Soviet history, tended to focus exclusively or predominantly on Jews.

The mass purges conducted by the secret police before World War II, tragically affecting the lives of hundreds of thousands of people, did not specifically target Jews. The victims were presumptive opponents of the paranoid regime, thousands of whom *happened* to be Jewish. Even if some of them were accused of "Jewish nationalism," the emphasis usually was on *nationalism* rather than on its specifically Jewish variety. Now, by contrast, broad circles of Jewish intellectuals and professionals as well as members of religious communities faced baseless accusations of sedition, espionage, or other serious crimes. Beginning around 1948, the targeted Jews would be tagged as "nationalists," "cosmopolites," or—in the latest and most sinister campaign—"murderers in white gowns," as the Soviet media portrayed the physicians and other medical professionals suspected of acting on behalf of hostile foreign interests.

On 13 January 1953, a group of foremost authorities in the Soviet medical community had figured in a historically unforgettable editorial published in the major, tone-setting Communist Party daily *Pravda* (Truth). Entitled "Despicable Spies and Murderers Disguised as Professors of Medicine," the editorial made it clear that the conspirators, aiming to cut short the lives of leading Soviet functionaries, had been recruited by the "bourgeois-nationalist" American Jewish Joint Distribution Committee (JDC). The JDC, which had distinguished itself with effective aid programs in many countries, including the Soviet Union, was dubbed a branch office of American intelligence and figured in the Soviet media as a conspiratorial operation.[3]

The ensuing smear campaign in the media found an approving or even gratified response among parts of the population. Rumors buzzed that Jewish physicians sought to poison or otherwise harm non-Jews, both children and adults.[4] In Vilnius, the capital of the Lithuanian Soviet republic, the chief accountant at the Ministry of Agriculture, named Venderis, called for the further examination of traces of "villainous kikes' deeds." He did not find it surprising that the "doctors-murderers" had sold themselves to Western secret services, because "their relatives sold Christ for thirty pieces of silver."[5]

A strictly confidential report of a Kyiv district Party committee from 16 January 1953, noting "the reactions of the public towards the detention of a group of murderer doctors," stated that the population in their part of the Ukrainian capital had "reacted with fury to the unmasking of a group of murderer doctors, who take advantage of the trust placed in them and carry out their criminal intent." The report quotes characteristic utterances on this matter. A Ukrainian female doctor said: "I have been appalled since my school days by the actions of the Jews. The arrested Jewish doctors should not only be shot, but slowly cut into pieces." A senior admissions-staff member of a polyclinic, a Russian woman, "was greatly disgusted by the actions of the Jewish doctors and announced that today, on 13th January 1953, sick people refuse to be treated by Jewish doctors, and demand to be received by doctors without Jewish nationality."[6]

The "doctors' plot" provided Soviet people, struggling with deprivation of various types, an outlet for their negative feelings, accumulated over time. After so many "plots" revealed in the 1930s and 1940s, people tended to be convinced that they lived surrounded by enemies and this mindset made them susceptible to believing virtually any tale of conspiracy. Religious and ethnic prejudice helped them to take the accusations at face value. In addition, for many people, Jews, and those whom they regarded as Jewish, embodied the deficiencies of the entire Soviet system, including the far from perfect healthcare system. This mood of the population caused worries among local functionaries, who in some places hastened to organize lectures aimed at bringing the situation under control by explaining that several Jewish doctors did not represent the entire Soviet Jewry. However, such public presentations could not stop some people from talking openly about their desire to see the Jews evicted one and all to Birobidzhan or Israel, or expressing their displeasure with the German "failure" to finish them all off during the war.[7]

The denouncers were not exclusively medical professionals. Moreover, Jewish zealots and fawners also participated in public castigations. Thus, E. A. Kopran, a teacher in the city of Gorky (Nizhni Novgorod since 1990), expressed her grievance against those Jews who "sold the honor of their people for money and thus stained the reputation of our nation." She believed or claimed, however, that by working selflessly and honestly for the greater good of their country, Jews would prove their devotion to the Soviet state.[8] Mark Mitin, the leading Soviet Marxist-Leninist philosopher, wrote an article in which he characterized Israel as an outpost of American imperialism and linked Zionists' "atrocities" to the arrested doctors, whose "names deserved to be eternally cursed."[9]

The actual objective for fabricating the doctors' conspiracy is up for debate. Much has been written about the rumors, circulated shortly before the end of Stalin's life, that the Soviet leader planned to expel the entire Jewish population to remote territories in the east, including the severely underpopulated territory of a never-finished project of social engineering and nation building—the Jewish Autonomous Region, established in 1934 and better known as Birobidzhan. Historians usually point to the complete absence of any shred of documented evidence related to preparing an exceptionally complex operation, involving relocating over two million people living all over the country.[10] Still, "reliable witnesses" claimed that in March 1953 Stalin suffered his fatal stroke while in a fit of rage over the opposition of his closest lieutenants to a plan he had to deport all Jews.[11] Indeed, some people seriously referred to Stalin's death as a divine intervention, pointing to the timing of the dictator's stroke: it occurred on the holiday of Purim, "and just as in the Book of Esther, the anti-Semitic intentions of a modern-day Haman were suddenly undone."[12]

The question is whether such a plan could even be considered by Stalin and his inner circle. On the one hand, they could rely on the experience the Soviet regime had gained from summarily expelling, with a high rate of death among the expellees, entire ethnic groups such as the Chechens and the Crimean Tatars, accused of collaboration with the Nazis. On the other hand, they certainly had unlimited access to statistics (Lenin taught that "socialism is accounting") and could see the state's heavy dependence on Jews who, nationwide, made up over 10 percent of all specialists with higher and specialized secondary education.[13] In addition to a grueling logistics exercise, such an operation—which, in the end, never occurred—would have engendered the challenge of replacing tens of thousands of scholars, managers, engineers, physicians, pharmacists, teachers, journalists, and other qualified workers, including unique specialists in their field.[14] A somewhat similar but smaller-scale "experiment" conducted by the Nazis, which resulted in the loss of a considerable proportion of experienced medical practitioners, had contributed to an increase in the death rate in prewar Germany, among other effects.[15]

CIA analysts, who closely followed events in the Soviet Union, had concluded that a conceivable purpose of fabricating the "doctors' plot" could be "to discredit Jews (who remain internationalists) and the West, and to alienate the Soviet people from the West through fear of their own government."[16] (The argument that Soviet Jews remained "internationalists" begs qualification, unless the CIA meant a subset of Jewish intellectuals.) According to the CIA analysis, the doctors, and Jews in general, served after all as proxy targets in the Cold War "hate-America" campaign purported to demonstrate "US hostility directly to the Soviet people by proving that this country had many agents *inside* the USSR."[17] The revelations about the "plot" came against the backdrop of the Korean War, a watershed in Soviet-American relations.

Stalin and people in his immediate surroundings might in fact have had other, more personal than political, intentions associated with the "doctors' plot." And one cannot rule out the possibility that even the initiators of the campaign failed to fully foresee its consequences.[18]

David Stavitsky finished writing his letter in the morning and very soon, at six o'clock, before he had time to seal and mail the envelope, the radio—in the voice of Iuri Levitan, the legendary Soviet radio announcer during and after World War II—brought the thundering news that Stalin had died late in the evening of the previous day. Incidentally, David's story is historically questionable. It is hard to believe that he addressed his letter to Stalin because by that time he certainly knew that on 2 March the Soviet leader had suffered a brain hemorrhage. The Soviet media did not make any secret of the fact that the Leader was gravely ill. Like many oral-history testimonies, David's narrative is faulty in its details, though it captures the spirit of the time.

I do not know whether David shed a tear on hearing about Stalin's death. My father, a political officer during the war who after the demobilization returned to his teaching profession, did cry. In later years, when he—and, for that matter, David—became better equipped with historical information that turned them into convinced anti-Stalinists, he scornfully laughed at himself for doing so. Back then he certainly was not the only one to mourn. Boris Pasternak, the future Nobel Prize winner for literature (who in 1936 described Stalin as "a genius of action"), wrote four days after the funeral: "Each wept the same instinctive and unconscious tears that stream and stream and you don't wipe them away, drawn aside by the flow of common grief that has outstripped you, that has affected you also, has dragged along the length of you, and dampened your face and permeated your soul."[19]

On 7 March 1953, two days after Stalin's death, the Soviet press carried the words of Ilya Ehrenburg, then arguably the most popular press commentator in the country, about the loss of a man who embodied "the wisdom, heart, and conscience of mankind."[20] On 8 March Ehrenburg stood in the guard of honor near Stalin's coffin.[21] Then, on 11 March 1953, *Pravda* featured his long article eulogizing Stalin as "A Great Defender of Peace."[22] Lazar Kaganovich, a deputy prime minister and a loyal lieutenant during all the years of Stalin's rule, was among the organizers of the state funeral. In 1943 the American magazine *Life* characterized Kaganovich, "a Ukrainian Jew," as "Stalin's trouble shooter." It also wrote that Kaganovich's sister Rosa was "supposedly married to Stalin."[23] In 1953 persistent rumors put the blame for Stalin's death on this woman, who, in fact, never existed, at least neither as Stalin's wife nor as Kaganovich's sister.[24]

Thousands of Jews were overwhelmed with sorrow and fear. Some were afraid that, being left without the protection of the all-powerful Leader, they faced an unknowable future. This was a future in which they felt defenseless against Jew-haters emboldened by the media and the ubiquitous public gatherings that condemned the doctors, and by extension all Jews, as agents and sympathizers of the hostile West.[25] For probably many more Jews, the distress came from their sincere devotion to Communism and to Stalin who, in their reckoning, embodied the mind and will of the Communist state and party, was in charge of the victorious Red Army, and had played an important role in the establishment and recognition of Israel.

During the entire Soviet period, Jews had the highest proportion of card-carrying Communists, though, by the time of Stalin's death, the number of Jews in the top echelons of Soviet power had significantly declined as a result of purges and demotions. In mid-February 1953 Lev Mekhlis, a Labor Zionist turned one of Stalin's close associates, was accorded an official Soviet funeral of the first class, buried in Red Square. By the early 1950s a quarter million Jews, or approximately 15 percent of all Jewish adults aged twenty and over, continued to carry Party membership cards.[26] While some of them had successfully passed the vetting process and joined the Party for career purposes or had been driven by an evanescent impulse at a particular point in their lives, notably in the patriotic atmosphere of

World War II, no doubt profound believers in the bright future of Communist ideals were by no means exceptional among them. A person who was both a Party member and a *frontovik*, or a frontline war veteran, belonged to a respected cohort of Soviet citizens well positioned for promotion.

At the same time, there were people who could not hide their satisfaction with or indifference to Stalin's death. Thus, according to judicial cases of the time, L. M. Olinskaia, a fourteen-year-old Jewish schoolgirl from Lviv, Ukraine, said during a memorial rally: "Good riddance to bad rubbish." For that she was severely beaten by her fellow students. Z. E. Levin, a thirty-four-year-old Jewish man, a Party member with higher education, was reported to comment about those who sought to bid farewell to Stalin: "It's not surprising. People run to see a dog driven over by a car. And now there's a funeral of the leader."[27]

Archival documents tell a tragicomic story about a case that was seriously investigated by the secret police and the Party's Central Committee in Ukraine. The events developed a couple of days before Stalin's death, at a kindergarten belonging to the chocolate factory named after Karl Marx, situated in the Kaganovich District of Kyiv. Six-year-old children were placed in front of a radio to listen to news about Stalin's health. In the meantime a Jewish boy, Alik, said that his family would move to America. Other children said that they would not give him a boat for the journey and one boy even promised to beat Alik if he really went to America.[28]

On 9 March a sarcophagus with Stalin's embalmed body was placed next to Lenin's sarcophagus in the mausoleum on Red Square, next to the Kremlin Wall. A month or so later, Raisa Stavitsky had her job back. The campaign of dismissing Jewish doctors—and not only doctors—from their jobs was put on hold. On 4 April 1953, merely a month after Stalin's death, *Pravda* informed the Soviet public that the Presidium of the Central Committee, then the apex of the Communist Party and de facto the ultimate decision-making authority of the regime, had exonerated the distinguished doctors, all but three Jewish. Soviet people were confounded to learn that the new leadership had hastened to admit that the charges had been a blatant act of criminalized "justice," and that the investigators had extracted confessions from the doctors by using "illegal" (though in fact widely practiced) means of pressure and torture. This stunning statement was a harbinger of more revelations to come.[29] The statement employed the term "judicial *rehabilitation*," widely current in the post-Stalinist years though it did not find a place in the vocabulary of Soviet legislation. Rather, the fabricated cases would be routinely closed "for lack of legal components of crime."[30]

The early post-Stalinist period, from 1953 to 1964, is conventionally, and to a large extent rightly, associated with Nikita Khrushchev, despite the fact that for the first two years Georgy Malenkov rather than Khrushchev succeeded Stalin as the top figure in the so-called "collective leadership," established after a quarter century of one-man rule. It was a stormy period, in which Khrushchev displayed remarkable Machiavellian abilities in gradually removing his rivals who, like him, had previously belonged to Stalin's inner circle and had given ringing endorsements to the murderous regime. The fearsome security chief Lavrenti Beria, who had concentrated too much power in his hands, was the first one to be disposed of June 1953. While other luminaries of the Kremlin, including Malenkov and Kaganovich, in a few years would be sent to retirement or lower-level positions, Beria was the only one among that cohort to be arrested in June and executed in December of the same year.

In the first phase of de-Stalinization, that is, between the 20th and 22nd Congresses of the Communist Party, held in February 1956 and October 1961 respectively, the propaganda cast Beria as a particularly monstrous villain. Characteristically, Boris Polevoy, chairman of the Foreign Commission of the Soviet Writers Union and, as such, one of the major globe-trotting players in Soviet cultural diplomacy, included in his misinformation stories the tale that pinned the blame on Beria for taking all power into his own hands during the last years of Stalin's life. Moreover, as the story went, Beria had discussed some questions with Stalin in Georgian, the two men's native language, thus making decisions unknown to other leaders. In this carefully constructed gossip, clearly aimed at whitewashing Khrushchev's and other top figures' reputation, Jews had been selected by Beria as a special target with a view to sparking outrage in the West and, thus, discrediting the Soviet Union abroad.[31]

Ironically, Beria meanwhile gained among some foreign observers a reputation of a slain progressive reformer. Raphael Abramovitch, a leading figure in the aging and shrinking circles of Russian—and heavily Jewish—anti-Soviet socialist emigration, hailed Beria's prompt decision to terminate the prosecution launched against the "murderers in white gowns."[32]

A strident critic of the Kremlin regime, Abramovitch, who had been living abroad since 1920, built his understanding of Soviet life on reading the press. Indeed, on 7 April, Moscow censors cleared a United Press International dispatch attributing the release of the doctors to Beria's personal initiative.[33] The decision to stop the prosecution case might have been used by Beria, at least partly, to rebuff the innuendos that his people had not paid heed to the conspiracy, and also as an excuse for getting rid of his detractors responsible for running the case, so that the security forces could be rendered an absolutely secure instrument.[34] In the event, this instrument failed to protect him.

The removal of Beria was essentially a coup d'état. Apart from him, people considered to be his aides were put in jail, including a number of Jewish senior secret-police and intelligence officers. A few had been detained earlier, accused of a concocted Zionist conspiracy. Some, such as Generals Leonid Raikhman and Mikhail Belkin, survived and were freed from prison in the months or years after Stalin's death, but lost their military ranks and Party membership. Lev Shvartsman, a colonel as well as an infamously ruthless torturer, was shot in April 1955. Earlier, in January 1955, General Solomon Milshtein, Ukraine's deputy minister of internal affairs, was executed. In his sensational February 1956 "Secret Speech" to the 20th Communist Party Congress, which launched the de-Stalinization campaign, Khrushchev paid special attention to the brutal investigator, Colonel Boris Rodos (without mentioning directly his Jewish origin): "He is a vile person, with the brain of a bird, and morally completely degenerate. And it was this man who was deciding the fate of prominent Party workers."[35] Rodos was sentenced to death on 26 February, the day after Khrushchev's speech.

Among those who were under threat of being arrested or at least removed during the purge of Beria's close associates was Boris Vannikov, a highly decorated three-star general, born into a Jewish family in Baku, Azerbaijan. Known for his effective, if brutal, organizational skills, Vannikov was in charge of overseeing the atomic project, working under the direct supervision of Beria. However, he remained unharmed and, until his retirement in 1958, continued to work as a deputy minister of "medium machine-building," a euphemism for the nuclear industry.[36]

After all, such people as Vannikov were certainly replaceable. It was different with numerous scientists of Jewish background whose services could not be spared. Yulii Khariton, one of the top physicists in the project, remained highly valued despite the fact that his father had been arrested and died in the Gulag, and his mother lived with her second husband in Germany and then in Palestine. Lev Landau, who would win the Nobel Prize in Physics in 1962, was considered so important to the atomic bomb project that the authorities tolerated his eccentric antics (including, for instance, propagation of free love) and openly critical view of certain aspects of the Soviet regime.[37]

The purge of Beria's cadres did not affect George Koval, the only Soviet citizen who managed to get direct access to American secret sites. He was born in the United States in 1913 into a family of Russian Jewish immigrants, who in 1932 moved to Birobidzhan. Koval later studied in Moscow, where the intelligence service recruited him and sent him back to America. Drafted into the US army, he received specialized training and was assigned to work for the atom project. This gave him a chance to provide the Soviet team with extremely valuable information. In 1948 he returned to Moscow.[38]

The End of the "Doctors' Plot"

As with many other decisions taken within the impenetrable walls of the Kremlin, we can only conjecture about the key motives for the hasty termination of the frame-up against the doctors. In mid-1953 Israel's prime minister David Ben-Gurion admitted to the government that "we do not know what the doctors' release means."[39] It is still hard to untwine the intricate webs of intrigue spun around this affair. To all appearances, apart from Beria's personal motives, the need to calm international public opinion became the imperative for discarding the alleged Jewish conspiracy. The prosecution and defamation campaign had resonated well beyond Soviet borders and was often perceived in parallel with the still recent events in Nazi Germany. The campaign led inter alia to an interruption of Soviet-Israeli diplomatic relations in February 1953, which were restored, however, in July of that year.[40] In December Shmuel Eliashiv (born Fridman), the Russian and French university-educated Israeli ambassador, returned to Moscow.

The campaign to unmask an imagined conspiracy of Jewish doctors had collaterally brought significant changes in the perception of the Soviet Union abroad. Whereas previously foreign observers had widely praised the Soviet regime for its fight against anti-Semitism and, in general, for being rather benevolent toward Jews (albeit certainly not toward Judaism and non-Communist Jewish ideologies), the "doctors' plot," as well as the general change of the government's attitude toward Jews, particularly following the establishment of the state of Israel, had altered this image radically and, as it turned out, irreparably.

The abrupt change of course in dealing with the "doctors' plot" astounded people holding positions at various levels of the Soviet state apparatus. Iakov Rapoport, one of the arrested top Moscow doctors, was puzzled that, when he first reappeared at the academic institute where he headed a research unit, his colleagues looked at him rather indifferently, as if he had returned from a business trip rather than from a prison. Soon he found out that they had obediently followed the strict instructions received on the morning of 4 April. Their Party bosses felt disoriented and confused by the overnight reevaluation of the matter, and therefore, as Rapoport described it, followed the French maxim: *dans le doubte, s'abstenir*—when in doubt, abstain.[41] Some people were presumably upset that they had ultimately ended up in an awkward position. Before the announcement disavowing the persecution, a slew of physicians and other medics had enthusiastically or dutifully participated in various meetings and rallies aimed at publicly denouncing their colleagues. Now, after a shift in the political wind, their zeal embarrassingly backfired. On top of that, some had to work under the leadership of those whom they had publicly maligned.

In the coming days and months, an unknown number of Jewish medical practitioners, scientists, and pharmacists, who had been incarcerated, demoted, or rendered jobless in various places of the country, returned to normal life and, reluctantly or not, were in most cases reinstated in their jobs.[42] In the city of Rostov-on-Don in southern Russia, for instance, a large group of Jewish physicians were released from prison from April to July 1953.[43] Also released were those who had nothing to do with medical professions but had been persecuted in the climate of campaigns that tended to target Jews. Thus, Stalin's death liberated the leaders of the religious community of the Ukrainian city of Proskurov (the next year it would be renamed Khmelnitsky), although the community was unable to repossess its confiscated synagogue.[44] Not a few doctors, often elderly people, never physically recovered from the upheaval.

Many people were delighted to see the full exoneration of the doctors as a sign of remedying the moral crisis that had gripped society. Significantly, officeholders and administrators did not necessarily receive from their superiors any direct orders to sack Jewish employees. However, in addition to clear directives, a kind of an unwritten code defined their course of action. Updates and interpretations of the "code," based on reading *Pravda* and putting one's ear to the ground, would spread like lighting among people working at various levels of authority.[45] In some cases, however, moral principles prevailed over the strategy of checking to see which way the wind was blowing.

Nikolai Masalkin, a seasoned Party functionary recently appointed to head the Agricultural Institute in the city of Molotov (as Perm, seven hundred miles east of Moscow, was called from 1940 to 1957), was one of those administrators who refused to follow suit. As a result, his Jewish employees were able to keep their jobs.[46] Nikolai Pankin, director of a construction enterprise in Kyiv, commended the April 1953 announcement as an act of self-criticism, which was "previously unheard of in the history of our Party." A card-carrying Communist from 1933, Pankin observed the "horrible antisemitism planted among people, making Jews feeling oppressed and humiliated, with the sword of Damocles hovering over their heads." It seemed to him as if the dark times of czarism had returned. Trying to understand what was going on, he reread Stalin's writings on the nationalities issue and was proud that, notwithstanding the pressure exerted on him, he had not fired any of his Jewish subordinates.[47]

Pankin was right: the "doctors' plot" and, generally, the atmosphere of the time left deep scars in society, contributing strongly to perpetuating the image of Jews as an alien and probably harmful element. The ideological and security apparatus looked at Jews with suspicion—and encouraged people to do the same—simply because of their Jewish origins.[48] This clearly echoed the situation in late Imperial Russia, when even conversion could not remove the sense of difference from "real" Christians.[49]

Small wonder that many people, most notably those with an anti-Jewish animus, resisted believing that the doctors—and Jews in general—were really innocent.[50] Some remained convinced that Jews had had a hand in Stalin's death.[51] As a rule, Jewish doctors and nurses were not directly accused of using Christian blood for ritualistic purposes, but the accusation that they conspired to poison leading Kremlin officials as well as people all over the country borrowed motifs from the blood-libel trope.[52] Beria's execution added fuel to the suspicion because it could, if desired, be interpreted as proof that the former security head (who some people believed was Jewish or half-Jewish) had acted as the doctors' accomplice, which explained why he had rushed to save them.[53]

Lev Druskin, a Leningrad poet and translator, wrote in his memoirs:

> Ten year later [after 1953], an intelligent woman, a teacher, told me, a Jew:
>
> "But they did infect children with cancer. I know this for sure."
>
> . . . To all our arguments she had but one reply:
>
> "A friend of mine ignored what people had been telling her and took her son to a Jewish doctor, and a month later the child died."
>
> "Because of cancer?"
>
> "The diagnosis was a different one, but it had been made by a doctor who also was Jewish. Yet the child died, no doubt, from cancer."
>
> And no matter what you say, she won't listen![54]

Overtly, in the media and public gatherings, the repression and smear campaign associated with the "doctors' plot" lasted less than three months. Despite its brevity, however, the affair carved deep wounds in many lives. In addition, among many Jews the hostile climate of the time fostered or, with the memories of the war still fresh, reinforced the feeling of victimhood, which in turn led to an increased national assertiveness.

Ilya Ehrenburg, a poet and novelist with a nationwide and international reputation, thanks mainly to his well-crafted, emotive, and inspiring wartime journalism, wrote later: "I cannot say how many times I read and reread the brief announcement printed on the second page [of *Pravda*]. I knew none of the doctors involved but I realized that something extraordinary had happened. The statement said that the doctors had been wrongfully accused, that they were completely innocent and that their confessions of guilt had been obtained 'by impermissible methods of inquiry, the use of which is strictly forbidden by Soviet law.' This was published in *Pravda*, it was said openly for all the world to hear."[55]

In February 1956 the "doctors' plot," without being characterized as a "Jewish" affair, figured in Khrushchev's historic "Secret Speech," delivered to the delegates of the 20th Congress. According to Khrushchev, he and other people in Stalin's surrounding felt

> that the case of the arrested doctors was questionable. We knew some of these people personally because they had once treated us. When we examined this "case" after Stalin's death, we found it to have been fabricated from beginning to end.
>
> This ignominious "case" was set up by Stalin. He did not, however, have time to bring it to a conclusion (as he imagined its conclusion), and for this reason the doctors are still alive. All of them have been rehabilitated. They are working in the same places they were working before. They are treating top individuals, not excluding members of the Government. They have our full confidence; and they execute their duties honestly, as they did before.[56]

Cosmopolitanism

No doubt, rumors about the ominous danger emanating from Jewish doctors and pharmacists affected directly or indirectly a much broader segment of the Jewish population than the hysteria about intellectuals who ostensibly spread the malaise of "cosmopolitanism," of "bowing down before the West." The campaign began in 1949 and, initially, was a reflection of internal conflicts in top circles of Soviet writers and critics competing for the status of guardians of Soviet—with strong emphasis on Russian—patriotism. Very soon, however, the implications of the campaign transcended the literary context. In addition, specifically "rootless cosmopolitanism" became a dominant theme in Soviet propaganda, with a particular focus on Jewish intellectuals and specialists as a prominent group among the culprits charged with serving foreign, notably American and Zionist, interests.[57]

Most probably, the idea that Jews, or some of them at least, were cosmopolites could register in the mind of average Soviet citizens, but normally without causing them to become emotionally charged, panic, or turn aggressive. Presumably, less-educated people never really knew what it meant to be a cosmopolite. It was quite another thing to have concerns about the doctors' reliability, especially since Jewish medical professionals were customarily suspected of preferentially helping their own people and ignoring the needs of the others. At the same time, paradoxically, many people held Jewish doctors in high esteem.

Still, in literary, artistic, and academic circles it was a serious matter to be accused of being a carrier of cosmopolitan ideas. This could easily make a person, even a distinguished one, unemployable and unpublishable. True, as a rule it did not lead to imprisonment, let alone capital punishment. Those labeled as "cosmopolites" often had conspicuously Jewish surnames, sometimes hidden under "innocuous" pseudonyms, which the vigilant press was happy to reveal. Indeed, the targeted groups of literati, artists, and academics were heavily Jewish, most notably in the capital and other large cities, which had the highest concentration of intellectuals. It was they whom the authorities primarily suspected as falling under the influence of what was considered ideologically unacceptable and harmful. Among Jews, the number of people suspected of being potentially susceptible to detrimental foreign influence was high for the simple reason that many of them were highly educated and lived in major cultural and academic hubs of the country. For all that, accusations of spreading or practicing cosmopolitan ideas could have little or even nothing to do with Jews, particularly in some ethnic areas of the country.[58] Importantly, the fight against cosmopolitan "kowtowing" encompassed a broad range of issues. Ehrenburg recalled that period from the vantage point of 1957:

> Seven or eight years ago much was said among us about the struggle against "kowtowing." The struggle against "kowtowing" was going on in all sorts of ways: workers in the food industry hurriedly changed the names of pastries; literary scholars argued that neither Indian tales nor Greek epics could possibly have been known to us in ancient times, and that neither Shakespeare, Moliere nor La Fontaine had any influence on any Russian author; the playwrights depicted Soviet scientists, composers, architects as supposedly slavishly devoted to Weismann, to jazz or to skyscrapers, respectively. The struggle was an energetic one, but no one could say with any clarity against whom or what it was being waged.[59]

For ideological reasons, Communist dogmatists opposed genetics (hence the mention of the German evolutionary biologist August Weismann) and cybernetics as "foreign influences" and harmful forms of "bourgeois pseudoscience."[60] In many cases researchers and professors, often Jewish, lost their jobs, accused of advocating theories deemed ideologically suspect.[61]

There is no way of knowing how many Jewish writers, composers, painters, artists, and other intellectuals felt at risk of being blamed for espousing views contrary to Soviet values. The atmosphere created by attacks on "cosmopolites" and "murderous doctors" clearly did not apply such labels to all Jews, especially as some Jews distinguished themselves as righteous activists. Characteristically, the 1948 film *Court of Honor*, one of the first propaganda salvos in the anticosmopolitan campaign, was directed by Abram Room and based on the play written by Alexander Shtein (Rubinstein). Of the sixteen Soviet movies released in 1953, seven had Jewish directors, including Mikhail Romm, Fridrikh Ermler, and Ian Frid. Songs by Isaac Dunaevsky, Matvei Blanter, and other acclaimed composers remained in the repertoire of concert and other performances. Books by Russian-language writers of Jewish background continued to come out in Moscow and other cities. Samuil Marshak, who studied in England and wrote Zionist poems in his youth, established himself as one of the most popular—or even the most popular—among Russian children's poets, and a foremost translator of William Shakespeare and Robert Burns. His books would come out each year, also in the heat of the anticosmopolitan campaign.

An interesting case was that of Emmanuil Kazakevich. A decree of the Communist Party's Central Committee criticized inter alia his 1948 story "Dvoe s stepi" ("Two in the Steppe"),[62] which essentially questioned the fairness of a death sentence issued by a military court during World War II. As a result, the author received a reprimand for basing his narrative on premises unacceptable to the official moral value system. That was a heavy blow for the thirty-five-year-old writer. In 1940 Kazakevich had been admitted to the Writers Union as a promising Birobidzhan Yiddish author, though by that time he already lived in Moscow after narrowly escaping arrest in the Far Eastern Jewish Autonomous Region during the mass purges of 1937–38.[63] When the war broke out, Kazakevich, whose poor eyesight exempted him from military service, volunteered to fight the Nazis and distinguished himself as a brave frontline intelligence officer. This experience found reflection in his postwar literary works, which lacked any Jewish content.

In 1948 Kazakevich's 1947 novel *The Star*, the only one he wrote in both Yiddish and Russian, had received (for the Russian version) a State Stalin Prize, awarded annually from 1940 to 1954. The Moscow Yiddish publishing house Der Emes (Truth) brought it out under the title *Green Shadows*. The Russian book had numerous reprints, was adapted into a film in 1949, and in the same year came out in Paris with an introduction by Louis Aragon, a prominent Communist-affiliated French writer married to Russian-born author Elsa Triolet (Ella Kagan). Notwithstanding the severe rebuke, Kazakevich once again won a Stalin Prize in 1950. His books continued to come out during the anticosmopolitan drive. In 1953 the Moscow Foreign Languages Publishing House released an English translation of his second prizewinning novel *Spring on the Oder*.

Some Jewish intellectuals and managers made use of the anti-Western climate of the time in order to realize their ambitious projects. Thus, in 1949 Iuri Iurovski, who worked in various capacities in the Soviet apparatus, including several years as a secret-police operative, cut an incongruous figure to get an appointment to head the Philharmonic Society in the Omsk Region, southeast of Russia. In 1950 he played the key role in organizing the Omsk State Russian Folk Choir, which became the best troupe of this kind nationwide and would often be sent on foreign tours (including to Israel in 1965) as part of the USSR's cultural diplomacy.[64]

Even more successful was the Moscow-based choreographic ensemble Berezka (Birch Tree), famous for its flowing, slow, "authentic Russian" dances.[65] The ensemble's style, developed by Nadezhda Nadezhdina (Brushtein) and later Mira Koltsova (Miriam Ravicher), began to embody Russian folk dance. In 1964, in Israel, the ensemble's performances attracted a hundred thousand people, including President Zalman Shazar and Prime Minister Levi Eshkol.[66] For unknown reasons Nadezhdina, who organized this quintessentially Russian collective in 1948, distanced herself from her Jewish mother, Aleksandra Brushtein, a well-established writer in her time.[67]

In March 1953 Alexander Fadeev, secretary general of the Writers Union (he would commit suicide less than three months after Khrushchev's February 1956 anti-Stalinist speech), wrote: "We have honorably waged a struggle with the ideologists of cosmopolitanism, we are waging it and we shall continue to wage it. . . . We have encountered and are encountering Jewish bourgeois nationalism. In our time bourgeois nationalists do not differ fundamentally from cosmopolitans, because both are hirelings of foreign capital and work for it, though only under a nationalist flag."[68] Indeed, "cosmopolitanism"—as a "bourgeois" antipode to "proletarian internationalism"—had not disappeared from the Soviet ideological vocabulary, remaining a term of opprobrium.

The 1961 program of the Communist Party stated: "The party will persist in its fight against the reactionary ideology of bourgeois nationalism, racism, and cosmopolitanism."[69] In post-Stalinist rhetoric, the concept of "cosmopolitan," which developed as a synonym for the word Jew even before the revolution, sometimes merged into the anti-Zionist concept.[70] Nevertheless, the Jewish-related usage would become rather marginal. Former "cosmopolitans" could restore their position in the Writers Union and other organizations. The term would mostly appear in a historical context—for instance, about Ukrainian or other literati gravitating to the West, or—most often—about the worldwide invasion of American lowbrow culture.

It is hard to tell whether or to what extent the Jewish context of "cosmopolitanism" was meant in the angry rhetoric against Boris Pasternak when his novel *Doctor Zhivago*, published abroad, led to him winning the 1958 Nobel Prize. The decision of the Swedish Academy ignited a grandiose scandal in the Soviet Union and forced Pasternak—in Ehrenburg's words, "an unfortunate victim of the Cold War"—to decline the prize.[71] A meeting of Moscow writers (who, incidentally, did not have a chance to read the novel and, at best, heard excerpts on Western broadcasts) issued a resolution condemning Pasternak and calling for him to be expelled from the country and stripped of Soviet citizenship. "Let him endure the unenviable fate of an emigrant cosmopolite, who betrayed the interests of his homeland!"[72] Ultimately he was expelled from the Writers Union, but not from the country, and died two years later.

In the late 1950s and early 1960s, Italian exchange students would bring copies of *Doctor Zhivago* to Moscow, where local students, eager to get the book, were ready to pay a price equal to two monthly scholarship stipends per copy.[73] According to an apocryphal story, in the early 1960s Khrushchev finally had read Pasternak's novel and then told Ehrenburg that he could not understand why it was necessary to make a scandal around it.[74] The 1965 Metro-Goldwyn-Mayer film *Doctor Zhivago* shared multiple Oscar nominations and awards with *The Sound of Music* and became one of the highest-grossing movies of all time in America.

The Name-Giver

In a country where the line between literature and politics always remained blurry, the so-called "thick" monthly journals often acted as the principal forums for publications testing the limits of what was permitted by ideological overseers and, in the absence of other forums, playing the role of surrogate for public opinion. Such literary periodicals had their own literary strategies, aesthetic programs, and even worldview—of course, kept strictly within the framework of official ideology.[75] Their editors, always powerful figures in deciding what was to be printed, gained prominence in the 1950s.[76]

The relaxation in the ideological overseers' attitude toward writers had already become clear in the year of Stalin's death. The Moscow literary monthly *Znamia* (The banner), which used to dedicate most of its pages to short stories and novels with military themes, appeared as one of the standard-bearers of the change, publishing trendsetting works. In its April 1954 issue, the journal introduced its readers to Boris Pasternak's poems from the novel *Doctor Zhivago*. True, it was years before the scandal around the novel; at that time of their first publication, the poems did not strike people as being particularly controversial.

This was quite remarkable since Vadim Kozhevnikov, editor of the journal, was hardly known as a liberal. Rather, he had a reputation as an ideologically impeccable literary and journalistic craftsman. He had been appointed to the editorial position in 1949, in the aftermath of a high-profile scandal caused by the journal's publication of several works, including Emmanuil Kazakevich's story "Two in the Steppe."[77] Kazakevich's 1950 novel *Spring on the Oder* also first appeared in *Znamia*, already under the editorship of Kozhevnikov. Kazakevich's success was particularly striking when compared with the tragic situation in the Yiddish literary guild. It is not out of the question that if Kazakevich had remained categorized as a Yiddish author, he might, by that time, have been incarcerated in a labor camp somewhere in a remote corner of the country, together with dozens of the literati who shaped the milieu of the Jewish Anti-Fascist Committee, brutally liquidated in November 1948.

Whereas Kazakevich was only cursorily involved in the activities of the Jewish Anti-Fascist Committee, Ehrenburg, also a contributor to *Znamia*, took part in the committee's work during the war, but distanced himself from that body in the years leading up to its liquidation and seemingly disliked what he considered its parochialism.[78] For their part, Yiddish writers were taken aback by Ehrenburg's militant assimilationism.[79] Indeed, while he never hid his Jewish origin and on numerous occasions decried anti-Semitism, Ehrenburg was at pains to stress, apparently sincerely, that his worldview rested on assimilation and internationalism. He would refer to Kazakevich's switch from Yiddish to Russian as a distinct example of Soviet Jews' successful cultural transformation.[80] Ehrenburg's September 1948 *Pravda* article, "Concerning a Certain Letter," sent a clear and unambiguous message that people in the Soviet Union, notably Jews, had no reason to show excessive enthusiasm for the establishment of Israel. The article was commissioned by the ideological apparatus, but most probably it also reflected the author's own standpoint.[81]

Ehrenburg later spoke with some bravado about the repressions that targeted people associated with the Jewish Anti-Fascist Committee, but bypassed him: "I have lived through too many stormy events to be afraid. But it was a dreadful period, and I was very depressed and gloomy. The turning point came with the rehabilitation of the doctors."[82] His own survival he explained as a lottery, in which he "just happened to draw a lucky ticket."[83] Moreover, in 1951, his sixtieth birthday was grandly celebrated by the Writers Union, while his collection of state awards saw the addition of the Order of Red Banner of Labor, a high Soviet decoration.[84]

No doubt, the anti-Jewish drive of the time caused him anxious days and nights, but ultimately it did not affect Ehrenburg's privileged status among the Soviet intellectual elite close to the Kremlin. He "was in a class of his own," valued as a well-connected cultural mediator, "shaping the cross-border contact between interested foreigners and the Soviet system."[85] In particular, he continued to act as a member of the prestigious international committee responsible for awarding Stalin Peace Prizes. When he himself became a winner of such a prize in 1953, the foreign press interpreted this distinction, along with a handsome monetary award, as a lame attempt to downplay the concurrent campaigns, which had an unmistakable anti-Jewish bent. A fortnight after the Soviet media made public the "doctors' plot," the Moscow radio quoted Ehrenburg saying: "No matter what is the national origin of any Soviet man, he is above all a patriot of his country, a genuine internationalist."[86] Exactly around that time he received editorial queries from the State Publishing House of Belles-Lettres, pointing, in particular, to the problem of numerous "non-autochthonous" (i.e., Jewish) characters in his writings.[87]

During February 1953, the ideological apparatus of the Kremlin's agitprop worked on preparing a letter signed by scores of distinguished Soviet Jews. The letter was supposed to appear in *Pravda*. Various drafts carried strong words of condemnation of Israel, the United States, and those Soviet Jews who had given themselves over to nationalism and Zionism. Ehrenburg was one of several dignitaries who dared to disagree with the suggested text. Moreover, he wrote to Stalin urging him to forbid *Pravda* from printing any sort of communiqué that might embarrass the USSR abroad. Ultimately, he succumbed to the pressure and put his signature on the amended version of the letter, but, for unknown reasons (Ehrenburg might take credit for this), Stalin did not give his permission for its publication.

Two weeks after Stalin's death Ehrenburg went to Vienna, sent there as a Soviet representative to the meeting of the World Congress of Intellectuals in Defense of Peace, established in 1948 in Wrocław on the initiative of Jerzy Berejsza (a nephew of the American Yiddish writer Menachem Berejsza), a top Communist propagandist in Poland.[88] In his speech Ehrenburg expressed strong anti-American sentiments, accusing "the Yankees" of bringing to postwar Western Europe "not Einstein, Faulkner, Fast, Chaplin, but the standardized thriller novels, the standardized gangster movies, all sorts of opium, that is."[89] He continued to make appearances abroad, mainly as a high-profile peace activist and a frequent spokesman on cultural matters.[90] Anti-Americanism remained an important ingredient in his writings and pronouncements.[91] In 1953 the over one hundred libraries of the Amerika Häuser (American houses), run by the US government as cultural outposts in Germany, removed his books from their shelves.[92]

In December 1953, less than a year after Stalin's death, *Znamia*, still under Kozhevnikov's editorship, published Ehrenburg's major article "On the Writer's Work," which called for granting greater freedom to Soviet writers by allowing them to extricate themselves from the shackles of minute Communist direction.[93] This can be seen as an indication of a seemingly impossible ransformation rapidly undergone by the seasoned survivor of the Stalinist era. It is doubtful, however, that his about-face into a leading voice of the liberal intelligentsia could have occurred in the span of several months. He later claimed that before 1953 he learned how to "live with clenched teeth."[94] In 1958 Stalin's daughter Svetlana would write to Ehrenburg, thanking him for his attempts to demonstrate a path of truth to "the contemporary Soviet fake intelligentsia."[95] This role was hardly surprising for a man of letters who spent his youth in Paris as a revolutionary student exile, a poet, and a habitué of Montparnasse cafés, where he rubbed shoulders with trendsetting modernist writers and artists. A 1959 CIA report summarized the transformation taking place at the time:

> Writers who in the past were consistently conformist have in the more relaxed conditions of the post-Stalin period appeared as ardent advocates of greater freedom in the arts. Ilya Ehrenburg has stood at the forefront of the erstwhile official apologists who, while continuing to render Caesar his due at international conferences and official functions, have plugged for a widening of the frontiers in their own professional life. Capitalizing on their international prestige and loyal service to the regime, these veterans have sought to remove the trammels on creative initiative and place Soviet literary activity on a sounder footing.[96]

A few words of disagreement would be voiced by Ehrenburg even earlier. Thus, in 1950, while in London, he categorically refused to discuss reports about the position of Soviet Jewry and the fate of its cultural figures, but said, to the surprise of foreign observers, that some Soviet press articles attacking "cosmopolitanism" were "stupid and idiotic."[97] The Hungarian Jewish-born political scientist François (Ferenc) Fejtö contended that, in the post-Stalin 1950s, Ehrenburg "rediscovered the youthful and romantic inspiration of his early years."[98] Whatever was happening in Ehrenburg's mind, he was ready to commit to paper his understanding of what was going on in Soviet society.

The May 1954 issue of *Znamia* carried the first part of Ehrenburg's novel *The Thaw*, "a shoddy piece of literature but, in spite of its equivocations, a timely and significant human document."[99] Ehrenburg briefly touched on the sensitive point of the "doctors' plot," but neither this nor anything else in the novel's content formed the reason why this literary work carved for itself a unique place in history. The novel's metaphoric name accorded with the image of a society—at least its more sophisticated parts—striving at that time to discern signs of being permitted to live a life less suppressed than during the long Stalinist freeze. The notion of the "thaw" firmly stuck to the post-Stalinist period, mainly to the time when Khrushchev occupied the top position in the Soviet pyramid of power.

Khrushchev recalled that, at first, he did not "greet this expression with favor" and that, during the Thaw period, "there were two conflicting feelings fighting inside us. On the one hand, this relaxation of controls reflected our inner state of mind; that's what we were striving for. On the other hand, there were people among us who didn't want a thaw at all."[100] Characteristically, in the United States the novel came out in the beginning of 1957 under the imprint of Henry Regnery Co., described by Howard Fast, then the top literary figure among American Communists, as one of "the most reactionary" publishers in the country.[101]

Allegations, Smears, and Rumors

Lack of reliable information about the gruesome destiny of scores of people associated with the Jewish Anti-Fascist Committee gave rise to concoctions, usually wildly inaccurate. In some of them, Ehrenburg appeared as a sinister figure. Particularly hurtful was the fiction penned by Bernard Turner, formerly a correspondent for the British and Palestinian press, who endured years of incarceration in labor camps and later was allowed to leave the Soviet Union. In his memoirs, published in 1956 in the Tel Aviv Yiddish literary journal *Di goldene keyt* (The golden chain), Turner described inter alia his conversation with the prominent Soviet Yiddish writers David Bergelson and Itsik Fefer in a camp near the Siberian town of Bratsk. Allegedly, both accused Ehrenburg of having denounced them.

One can only speculate why Turner decided, or was encouraged, to violate the truth. In reality, his conversation with the writers simply could not have taken place. Bergelson and Fefer, as all the other members and employees of the Jewish Anti-Fascist Committee put on trial and executed on 12 August 1952, remained imprisoned in Moscow until the last moment of their lives. At the time of the publication, however, Turner's fabrication or delirious fantasy could be neither convincingly verified nor disproved, and this "piece of evidence" began to be quoted as a historical fact.[102]

The driving force behind at least some such publications was the Liaison Bureau (Lishkat ha-Kesher), also known under the codename Nativ (Path), the highly secretive Israeli governmental office formed in 1952 at the initiative of the prime minister of Israel, David Ben-Gurion, in order to preserve the ties with Jews in other countries and, in particular, to encourage emigration from Eastern and Central Europe. One of the Nativ-inspired publications, Manès Sperber's article "Tué, je vivrai" ([Despite Being] Killed, I Will Live), appeared in the Parisian journal *L'Express* on 30 March 1956 and carried disparaging remarks about Ehrenburg.[103] In December 1962, at a conference of Soviet writers in Moscow, Galina Serebriakova, a writer who experienced years behind barbed wire during the Stalin era, also publicly accused Ehrenburg of being culpable for the liquidation of prominent Yiddish writers and members of the Jewish Anti-Fascist Committee.[104] The concocted allegation and its associated character assassination cast a dark shadow over Ehrenburg for many years to come, and fully evaporated only in the 1990s following publication of archival materials of the 1952 trial. The vindication came only after his death.

Ehrenburg's ancestral rather than spiritual Jewishness (he did not know any Yiddish or Hebrew nor did he ever practice Judaism) continued to haunt him. Joshua Rubenstein, a biographer of Ehrenburg, contends that "aside from Lazar Kaganovich, Ehrenburg remained the most prominent Soviet Jew to survive Stalin, a fact that was often used against him."[105] Indeed, Ehrenburg occupied a distinguished position in Soviet society. In 1954 he was reelected—or, in fact, appointed—as one of the Jewish deputies to the Supreme Soviet of the USSR, the Soviet parliament. Apart from him and Kaganovich, the others were the physicist and key figure in the nuclear bomb project Iuli Khariton, the Marxist-Leninist philosopher Mark Mitin, the aircraft designer Semen Lavochkin, and the agronomist from Valdgeim, a collective farm near Birobidzhan, Rakhil Freidkina.[106]

Although the Supreme Soviet was a decorative body in the peculiar system of Soviet "democracy," the status of deputy lent additional weight to Ehrenburg's position. For reasons unknown (probably to Ehrenburg as well), he represented various locales in Latvia, with which he, a Kyiv-born thoroughly Russified Jew, had very little to do.

There was something ironic about Ehrenburg becoming a "prominent Jew," though he definitely never vied for this status. During his frequent foreign visits, he regularly faced journalists' questions about his own identity and the situation of Soviet Jews. In May 1959, when Ehrenburg was in Paris, he described his Jewishness as a posture of defiance to be retained as long as there was still anti-Semitism in his country. Once anti-Jewish feelings disappeared in the USSR, he would see no reason to call himself a Jew. Asked about the possibility of Jewish emigration from the Soviet Union, he was reported to have said that the Soviet Union would not allow its citizens to move to countries with capitalist regimes. In his estimation (seemingly out of whole cloth), of the more than two million Jews in the Soviet Union, less than 5 percent might be willing to emigrate if permitted to do so.[107] He held a low opinion of Israeli culture: "I was told that they have not produced a novelist of the stature of Sholem Aleichem nor a poet who could equal Bialik. The work of Israeli painters I have seen for myself, and so far there is no Chagall or Soutine among them."[108]

Ehrenburg certainly had strong supporters in the highest echelons of the state and Party hierarchy. In 1961, on the occasion of his seventieth birthday, he was decorated with the highest Soviet award—the Order of Lenin—"for services in developing Soviet literature."[109] At the same time, Khrushchev did not particularly like him. Their strained relations came to a head during Khrushchev's meeting with Soviet intellectuals in March 1963, when Khrushchev accused him of betraying ideals of the revolution and deviating from Communist criteria in his literary work (which the Soviet leader, most probably, had not read).[110] At a meeting of top Soviet functionaries that took place the next month, Khrushchev, wary of emerging dissent, especially in intellectual circles, called Ehrenburg a "fraud" who had "artfully added" "the concept of a thaw," which the Soviet leader characterized as ideologically aberrant.[111]

Ehrenburg's adversaries among conservative literati and artists were annoyed or even dismayed by reading *The Thaw*, which juxtaposed, in particular, a socialist-realist artist with his colleague, who preferred to be independent of the official artistic establishment even if that meant living in poverty. The author's sympathies were clearly with the latter rather than the former. In 1956 Ehrenburg played a central role in organizing a Soviet exhibition of Pablo Picasso's artwork. A broad range of lay and professional viewers were unable to separate themselves from the dogmas of socialist realism, the official doctrine of Communist aesthetics, and responded to such art with hostility and suspicion.[112]

Ivan Shevtsov's book *Plant Louse*, defined by the author as a "novel-pamphlet," reflected the mood in those circles of literati and artistic intelligentsia that continued to see the world around themselves through the dichotomy of Soviet Russian patriotism versus Jewish conspiratorial cosmopolitanism. The novel was published in 1964, with a print run of one hundred thousand, after Khrushchev's attack on avant-garde artists. Shevtsov described the ideological struggle between a group of Russian "realists" and advocates of abstract art. Most of the "abstractionists" were Jewish and gathered under the auspices of Lev Barselonsky, a clear allusion to Ehrenburg, whose reportage from Barcelona during the Spanish Civil War was still remembered by many Soviet readers.[113]

The Soviet press made a mockery of Shevtsov's book.[114] This did not mean, however, that these same critics welcomed deviations from what was considered proper art. Picasso's exhibitions in Moscow and Leningrad were not followed—at least during Ehrenburg's life (he died in August 1967)—by similar exhibitions of, for instance, Marc Chagall. Not only was Chagall, Ehrenburg's old friend, not a Communist, whereas Picasso did belong to the Communist movement, Chagall also was, in the words of the Soviet writer Marietta Shaginian, "a renegade [*otshchepenets*], who lost his homeland" and one of those who contributed to developing abstractionism and other isms, "cultivated without roots in a foreign land, detached from historical traditions of the native art."[115]

True, Shaginian's article appeared in 1958 and later the attitude toward the "renegade artist" gradually mellowed. In 1960 the writer Viktor Nekrasov noted in his American travelogue about visiting the Guggenheim Museum in New York: "The museum's collection is rich and diversified. Cezanne, Modigliani, Leger, Picasso, Paul Klee, Kandinsky, Chagall, sculptures by Lipchitz and Brancusi—in a word, all the most interesting artists the West has had since the end of the 19th century."[116] Seven years later, the Moscow Yiddish journal *Sovetish Heymland* did not find it problematic to publish a memoir, "My Friend Marc Chagall," by the Soviet artist Amshei Nurenberg, who in his youth had lived in Paris and for a while shared a studio with Chagall.[117] Also, Aron Vergelis, the journal's editor, visited Chagall at his home near Saint Paul de Vence in the South of France.[118] In 1968 *Sovetish Heymland* became arguably the first Soviet journal to publish reproductions of works by Chagall, and its arts editor even received a thank-you letter from the artist.[119]

There is no way to gauge precisely Ehrenburg's status and popularity among Soviet Jews. No doubt, he was known among the well-read population, and many Jewish readers even wrote to him seeking help, advice, or simply sharing their thoughts and concerns.[120] A strong boost to Ehrenburg's popularity, particularly among younger people who did not remember his wartime journalism, came with the publication of his memoir *People, Years, Life*, serialized from August 1960 to April 1965 in the Moscow literary journal *Novyi mir* (New world), whose print run fluctuated between 90,000 and 125,000. The memoir irked dogmatic Communist critics. One of them welcomed Ehrenburg's detailed denunciation of various manifestations of anti-Semitism, including the persecution of "murderous doctors," but found it regrettable that the writer demonstrated a bias by forgetting to equally chastise Jewish nationalism.[121]

Meanwhile, each installment of *People, Years, Life*, having fought its way through censorship at various levels, including the author's self-censorship, would be passed from hand to hand, eagerly read and discussed. Ehrenburg was the first one after 1958 to write and to be allowed to publish a few good words about Pasternak. Thanks to Ehrenburg's travels across his eventful life, readers discovered—or rediscovered—for themselves the names of scores of Soviet and foreign writers, scholars, actors, and painters who had shaped modern culture but later had been removed from cultural memory. Many of them, including the writers Isaac Babel, Osip Mandelstam, and Perets (Peretz) Markish, were victims of repression in the years of Stalinist terror.[122] The impact of *People, Years, Life* in challenging and shaping the worldview of, without exaggeration, hundreds of thousands of people cannot be overestimated.

2

REHABILITATION

Early Releases

It took Khrushchev and his associates three years to come to the decision to start the dethronement of the dead leader. Daniil Granin, one of the most popular Soviet writers from the 1960s to the 1980s, recalled that a year after Stalin's funeral and the transformation of the Lenin Mausoleum on Red Square into the Stalin-Lenin Mausoleum, virtually everything remained the same as before: the discourse, the ubiquitous monuments to the Leader. Everything said by Stalin continued to be perceived as universal truth. "History only began to make itself ready for a leap."[1] And yet, following the profound shock of losing the idolized father figure, Stalin's departure brought positive, if not uniformly welcomed, changes in the lives of the majority of Soviet people in general and the Jews in particular. Tellingly, the cases of L. M. Olinskaia and Z. E. Levin, noted earlier, accused of disparagingly commenting on Stalin's death, were closed a few months after the funeral.[2]

Crucially, the attitude of the state toward real or perceived dissent changed. The Gulag, which is the Russian abbreviation for Main Directorate for Corrective Labor Camps, began to shrink rapidly in the 1950s. (The term Gulag itself has been widely used in public discourse retrospectively, following the 1973 publication of Alexander Solzhenitsyn's *The Gulag Archipelago*.) The nightmarish world behind the confines of prisons and camps was inhabited, in addition to criminal offenders, by political prisoners—over 425,000 by mid-1954 and still over 100,000 by the beginning of 1956.

In May 1956 the Main Directorate was closed down.[3] Later the number of political prisoners held in labor camps and "corrective penal colonies" shrank considerably: from Jauary 1952 to January 1959, their number had fallen more than fifty times, to eleven thousand.[4]

The dismantlement of the system of mass repression gradually returned surviving Gulag prisoners to society. Jewishness of the inmates usually did not play any role in the process of their rehabilitation. Some small number of the released Jewish inmates were former citizens of countries that after World War II became socialist satellites of the USSR (e.g., Poland and Hungary) and as such had a chance for repatriation. The vast majority, however, had to try to rebuild—at least partially—their lives in the Soviet environment, and, it seems, usually succeeded. Still, they were not the same people they had been before their arrest, and their fear, disillusionment, anger, or hatred often passed on to their family members and friends. The Gulag survivors' devastating experience added to their and other Jews' traumas of the war, the Holocaust, and the anti-Jewish Stalinist campaigns. For some people, the de-Stalinization turned into a traumatic experience too. How the burden of the past weighed on their daily life depended on the person's character and circumstances, and clashed with the future-oriented present, described in the official propaganda products as the last stretch toward Communism.

Although many people in the West believed that some Soviet forced-labor camps contained 30 or 40 percent Jews, the real mean incarceration rate for Jews did not exceed 1.2 percent in the late 1940s and thus was close to the proportion of Jews in the general population of the country.[5] No information is available for distinguishing, among them, those who were effectively political prisoners. In general, in terms of the rate of incarceration, the Jews certainly did not represent the most underprivileged ethnic group, especially compared with the Chechens, Crimean Tatars, ethnic Germans, and other peoples summarily deported for actual or anticipated collaboration with the Nazis. In addition, authorities hardly considered the Jews en masse less loyal than the local population of the Baltic republics and the western areas of Ukraine, where anti-Soviet partisans fought for many years after the end of World War II. In Moldavia the Jews were deemed more politically trustworthy than ethnic Moldovans because the latter were perceived as having strong sympathies with Romania.[6] True, following the establishment of Israel, which disappointingly for the Kremlin turned out to be "an outpost of capitalism." Jews began to be increasingly looked at with suspicion, as people whose sympathies with the Jewish state and its "imperialist partners" might be stronger than their loyalty to the Soviet Union. An institution with a high percentage of Jews among its employees would often be described as having "soiled personnel."

We don't know how many Jews were among those who received death sentences in the last years of Stalin's rule. Abolished in May 1947, capital punishment was reintroduced in January 1950 for particularly grave crimes such as treason and espionage. In Soviet practice this meant that, "in order to follow due process of law," prosecutors and judges often constructed farcical cases for people whose death sentences were dictated in advance of the trial. For instance, in Kyiv in the fall of 1952 several Jewish shadow-economy entrepreneurs were sentenced to death by firing squad for "economic counterrevolution."[7] Among the 1,612 people who received capital punishment in 1952 were thirteen members and staff employees of the Jewish Anti-Fascist Committee, established in the early phase of the Soviet-Nazi war and closed in November 1948. One of those executed, Solomon Lozovsky, was in fact not a member of the committee but rather their superior, chairman of the news agency Sovinformburo, the committee's umbrella organization. Those executed were spuriously accused of nationalism and espionage. Five of them were leading Soviet Yiddish authors: David Bergelson, Itsik Fefer, David Hofshteyn, Leyb Kvitko, and Perets Markish. In the 1950s someone described this execution as the "Night of Murdered Poets" and thus unjustly relegated the other eight victims to secondary characters in this cultural and human tragedy.

Among the accused members of the Jewish Anti-Fascist Committee was Lina Stern, a Lithuanian-born biochemist and physiologist, the first woman professor at the University of Geneva. In 1925 she emigrated to the Soviet Union and in 1939 became the first woman to be a full member of the Soviet Academy of Sciences. Stern was spared death in 1952 and instead exiled to Kazakhstan. Stalin's clemency toward her probably stemmed from his keen interest in issues of longevity; gerontology was one of Stern's fields of research. Upon her return to Moscow, in May 1953, she continued to be active as a scholar. In 1960 she was awarded the degree of doctor honoris causa by the University of Geneva, her alma mater.[8]

Only in a small number of cases, most conspicuously concerning the leading Moscow doctors, were acquittals announced in the press. The process of releasing and rehabilitating (often posthumously) political prisoners usually occurred covertly. This was characteristic also of the three post-Stalinist years, before the 20th Party Congress, which issued the first official condemnation of the Stalin-era repressions. Even the "doctors' plot" was not openly discussed after the first announcements.

The doctors were not the only Jewish intellectuals, officials, and officers rehabilitated in the early weeks and months after Stalin's death. On 21 March 1953, the Presidium of the Central Committee exonerated Polina Zhemchuzhina (Perl Karpovskaya). By that time Beria had already released her from captivity so that she could reunite with her husband, Vyacheslav Molotov, first deputy chairman of the Council of Ministers, whose name left a trace in the Molotov-Ribbentrop Pact (which effectively touched off World War II) and, rather irrelevantly, in the Molotov-cocktail petrol-bottle bomb. Molotov received his wife's liberation as a gift on his birthday, which coincided with the day of Stalin's funeral.[9] Zhemchuzhina, who in the 1930s occupied various positions in the Soviet government, had been arrested in January 1949 and accused of contacts with "Jewish nationalists," most notably Solomon Mikhoels, chairman of the Jewish Anti-Fascist Committee and director of the Moscow State Yiddish Theater.[10]

On the same day, 3 April 1953, when the Presidium of the Central Committee reassessed the "doctors' plot," it issued a decree condemning the January 1948 assassination of Solomon Mikhoels as a "blatant violation of the rights of a Soviet citizen guaranteed by the Constitution of the USSR." The decree also instructed punishment for those culpable for the "violation."[11] However, the decree did not appear in the press. A front-page editorial, "Soviet Socialist Legality Is Inviolable," published in *Izvestiia*, the second most important Soviet daily after *Pravda*, and reprinted in other newspapers, stated that Mikhoels, "an honest public figure and a People's Actor" (no mention of "Jewish"), had been defamed by "criminal adventurists" from the former Ministry of State Security, the same "adventurists" who were responsible for persecuting "a group of doctors." There was no mention that Mikhoels had been *murdered*.[12] Mikhoels had reemerged in the official narrative as a brilliant actor and director rather than a figure in

Jewish history. A collection of his essays and speeches came out in 1960 and, in an expanded edition, in 1965.

Earlier, in 1959, a bronze bust of Mikhoels was unveiled on his grave at the Donskoy Cemetery in Moscow.[13] Nearby, in the Donskoy Crematorium, built in 1927 as the first crematorium in Russia, the bodies of the thirteen people associated with the Jewish Anti-Fascist Committee had been burned after their execution in August 1952.[14] In the 1960s the iconic 1936 Soviet film *The Circus* once again included a short scene with Mikhoels, which in the late 1940s had been cut from copies then in circulation.[15] In January 1963, fifteen years after the murder, the newspaper *Sovetskaia Litva* (Soviet Lithuania) published a commemorative article by Leonid Lurie, a director at the Russian Dramatic Theater in Vilnius. In the 1940s he had worked as an assistant director in the Moscow Yiddish Theater. Lurie wrote that Mikhoels had fallen victim to the "Beria clique, those who calculatedly and pitilessly crushed the material and spiritual culture of the people."[16] It remained unsaid, however, that Mikhoels to all appearances was killed on direct orders from Stalin.

Miron Vovsi, Mikhoels's cousin, the chief internist of the Red Army (Soviet army from 1946) from 1941 to 1950 with a rank of general and a distinguished member of the medical scientific community, was among the leading doctors arrested and released in 1953. In the phantasmagoric script of the "doctors' plot," Mikhoels acted as his link to foreign intelligence. The authorities tried to make things right with Vovsi after his liberation and full exoneration in April 1953. He received an apartment in one of the most prestigious residential buildings in Moscow, was awarded the Order of Lenin on his sixtieth birthday in 1957, and was allowed to travel to Berlin and Brussels to present academic papers.[17]

This was not the only "family link" between the "doctors' plot" and the case of the Jewish Anti-Fascist Committee. The Yiddish writer Shmuel Gordon was arrested in December 1950, while his wife Evgeniia Reznik, a physician, also became a Gulag inmate, accused of plotting to poison top Soviet leaders. Reznik was sentenced in December 1953—eight months after the official end of the "doctors' plot"—to ten years' imprisonment. She was released in January 1954, though her case would be finally closed only in October 1962. In August 1955 Gordon returned from a camp in Abez, a settlement not far from the Arctic Circle in the Autonomous Soviet

Republic of Komi, to Moscow. He would later visit the polar area where he and a number of other Yiddish writers had served time as inmates of the Gulag. Toward the end of his life, in the 1990s, he wrote an autobiographical novel, *Yizker* (Commemorating the dead), which is matchless for a background understanding of the atmosphere in the milieu of Moscow Yiddish literati in the 1940s and 1950s. In his preface Gordon defined the genre of the novel as "a work documentary to some degree." Indeed, it was partly based on a document from the writer's personal archive: the fifty-six-page copy of the appeal that Gordon, then an inmate of a labor camp, submitted on 17 July 1954.[18]

Among those rehabilitated in March 1953 was Naum (Leonid) Eitingon, a Soviet master spy, one of the chief organizers of the 1940 assassination of Leon Trotsky, Stalin's influential opponent living in exile in Mexico who enjoyed a strong following worldwide. Arrested in 1951, Eitingon was accused of providing training to the doctors who participated in the alleged plot against Stalin and other governmental figures. In August 1953 he was arrested once again, this time as part of Beria's entourage. Finally, in March 1964, Eitingon was able to return to life outside the prison walls and, albeit remaining officially unrehabilitated, worked as a translator (he knew English, French, Spanish, and German) at a Moscow publishing house specializing in foreign literature.[19]

In December 1953 Grigori Kheifets left the prison confines. In his last foreign assignment, from 1941 to 1944, as the Soviet vice-consul in San Francisco, Kheifets played an active role in gaining access to atomic secrets. In 1947 he was appointed assistant secretary of the Jewish Anti-Fascist Committee. Arrested following the committee's liquidation, he was sentenced to death, but Stalin died first and this saved his life.[20]

In May 1954 the prison gates opened to release Leopold Trepper, a leading figure in the Soviet espionage network in Nazi-occupied Europe. Born in Poland, Trepper lived in Palestine and France before coming to the Soviet Union, where he studied in Moscow at the Yiddish Department of the Communist University for the National Minorities of the West, and joined Soviet military intelligence in 1937.[21] Sándor Radó, born into a Hungarian Jewish family, was released in November 1954. He had overlapping careers as cartographer, journalist, publisher, and Soviet agent.[22] Trepper and Radó later returned to their homelands, now Soviet satellites. Trepper would head the Warsaw-based publishing house Yidish Bukh (Yiddish book) and finally settled in Israel in 1974; Radó secured an academic appointment as a professor of geography and cartography in Budapest.

Lev Sheinin, who emerged from prison in November 1953, in the remaining years of his life (he died in 1967) focused on literary work, especially as he enjoyed the reputation of a bestselling Russian-language crime writer, whose stories and plays also came out in numerous translations. Before his arrest he had a remarkable career as a top investigator at the central procurator's office, and he was a member of the legal team at the postwar Nuremberg trials of Nazi war criminals. He was also notorious as a reveler and sybarite. Fired from his investigator's job in 1949 and arrested in 1951, Sheinin was accused inter alia of sympathizing with the Jewish Anti-Fascist Committee. It seems that in 1948 he showed reluctance to confirm the notion that Solomon Mikhoels had died in a random road accident.[23] In the 1960s Sheinin worked as editor-in-chief at Mosfilm, the main Soviet film studio.

Even more adventurous and scandalous was the story of Aleksei Kapler, a scriptwriter of the enormously successful films *Lenin in October* (1937) and *Lenin in 1918* (1939). He walked free in 1953 after spending ten years in the Gulag for having an affair—to all appearances a chaste one—with Stalin's sixteen-year-old daughter Svetlana.[24] Thanks to his status as a "privileged" inmate, he lived and worked as a photographer outside the camp.[25] Kapler's release did not lead to a happy ending with Svetlana, although by that time she was already twice divorced. Her first ex-husband was Jewish (Stalin made a point of never meeting him); her second ex-husband was the son of Andrei Zhdanov, the notorious advocate of purified Communist ideology during his 1945–48 tenure as the Party's "propagandist-in-chief." In 1966 Kapler, who by that time had reestablished himself as a successful scriptwriter, embarked on a new career as the anchor of the TV program *Kinopanorama*, which made him a household name in the USSR.

Among those released in 1954 was the Berlin-born popular jazz musician Eddie (or Ady) Rosner, who lived in Poland after Hitler's rise to power. In 1939 Rosner settled in the Soviet Union, where he developed a successful career. However, in the heat of the campaign against cosmopolitanism, jazz became essentially outlawed in the country. In the late 1940s and early 1950, tango, a "relic of the decadent West," also fell under disrepute, which severely affected the careers of such composers of hit songs as Oscar Stok and Efim Rosenfeld. The only band that continued to perform in the genres deemed non-Soviet was one led by Leonid Utesov (Lazar Vaysbeyn). The received wisdom is that Stalin liked his repertoire. Importantly, however, Utesov distanced himself from being called a jazz singer. Moreover, in his writings and public statements he repeated ad nauseam, probably half-jokingly, that Odessa rather than New Orleans was the real birthplace of this style of music.[26]

Given the hostile ideological and cultural climate, Rosner decided to leave the country, but was arrested after attempting to repatriate illegally to Poland. As a result he wound up in Kolyma, in the farthest northeastern extremities of Russia, where the local Gulag administration made it possible for him to form and lead a jazz orchestra for entertaining the guards, officials, and their families. After his release and move to Moscow, Rosner formed a large symphonic jazz orchestra, which at times had over sixty members.[27]

In April 1955 Georgy Zhukov, minister of defense, successfully petitioned the Central Committee to authorize the promotion of two Jewish veterans, both survivors of the purges in the late 1930s, to the rank of major-general.[28] Neither was in active service anymore, so the high military rank provided them with an honorable and substantial pension. One of them, Pavel Kolosov (Zaika), had been a leading figure in Soviet military espionage and later in military censorship.[29] The second, Yakov Fishman, had headed the chemical-weapons directorate. His success in building huge chemical-weapons production capacities had a major impact on the course of World War II, because this was what probably deterred the Germans from using such weapons.[30]

In 1955, the same year that Yosef Avidar succeeded Shmuel Eliashiv as the Israeli ambassador to the Soviet Union, the former's cousin, Zvi Preigerzon, was rehabilitated after spending six years in a labor camp. Preigerzon, a well-established scientist in the mineral-processing field, was also one of the last Hebrew writers remaining in the country. In 1948 and 1949, the secret police arrested several Hebrew literati who were enthused by the establishment of Israel and the positive role that the Soviet Union played in the realization of the Zionist dream. Some of Preigerzon's works reached Israel with the help of the Israeli embassy and were published there under the pen name A. Tsfoni.[31] In the meantime, the secret police tried to block attempts to send to Israel manuscripts of the late Hebrew author Avraham Friman, who was twice arrested in the 1930s. This operation involved the Yiddish writer Hirsh Bloshtein, recruited as an agent in the late 1930s.[32]

As we can see, the Gulag survivors had a chance to rebuild their lives after their liberation, especially if they had enough physical and psychological strength to do so. Some, such as Vovsi, Sheinin, Kapler, and Posner, managed to reclaim their place in the cultural and professional elite. Among the liberated were surviving veterans of the revolutionary movement, who had been active during the 1917 revolution, the ensuing civil war, and the later years of Soviet rule. Thousands of such veterans, often senior figures, were targeted during the purges in the second half of the 1930s. Some of those who survived remained staunch Communists throughout fifteen or more years of detention. "Lenin," "Leninism," and "restoration of Leninist norms" were invocations reiterated by them and many other Soviet and foreign Communists in an attempt to draw a line between their unfulfilled beliefs and the Soviet reality.

Aleksei Snegov (born Iosif Falikson) was arguably the most active and influential representative of those who remained committed Communists. In December 1953 he was brought from the Gulag to testify at Beria's perfunctory trial, but then sent back after sharing details of the latter's crimes. Only several months later did Khrushchev order Snegov's liberation and then place him in charge of the liberation of victims of political repressions. Snegov played an important role in persuading Khrushchev that denouncing Stalin would redeem and even strengthen the party.[33]

Voices of surviving veterans could be heard in 1961, during the 22nd Congress of the Communist Party, which became a moment of Stalin's conspicuous desacralization, with the removal of his embalmed body from the mausoleum on Red Square and the renaming of thousands of geographical and institutional objects in the country. Dora Lazurkina, who spent seventeen years in the Gulag, spoke most emotionally. Her husband, Mikhail Lazurkin, also a veteran Bolshevik and, like his wife, Jewish, had not survived imprisonment. Lazurkina told the delegates, who were supposed to be materialists rather than spiritualists, that Lenin's ghost had spoken to her: "It is unpleasant to be [in the mausoleum] next to Stalin, who did so much harm to the Party."[34]

Meanwhile, the process of releasing prisoners and their rehabilitation took place very slowly. Maria Zeifman, mother of the writer Georgy Vladimov, was arrested in the dying days of Stalin's rule and kept in a cell of the Leningrad branch of the secret police, accused of criticizing Beria. Even the execution of the latter did not save her from imprisonment in a labor camp, because investigators detected in her criticism an underlying anti-Soviet motive. Finally, she was released in January 1955 due to her physical condition; she had begun to lose her sight after an accident in the camp. However, full rehabilitation, which entitled her to a pension and housing, came only in 1957 thanks to the help of Konstantin Simonov, one of the most acclaimed and influential writers.[35]

Miron Bershadski, a twenty-six-year-old pianist at a Young Pioneers club (a Party youth center) in the Siberian city of Omsk, was arrested on 17 February 1953 as a "fervent Jewish nationalist." He was accused of being actively engaged in anti-Soviet agitation, praising the conditions of life and human rights in the United States, and maligning the Soviet leadership. In addition, he questioned the validity of the information published about the "doctors' plot" and spoke about specifically anti-Jewish persecution. On 27 March 1953, he received a sentence of ten years in a labor camp. In November 1955 the court took into consideration the six years of Bershadski's military service and the fact that he had two little children, and his sentence was reduced to six years. Finally, in May 1956, he was released, but his full rehabilitation came only in 1990.[36]

Echoes of Yiddish

In the Soviet Union, as previously in czarist Russia, the term Yiddish (*idish* in Russian) was hardly used in publications coming out in such languages as Russian, Ukrainian, and Belorussian. Instead, "Jewish language" (*evreiskii iazyk* in Russian) usually meant Yiddish, and the terms "Jewish culture" and "Jewish literature" normally referred to Yiddish culture and Yiddish literature. The same applied to actors, but not to artists, especially Soviet ones—they, creators of nonverbal art, would not, as a rule, carry the tag of "Jewish." The linguistic principle of classification had been adopted for all Soviet literatures. For instance, Ukrainian authors were those who wrote in

Ukrainian, including such writers as Natan Rybak, Abram Katsnelson, and Grigorii (Hryhorii) Plotkin, Jewish by origin. Zmitrok Bialdula, who under his real name, Shmuel Plavnik, compiled the first Yiddish-Belorussian dictionary (1932), but wrote his literary works in Belorussian, was characterized as a prominent Belorussian author. Applying this yardstick, Isaac Babel and Vasily Grossman were Russian writers, despite the fact that the themes and settings of their works tended to be Jewish. Only Yiddish writers could be members of the Jewish sections formed at the Moscow, Ukrainian, and Belorussian branches of the Writers Union in 1934, the year of its founding as an influential state-run organization. While the sections maintained their presence in the Writers Union until 1948, they blended to a large degree into the Jewish Anti-Fascist Committee, liquidated concurrently with the liquidation of the sections.

In 1954, among foreign visitors to the Soviet Union—whose number increased significantly after Stalin's death—were Leah Goldberg, a well-known Israeli poet, and Haim Shurer, editor of *Davar*, the Tel Aviv newspaper of the centrist labor party Mapai, then the dominant political force in Israeli politics. They came separately: Goldberg spent two weeks in the Soviet Union as a member of a delegation of Israeli women, while Shurer traveled in the country for a longer period of time. However, the hope that one or both of them would bring information about the fate of Bergelson, Markish, and other vanished Yiddish writers remained unfulfilled. Foreign activists, even such as Goldberg and Shurer who had no direct connections to the Yiddish literary world, were particularly concerned about their fate.[37] The first information on this issue would come out only at the end of 1955, when widows of the executed writers received information about the fate of their husbands. Earlier, in April 1955, the rehabilitation process was launched for the families of the executed members of the committee and they could return to Moscow from the remote and inhospitable places of their exile. Thus, Fefer's wife and sister were kept for seven years in labor camps, while his daughter and son-in-law spent three years in exile.[38]

On 22 November 1955, the Supreme Court of the USSR annulled the judgement taken on the case of the Jewish Anti-Fascist Committee and rehabilitated all the victims of that fabrication.[39] On 27 November the next of kin were summoned to the Military Collegium of the Supreme Court.

Surprisingly, the official of the collegium did not hide either the date of the victims' death, 12 August 1952, nor the fact of their execution.[40] In many other cases, families would get misleading information. Officials had a list at hand of forty-seven causes of "natural death," from peritonitis to congenital heart failure, recommended for using instead of the actual information about executions.[41]

Among the unsolved puzzles of Soviet decision-making is one that has to do with Yiddish. What could be the precise reasons for Stalin's destruction not only of the Jewish Anti-Fascist Committee chaired by Mikhoels, but of Yiddish culture in general, whose active constituency had been declining anyway? It is more or less graspable why the committee had fallen foul of the authorities. Established with a remit to generate pro-Soviet propaganda, it—to the dismay of watchful ideological overseers—developed some features of a centralized, internationally linked (and hence, through the prism of paranoid delusion, conspiratorial), quasi–civil society organization. A body of this kind had no place in the Soviet system and, therefore, was doomed to disappear from the landscape of Soviet organizations.

Nonetheless, other factors must have contributed to the destruction of virtually the entire infrastructure of Yiddish culture, which previously, especially before 1938, the year of the closing of vital cultural and educational programs in minority languages, was generously sponsored by the state. It seems that, by the end of the 1940s, any activity in Yiddish began to be considered at least potentially nationalist. In a country where people had been preemptively and routinely sentenced because of "*suspicion* of espionage" or "*unproven* espionage" (Article 58-6 of the Russian republic's Criminal Code), the difference between "potentially nationalist" and "nationalist" was of little or no importance. Characteristically, Yiddish literati made up the majority of those persecuted in the case of the Jewish Anti-Fascist Committee. The status of "outsiders" to Yiddish/Jewish literature may have saved Ehrenburg and Grossman. Other prominent Russian Jewish cultural figures who were members of the Jewish Anti-Fascist Committee also escaped arrest, including the renowned violinist David Oistrakh and the film director Fridrikh Ermler. Perhaps they were spared because the regime considered them useful as famous contributors to Russian or generic Soviet culture.[42]

Nineteen fifty-four was the year when imprisoned writers began to return from prisons and labor camps, and were trying to adjust to their new circumstances after years of isolation and privation. Some of the writers were released from the Gulag earlier than the others. Among the fortunate ones was Aizik Platner, a poet who from 1921 to 1932 lived in the United States, but then moved to the Soviet Union and settled in Minsk, eager to live and work in the first socialist state. To all appearances, the legal team that dealt with his case paid attention to the absurdity of the charges against him: the American "master spy" allegedly responsible for recruiting Platner was Moyshe Olgin, the staunchly pro-Soviet editor of the New York Communist daily *Morgn-Frayhayt* and an American correspondent of *Pravda*. To make matters even more absurd, Olgin had died a decade before Platner's arrest.[43]

Some writers established contacts with their foreign colleagues. Zalman Wendroff, the oldest Soviet Yiddish writer, born in 1877, came out of prison (he was not sent to a camp) in 1954. From 1900 to 1908 Wendroff lived in Britain and the United States. In the 1920s he was known as a "dollar correspondent," working—with approval by Soviet authorities—as a Moscow correspondent for foreign press outlets, most notably the New York Yiddish right-socialist daily *Forverts* and the Jewish Telegraphic Agency. In October 1956 Wendroff wrote to Paul Novick, who replaced Olgin as editor of *Morgn-Frayhayt* and also figured in the legends of the Soviet secret police as an American spy. The veteran writer explained that he had found himself in the situation of losing his whole archive accumulated during over fifty years of his journalistic and literary work, including all his books, articles, stories, and diaries. "As a result, I am left, to borrow a phrase [from a Christian tradition], naked on a naked earth." After euphemistically explaining the results of his arrest and its associated confiscation of his private archive, Wendroff asked Novick to help him obtain clippings of his writings published in the New York newspaper.[44]

Rehabilitation could come later than liberation. Only a minority of those released in 1954–56 would concurrently receive a full legal exoneration.[45] Meanwhile, former inmates often could not return to their home cities or sometimes even continued to live next to the prison camp.[46] Itsik Kipnis, the Yiddish writer arrested in Kyiv in June 1949, celebrated the New Year of 1956 outside the confines of the Gulag, but his official rehabilitation, and permission to return to Kyiv, came only eighteen months later.[47]

Many of those released from the camps needed serious medical care. The poet Shmuel Halkin (Samuil Galkin), arguably the most venerable figure among the surviving Yiddish writers, got a spot at a sanatorium situated not far from Moscow.[48] In 1957 his sixtieth anniversary was celebrated in a fitting manner, both officially, in Russian, and in the circle of his Yiddish colleagues.[49] The government decorated him with the Order of the Red Banner and the State Publishing House published a massive volume of his poems translated into Russian. The Yiddish poet Naftali Herts Kon, who tasted the Gulag twice, before and after World War II, was outraged by Halkin's readiness to accept these honors.[50]

Although the November 1955 decision annulling the judgment on the case of the Jewish Anti-Fascist Committee remained unknown to the broad public until its official publication thirty-four years later, in December 1989, the information went around in the circles close to the families of the victims. On 6 December 1955, three former leading figures of the Moscow Jewish (predominantly Yiddish) publishing house Der Emes, closed in November 1948, wrote to the poet Aleksei Surkov, who headed the Writers Union from 1953 to 1959:

> Now, when the Supreme Court has rehabilitated Yiddish writers, the Soviet Writers Union faces the urgent task of rehabilitating Yiddish Soviet literature. The Writers Union has to undertake measures to publish the tragically perished writers' works in their original language and restore publication of works by other Yiddish writers, who in recent years have been robbed of the possibility to see their writings in print. Such steps are expected by many thousands of Jews, whose proud feeling of being Soviet citizens was hurt in the last several years, because of the actions of the enemies of the people.

The signatories identified the positions they held at the liquidated publishing house: Moyshe Altshuler, head of the department of Marxist-Leninist literature; Moyshe Belenky, editor-in-chief (liberated from the Gulag in 1954); and Eli Falkovich, head of the department of belles-lettres.[51] A leading Soviet Yiddish grammarian and lexicographer, Falkovich was awarded the Order of Lenin for his valiant deeds during the battle for Moscow in 1941–42, in which he took part as a soldier in the people's militia (*opolchenie*).[52]

On 16 December 1955, most probably in reaction to that letter, Surkov wrote to the Central Committee of the Communist Party, focusing mainly on the situation regarding Yiddish literature:

> Since the recent rehabilitation of a large group of Yiddish writers, the Writers Union keeps getting numerous letters and oral inquiries from the writers' relatives and various other persons. They want to know what is going to happen to the literary legacy of the rehabilitated dead writers as well as to the relatively large group of Soviet literati who write in Yiddish.
>
> . . . issues concerning, first, the current status and future of Yiddish literature as one of the Soviet national literatures and, second, its publishing base . . . have an all-Union significance and are therefore outside the competence of the Writers Union.
>
> The Secretariat of the Writers Union is therefore raising these questions with the Central Committee and requesting instructions and advice on how to solve them in the life of our writers' organization.[53]

The 29 December 1955 issue of *Literaturnaia gazeta* (Literary newspaper), published by the Writers Union, informed its readers about a commission responsible for Perets Markish's literary legacy. While David Bergelson and Itsik Fefer were best-known to foreign Yiddish readers, Markish carried the reputation of the most prominent author in the "domestic" hierarchy of Soviet Yiddish writers, especially in the all-Soviet rather than the internal Yiddish ranking. It is no coincidence that information about a commission authorized to oversee his legacy appeared before other similar news items. Proceeding from this information, editors of *Morgn-Frayhayt*, who previously discounted as malicious fabrication any mention of Soviet repressions against Jewish cultural figures, drew the logical conclusion that, first, Markish was no longer alive, and, second, that his name was "stainless."[54] Still, they, American Communists, remained baffled by what actually had happened to Markish and other writers.

On 24 January, 29 March, and 15 May 1956, *Literaturnaia gazeta* wrote about commissions formed in Moscow by the Writers Union to deal with legacies of several posthumously rehabilitated Yiddish men of letters:

David Bergelson, Leyb Kvitko, Isaac Nusinov, Shmuel Persov, and Itsik Fefer. These and other similar commissions became an important phenomenon in literary and, generally, cultural life. Thanks to them, writers who otherwise had nothing to do with Yiddish literature became involved in preparing various memorial events and book publications. Typically, each commission included several representatives of the literary community, Russian and Yiddish, as well as the murdered writer's widow. A well-established Russian author (Yiddish authors were, apparently, considered less weighty) chaired such a body. Thus, the prose writer Vsevolod Ivanov, who chaired the Bergelson commission, used to be a neighbor and friend of the slain writer. Mikhail Khrapchenko, a historian of literature, chaired the Nusinov commission. Nusinov, who died in prison, specialized both in Yiddish and West European literatures and was, arguably, the first direct target of the "cosmopolitanism" campaign. Nusinov's book *Pushkin and World Literature* faced condemnation as an alleged attempt to present the great Russian poet's writings as derivative and imitative.[55]

The popular children's writer Lev Kassil volunteered to chair the commission of his friend Lev (Leyb) Kvitko, who was, uniquely among non-Russian-language authors, widely known thanks to numerous translations of his children's poetry.[56] Kassil's book in two parts, *Konduit* and *Shvambrania*, set in his Jewish childhood home, came out in new editions from 1957 onward, following the rehabilitation of his younger brother Osia, or Iosif. Osia, the second protagonist of Kassil's autobiographical book, was executed in 1938. Many readers remembered Osia's juicy punch line when he, a child of assimilated parents, finds out that he and his entire family were Jewish: "Is our cat also a Jew?"[57] Kvitko's books began to appear in 1956. In November 1960 Kassil chaired a gala devoted to the seventieth anniversary of Kvitko's birth. He said: "The enemies culpable for Kvitko's death—are our enemies, enemies of our culture and our Soviet state."[58]

Surviving former "cosmopolitans," "spies," and "nationalists" could restore their positions in the Writers Union and other organizations. Yiddish writers, meanwhile, were kept in ideological quarantine. None of them were present at the congress of the Writers Union in December 1954, though, paradoxically, Alexander Pen, a Communist Israeli Hebrew poet ("a talentless rhymer" according to the Soviet poet David Samoilov), was one of the foreign delegates.[59] Also, none of them figured on the list of thirty-four distinguished people (scholars, generals, actors, etc.) purported to represent Soviet Jews who—judging by their collective letter in *Pravda* on 6 November 1956—"together with the entire Soviet people and the peoples of all other countries" condemned the "aggression of Israel, England, and France against Egypt" during the Suez Crisis.

Outside the Soviet Union, the moment of shocking clarity came in April 1956 when an article, entitled "Our Pain and Our Consolation," appeared in the Warsaw Yiddish newspaper *Folks-Shtime* (People's voice). This was the first publication in the Communist press that focused on the specifically Jewish aspect of Stalinist repressions. Strictly speaking, the *Folks-Shtime* article was a paraphrase of what Leon Crystal, a writer for *Forverts*, had brought from his fact-finding trip to Moscow in the beginning of 1956. Israeli operatives helped the American journalist "discover" the first dose of truth about the tragic destiny of the Jewish Anti-Fascist Committee. Crystal's information was rather vague. Even the number of those executed on 12 August 1952 remained unknown and for many years was believed to be twenty-four.[60]

During a stopover in Warsaw on his way back from Moscow, Crystal shared his scoop with Hersh (Grzegorz) Smolar, editor of *Folks-Shtime*, who was eager to get information about Soviet writers and journalists. Smolar used to be in constant touch by telephone with Fefer, managing secretary and, following Mikhoels's death, chairman of the Jewish Anti-Fascist Committee. In November 1948, however, a stranger responded rudely to Smolar's routine Friday telephone call: "There is no Itsik and no Fefer here." Smolar immediately understood that something truly calamitous had taken place in Moscow. This had a devastatingly demoralizing effect among Polish Jewish Communists and their sympathizers. In addition to worrying about their Soviet friends and colleagues, they feared that a similar situation could arise in Poland.[61] Crystal's update brought some clarity to what had happened to Fefer and other writers.

While the American and other Western Communists initially dismissed Crystal's report, there was no way to brush aside the information from the newspaper of Polish Communists. As it happened, the publication of "Our Pain and Our Consolation" inadvertently turned into a defining moment in the history of Jewish Communism in the Western world, marking its decline as a relatively widespread phenomenon.[62] At the same time, the article generally remained unknown in the Soviet Union. Moreover, it seems that the majority of Soviet Jews not only did not know about the destiny of the leading figures of the Jewish Anti-Fascist Committee, but in all likelihood had no idea about the former existence of the committee, whose single periodical, the Yiddish newspaper *Eynikayt* (Unity, 1942–48), was allowed to print only ten thousand copies, almost a third of which went abroad.[63] Most importantly, the committee did not have a periodical in Russian, by that time the language of the majority of Soviet Jews. The silence that surrounded the liquidation and the rehabilitation of the Jewish Anti-Fascist Committee contributed to its almost total absence from collective memory, particularly among younger people.

In 1954 Yiddish books appeared in Moscow secondhand stores. Optimists took it as heralding the rehabilitation of Yiddish literature.[64] Indeed, bookstores had to follow instructions of the General Directorate for the Protection of State Secrets in the Press under the Council of Ministers of the USSR, known as Glavlit, whose censors ubiquitously controlled the contents of all books, periodicals, recordings, films, radio and television programs, repertoires of performers (from top professional theaters to restaurant ensembles), and posters. Glavlit also regulated the return of previously banned books. Significantly, the rehabilitation of a writer did not necessarily mean that his or her writings would be made immediately, or ever, accessible.[65]

Another encouraging development in 1954 was the publication of a Russian translation of Sholem Aleichem's novel *Motel the Cantor's Son*, which came out in Moscow with a print run of thirty thousand. This was followed by publications of numerous translations from Yiddish. Thus, from 1956 to 1959, Moscow publishing houses produced books by the five writers executed on 12 August 1952 as well as dozens of titles by other Yiddish authors, some of them still active.

The 1958 additional volume, no. 51, of the *Great Soviet Encyclopedia* came out with four articles on "Jewish writers." Those on David Bergelson (pp. 36–37) and Shmuel Halkin (p. 70) did not carry the writers' photos, which indicated their lower hierarchical status than that of Lev Kvitko (p. 148) and Perets Markish (p. 189), whose photos accompanied the corresponding entries. The article on Kvitko—"an author of wonderful poems about children and for children," translated into thirty-three languages of the Soviet Union—also contained information pointing—surprisingly—to his membership in the Jewish Anti-Fascist Committee. Judging by the general list of contributors to the encyclopedia, it was, most probably, Moyshe Belenky, editor in chief of the liquidated Moscow Jewish publishing house, who wrote the four articles. Characteristically, Jews are absent from the long list of nationalities of the contributors, despite the presence of six people with the surname Abramovich, twelve Kogans, sixteen Rabinoviches, as well as many other distinctly Jewish surnames. Indeed, as Petr Vail and Aleksandr Genis, the historians of Soviet culture, wrote with some sarcastic exaggeration, Jews would become "virtually the main secret of the Soviet Union. Perhaps only sex was shrouded in mystery more zealously."[66]

Returning the Names of the Perished

As in many if not the majority of similar cases, it remains unclear what the real reason was for persecuting the writer Isaac Babel, especially as it happened after November 1938, when Stalin scaled down the purges. Babel was considered important and reliable enough to be sent as one of the Soviet representatives to the Congress of Writers in Defense of Culture, convened in Paris in 1935. In the indictment, he was accused of being a member of a Trotskyist organization in the 1920s and acting as a French and Austrian spy in the 1930s.[67]

According to one apocryphal theory, his arrest was, in fact, triggered by the suspicion that in his new stories he planned to portray Soviet secret-police officers in the manner in which he had previously depicted, rather controversially, the Red Army during the civil war in Russia. Characteristically, around the time of Babel's arrest, Semen Gekht, a writer close to him, published a story entitled "An Instructive Story," which described the unfair repression of the story's protagonist. At that time of temporary "liberalization," later sometimes called "the Beria thaw," such publications were permissible. (In 1944, when the secret police arrested Gekht, "An Instructive Story" became one of the incriminating documents.)[68] On the other hand, also during the same "liberal" period, the repressive machinery had consumed the life of Mikhail Koltsov (Fridlyand), a towering figure in the world of Soviet journalism who had nothing to do with portraying the secret police. In fact, the secret police had numerous reports citing Babel's criticism of what was going on in the country, including his ridicule of Stalin's Russian usage.[69] Significantly, there was no Jewish aspect to these arrests.

One way or another, all the manuscripts of Babel's works in progress either were destroyed or, less probably, remain hidden in inaccessible files.[70] Among the confiscated manuscripts were drafts of Babel's translation of Sholem Aleichem's *Tevye the Dairyman.* According to his contractual obligation, Babel was to prepare the new translation for a publication planned in conjunction with the eightieth anniversary of the classic Yiddish writer's birth. In February 1939, Babel, a member of the jubilee committee, spoke about the "generally terribly misinterpreted and distorted" Russian translations of Sholem Aleichem works and that "even those that are correct still don't reflect the spirit of Sholem Aleichem."[71]

Arrested in May 1939 and executed in January 1940, Babel was legally rehabilitated in December 1954 following the review of his case by the Military Collegium of the Supreme Court. The investigating judicial team could find no basis for legal action against him. Nevertheless, character witnesses had to participate in the procedural formalities of the rehabilitation process. Ehrenburg, one of them, wrote in his testimonial: "I consider Babel to be an outstanding Soviet writer; his works are widely known abroad and have always been placed, by our foes as well as our friends, in the pantheon of Communist literature."[72] In the commission, formed in April 1956 by the Writers Union to deal with Babel's literary legacy, Ehrenburg played the major role.[73] He explained later that Babel "was the greatest friend I had in my life."[74]

It did not mean, however, that following Babel's exoneration his stories immediately reappeared in print. His first posthumous collection of stories (with Ehrenburg's introduction) came out in 1957. After over two decades of complete obscurity, the younger generation did not know him at all, and initially did not rush to buy the book.[75] T. S. Gorbshtein, a thirty-nine-year-old reader from Tashkent, wrote to Ehrenburg: "Your book [*People, Years, Life*] is great and thrilling. It offers much to those of my age and to me, who have received a one-sided education, because it opens our eyes. . . . Effectively, we do not know the history of literature and art in this century, be it Western or our own. . . . Babel's stories have stunned me—but those my age and I did not even know his name. I repeat: yours is a great book."[76]

Boris Frezinski, whose studies of Soviet literary life have a special focus on Ehrenburg's life and work, recalled that his first encounter with the name of Babel occurred through reading Ehrenburg's 1957 article in *Literaturnaia gazeta*.[77] In that long article, aimed at stressing Babel's loyalty to Communism, Frezinski read inter alia: "Babel's destiny is tragic: unworthy people slandered and destroyed him. His writings will soon see the light of day and, after reading them, everyone will see how intimately he associated himself with the Soviet perception of the world and how unfair it would be to juxtapose him with other Soviet writers."[78] The 1957 collection of stories, whose seventy-five thousand copies found a place in private and public libraries all over the country, and Ehrenburg's praise for his perished friend's literary legacy, attracted the interest of (predominantly Jewish) literary scholars and lay enthusiasts. The literary scholar Lev Livshits, a pioneering student of Babel's work, was a war veteran and a Gulag prisoner in the early 1950s. His friend, the poet Boris Slutsky, introduced him to Antonina Pirozhkova, Babel's widow.[79]

To the alarm of conservative ideologists, the less orthodox members of the Soviet cultural elite promoted Babel's name and his writings. In November 1957 Aleksei Surkov lamented that "some critics went to other extremes, exaggerating the significance" of such writers as Babel and "granting full amnesty to their generally recognized mistakes and misconceptions."[80] Dmitri Starikov, the twenty-seven-year-old abrasive critic then on the staff of *Literaturnaia gazeta*, opined that Ehrenburg's "views contradict[ed] the entire experience of our literature, including Ehrenburg's own experience" and noted that Ehrenburg "avoided speaking about contradictions of Babel's, which resulted in a flagrant bias revealed in this case by the authoritative writer."[81] Leonid Novichenko, an influential Soviet literary critic and theorist, characterized Babel's humanism as bourgeois, in contradistinction to socialist humanism.[82]

Over the years there was less appetite for questioning Babel's place in the Soviet literary canon. However, a negative attitude continued to be apparent. In 1964, during an event marking the seventieth anniversary of Babel's birth, Ehrenburg spoke with bitter scorn about the obstacles to publishing books by Babel. He claimed readiness to beg on his knees for permission to issue a new edition of Babel's writings, even instead of publishing his own book.[83] Two years later a larger collection of Babel's works came out in

Moscow. In the same year the Moscow Vakhtangov Theater staged a dramatized version of Babel's *Red Cavalry*, previously violently anathematized by his critics.[84] In 1962 the Moscow chapter of the Writers Union expelled the well-known literary critic Iakov Elsberg (born Shapirstein), who was blamed for working as a secret-police agent assigned to collect compromising information about several writers, including Babel. However, a year later, after Elsberg's appeal, his membership was restored by the central apparatus of the union.[85]

In 1964 the CIA reported that Western critics considered Babel "to have been the greatest of the post-revolutionary prose writers."[86] Nineteen sixty-four was also the year when the first book of Babel came out in East Germany, whose readers had broad access to translations of books by Soviet authors. Babel's stories, however, were previously deemed unsuitable because, as the East German decision-makers concluded in 1958, they carried "a frightening image of Communism."[87] The situation was somewhat different in Poland, where the Warsaw Yiddish periodicals—the journal *Yidishe Shriftn* and the newspaper *Folks-Shtime*—began to publish Babel's stories in December 1956.[88] True, in Polish translation his books appeared later, starting in 1961.

The strong Jewish coloration of Babel's prose made his writings particularly appealing to Jewish readers.[89] Babel's persona and writings challenged the Soviet convention of defining only Yiddish writers and, sometimes, writers in the languages of other ethnic Jewish groups as "Jewish," Sergei Dovlatov, a popular Russian writer of the late twentieth century, fully agreed with such conventional classification, arguing that Babel's Jewish origin and the Jewishness of his literary characters were not enough to justify calling him a Jewish author.[90] In contrast, Shimon Markish, Perets Markish's son and a litterateur in his own right, considered Babel the principal founder of Soviet Russian-Jewish literature.[91] Babel's stories, set in Odessa of the first two decades of the twentieth century, contributed strongly to creating the image of Odessa as the capital of Russian—and considerably Jewish—humor. An *odessit*, a witty and resourceful native of Odessa, speaking a peculiar—"Jewish"—kind of Russian, became a staple of the caricatured Jew appearing in writings, films, and various performances. Such an *odessit*, Buba Kastorski, performed by Boris Sichkin, appeared in the 1967 action film *The Elusive Avengers*, one of the highest-grossing Soviet films. Sichkin even inserted the Yiddish word "schlimazel," meaning a consistently unlucky person, in the secret password, ostensibly in Spanish: "Buenos-Aires-schlimazel-besame-mucho."

Whatever category Babel belonged to, his books occupied a place of honor on Soviet Jews' bookshelves, often next to the sets of volumes of Russian translations of Sholem Aleichem, a long-established figure in the Soviet literary canon, and Lion Feuchtwanger. Little known in the United States where he settled in 1941 as a refugee from Nazi Germany, Feuchtwanger was canonized as a progressive novelist in East Germany and the Soviet Union. His novels were present in non-Jewish homes as well, but they, most notably *The Josephus Trilogy*, *Jew Suess*, and *The Spanish Ballad* (or *The Jewess of Toledo*), stood prominently on Soviet Jewish shelves as a signifier of Jewish space. Moreover, the Jewish perception of Feuchtwanger tended to be markedly different from the non-Jewish one.[92] Russian translations from Yiddish, including collections of Perets Markish's poetry and of Sholem Asch's stories, might sit on the shelves of the same family bookcase. However, a volume of the poet Osip Mandelstam could not be found on such shelves, except, perhaps, when a person demonstrated bravery or naivete by keeping an old publication of Mandelstam's poetry.

In contrast to Babel, Mandelstam received a full posthumous rehabilitation only in 1987. Even after the de-Stalinization process, the authorities could not forgive the poet his 1933 satirical poem that described the climate of fear in the Soviet Union under Stalin's rule. Not long before Mandelstam's arrest, Perets Markish warned him: "You are taking yourself by the hand and leading yourself to your execution."[93] Ehrenburg's *People, Years, Life* included the first mention of the circumstances of Mandelstam's death "10,000 kilometers away from his native city." Although Ehrenburg did not elaborate, it was clear that the poet died in a labor camp.[94]

Mandelstam's status as an unrehabilitated person made it difficult to publish his poetry. As a result, his poems circulated informally or appeared in print only occasionally in various periodicals. One of the most significant publications came out, with Ehrenburg's introduction, in the April 1965 issue of the journal *Prostor* (Expanse), based in Alma-Ata, the then capital of Kazakhstan.[95] In May 1965 Ehrenburg chaired a literary event devoted to Mandelstam, the first in post-Stalinist Moscow. It was initiated by Valentin Gefter, whose father, Mikhail Gefter, would later become a well-known nonconformist historian and philosopher. The younger Gefter, who was at that time studying at the Mechanic-Mathematical Faculty of Moscow State University, and several other students formed a group that staged the event on the premises of the university.[96] Notably, this took place before 1968, the year when Moscow University and especially its Mechanic-Mathematical Faculty became known for their anti-Jewish sentiment.[97]

In all, against the backdrop of less rigid cultural policy, rehabilitation of cultural figures and posthumous rehabilitation of those executed contributed to broadening the cultural horizon of the Soviet population in general and in particular that of Soviet Jews. Importantly, the state perceived the growth of cultural needs of the population as a positive side effect of better standards of living, and sponsored ideologically approved publications, art projects, and events. Denizens of Communist society were supposed to have strong and variegated cultural interests. In this sense, those Soviet Jews who regularly went to theaters and museums and whose (typically cramped) dwellings were full of books and literary journals could be already qualified to live in a more advanced society, though they did not necessarily envision it as a Communist one.

3

BIROBIDZHAN

An Almost-Lost World

The Soviet project of building a Jewish territorial unit in the Far Eastern area of Russia, over five thousand miles from Moscow, was launched with a great deal of fanfare in 1928 and remained, most notably in the early and mid-1930s, a focus of attention in the press and wider public, both in the USSR and abroad.[1] This formidable and challenging undertaking was intended mainly to "normalize" the Jews, historically living dispersed among other ethnic groups, by turning them into a "proper" Soviet nation with a titular homeland. In addition, the development of the severely underpopulated territory aimed to help solve the strategic problem of economically and militarily buttressing a stretch along the troublesome border with China.

The geographic name, Birobidzhan, spelled also *Birobidjan* or *Biro-Bidjan*, was assembled from two local toponyms—the Bira and the Bidzhan, tributaries of the Amur River, the chief waterway of the Far East. The word was coined to define the entire allocated tract, but later its official usage narrowed to denote the newly built town and administrative center of the Jewish Autonomous Region (JAR), the status that the area received in May 1934. Yet the initial name, sometimes spelled as Birobidjan in English-language publications, continued to be widely used for the entire region, sometimes even as "the Jewish Autonomous Region of Birobidzhan."

It was not a new idea to make Jews look bureaucratically less abnormal, at least by the yardstick of Stalinist rules for elevating ethnic groups to the status of bona fide nations. An earlier, curtailed attempt to construct a Jewish republic on the Crimean Peninsula was, to a degree, grassroots-initiated and therefore appeared more "national(ist)" and less "Soviet" than the Birobidzhan project, conceived by Moscow functionaries. Moreover, the Crimean Jewish project encountered discontent from the local population, notably the Tatars, and in general never developed beyond establishing two contiguous rural Jewish districts, named after their central villages, Fraidorf and Larindorf. They were renamed Novoselovka and Krestianovka in 1944 as part of a process of removing Jewish toponyms from the Soviet map.

In February 1944 the Jewish Anti-Fascist Committee attempted to lobby for a Soviet Jewish republic in Crimea as a place of ingathering for the surviving Jews who were scattered all over the country. Clearly, after years of failed attempts to build something significant in the Far East, the committee did not consider Birobidzhan a place suitable and appealing for such a purpose. Some sources blame the committee's demise, in particular, on that initiative.[2]

It seems that there were attempts to populate the JAR not only with Yiddish-speaking migrants from the Slavic republics but also with Jews from Georgia and the Caucasus. However, such attempts came to naught.[3] Similar attempts with Central Asian Jews were also unsuccessful.[4] In the 1930s hundreds of foreign Jews came to the JAR. Many more foreigners, usually emigrants from Russia or those who lived in the territories formerly belonging to pre-1917 Russia, wanted to move to the Soviet Far East, but the hyperparanoia of spying stopped Soviet authorities from allowing them to enter the country.

The Birobidzhan project also attracted an unknown number of Subbotniks, or Sabbatarians, Russian converts to rabbinic Judaism.[5] Their arrival hardly affected the composition of the Jewish segment of the local population, though it implanted a group of devotedly observant practitioners into what was otherwise predominantly an emphatically secular population. A Polish Jewish activist who visited the area in 1934 found, or chose to find, only several men who kept the Sabbath and abjured pork; all of them were Subbotniks.[6] According to David Khait, a Russian Jewish writer, by the mid-1930s young Birobidzhaners knew, and preferred to know, very little about Jewish traditions and were bemused watching a group of Subbotniks who had settled in one of the villages of the JAR. Some local Jews even offered in jest their services as *shabes-goyim*, or Gentiles, hired to perform domestic chores forbidden to Jews (including the pious converts) on the Sabbath.[7]

As in other areas of the Soviet Union, the agricultural sector of the JAR had two forms of organizations—collective farms and state farms, which reflected two kinds of property recognized by the Soviet Constitution: cooperative property and (ideologically more preferable) state property. The private sector had been effectively eliminated, though village dwellers were allowed, with a plethora of restrictions, to have a small private plot.

In 1934, when the JAR appeared on the map, the area's status as a "region" was considered a temporary designation prior to the proclamation of an autonomous republic. The latter was the status one notch lower than that of a union republic, or the ultimate in the national-territorial hierarchy of the USSR. Nonetheless, the status of the JAR remained untouched throughout the Soviet period and later on. In addition to the general difficulties of getting large numbers of people to relocate to remote areas of Russia, the voluntary resettlement of Jews to the Far East, which underwent a brief revival after the end of World War II, was undercut in particular by the authorities' chronic fear of Jewish nationalism.[8] Repressions aggravated the situation. In the 1930s, 1940s, and 1950s, the police arrested hundreds of Jewish and non-Jewish residents of the JAR, notably top officials, intellectuals, and recent immigrants, after accusing them of anti-Soviet activities. Many of those arrested were executed.[9]

During the rallies and private conversations in the last months of Stalin's life, in the heat of the "doctors' plot," people in various corners of the country called for removing all Jews to the JAR. In Birobidzhan, like elsewhere in the country, even the official condemnation of the "doctors' plot," published on 4 April 1953, did not immediately stop the repressions targeting "Jewish nationalists." On 6 and 7 April, two accountants working in one of the collective farms of the JAR received sentences of ten and eight years for "anti-Soviet, bourgeois-nationalist agitation." In November 1954 their punishment was reduced to five years' imprisonment, and only sometime later were they freed by an act of clemency rather than by annulment of the accusations against them.[10]

Around the same time in the West, Birobidzhan constituted one of the central topics concerning Soviet Jewry. In May 1951 a (British) *Observer* article by Edward Crankshaw carried the news that the Kremlin had merged the JAR into the Khabarovsk Province, thus downgrading it into a region "administered as an integral part of the Russian Federated Republic."[11] An intelligence officer at the British Military Mission in Moscow from 1941 to 1943, Crankshaw later turned to journalism and gained a reputation as an expert on the Soviet Union. Yet, on this occasion, he was mistaken in his conclusions. Already since its establishment, the JAR had been part of the Khabarovsk (until 1938, Far Eastern) Province of the Russian republic.

The rumor, however, prevailed over the facts. A 1954 article by Maurice Friedberg, a specialist on Soviet literature, also mentions the "abolition" of the JAR.[12] The *American Jewish Year Book*, published annually by the American Jewish Committee, reported in its 1954 edition that "nothing had been heard for years about Jewish life" in the JAR and that, according to rumors, "the territory had been transformed into a district of slave labor camps."[13] It was an open secret that Gulag prisoners had built many facilities in Birobidzhan, including the railway station and the movie theater.[14] Even so, regular citizens, rather than inhabitants of labor camps, made up the core majority of the region's population.

In September 1954 Hershl Weinrauch, also known as Vinokur, from 1932 to 1938 a journalist on the regional Yiddish newspaper *Birobidzhaner Shtern* (Birobidzhan Star), appeared in the United States as a witness before the House Committee on Communist Aggression. In the postwar 1940s Weinrauch managed to leave the Soviet Union among the stream of repatriates to Romania and then lived in Israel for a short time before moving to the USA. The House Committee learned from him that "Birobidzhan was fake" and that Soviet authorities "didn't officially liquidate it, but they closed the Jewish schools and eliminated Jewish cultural life."[15]

In the meantime, the JAR did not warrant mention in the Soviet press, except in such materials as postelection lists of deputies of the Supreme Soviet (parliament) of the Soviet Union. After 1946 the JAR usually had one Jew in its constitutionally guaranteed five-person decorative parliamentary representation.[16] Rakhil Freidkina, an agronomist, filled the slot from 1954 to 1958, and was replaced by Vera Gleizer, a pedagogue, from 1958 to 1962. The JAR remained almost invisible in the media also because, from 1949 to 1955, there was no industrial development in the region and no significant investments were made in its inefficient agricultural sector. Until the early 1960s, the population of the JAR was declining; people were leaving for regions with better job prospects.[17]

Birobidzhan did surface in some Soviet newspaper articles, typically referred to as one of the towns in the Far Eastern part of Russia without indicating its status as capital of the JAR. Strikingly and tellingly, no JAR residents figured on the list of distinguished Soviet Jews whose collective letter in *Pravda* on 6 November 1956 condemned the "aggression of Israel, England, and France against Egypt" during the Suez Crisis.

The writer Andrei Prishvin, or perhaps the editors of *Pravda* who had doctored his article, refrained from using the words Jew and Jewish in his long description of the "fertile land" in the Birobidzhan area.[18] Prishvin's piece of reporting brought home to readers Khrushchev's reference to Birobidzhan as a propitious locality for his pet campaign of reclaiming virgin lands and thus increasing agricultural cultivation in large Siberian territories. In January 1956 the Soviet leader mentioned Birobidzhan, without specifying its "Jewishness," as an area rather than a town: "Let's take, for instance, Birobidzhan. Rice has been cultivated there, watermelons and melons can grow, tomatoes, orchards! This is a wonderful place! It means that we have to move there. When? We'll discuss it, we'll see."[19]

Indeed, it was not a barren land by any means. The geologist Iuri Kapkov, who in 1954 spent several months in the JAR and portrayed Birobidzhan as "a usual provincial little town" with "several factories and produce cooperatives," was impressed by the state of affairs in the collective farm, named Twenty Years of October (meaning the October Revolution of 1917), all or almost all of whose members were Jewish. Their industry and resourcefulness, as well as advantageous climatic conditions assured success in running the farm. Apart from the "usual vegetables," they cultivated watermelons, melons, grapes, and even cork trees.[20]

The virgin-land campaign started in the JAR even before Khrushchev's 1956 speech. In 1954 a new village—later called Tselinnoe (a derivative of *tselina*, the Russian word for "virgin land")—was established in the region. Although ethnic Russians formed the predominant majority among Tselinnoe's villagers, and generally in the rural areas of the JAR, it was Israel Umanskii, a war veteran and formerly a member of a Jewish collective farm in Ukraine, who made the first symbolic furrow in the field.[21] Collective farms of the region took an active part in cultivating maize, "the queen of the fields" (a contemporary Soviet moniker for the crop), seen in Khrushchev's visionary plans as a panacea for the USSR's agricultural ills.[22]

The best-known collective farm of the JAR, Legacy of Lenin, was based in Valdgeim (or Valdheim, "Forest Home" in Yiddish), a village less than ten miles from Birobidzhan. It was chaired by Vladimir Peller, a heroic World War II veteran. Riva Vishchinikina, a member of the farm, filled the "Birobidzhan Jewish slot" in the Soviet parliament from 1962 to 1966. Peller, who had demobilized as a Full Cavalier of the Order of Glory[23] and in 1966 became a Hero of Socialist Labor, would fill this slot from 1970 to 1974. From 1971 to 1976 he was one of the two Jewish members of the Communist Party's Central Auditing Commission, the group one step lower in prestige than the Central Committee.

Although only a small minority of Soviet Jews lived in rural areas in the 1950s and 1960s (around 5 percent in 1959), quite a few Jewish agricultural specialists worked in various parts of the country. Many, if not the majority of them, were holdovers from pre–World War II Jewish collective farms and some had been trained in those years at Jewish agricultural schools. Peller was one of the most prominent figures in that cohort. Ilya Yegudin was another high-profile Jewish chairman of a collective farm, in Crimea, where the Yegudins settled in the mid-1920s. Like Peller, he was a Hero of Socialist Labor, had numerous other state decorations, and a seat in the Ukrainian parliament. Yegudin became the prototype for Megudin, the protagonist of the novel *Under the Hot Sun* by the Yiddish writer Eli Gordon. The novel appeared in both Yiddish and Russian. In 1961 Shmuel Gordon (the two Gordons were not related) published a story, entitled "Virgin Land," about Lea Goldberg, director of a state farm in Kazakhstan that was one of the best in the republic.[24] In 1964, not long before his ouster, Khrushchev visited the farm together with the British media mogul Roy Thomson.[25]

A Yiddish Newspaper

The Soviet press's focus on Birobidzhan as an area of industrial and agricultural projects rather than a Jewish habitat reflected the conspicuous silence that usually surrounded Jewish-related issues. The local press was largely inaccessible outside the region, and in the early 1950s foreign observers did not know for sure whether the *Birobidzhaner Shtern* was still being published.[26] Established in 1930 as a bilingual—Yiddish and Russian—publication, it later split into two newspapers. The title of the Russian newspaper, *Birobidzhanskaia zvezda*, had the same meaning of "Birobidzhan Star."

After 1948, *Birobidzhaner Shtern* endured as the only remnant of the Soviet Yiddish literary and journalistic scene. In 1954, when Harrison E. Salisbury, the first regular correspondent of the *New York Times* in post–World War II Moscow, received permission to make a stopover in Birobidzhan, he was told that *Birobidzhaner Shtern* came out three times weekly in a circulation of one thousand copies.[27] In reality, only five hundred copies of the paper were printed (but not necessarily sold) at the time, whereas *Birobidzhanskaia zvezda* boasted a circulation of twenty thousand.[28] Meanwhile, Salisbury inadvertently refuted the misinformation, spread among foreign Communists, that Yiddish writers had been sent from Moscow and other cities in the European part of the Soviet Union to Birobidzhan in order to reinforce the JAR as the main Jewish cultural center in the country. Salisbury did not see any of them during his visit.[29] He was not informed that several local Yiddish literati, arrested five years earlier, still had not returned to the city.

In June 1956 Yosef Avidar, the Israeli ambassador to Moscow, and his wife, Yemima Tchernovitz, had an unprecedented opportunity to spend two days in Birobidzhan. Tchernovitz, a distinguished Hebrew children's writer, described in her diary their visit to the editorial office of the Yiddish newspaper:

> We entered the office of *Birobidzhaner Shtern*. A young man with curly hair and a repulsive face received us quite coldly. He seemed as if his tongue, hands and legs were tied, afraid to utter a word. The corpse itself was thrown in front of us, the remnant of what had perhaps once been a Yiddish newspaper, but now was a pitiful copy of the local Russian paper, which itself was a copy of *Pravda*. When we asked him where he got his material from, he shamelessly lied and said: "Mainly from readers' letters. We print everything sent to us." We asked about the number of copies distributed. At first his answer was evasive like all his answers, but finally he stuttered: 3000.[30]

Soviet journalists had to be, in Khrushchev's words, "not only the loyal helpers of the Party, but literally the apprentices of the party," fulfilling the function of "the most trusted transmission belt," taking decisions of the Party and carrying them "to the very midst of the people."[31] While leading writers of major Soviet periodicals could make their "transmission belt" journalism more or less readable, provincial newspapers usually filled their pages with reprints and dull articles describing achievements of local factories and collective farms. The *Birobidzhaner Shtern* was in a particularly disadvantaged position, having an exceptionally limited choice of local people able to work as Yiddish journalists.

It seems Avidar presumed that many, if not the majority of young Jews were married to non-Jews, predominantly of Cossack origin.[32] In fact, only a small percentage of non-Jewish Birobidzhaners had their roots in the old Cossack settlements, established in the nineteenth century to patrol the border along the Amur River.[33] Like many foreigners, the ambassador (he was born in Ukraine but left as a young boy) may have had a foggy understanding of who the Cossacks—historically farmers-cum-warriors—were. People often conflated Ukrainian Cossacks of the seventeenth century with contemporary Russian ones, living in border arears of the former Russian Empire. The alleged Jewish-Cossack symbiosis became a symbol of Birobidzhan following the release of the 1936 Soviet film *Seekers of Happiness*, with the wedding of Rosa, a Jewish woman, and Kornei, a Cossack, in its final scenes. At the time of production of this piece of cinematic propaganda, the Jewish-Cossack friendship was on the agenda of Soviet ideologists, who sought to find an antidote to the centuries-old reciprocal mistrust and hatred between the two groups of the population. For many Jews, the word Cossack was associated with the word "pogrom."[34]

Upon his return to Moscow, Avidar shared his observations with the British ambassador, who reported to London:

> He said his impressions could be summarized by saying that of the three words in the title of Birobidjan, only the last [i.e., "region"] had any reality. There was of course no question of autonomy, and there was very little that was really Jewish about the area. There was no school in which instruction was carried on in Yiddish and Yiddish was not even taught as a language in any of the schools. There was no Jewish theatre. In the bookshop in the capital of the area

> General Avidar could find only four books in Yiddish; the works of well-known Yiddish writers such as Sholem Aleichem were not available. There was one little paper in Yiddish which appeared twice a week; it was merely a reproduction of *Pravda*. There was one synagogue; this had been burnt down two months ago but General Avidar thought it was going to be repaired. Practically none of the Jewish children spoke or understood Yiddish, though the older Jews in the area seemed to speak it among themselves.
>
> . . . His impression was that there was a much higher proportion of Communists among the Jews of Birobidjan than in other Jewish communities which he has come across here in places like Kiev [Kyiv] and Homel [Gomel, the second largest city in Belorussia].[35]

Two decades later, a British journalist came to a similar conclusion—that local Jews were "a breed apart. They are uniformly not dissidents and—unlike numbers of Jews in cities such as Moscow, Leningrad, and Odessa—they do not wish to emigrate to Israel or elsewhere. Jews were the pioneers here. As a result, some self-glorification is evident. You get the impression that the Jews of Birobidzhan are very patriotic and loyal Soviet citizens."[36]

The rare visits of journalists and the unique visit of the Israeli diplomat were meticulously orchestrated by the local apparatus of government, including the KGB. According to Salisbury, during his visit he "was unable to take a single step in the streets of Birobidzhan without the company of the agents. . . . Their role was obvious. They were to make it evident to the local residents that I was being followed and that it was more healthy not to talk to me. The lesson was easily understood by the populace."[37] Foreigners had a chance to talk almost exclusively to carefully vetted people. As a result: "Never during question periods, which uniformly occurred when this correspondent was escorted through schools, factories or other institutions, were questions asked about Jews abroad, Israel, Zionism or other matters of Jewish interest. Officials said this reflected a lack of interest on the part of Jews in such matters."[38] It remains unknown if the several lovers of Hebrew who visited the Israeli ambassador and his wife at the hotel did so on their own initiative or—which seems more probable—knowingly or inadvertently acted as extras in an authorized performance staged for the foreign guests.[39]

Judging by the minutes of a meeting of Communists working for *Birobidzhaner Shtern*—whose leading authors had been arrested in the last spate of Stalinist purges—the climate in the collective was tense, and the journalists were "stewing in their own juices."[40] One of them, Max Riant (he was not arrested), recalled that they were wary of speaking Yiddish even in the office, let alone in the street. In general, they "had the feeling of being trapped and, to be honest, were afraid that the authorities would close the newspaper."[41] Indeed, there was an attempt to do so. Pavel Simonov, a non-Jewish functionary sent from Moscow in 1949 to replace his soon-to-be-arrested Jewish predecessor Aleksandr Bakhmutskii as the Party boss of the JAR, suggested turning the newspaper into a weekly Yiddish supplement to its Russian-language sister publication.[42] However, Simonov's plan did not get the go-ahead from the central Party apparatus.[43]

In the atmosphere of fear that stalked the JAR, the actual circulation of *Birobidzhaner Shtern* declined to virtual extinction in 1949–50.[44] As was the way of things in the Soviet Union, there was no overt prohibition of Yiddish, but risk-averse people nevertheless preferred to keep a distance from it. It is hard, if possible, to measure the level of fear among Jews in various areas of the Soviet Union. Presumably, however, in Birobidzhan it was particularly high, because no other place was so spectacularly affected by the arrests of Jewish functionaries and intellectuals. Birobidzhaners also knew that the majority of Yiddish books at the regional library had been destroyed, and the museum of local history had been stripped of its department of Jewish culture. Also shut down was the Yiddish theater named after Lazar Kaganovich, as well as the amateur Yiddish troupes. Yiddish disappeared from all educational institutions in the region. Even after Stalin's death, as late as 1956 and 1957, local censors continued to cleanse bookstores, rooting out hundreds of "harmful" volumes.[45]

Among the local intelligentsia imprisoned in the late 1940s and early 1950s was Buzi (Boris) Miller. Shortly before being arrested he was removed from his post as editor of *Birobidzhaner Shtern*.[46] Accused of authoring and publishing "politically harmful," "bourgeois-nationalist" works, he served almost seven years in the Gulag before returning to the city in 1956. In September 1956 the local court exonerated him along with the actor Faivish (Fayvl) Arones and the writers Israel Emiot (Goldwasser), Gessel Rabinkov, and Liuba Vasserman. Earlier, in November and

December 1955, several other literati were acquitted, including the poet Chaim Maltinsky and the journalists Mikhail Fradkin and Naum (Nokhim) Fridman. In various years the latter two edited *Birobidzhaner Shtern*.[47] Soon after Miller's liberation, the Writers Union reinstated his membership and invited him to Moscow to attend a cultural event marking the fortieth anniversary of Sholem Aleichem's death.[48] Miller would live in Birobidzhan until his death in 1988, cherished as the major local writer, a symbol of Yiddish culture in the JAR. One of the streets in Birobidzhan carries his name.

In the summer of 1956, after learning that the foreign press was citing material published in Birobidzhan, local functionaries sounded the alarm and reported the perturbing problem up the chain of command to the Central Committee of the Communist Party, pointing to the Warsaw *Folks-Shtime* as the source of the information leak. In fact, the Warsaw editors, veterans of the Communist movement, meant well: their reprint of an article from *Birobidzhaner Shtern* and the reproduction of the postmark bearing the official stamp of the JAR was aimed at refuting claims that the Birobidzhan area had lost its Jewish definition.[49]

The first contact between the Warsaw and Birobidzhan periodicals dated from August 1955,when Naum Korchminsky, editor of *Birobidzhaner Shtern*, received a letter from Warsaw asking for copies.[50] Korchminsky had been through the thick and thin of Soviet life. In his previous job as director of the local library he had had to participate in the liquidation of thousands of Yiddish books, including burning them in bonfires. (It seems that the Yiddish collection was later partly restocked with books sent from Alma-Ata and Lviv.)[51] He certainly knew the limits of his brief and would not start mailing complimentary copies to a foreign newspaper without the permission of his local Party overseers, who in turn made sure to secure consent from Moscow. Nonetheless, they panicked when their material attracted broader attention in the West, wary that such exposure could bring them trouble.

To local officials' surprise and relief, Moscow functionaries issued an instruction that, instead of walling itself off hermetically from the rest of the world, *Birobidzhaner Shtern* should expand contacts with "progressive Jewish newspapers." Soviet policymakers found it necessary to supply the foreign media with information about events, publications, and other activities demonstrating achievements in the field of Yiddish culture, effectively the only form of Jewish cultural activity permitted in the Soviet Union. Foreign audiences used to get this kind of information in the 1920s and 1930s. Yet back then Yiddish culture was sponsored by the state, first, for the domestic market—as part of the effort to address social and economic problems of the Jewish population—and second, and only second, in order to make an impression abroad. In the 1950s and onward, foreign audiences were, as a rule, the main targets for publicizing various Yiddish projects. Moreover, such projects would get the authorities' consent mainly or even solely for purposes of cultural counterpropaganda, aimed at rebuffing accusations of "alleged" restrictions on Jewish culture.

In this context, the quality of *Birobidzhaner Shtern*, whose contents now could be read abroad, became an important issue. Lev Benkovich, the head of the JAR's Party organization from 1955 to 1957, reported to the Central Committee that the paper was poorly designed and published hackneyed articles written in poor ("Germanized") Yiddish.[52] The result was that he, apparently, received permission and resources to improve the situation. In 1956 the *Birobidzhaner Shtern* began to appear three times a week with double the number of pages—four instead of two. New equipment mechanized its typesetting, previously done by hand.[53]

The orthography of *Birobidzhaner Shtern* reflected the results of the radical Soviet language reforms of the 1920s and 1930s, which meant, in particular, the application of phonetic-morphological spelling to all Hebrew and Aramaic elements and the elimination of the word-final forms for five letters used in Hebrew and traditional Yiddish writing systems. Absence of the final letters remained a hallmark of *Birobidzhaner Shtern* during the entire Soviet period, even following the restoration of these letters in Moscow Yiddish publications. The reason was purely technical: the Moscow printing shop, equipped with British-made linotypes, could print these letters, whereas the typographic equipment in Birobidzhan lacked them.[54] In addition, while only a few copies of the Birobidzhan newspaper were sent to addresses abroad, Moscow publications targeted a broader audience that included thousands of foreign readers, and these were likely to be put off by a Yiddish text lacking the final letters.[55]

The contents of the Birobidzhan newspaper had not improved enough to become appealing to a significant number of readers. A 1959 article by Max Frankel, then a Moscow-based journalist for the *New York Times* who gained permission to visit Birobidzhan, provided some details of its nonsubscription distribution: "Two newsstands had a few copies; a third, placed near a publicly posted copy of the paper, had not heard of it."[56] In his 1958 letter to a friend, a local Hebraist alluded to a biblical verse ("And the remaining trees of his forest shall be so few that a child could count them")[57] to signal the decline of *Birobidzhaner Shtern*'s readership.[58]

Not only did the newspaper remain unpopular in the region, but it was also downright unappealing in other places. Chaim (Henri) Sloves, the French Communist Yiddish writer who visited Moscow in 1958, went to the Lenin Library (since 1992, the Russian State Library), where the periodicals department gave readers access to recent issues of several Yiddish newspapers. While the foreign Communist newspapers were worn from being read over and over, readers sniffed at *Birobidzhaner Shtern*, leaving its issues untouched.[59]

Local newspapers were available only in the areas of their publication, because otherwise—as the state security maintained—they could provide rich fodder of information for analysts of foreign intelligence agencies. For the Birobidzhan newspaper, an exception would be made in 1970: since then *Birobidzhaner Shtern* could be subscribed to all over the country, following a special decision to use it as a counterpropaganda move in the anti-Zionist campaign of the time. Yet, in 1965, during a visit to Vilnius, capital of Soviet Lithuania, a correspondent of the *New York Times* found to his surprise the newspaper on sale at a hotel newsstand.[60] In a recycled form, *Birobidzhaner Shtern* also figured in the material prepared for foreign outlets willing to peddle Moscow propaganda.

The person responsible for this was Solomon Rabinovich, a veteran Yiddish journalist who, after serving six years in the Gulag, worked in the Sovinformburo (since 1961, Novosti Press Agency), the parent organization for his pre-arrest employer—the Jewish Anti-Fascist Committee. Some of his articles contained journalistic portraits of happy Jewish Birobidzhan dwellers, working at various factories and organizations.[61] The CIA, which monitored Rabinovich's activity, noted in a memorandum that, from 17 February 1959 to 6 January 1960, he submitted eighteen articles to New York's *Morgn-Frayhayt*.[62] Mordechai Gutman of Kfar Saba, Israel, wrote in his letter to the *New York Times* that Rabinovich's hailing of Soviet life was "hardly admissible testimony" because the Moscow journalist was "a man shattered by the Soviet Secret Police, tortured in its slave labor camps and fearful of further persecution." Gutman had known Rabinovich "extremely well" at the time when they were both incarcerated in a camp near the coal-mining town of Vorkuta, north of the Arctic Circle.[63]

Khrushchev's Interview

Khrushchev cut a disappointing figure to many Jewish left-wingers in the West. A conversation with him had left Joseph Baruch (Joe) Salsberg, a popular figure among North American Communists and their sympathizers, with a bad taste. This happened in August 1956 during a meeting of a delegation of Canadian Communists with several top Soviet functionaries. Salsberg inquired about the status of Soviet Jews, particularly whether they were regarded as a community entitled to have its own press, theaters, and schools. The Soviets took umbrage at Salsberg's question and enlightened the guests that, in the Soviet understanding, only Birobidzhan-based Jews represented a community, whereas in all other parts of the country the authorities treated Jews "like all other Soviet citizens." The Soviet policy-makers argued that the vast majority of the Jews had already joined the mainstream of society, and only some "backward elements had shut themselves up in their Jewish shell."

Salsberg was appalled to hear the Soviet leader's derogatory off-the-cuff remarks about Jews. Khrushchev's stereotype included such "Jewish traits" as shunning manual labor (the liberated city of Chernivtsi was filthy because the Jews living there showed no interest in cleaning up the streets), untrustworthiness (among thousands of Soviet tourists there were only three defectors, all of them Jewish), and clericalism (where Jews settled, they formed synagogues). Khrushchev mentioned that he supported Stalin's decision to reject the project of concentrating Jewish refugees from the Nazi-occupied Soviet territories in Crimea since the suggested Jewish republic would have created a springboard for attacks on the Soviet Union. Khrushchev also expressed his disappointment about the very poor results of the Birobidzhan endeavor.[64] Hurt by these remarks, Salsberg did not keep Khrushchev's words "in-house," but this information did not appear in thoroughly insulated Soviet media.

Following the 1956 publication of "Our Pain and Our Consolation" in the Warsaw *Folks-Shtime*, Paul Novick was quick off the mark to formulate in his *Morgn-Frayhayt* what he saw as principles of "consolation." In particular, he wrote that "the Jewish masses, the builders of Yiddish culture, the friends of the Soviet Union—they, the injured, will always ask: *What next?* . . . What news comes from Birobidzhan, where Yiddish is supposed to be the state language?"[65] After 1956 the New York newspaper adopted a critical stance on Soviet Jewish policy. Two years later it offered a strong reaction to Khrushchev's interview, in which the Soviet leader, according to the *New York Times*, had "singled the Jews out as the one major group not fitted for normal life in Soviet society."[66]

Published in the Parisian *Le Figaro* on 9 April 1958 under the headline "The Jews Do Not Know How to Organize Themselves Collectively," the interview made the Soviet leader look, in the words of the American public intellectual Irving Howe, like "a vulgar anti-Semite."[67] Although *Morgn-Frayhayt* did not label Khrushchev an anti-Semite, it struggled to digest the Soviet leader's answer to a question about the Birobidzhan project. According to *Le Figaro*, Khrushchev said the following:

> How many Jews remain in this beautiful region? In the absence of any documents before me, I would not be able to give you a precise figure. In actual fact, there must be quite a large number there. Look, in 1955, I myself passed through Birobidzhan. And . . . I noticed many signs in Yiddish there, in the stations and in the streets around the stations. This being granted, if one looks at the balance sheet, it is only right to conclude that Jewish colonization in Birobidzhan has resulted in failure. They alight there burning with enthusiasm, then, one by one, they return.
>
> How can one explain this disagreeable phenomenon? In my opinion, by historical conditions. The Jews have always preferred the trades of craftsmen. . . . But, if you take building or metallurgy—mass professions—you might not, to my knowledge, come across a single Jew there.[68] They do not like collective work, group discipline. They have always preferred to be dispersed. They are individualists.[69]

The version of the interview published in the Soviet press did not include the above section. The redacted version included several sentences relating to Jews, but in a completely different context: "National problems are being solved correctly only under socialism. In old czarist Russia, for instance, there were often anti-Jewish pogroms. . . . All such things have disappeared under Soviet rule."[70]

In essence, Khrushchev's words echoed what Stalin told Roosevelt in February 1945 during their meeting at the Yalta Conference: that the Soviet government had tried to establish a national home for the Jews but they, natural traders, had only stayed there two or three years and then scattered to the cities.[71] It seems that Khrushchev saw the failure of the Birobidzhan project as proof of the "inescapable fact" that Jews, at least the majority of them, had already assimilated or were prone to do so. A believer in the rapid advancement to Communism, he certainly regarded this as a positive development.

Morgn-Frayhayt, which had detached itself from uncritical subservience to Moscow, was not on the same page as Khrushchev, calling his statements "inconceivable" and "entirely out of tune with reality." The newspaper noted that Khrushchev's government had "no comprehensive approach on the Jewish question" and that it had so far only partly rectified the "injustices inflicted upon the Jewish people during the last years of the Stalin regime." American Jewish Communists rejected the charges brought by the Soviet leader that Birobidzhan had failed because of Jews' intellectual pursuits and opposition to collective discipline. In fact, stressed the editorial, Jews had succeeded in building agricultural colonies in pre–World War II Ukraine and Crimea. They had also worked as pioneers in Birobidzhan until the Soviet authorities began to persecute their leaders and liquidated Jewish cultural life in the region. The newspaper pointed to compelling examples of Jewish collectivism in Israel, in the American labor movement, and in the heroic struggles against the Nazis.[72]

The bias of Khrushchev's interview was not lost on Senator Jacob K. Javits, who had grown up in a tenement in the Lower East Side of Manhattan and was elected from New York in 1956 (later he would play a major role in campaigns for Soviet Jewish rights). The senator reacted by speaking about the need to overcome the Soviet government's ban on Jewish emigration.[73] Nahum Goldmann, president of the World Zionist Organization and the World Jewish Congress, suggested sarcastically that Khrushchev's remarks be welcomed as a recognition of the fact that "the Jews of the Soviet Union constitute a nationality, separate and distinct from other nationalities in the Soviet Union, and that this nationality does not live in similar conditions to the other nationalities of the USSR. This admission, albeit in negative terms, is essential to a serious dialogue on the implications of the Soviet Jewish problem."[74]

Soviet ideologists realized that Khrushchev's uncareful words had caused an undesirable reaction in many quarters of Western society. The article "Jewish Autonomy," published in the Moscow newspaper *Sovetskaia Rossiia* (Soviet Russia) on 6 August 1958, aimed squarely at calming the Western public's concerns. Novick, who at the beginning of 1959 happened to be on a visit in Moscow, tried unsuccessfully to meet V. Pakhman, the author of the article. He took, or preferred to take, at face value the fanciful explanation, given him at the office of *Sovetskaia Rossiia*, that Pakhman was a professional pilot, here today, gone tomorrow, but from time to time he wrote for the press. It just so happened that he had recently visited Birobidzhan—which, incidentally, did not boast an airport—and this experience had inspired his journalistic fire.[75]

Whoever Pakhman was in reality (on 29 March 1962, an article entitled "Israeli Racists" appeared under the same byline in the central trade-union newspaper *Trud*), this piece was the first description of the JAR in the Soviet press since the late 1940s. The article emphasized distinctions between the happy life of Birobidzhan Jewish residents and the unhappiness of those former Birobidzhan residents who, "under the influence of Zionist propaganda, left for Israel." By that time several Birobidzhaners had reached Israel either directly from the Soviet Union or after first repatriating to Poland as erstwhile citizens of the Second Polish Republic.[76] According to the flying journalist Pakhman, Israeli authorities treated all immigrants as unwelcome guests, but this was especially true of those who had arrived from the Soviet Union, the People's Democracies, India, and some other countries. Pakhman asserted, as if he had witnessed it with his own eyes, that the immigrants were crammed into barracks, often could not find work, and dragged out a half-starved existence, constantly scoffed at by local Jews.

In clear contradiction to Khrushchev's claim that the Birobidzhan project had not fulfilled its purpose, the article portrayed the JAR in glowing terms. Jews appeared in it in several different capacities: Iosif Bumagin and

Aleksandr Kudryavitski, the two fallen brave Red Army soldiers awarded the title of Hero of the Soviet Union; Iosif Bokor, the head of the Birobidzhan city Communist Party organization; Naum Korchminsky, editor of *Birobidzhaner Shtern*; and Buzi Miller, the Yiddish writer. The article claimed with a good deal of exaggeration that Miller's name was "known far beyond the borders of Birobidzhan."[77] It also mentioned that a Moscow publishing house was producing one of his books, translated from Yiddish into Russian. In reality, Miller's name recognition did not, despite claims, stretch much beyond the JAR.

In his Russian book *Pod radugoi* (Under the rainbow), published in 1959, Miller included his heavily revised long story, whose title in its original 1947 version was "Birobidzhan." Censured then as "nationalist," it now carried the title "Brothers" and was deprived of specifically Jewish traits of the Yiddish original. Its characters, originally recognizably Jewish in the "Birobidzhan" version of the story, now turned into simply "people," re-settlers in the ethnically generic "Far East."[78] It is known that Soviet editors practiced "de-Judaization" of translated literary texts.[79] However, most probably Miller had done it himself, as an act of self-censorship, rather than under the direct pressure of the publisher. In a similar case of de-Judaizing a translated story, the little-known Yiddish writer Chaim Zilberman, also a traumatized former Gulag prisoner, brought trouble to the same publisher, Sovetskii pisatel (Soviet Writer). Judging by the minutes of the meeting of the publishing house's governing board of the on 6 July 1963, the editors were oblivious of the introduced revisions until the New York *Forverts* published an article pointing to Zilberman's de-Judaized story as an example of "anti-Semitic" misrepresentation of Jewish literature in the Soviet Union. Moreover, the publisher had to react somehow to an official request for explanation received from the American Communist Party.[80]

Ben Zion Goldberg (Waife), a left-wing American Yiddish journalist and a son-in-law of Sholem Aleichem, contended that the *Sovetskaia Rossiia* article, reprinted by pro-Soviet periodicals in a number of countries, "was not merely just another piece published in a newspaper." With the benefit of a couple of years' hindsight, he observed that it "represented a new turn in Soviet public relations" because it put Birobidzhan back into circulation as a touted propaganda item.[81] Goldberg knew the subject well and traced correctly the change in the Soviet handling of the issue. He had spent three weeks in Birobidzhan in 1934 during his trip to the Soviet Union and later acted as vice president of Ambijan, an organization of American supporters of the Birobidzhan project. (In November 1950, disappointingly to pro-Soviet circles, Moscow informed Ambijan that the JAR no longer required nor wanted any outside help.)[82]

Goldberg either did not realize, or at least did not specify, that the change in the attitude toward Birobidzhan was aimed almost exclusively at foreign audiences. In the domestic information space, not counting the *Sovetskaia Rossiia* article, Birobidzhan remained nearly invisible. For instance, few people, Soviet or foreign, had access to the 1959 article by Filipp Klimenko, chairman of the administration of the JAR. His article appeared in the obscure Khabarovsk-published journal *Dal'nii Vostok* (Far East) to mark the twenty-fifth anniversary of the JAR. Let alone that Klimenko's text carried very little meaningful information about the region, its bombastic leitmotif was that toilers of the JAR were determined to contribute to the further strengthening of the Soviet Union.[83]

In February 1959, in a small-talk conversation with British prime minister Harold Macmillan, Khrushchev more or less repeated, even if in a milder form, his 1958 statement about Jews—"a very vital and tough race"—and Birobidzhan: "An experiment had been made in settling them in their own area but this was mainly agricultural. The Jews were chiefly tradesmen and artisans and the experiment had not been very successful and there were few Jews left there. Jews were very talented; some of them were engaged in atomic and rocket research."[84]

Those foreign observers, who penned their comments hard on the heels of the publication of the Pakhman article, usually jumped to a conclusion that differed from Goldberg's. Harry Schwartz, a journalist with the *New York Times* who taught himself Russian and wrote prolifically on Soviet affairs, mentioned "speculation in some Jewish circles" in America that "the decision to paint a glowing picture of Jewish life in Birobidzhan may be intended to initiate a new campaign to induce Soviet Jews to move to that area."[85] It did not take long before Jewish organizations received "reliable information" from Israeli sources that "the Soviet Jews appeared in peril of their lives" because the Soviet government was purportedly considering a massive forced resettlement of Jews to the JAR. Furthermore, the same source claimed that the plan would be placed before the 21st Congress of the Soviet Communist Party scheduled to be convened on 27 January 1959.[86]

Rumors about Expulsion

Only people with a shallow understanding of Soviet realities could come to, or accept as true, the idea that the Kremlin would choose an open "democratic" way to legitimize expulsion of a segment of the Soviet population, particularly after Khrushchev's condemnation of the deportations of Chechens, Crimean Tatars, and other ethnic groups in Stalin's time as "monstrous acts."[87] The 21st Congress—a midterm or "extraordinary" one—was supposed to consolidate Khrushchev's grip on power and adopt the Seven-Year Plan of economic development, with a particular emphasis on strengthening the economy in Siberia. The Siberian agenda might form the "factual basis" for the disturbing rumors about a planned expulsion.[88] Perhaps there was no smoke without fire: some people in the Kremlin corridors of power might have broached the idea of a limited-scale and not necessarily Jewish resettlement to the JAR, encouraged and sponsored by the government. They could have suggested it as part of an attempt to find human resources for the region.

Rumors were generally a powerful force within Soviet society, which was devoid of independent media or other public institutions able to verify, analyze, and interpret the news.[89] The impenetrability of the Soviet policymaking mechanism sparked guesswork and conspiracy theories. The speculation about forced removal of Jews to Birobidzhan echoed the resonant, if historically unsubstantiated, narrative about the deportation of Jews, which, as the story goes, failed to occur only because Stalin died before he could make it happen (see chapter 1, p. 10).

The 1958–59 rumor differed significantly from the one that had gone around a decade earlier: it circulated outside the country even though Novick pointed to the *Sovetskaia Rossiia* article as the initial source of the miscue.[90] In January 1959 Sloves wrote to Maurice Thorez, secretary general of the French Communist Party: "The bourgeois press of diverse countries has recently become the conveyor of so-called plans for a 'territorial solution' that would currently be under consideration in Moscow, plans that would be centered on the Jewish autonomous region of Birobidzhan."[91] True, some observers remained unconvinced that the Soviets had in mind an all-embracing deportation. They were more prepared to believe that the government might organize a campaign of partly cajoling and partly brow-beating some Jews, particularly the young, to make them agree to move "voluntarily" to the Far Eastern region.[92] Yet even a milder version of the predicted plan caused serious consternation.

On 14 January 1959, the Soviet ambassador to the United Kingdom received a memorandum of the Anglo-Jewish Association on "Reported Renewal of Settlement of Soviet Jews in Birobidjan." An influential organization of the British Jewish establishment, the association urged "that no transfers of populations by compulsion, direct or indirect, of Jews or others be undertaken in the Soviet Union."[93] Two weeks before the opening of the 21st Congress in Moscow, representatives of the American Jewish Committee, established in 1906 by people concerned about pogroms in Russia, had a meeting with Anastas Mikoyan, the first deputy chairman of the Council of Ministers and, generally, one of the key figures surrounding Khrushchev. This unprecedented encounter became a momentous, if little-mentioned, episode in Soviet Jewish history. Never before had representatives of a Jewish organization been given a chance to meet with a visiting top Soviet official to discuss the situation of Soviet Jews.

Mikoyan, ostensibly on a two-week vacation, "toured the United States and smiled through the vilifications he was subjected to during several public appearances."[94] His mission was a reconnaissance-in-force before Khrushchev's historic visit to the United States in September 1959. Mikoyan's son Sergo, a historian, who accompanied his father during the trip, recalled: "Khrushchev asked my father to go to the United States and to improve relations, to let them know that we were not aggressive and so on."[95] Oleg Troyanovsky, later a Soviet ambassador, traveled with Mikoyan as his adviser and interpreter. In retrospect, Troyanovsky described the trip as a difficult one, during which Mikoyan, with his emollient style, "combined irony, sarcasm, humor, and calm refutation," and was also not afraid of facing the media and the public.[96] Ironically, Mikoyan, an Armenian, had some connection to Birobidzhan. In 1948 his name for an unknown reason appeared on the JAR map, but after the September 1957 decree, which banned naming towns, streets, and so on after live people, the settlement Mikoyanovsk was renamed Khingansk.

Like the Anglo-Jewish Association, the American Jewish Committee did not represent a mass-based constituency. Its membership was made up largely of prominent and wealthy individuals, and, in the opinion of KGB experts, "played an important role among dyed-in-the-wool anti-Communist organizations."[97] In particular, the committee sponsored the 1951 book *The Jews in the Soviet Union* by the well-informed veteran anti-Communist socialist (Menshevik) historian Solomon Schwarz, and a number of other publications on this topic. To all appearances, Mikoyan and his advisers thought out of the box, which led them to the conclusion that it would be unwise to avoid contact with this influential body. Among the committee's four representatives who participated in the meeting on 15 January 1959 were Herbert H. Lehman, the former New York governor and senator, and Jacob Blaustein, a prominent American entrepreneur.[98] Characteristically, Mikoyan avoided contact with representatives of the Jewish labor movement. As he explained later, American labor leaders turned out to be more hostile to the Soviet Union than some capitalists.[99]

The memorandum, written on 2 January 1959 by Eugene Hevesi, who served as foreign affairs secretary for the American Jewish Committee, outlines the background knowledge that the four American Jewish establishment figures possessed about the plan, "discovered by Israeli intelligence in Russia" and relayed to the committee confidentially by some official Israeli sources:

> The only further detail that the Israelis could add to this information was some indication that the Soviet authorities may apply educational or economic "inducements" in furthering the resettlement plan but would abstain from the use of direct administrative compulsion. For this reason, the Israelis urged us to avoid, in our public comments on the problem, any references to the possibility of compulsory "mass deportations." implying that any exaggeration on our part would make it easy for Soviet propaganda to brand our statement untrue.
>
> Meanwhile, circumstantial evidence was growing in confirmation of the news received from Israeli authorities. Recently in the Soviet press, several articles have again appeared, after decades of silence, singing the praises of

> Biro-Bidjan as a "national home" for Jews. Cairo Radio greeted the renewal of the idea of a "Jewish state" inside the Soviet Union with great satisfaction, and expressed the hope that Mr. Ben-Gurion himself would soon find his way there. And finally, on December 30, the first direct anti-Semitic Soviet propaganda blast since the establishment of the Khrushchev regime was broadcast by the Ukrainian Radio.[100]

During the two-hour-long luncheon-conference at the Carlyle Hotel at 35 East Sixty-Sixth Street, Mikoyan flatly denied the existence of a plan to start expulsions to the JAR. The Americans tried to get Mikoyan to make a statement for public release. Though initially unwilling to do so, he ultimately authorized Lehman to state to the press in no uncertain terms that the entire story was altogether false: "The reported plans for recreation of a Jewish state in Birobidzhan and the transfer of the Jewish population in Russia to that area is without foundation."[101] It remains unclear to what degree the American Jewish Committee, and the American public in general, took Mikoyan's words as truth or whether they did not believe him and considered themselves saviors of Soviet Jews.

The London *Jewish Chronicle* pointed to Mikoyan's decision to speak with Jewish representatives, on the eve of his meeting with President Dwight D. Eisenhower, as a sign that the image-conscious Soviet leaders were fully aware that they could not disregard the reaction abroad to their policy concerning the Jews. It also opined that, as a result of his American visit, Mikoyan might "advise the Kremlin of the need for greater discretion in the handling of Jewish affairs."[102] Indeed, as we'll see later in this book, Mikoyan's American visit brought a rapid change in the Soviet leadership's views on reviving Yiddish publishing. It is beyond coincidence that the first Yiddish book in the post-Stalinist period came out in Moscow with remarkable speed of preparation and production.

The Situation on the Ground

In 1959 Max Frankel went to Birobidzhan and brought back pleasant memories of eating gefilte fish, a staple of Jewish holiday dinners, with horseradish, and cheese blintzes with sour cream. From the late 1930s,

Jewish recipes appeared on the menu of the local restaurant and other eateries (*stolovye*). In February 1936, when Lazar Kaganovich, then a top party functionary and a minister, visited Birobidzhan, housewives cooked gefilte fish for him. In the event, the guest—who traveled in style, accompanied by a cook—did not touch the local food. Nevertheless, the next year, when the secret police arrested the Party boss of the JAR in the wave of Stalinist purges, his wife was grotesquely accused of trying to poison Kaganovich with her gefilte fish. The issue of gefilte fish reemerged during the visit of another Jewish guest—Polina Zhemchuzhina, who at that time headed a department at the Ministry of Food Industry. She expressed her disappointment that this quintessential Jewish dish did not appear on the menu of the—apparently only—Birobidzhan restaurant.[103]

Frankel could not find any indication that the city anticipated the arrival of new settlers: "The Soviet government has denied rumors abroad that it intends to direct more Jews to the province. There is no evidence of such plans in Birobidzhan."[104] Probably this was the main reason the Soviet authorities allowed him to visit the city—to convey to the American public that he could not detect any new Jewish settlers. The New York *Forverts* reported that one Aron Liblikh, who had lived in Birobidzhan before repatriating to Poland, had also never heard of any new resettlements to the JAR and knew nothing about any preparation for such a campaign. Moreover, he saw a different direction of migration, namely *from* Birobidzhan.[105]

Frankel made interesting observations on mundane details of life in the city, which struck him as a rather agreeable place, with people dressed as elsewhere in the Soviet Union or perhaps a bit more stylishly, thanks to locally produced shoes and accessories. Indeed, Birobidzhan had been selected to become the center of consumer manufacturing in the Soviet Far East. As a result, local factories and produce cooperatives would increasingly supply the area with fabrics, garments, footwear, and knitted goods. The newly built or expanded clothing and furniture factories, and the plants producing power transformers and agricultural machinery, created new positions of employment, but it was predominantly non-Jews, often recent migrants to the region, who filled new job openings.[106]

Frankel left the city with the impression that its job market did not appeal to young Jews. Many of them preferred to leave for education and career possibilities elsewhere, notably to Khabarovsk—many, if not the majority, of its Jews had "defected" there from the JAR—and returned "only to look up old girl friends."[107] Indeed, Birobidzhan, a town without a university or other higher schools, could not be an appealing place for young people with strong educational values. Daniel Patrick Moynihan, an American intellectual and public servant, once famously quipped, "If you want to build a great city, create a great university and wait 200 years."[108] Birobidzhan had neither a university nor enough time allotted for a long-standing experiment. As a result, by the end of the 1960s, in a striking contrast to the rates of higher education for Jews nationwide, the same rate for Jews in the JAR was almost eight times lower and almost equal to average Russian rates.[109] If we define the shtetl in particular as a parochial place from which, in modern times, dynamic, self-motivated Jews tended to (e)migrate, then Birobidzhan had been built as a new shtetl.

Frankel noted also that "no youngsters ever show up at the shack that serves as a synagogue. Friday nights and Saturdays . . . Cantor Kaplan (there is no rabbi) leads prayers for thirty persons, more women than men." He was told that on Yom Kippur the number of worshippers was much larger—four hundred, and that a few packages of matzo arrived from Israel each Passover. The Polish journalist Dominik Horodyński, who described his impression of visiting Birobidzhan in a December 1958 article that appeared in the Warsaw weekly *Swiat* and then in his 1959 Siberian travelogue, had learned that the congregation numbered only twenty-four, none of them young, but "more than 50" would come on the High Holidays.[110] Judging by a 1967 article in a Soviet antireligious journal, the Birobidzhan Jewish religious community had forty-three members, all between the ages of sixty-three and eighty-four. A survey involving three hundred Jewish residents of Birobidzhan, "mainly those who for some reason could be considered religious" (the criteria used in the research remain unknown), found only eight believers, all but one over sixty years old. The author of the article, a sociologist, pointed to the fact that the builders of the JAR in the 1920s and 1930s were, as a rule, young secular enthusiasts, and hence religion had not taken root in the city.[111]

In December 1935 one of the streets in Birobidzhan was named after Emmanuil Kazakevich's father, Henekh, one of the first editors of *Birobidzhaner Shtern*, but in May 1938 this name disappeared from the map of the city because the late editor was retrospectively branded a "nationalist."

In the topsy-turvy world of Soviet propaganda, Sholem Aleichem, by contrast, did not get the label of a nationalist. As a result, the local library was named after him shortly before its opening in February 1941, whereas the Sholem Aleichem Street appeared on the town's map in May 1946, marking the thirtieth anniversary of the writer's death. This was the time when Birobidzhan functionaries hoped, in vain as it turned out, to revive the campaign of building a strong Jewish polity in the region. In this climate it seemed appropriate to have a "Jewish" thoroughfare.[112] Thanks to the extraordinary status of Sholem Aleichem in the canon of Soviet culture, the library and the street could keep their names even during the purges, which followed within several years. In 1959 two Birobidzhan Yiddish journalists wrote on the occasion of Sholem Aleichem's centenary that, were the writer alive, his love of people would give forth "bright and elated words about the new, happy life of his brethren in the brotherly family of Soviet peoples in the entire country, including Birobidzhan."[113]

The 1959 census brought some statistical clarity to the composition of the local population. The returns gave the lie to the information provided in the previous years. For instance, Salisbury had relayed the misinformation that Jews constituted about half of the population of the JAR, and Moscow Radio had broadcast an even higher estimate, about 60 percent.[114] By contrast, the census statistics revealed 14,269 local Jews (8.9 percent of the JAR's population and 0.7 percent of Soviet Jewry), 5,597 of whom claimed Yiddish as their first language.[115]

The relatively high proportion of Yiddish speakers among Birobidzhan Jews reflected the essentially negative fact that young people tended to move to other places, in particular not returning to the JAR after getting a higher educational qualification in Khabarovsk or other cities, and leaving behind an aging sedentary population. In addition, the postwar migration brought to the region Yiddish speakers from Crimea, Ukraine, and Belorussia, often former members of prewar Jewish collective farms, let alone that thousands of Yiddish speakers had arrived in the early years of the Birobidzhan endeavor, when, until 1949, schoolchildren had access to Yiddish.

Soviet ideologists expected Jewish re-settlers to the Far East to abandon all residues of the shtetl.[116] In reality, however, features of traditional shtetl life were upheld in the JAR. In 1948 the following description by Yiddish writer Shmuel Gordon angered the Birobidzhan Party leadership:

> The peace of the eve before the day off [i.e., Sunday] rather than [the view of the] streets and houses reminded me today of the distant shtetls of Ukraine and Belorussia. . . . Around the houses, smartly dressed women were sitting, cracking dried hazelnuts, and waiting for their husbands and children to return from the bathhouse. In the heat of the day—the sunset just started—these women were sitting muffled in silk shawls, in which they perhaps once paid visits on Sabbath or holidays. From the open doors and windows one could feel a strong scent of gefilte fish and carrot tzimmes. The houses and gardens looked festive.[117]

Jewish residents of the JAR tended to live in the town of Birobidzhan, where a quarter of the approximately forty thousand residents identified themselves during the census as Jewish. Close to a third of the deputies of the Birobidzhan city soviet (council) elected—or, given the reality of Soviet "elections," chosen by the authorities—in 1961 had Jewish-sounding names, which was a proportion twice as high as in the regional soviet of the JAR.[118] In 1959, compared with 1939, the Jewish population of the JAR had shrunk by almost 20 percent. This decline continued in the coming years. As a result, Jews had slid to the third position among the largest ethnic groups in the region, after Russians and Ukrainians.[119] While Soviet propaganda agencies continued to use Birobidzhan as a gimmick for credulous foreign enthusiasts of Communism, it did not play any practical role in the self-identification of Soviet Jews living outside the JAR.

As for Birobidzhan proper, Horodyński stated that Jewish ethnic identity had been vanishing there, persisting only in certain traits, such as the attitude toward hunting: Jews did not hunt. Yet even this difference began to disappear with the increase of mixed marriages.[120] The Yiddish writer Tevye Gen, who lived in Birobidzhan in the 1930s, tried to paint an attractive picture of the city as he saw it during his short stay there in 1963. However, the resulting image came out bleak and, despite his efforts, only superficially Jewish—in the name of Sholem Aleichem Street, in distinctly Jewish names of local residents mentioned in the narrative, and in their and the writer's flashbacks to the early years of the Birobidzhan campaign.[121]

In 1961 two diplomats from the British embassy visited Birobidzhan. They found that it was

> in fact little more than a village, consisting largely of huts and unsurfaced roads. It is pleasantly, though probably unhealthily situated as it is surrounded by marshy land which breeds a particularly aggressive type of mosquito. A large proportion of the town's population is obviously Jewish but there are few signs of national culture. In the bookshops only Russian books were displayed and further efforts to discover what was available in Yiddish revealed that there was nothing more than a few school textbooks. Only a few people seemed to have any idea of the whereabouts of the synagogue. This was perhaps not very surprising since it is housed in a wooden hut similar to others in the same rather muddy road. The Rabbi was away and the caretaker said that the services were attended by only a few, usually old, people.
>
> A considerable amount of discontent was discernible in Birobidzhan. Jews complained of being isolated and out of touch with civilization. Several had apparently tried unsuccessfully to move away from the town. Russians complained, in traditional anti-semitic fashion, of the way in which "honest workers" were frequently outdone by Jews, particularly at the market (which was incidentally reasonably well stocked).[122]

After 1949 the government did not encourage any more Jewish migration to the JAR. On the other hand, there were hardly any Jews willing to move to the Far Eastern corner of the country. In an attempt to explain the situation, Solomon Rabinovich, who "was in Birobidjan when the first settlers arrived," wrote in his 1965 propaganda pamphlet *Jews in the Soviet Union*:

> Year after year the Government allocated large sums of money for the building of industrial enterprises, the cultivation of taiga [forest] land and the building of new towns and settlements in the Jewish Autonomous Region. All this yielded wonderful results.
>
> "But why are there so few Jews in the Region?" the reader may ask.
>
> It seems to me that one of the main reasons is this: by the end of the thirties, especially in the war years, there was no longer any need for Jews with jobs to move. Why should a person living in Vinnitsa [Vinnytsia], Kiev [Kyiv] or Sverdlovsk leave a place where he has lived for a long time, give up his permanent job and abandon his friends and acquaintances? There may have been other reasons. And of course, Soviet power is not to blame for the fact that tens of thousands and not hundreds of thousands went to Birobidjan.[123]

Soviet authorities were reluctant to allow foreigners to visit the JAR. In 1971 an eighteen-member pro-Soviet delegation led by Dr. Thomas Matthew, the president of a Black self-improvement group called NEGRO (National Economic Growth and Reconstruction Group), came to evaluate Soviet racial progress and get to the truth behind the situation of Jews in the country. The trip deteriorated, however, when the Soviets did not allow the American visitors to go where they wanted—to visit the JAR. Angered by the restraints placed on his movement, Matthew left the country early but not before calling two separate press conferences.[124]

The lackluster state of the Birobidzhan project does not mean that its import and impact can be nullified entirely. While demographically and culturally insignificant, the JAR played a key, and predominantly detrimental, role in determining Jews' place in the Soviet pecking order. According to anthropologist Igor Krupnik, they "were condemned to a second-rate status in Soviet society, even without an anti-Semitic stance on the part of the regime." The national-territorial categorization did a disservice to the Jews by giving them a ranking along with other peoples of autonomous provinces, "somewhere between the 44th and 50th position, among some hundred Soviet nations."[125] Crucially, Soviet Jews neither had nor were permitted to have any recognized voice of leadership to argue their case regarding the central authorities. As for Birobidzhan officials, they, like their counterparts in other ethnic territories, were not supposed to have any pan-Soviet agenda to advocate before the party and state leadership.

While in the general landscape of Jewish life the Birobidzhan project had turned into one of the rather hollow Soviet-built facades, or "Potemkin villages" (named after an eighteenth-century precedent in Imperial Russia), the Far Eastern Jewish "village" was populated by many thousands of real people. Moreover, as a constituent of the ethnoterritorial patchwork of the Union of Soviet Socialist Republics, the JAR was supposed to have some national spice. A late-Soviet cookbook, William Pokhlebkin's *National Cuisines of Our Peoples*, represented Jewish fare (gefilte fish, carrot stew or tzimmes, and chopped herring or *forshmak*) as an ethnoterritorial phenomenon—in a chapter dedicated to food traditions of the Far East.[126] This reflected the Birobidzhan-centered ideological model, which dogmatically linked the entire Soviet Jewish population to its "heartland" in the JAR. Characteristically, according to the universal system developed for Soviet library catalogs, Yiddish books and their translations were placed among the "literatures of Far Eastern peoples."

The JAR also provided some meaningful "national spice" for other aspects of Soviet Jewish life. Thus, as we saw earlier, the rumors about an expulsion to Birobidzhan inadvertently triggered the revival of Yiddish publishing. It is also no coincidence that, as we will see, the poet Aron Vergelis, chosen by the authorities to play the leading role in Soviet Yiddish life, had a Birobidzhan pedigree. Two decades later this would be one of the criteria for training and appointing Adolf Shayevich as the new chief rabbi in Moscow.

4

THE "KHRUSHCHEV ALIYAH"

Polish Jews on the Way

While World War II affected Russia's Far East only indirectly, the European areas along the western borders of the Soviet Union bore the first devastating brunt of the German onslaught, whose consequences would be felt for many years to come.[1] Until 1941 all these areas were, as a rule, densely populated by Jews. Thus, in the fall of 1939, when the Soviet Union, in accord with Nazi Germany, annexed the eastern half of the Second Polish Republic, the Soviet Jewish population increased overnight by close to 1.3 million. In addition to the Jewish residents of these areas, there were between 200,000 and 300,000 Jewish refugees who fled to the Soviet side from parts of Poland that fell under German control. Expulsion of "unreliable elements" from the border regions, migration to "old Soviet" areas for work and study, and, from 22 June 1941, evacuation had removed about a fifth of these people from the theater of the Soviet-German war.[2] A much smaller number of Polish Jews had survived under the German occupation or in the ranks of the Red Army. In all, the survival and other statistics of Polish Jews in the Soviet Union remain vague.

The Polish-Soviet agreement, signed on 6 July 1945, gave surviving former Polish citizens a chance to renounce their Soviet citizenship, whether they had accepted it willingly or unwillingly, and return to Poland.[3] After spending six or more years in the Soviet Union, those who applied for repatriation usually had more or less blended into the general population and some of them had married locals. At the same time, among the repatriates were also the so-called "special settlers" (*spetsposelentsy*) who had been deported by the Kremlin from the new Soviet territories to Siberia or Central Asia. The agreement, which laid down the rules for repatriation, had a bearing on ethnic Poles and Jews but not on other ethnic groups, most notably Ukrainians and Belorussians. The agreement reflected a radical change in the position of the Soviet government, which at the initial stages of negotiations, in December 1941, recognized only ethnic Poles as eligible to return to their homeland.[4] We cannot reconstruct the train of thought that motivated Stalin to change his view on this issue by the end of the war. He may have agreed, for instance, with the view that there was no reason to keep Polish Jews in the USSR because they, or at least the majority of them, were unfit for Soviet society. Indeed, one Jewish refugee, formerly a member of an illegal Communist group in Poland, said in the fall of 1944 that after five years of living in the Soviet Union "all the Communist microbes have died in me by now."[5] Judging by the fact that among the Jewish repatriates from just one region in Ukraine (Stanislav, renamed Ivano-Frankivsk in 1962) there were twenty members of the Communist Party, it is easy to assume that hundreds of Jewish Communists had decided to emigrate from the Soviet Union out of disappointment (hence desire to build something better in Poland) or homesickness or a combination of both.[6] For all that, Soviet decision-makers may have presumed that Jewish refugees, or at least some of them, could be useful for the task of the Sovietization of Poland.[7]

By the end of the 1940s, over two hundred thousand Jews availed themselves of this arrangement. However, after a short stay they by and large left Poland. Their typical route took them to displaced-persons camps in Germany, Austria, or Italy and finally to Israel. Not all of them were bona fide former Polish citizens. Some left the Soviet Union as the repatriates' spouses (including via marriages of convenience), their children, or the spouses' immediate relatives. In addition, people would buy, steal, and doctor documents in order to prove their entitlement to repatriation. Orthodox Jews—most notably members of the Hasidic movement Chabad, whose centers emerged among the wartime evacuees in the Uzbek cities of Samarkand and Tashkent—exhibited remarkable ingenuity in finding ways to leave the country where they faced deep problems with sustaining their mode of life.

In the second half of the 1950s, both the Soviet Union and Poland were not the same countries as they were a decade earlier. The 20th Communist

Party Congress, which made public the break with Stalin's repressive methods and condemned the mass purges that ravaged virtually all segments of society in the years of his authoritarian rule, sparked enormous turmoil in all Communist circles. In October 1956 Władysław Gomułka, who had been imprisoned from August 1951 to December 1954 for deviating from the Kremlin line, regained his status as the country's leader. Troubled by mass demonstrations and strikes in Poland during what became known as Polish October, and wary of Gomułka's advocacy of a specifically Polish model of building socialism, the Soviet leaders considered military intervention to quell the unrest. Ultimately, a nonviolent compromise allowed the neighboring "brotherly" country to avoid fully copying the Soviet model yet still remain a steadfast member of the military alliance of Communist countries that even carried a "Polish name"—the Warsaw Pact, the Soviet answer to NATO.[8]

The organizational structure of Polish Jewish life, which was centered on the Jewish Social-Cultural Association (Towarzystwo Społeczno-Kulturalne Żydów, TSKŻ), also did not and, given the geography of the country, could not replicate the Soviet model with Birobidzhan as the illusory cultural linchpin of the Jewish population.[9] The TSKŻ was chaired by Hersh Smolar, a professional revolutionary, who also acted as editor of *Folks-Shtime*. Born in Poland, he studied and worked in the Soviet Union in the 1920s and 1930s, from where he was twice sent to Poland as an agent operating in the underground of the Communist movement, outlawed by the Polish authorities. In 1941 he became a leading member of the anti-Nazi resistance in the Minsk Ghetto and later fought as a political officer in a partisan group operating in Belorussian forests. His wartime memoirs came out in Moscow in Yiddish in 1946 (*Fun Minsker geto*) and in Russian in 1947 (*Mstiteli geto*).

Notwithstanding the Soviet-Polish agreement, tens of thousands of former Polish citizens did not want to or could not depart from the Soviet Union in the 1940s. The hindering reasons varied: ideological persuasion, satisfactory jobs, lack of information about the repatriation, family circumstances, health problems, or continued imprisonment.[10] Thousands preferred to remain in the Soviet Union at that time, but subsequent years convinced many of them that they had made a mistake.[11] Among those who could not be repatriated in the 1940s were also direct victims of the repressive machinery. Thus, Joseph Berger-Barzilai, a onetime leader of the Palestinian Communist Party (PCP), and Leopold Trepper, a member of the PCP and then a Soviet master spy in Nazi-occupied Europe, gained their freedom only after many years of incarceration.

In April 1955 the Central Committee of the Communist Party of the Soviet Union sanctioned the return to the "countries of people's democracy," including Poland, of the remaining special settlers, who had received more freedom around that time. Official Soviet documents described this process as "evacuation," because the term "repatriation" was usually reserved for *return* to the Soviet Union. We will, however, use the term "repatriation," which describes the nature of the process with greater accuracy and was also the term used by the Polish government. In November and December 1955, hundreds of the special settlers, including forty-one Jews, crossed the Soviet-Polish border.[12] In July 1955 and then in January 1956, the Presidium of the Supreme Soviet of the Soviet Union issued resolutions that regulated the repatriation to Poland of those who did not avail themselves of the right to return to their home country under the July 1945 agreement or, to be precise, the three agreements that Poland then had with Soviet Ukraine, Soviet Belorussia, and Soviet Lithuania. Back then the Soviet government sought to demonstrate "independence" of its republics, trying (and succeeding in the cases of Ukraine and Belorussia) to secure for them places in the newly built United Nations. In the 1950s, by contrast, only Moscow signed the repatriation agreement.[13]

On 19 November 1956, *Pravda* published a joint communiqué agreed by the Soviet and the Polish leaders at the conclusion of their talks in Moscow. Section 5 of the rambling text opened with a statement about a new stage of return to their homeland of Soviet residents who were citizens of Poland by 17 September 1939 and, "due to reasons not in their control," could not utilize their right in the 1940s.[14] The document did not explain that 17 September 1939 was the day when the Red Army had invaded Poland in accord with the Soviet-German Pact that led to World War II. In March 1957 both sides signed an agreement about the further repatriation of former Polish citizens and their spouses, children, and immediate family members. The process was supposed to be completed by 31 December 1958 but ultimately continued until the end of 1959. It involved an automatic change of citizenship, from Soviet to Polish.[15] However, this rule initially applied only to ethnic Poles, whereas Jews and people of other ethnicities had the choice of retaining Soviet citizenship.[16] Whereas Polish citizens who had settled in the Soviet Union before September 1939 generally were not part of the repatriation pool, a special exemption was made for political immigrants, such as Berger-Barzilai and Trepper.[17]

In the fall of 1956, Soviet-Polish repatriation negotiations sparked rumors of impending or already occurring expulsion to Siberia of Jews, as well as Poles, who had Polish or Lithuanian citizenship before the Second World War. The Jewish Labor Committee, which Yiddish-speaking immigrant labor leaders formed in the United States in 1934 in response to the rise of Nazism in Germany, urged the United Nations to intervene in order to stop the expulsion.[18] Even following the agreement signed in March 1957, rumors arose that Soviet officials had told some Jewish applicants for repatriation: "Sorry, we need you to go to Birobidzhan and reclaim the wilderness."[19]

In December 1956 the Polish government formed a committee to aid repatriates from the Soviet Union. Judging by press reports of the time, it took those on the Polish side several months to convince their Soviet counterparts to replicate the 1940s arrangement by extending the new agreement "to persons of Jewish nationality." Władysław Wicha, Poland's minister of the interior, appears as one of the persons instrumental in including the old clause.[20] The Soviet Red Cross and Red Crescent informed the public that those who wanted to find their relatives in Poland could contact its Moscow office.[21]

Out of the Fire and into the Frying Pan

By March 1957 some 3,500 Jewish repatriates had come to Poland. From the very beginning it was obvious that most considered Poland only the first leg of their journey to Israel or other countries: ultimately all but 500 of the 3,500 returnees applied for permission to emigrate from Poland.[22] Importantly, early in 1955 Poland liberalized its exit policy, making emigration to Israel and other counties relatively easy.[23]

Morgn-Frayhayt found the motive for the Jews' desire to leave the Soviet Union in the Khrushchev government's nationalities-policy mistakes:

> If these Jews are now emigrating, it is because Jewish cultural institutions had been wiped out and have not yet been restored. These Jews, as the Soviet Jews in general, still have no opportunity for self-expression as Jews. . . .
>
> Besides, it seems that there is also an additional reason for the desire to emigrate. The recent resolution of the American Communist Party points out that in the Soviet Union, where there is no official anti-Semitism, there are, however, vestiges of anti-Semitism. . . . So far no . . . public campaign against the vestiges of anti-Semitism has been initiated.[24]

There is, no doubt, a grain of truth in this assessment, proven by the fact that the repatriates who had chosen to stay in Poland usually felt compelled to maintain a distinctive Jewish milieu and, following the departure of many activists in the 1950s, played a larger role in the TSKŻ.[25] Nevertheless, it would be wrong to see exclusively *Jewish* grounds for disillusionment with life in the Soviet Union. As in the 1940s and the coming years of emigration, people saw repatriation as an opportunity to leave; they were *generally* dissatisfied with the Soviet system. Given the political and economic situation in Poland, repatriation was, in a way, a case of out of the fire and into the frying pan. Yet it gave people a unique chance to escape from the Soviet fire with the hope that the second leg of their journey, beyond Poland, would rescue them from the frying pan.[26]

The memoir of Yechiel Burgin, a leftist Yiddish cultural activist and resistance fighter in Vilna during World War II, describes how he and his family left the Soviet Union in March 1957. Before the war they lived in Vilna, then a city in Poland, which made them eligible for repatriation. The Burgins were by no means disadvantaged in Soviet society: Yechiel headed a department in the city's administration dealing with organizing concerts, while his wife worked as a teacher. Still, they felt themselves strangers in their city of Vilna, now Vilnius, capital of Soviet Lithuania. Once in Poland they straightaway applied for emigration to Israel, but the Polish authorities allowed them to depart only two years later. Meanwhile, they worked for Polish Jewish cultural and educational institutions and received support from the American Joint Jewish Distribution Committee (JDC).[27]

The majority of the Jewish repatriates, including the Burgins, were thoroughly secular.[28] Children in such families usually knew very little if anything about Jewish religious traditions but neither did they feel an affinity for Poland. Boris Smolar, the editor in chief of the Jewish Telegraphic Agency, warned that such children would pose a particular problem because they were "strangers in Poland and to the Polish language."[29] This echoed the 1957 reports of the JDC and the American Jewish Committee that the repatriates' children did not speak Polish and needed special preparation to enter Polish schools.[30] Children of the erstwhile Soviet citizens often "did not understand what had motivated their parents to leave Russia": "Repatriates related the touching scenes that had taken place when their children had to say goodbye to their school friends and to their teachers. . . . The children knew very little about Jews and Judaism. Their information about Israel came from official Russian sources taught in schools. One ten-year-old told us [American visitors]: 'Israel is a tool of colonialist power and wants to wage war upon the Arabs.'"[31]

The American rabbi and mohel (ritual circumciser) Zvi Bronstein spent six weeks in Poland in March and April 1958 and during this period circumcised 141 Jewish boys between the ages of eight and eighteen, almost three-quarters of them from families of recent repatriates. Among them was Burgin's eleven-year-old son. Children of repatriates would also be circumcised later. Thus, the sixteen-year-old son of Perl Sobol underwent circumcision in 1959. His father, whom Perl had met in a guerrilla detachment, was a Russian officer who had been killed in action. Prior to the Sobols' repatriation they lived in Birobidzhan, where a small number of former Polish citizens had settled in the 1940s.[32]

The KGB knew that some people, Jewish and non-Jewish, paid to enter a marriage with a person eligible for repatriation. Such arrangements usually involved payments of about five thousand rubles—roughly seven average monthly salaries or the price of two refrigerators. There was a danger of being caught in a scam or blocked by the KGB because of the questionable nature of the marriage.[33] Even so, Israel Mowshowitz, a prominent American rabbi who in the summer of 1957 visited camps for recent repatriates in Poland, "often noticed that young women were married to old men, and, conversely, that young men were married to old women"—clearly a sign of contrived marriages.[34] Hillel Zaltzman, a Lubavitch Hasid, described how he, then a Samarkand resident, tried to take advantage of the opportunity to leave the Soviet Union:

> There was a Jewish woman by the name of Luba who lived in our neighborhood. She . . . spoke Yiddish with a Polish accent. . . . I did some research and discovered that indeed she was a former Polish citizen. After I spoke to her, it turned out that she had a sensible reason for not leaving in 1946. Last but not least, Luba also had an only daughter by the name of Genia.
>
> My idea was to have the government register me as married to Genia and then to submit a request for my entire family to leave for Poland. This ruse was not my innovation: many of *anash* [here: Chabad Hasidim][35] had arranged similar fictitious marriages with Polish citizens during the previous wave of escapes.
>
> . . . I approached Luba with the proposal, adding that I would pay her if she agreed. She gave her general consent but said that the problem was that her daughter was a member of the Komsomol [Young Communist League]. . . . She wouldn't even discuss it with her daughter, fearing that her daughter's loyalty to the Party would supersede her family loyalties. . . .
>
> Having no other choice, I undertook the difficult and dangerous step of speaking to the girl directly. . . . I managed to convince her. There was an additional problem, though: she was only 16, and by law, you could not marry before 18. After much effort, we made some connections in the Ministry of the Interior to bribe the right people, and . . . we obtained a false identity card for her, stating that she was 18.
>
> Everything was proceeding according to plan, and we sincerely hoped that the day we had been yearning for would soon arrive and we would leave the Soviet Union.
>
> Although we kept the entire plan undercover, the mother was a big talker and spread the news that Hillel Zaltzman was marrying her daughter and then they were all going to Poland. Of course she didn't tell anyone that it was a phony marriage but since she and her daughter weren't religious, it was wholly obvious. Word spread, and explanation followed: Hillel Zaltzman is marrying into a secular family; surely, it's only in order to leave Russia!
>
> You can imagine how scared my father and our entire family were when the news spread throughout the Jewish section of Samarkand. Luba and Genia proceeded to leave, but before I would be caught, I aborted the deal.[36]

Shalom Skopas, a valiant scout in the Red Army's Sixteenth Lithuanian Division during World War II (a division that had an exceptionally high percentage of Jews in its ranks), hailed from Lithuania in its prewar borders and this did not permit him to apply for repatriation to Poland. Therefore, he entered a fictitious marriage with an ethnic Polish woman whom he then divorced after leaving the Soviet Union. Once in Warsaw, he registered at the Soviet consulate as a holder of a Soviet passport, which the Polish authorities eventually allowed to be stamped with an Israeli visa. Like the Burgins, he came to Israel, via Italy, in the spring of 1959.[37]

The Vilnius resident Ariana Jed fictitiously married a Pole because she and her sister (both survivors of the Kaunas Ghetto) and their father, a Red Army military doctor during the war, were former citizens of Lithuania, which rendered them, like Skopas, ineligible for repatriation in Poland. A friendly KGB officer, grateful to the sisters' father for healing his children, warned them that two Jewish residents had informed his agency about the fictitious nature of Ariana's marriage. He promised to put the investigation on hold but urged them to leave the country at the earliest opportunity. They managed somehow to do this.[38]

As in the 1940s, in the 1950s many people submitted fake documents. According to some accounts, an easily bribable or bighearted Vilnius archivist had furnished papers that certified former Polish citizenship and thus allowed many otherwise ineligible people to leave the country.[39] In all, it is estimated that about 15 percent of the Jewish repatriates were never Polish nationals.[40] In March 1957 Poland announced plans to send back those persons, predominantly Jews, who had "slipped into the country under the pretense of repatriation." Władisław Wicha described them as "persons who went to Poland without any right, who never lived in Poland and were not of Polish nationality."[41] However, apparently under international pressure, the threat of expulsion did not materialize: Romuald Spasowski, the Polish ambassador to the United States, soon disavowed the minister's statement.[42]

Meanwhile, Moscow began pressuring Warsaw to limit the number of departures for Israel. Sydney Gruson, the *New York Times* correspondent who received a Pulitzer Prize for his dispatches from Poland, observed in March 1957:

> A sudden change in Polish regulations has in effect halted the first numerically significant emigration of Jews from the Soviet Union to Israel.

> Large numbers of Jews have been among the Poles returning from the Soviet Union under the repatriation agreement. . . . Until last Monday virtually all of these Jews went on to Israel as soon as transport and other arrangements could be made for them.
>
> Since Monday, however, this situation has changed. Polish police headquarters had rejected all emigration applications of Jews from the Soviet Union. These Jews have been told that since they returned here as Poles they must assume Polish citizenship and apply for permission to emigrate "in a normal way."
>
> . . . There were speculations that the change had resulted from representations made by the Soviet Union, possibly after Egypt had brought the situation to the notice of the Soviet Government.
>
> The attitude of the Soviet Government seems to be that Jews wanting to go to Israel . . . should apply in the Soviet Union for permission to emigrate and not for repatriation to Poland. . . .
>
> Two thousand Jews recently arrived from the Soviet Union now are billeted in and around Warsaw. Many of them have already received permission to leave for Israel and the change in regulations does not affect them.[43]

An August 1957 JDC report explains the situation on the ground: "During the time when emigration was permitted, almost 100% of the repatriates from Russia registered for Israel on the day of their arrival. When Russia saw the stream of Jews flowing out of Poland to Israel, it threatened to discontinue the repatriation unless Poland would stop their emigration. Consequently, emigration of repatriated Jews from Poland to Israel was halted last March."[44]

Indeed, on 8 March 1957 the Polish authorities stopped issuing permission for the emigration of recent Jewish repatriates, and, although they later reversed this decision, many people, including the Burgins, had to wait for their turn to move to Israel. By June 1957, of the six thousand Jewish repatriates who came to Poland in 1956 and 1957, over two thousand had emigrated to Israel and nineteen hundred were awaiting a decision on their applications to leave the country.[45] In February 1957 the Soviet Ministry of Internal Affairs introduced a much more complex questionnaire for applications.[46] Still, by the beginning of 1958, the number of Jews who had arrived in Poland had exceeded ten thousand. According to Irving R.

Dickman, the JDC's public relations director, the majority of them hailed from Lithuania and other Baltic countries and had documents confirming their previously held Polish citizenship.[47] A November 1957 article by Milton Friedman, the Washington correspondent for the Jewish Telegraph Agency, states that the majority of the repatriates came from two formerly Polish territories: about 78 percent of them were from the "Vilna area" and 10 percent from Lviv.[48]

No doubt, in the coming years Lithuanian and Latvian Jews also played conspicuous roles in emigration, predominantly to Israel. This was a result of their closeness to traditional Jewish culture and of the relative ease with which they obtained permission for emigration, which perhaps reflected the desire of Soviet policymakers to minimize the destabilizing influence of those Jews whose outlook had taken shape in bourgeois societies.[49] The high level of national self-awareness, the relatively flexible policies of the local authorities, and contacts with Jews abroad led to Vilnius becoming an important source for emigration. The year 1956 saw a rise in religious activity among Vilnius Jews, which the head of the community explained by their preparation for emigration to Poland. According to another explanation, by a Soviet functionary, the temporary surge in synagogue attendance was related to support for Israel against the backdrop of the Suez Crisis. In any case, even nonreligious Jews went to synagogues on holidays, consumed kosher poultry and matzo, and circumcised their newborn boys. In the fall of 1956, visitors filled synagogues and their courtyards, spilling out onto the streets. Among the hundreds of visitors were people working at ministries, the film studio, publishing houses, and other institutions. Synagogue attendance declined somewhat in 1957 but still remained significant. By March 1960, 369 card-carrying members of the Party emigrated from Lithuania, of whom 173 were Jewish. While the majority of them went to Poland, three former Jewish Communists (emigration led to mandatory expulsion from the Party) were allowed to emigrate directly to Israel.[50]

For all that, Soviet sources paint a statistical picture that negates Dickman's and Friedman's conclusions that Jews from the Baltic republics dominated among the emigrants, as outlined in table 4.1.

On the other hand, Dickman's and Friedman's observations can be interpreted as an indication that a significant number of the Jews who came to

Table 4.1. Jewish Repatriation from the Soviet Union to Poland, 1956–1958

Soviet Republics from Which Jewish Repatriates Came to Poland	January–December 1956	January–April 1957	January–June 1958
Ukraine	671	1,842	368
Belorussia	40	113	290
Lithuania	249	1,365	265
Russia (not including Moscow)	211	147	109
Moscow	81	107	. . .
Kazakhstan	41	54	3
Latvia	26	214	90
Uzbekistan	22	74	34
Estonia	. . .	21	3
Kirgizia	14	. . .	5
Moldavia	12	28	25
Turkmenia	1	2	. . .
Georgia	3	11	. . .
Azerbaidzhan	2	1	6
Tadzhikistan	. . .	. . .	1

Source: Vialiki, *Belarus'—Pol'sha ŭ XX stahoddzi*, 220, 223, 228.

Poland from Russia and other places were, in fact, Litvaks or "Lithuanian Jews," that is, they were originally from the Baltic region or other localities populated by Jews who spoke the Lithuanian dialect of Yiddish. In addition, Lithuanian Jews were better organized. In June 1957 a landsmanshaft, or hometown association, was established in Poland to unite and represent those repatriates who hailed from Vilna/Vilnius, though by that time the majority of the recently arrived active or potential association members (278 of 320) had already emigrated to Israel. The president of the Union of Jewish Religious Communities in Poland, Dr. Alexander Libo, a survivor of the Vilna Ghetto who settled in Łódź after the war, and Abraham Morevski, a well-known Yiddish actor who came from the Soviet Union, took part in the inaugural meeting of the association.[51]

In 1958 the Soviet authorities slowed the repatriation of Jews and, in addition, rejected the applications of those individuals who had somehow disclosed their desire to emigrate to Israel.[52] It seems, for instance, that for this reason the Yiddish poet Joseph Kerler, later a prominent refusenik (the category "refusenik," or *otkaznik* in Russian, emerged in the early 1970s to characterize those people whose applications to emigrate had been refused by the Soviet authorities), did not get permission to leave the country. A relative of Golda Meir (she was then Israel's minister of foreign affairs) also failed to get permission to repatriate to Poland because the local KGB knew about his contact with Meir when she had served as Israel's ambassador to the Soviet Union.[53]

On 27 October 1958, during a meeting between Soviet and Polish leaders, Khrushchev stated that he was fed up with the issue of repatriation, especially because of the consequent Jewish emigration to Israel. Gomułka reassured him that the Polish government was mainly interested in the further repatriation of ethnic Poles.[54] Ultimately, this "annoying" process continued until the end of 1959, though the share of Jews in the repatriation stream—15 percent in 1957—plummeted to 5 percent in 1958 and 1959.[55]

Meanwhile, beginning in 1956, hundreds of Soviet Jews found themselves being denied permission to emigrate.[56] While Belorussia became known as a difficult place from which to get permission to repatriate to Poland, in Lithuania, too, Jews had a higher percentage of turned-down requests compared to ethnic Poles. Officially, the Soviet authorities opposed their emigration on the grounds of "inexpediency."[57] They would frequently use this semantically meaningless term in the coming years.

Emigration of Soviet Jews annoyed not only Khrushchev but the Polish Jewish Communist leaders as well. Benjamin Eliav, an Israeli journalist and later official ("about whom unfortunately little is known"),[58] wrote in March 1958 that the arrival of repatriates caused alarm rather than empathy among "members of the Stalinist wing" of the TSKŻ, who "explicitly insisted on appealing to the Soviet Union, requesting the delay of the departure of the Jewish repatriates, because there are amongst them 'nationalistic elements whose intention is not to remain here but to continue elsewhere.'"[59] When this request did not deter the Polish authorities from accepting Jewish repatriates, the same Communist zealots urged the government to speed up the repatriates' transit to Israel or elsewhere because they had misgivings about the revitalizing of Polish Jewish organizations and thereby creating a Jewish state within the state. They also sought to safeguard the existing Jewish community, wary that an increase in the Jewish population and the reestablished links with foreign Jewry could contribute to the further rise of anti-Semitism.[60]

In the often-quoted episode of his outburst at a session of the Central Committee of the Polish United Workers Party (Polska Zjednoczona Partia Robotnicza, PZPR, the official name of the Communist Party), Khrushchev urged his Polish comrades to correct the "abnormal composition of the leading cadres" as the Soviets had effectively done. Looking fixedly at the chairman of the session—Politburo member Roman (Rachmil) Zambrowski—Khrushchev declared: "Yes, you have many leaders with names ending in 'ski,' but an Abramovich remains Abramovich. And you have too many Abramoviches in your leading cadres."[61] To all appearances, ethnic Polish Communists were particularly active in scapegoating their Jewish comrades and thus effacing or obscuring their own role in the Stalinist system. In addition, the victory of Gomułka and his supporters over the previous group of leaders, among whom Jewish Communists had a visible role, had opened the Pandora's box of grassroots anti-Jewish feeling, which certainly reinforced the Jewish repatriates' resolution to leave Poland.[62]

The repatriation of the 1950s took place at the time of the second wave of Jewish emigration from postwar Poland, known as the "Gomułka Aliyah." While the anti-Jewish atmosphere in Polish society and severe economic difficulties were push factors for leaving the country, it also was a delayed emigration of those who were not allowed to move to Israel between 1950 and 1956. Lucjan Blit, a Bundist in pre-1939 Warsaw who later settled in London and built a successful career as a journalist and scholar, visited Warsaw in December 1956 as a correspondent for several periodicals, including the British newspaper *The Observer* and the New York *Forverts* (in which he used the byline V. Finsber). He wrote: "The Poland I knew before September, 1939, was not a rich country; now Soviet exploitation and doctrinaire planning have reduced it to the Balkan level. Only a tiny, privileged group of high officials, recognized artists and journalists can achieve what would be regarded in Britain as lower-middle-class standards. The rest work themselves to death on a subsistence level."[63] Summing up his three-week stay in Poland, he described the mood that prevailed among the Jews as "one of utter despair and panic." Many of them "were able to rise quickly, in the absence of other qualified personnel, to high party and government posts" in the pre-Gomułka regime, and this left them open to attack as Stalinists.[64]

The Repatriations

When interviewed by the American Yiddish journalist Samuel Loeb Schneiderman, Alexander Libo described the repatriates as a heterogeneous group. Some of them were young, practical, business-minded, and hardly destitute. On the other hand, hundreds of the newly arrived Jews—especially those who had been exiled to remote areas—came threadbare. In many instances the repatriates did not have professions in demand in the Polish job market. In addition, only a minority of them knew Polish well enough to function effectively in society; their languages were mainly Russian and Yiddish. A large number of them also needed serious medical attention.[65]

The repatriates brought to Poland a relatively limited, though not insignificant, amount of goods. Whereas in the 1940s they were allowed up to two metric tons, the new regulations restricted the allowance to "things for personal need," which included items for professional (e.g., academic or artisanal) activity. Nonetheless, well-to-do people brought refrigerators, washing machines, other appliances, and even cars (particularly valuable was the limousine ZIL-12), all of which were less expensive in the Soviet Union. Once they gained permission to leave the country, the repatriates were eligible to cash in their long-term state loan bonds, which Soviet citizens had to purchase as "voluntary" donations (usually 10–20 percent of earnings) toward the economic development of the country. They also could deposit money in a special account opened by the Polish embassy to receive later an equivalent amount in zlotys. Demobilized soldiers and officers as well as released prisoners would get free transportation to the Soviet-Polish border, whereas all other repatriates had to pay their travel expenses themselves.[66]

Although the Jewish immigration of the 1950s was of a lesser magnitude than the influx of returnees in the 1940s, the Polish government preferred to avoid carrying this additional burden. Significantly, the United States assumed that the maverick regime of Gomułka would weaken the Soviet coalition and, therefore, started a program of economic aid to Poland.[67] In this political context, the Polish Jewish leadership signaled that the authorities were to allow foreign Jewish relief organizations, most notably the JDC and the Organization for Rehabilitation through Training (known as World ORT), to renew operations in Poland. Both aid organizations, actively involved in rebuilding Jewish life in post–World War II Poland, had to leave the country in the early phase of the Cold War. In September 1957 an ORT delegation arrived in Warsaw. Hersh Smolar welcomed them as representatives of an organization whose idea was always dear to Polish Jews "because it was the idea of Jewish progress, of social restructuring and productivization."[68]

For foreign Jewish organizations, this new period was driven by an ideology different than the one that prevailed in the years immediately after the war. While the main objective then was to develop the economic foundation of Jewish life in the war-devastated country, this time the aim was to facilitate emigration to Israel. ORT trained and supported recent repatriates who had to stay in Poland before getting permission to move to Israel. Thanks to its help, Jewish cooperatives with almost two thousand Jewish workers appeared in several Polish cities. The majority of the new cooperatives produced goods, often from high-quality raw materials supplied by the JDC. Two cooperatives in Warsaw generated income from other services: one was a cooperative of translators; the other ran a Jewish restaurant.[69]

In Łódź, a cooperative located at 49 Kilinski Street in a building that had historically housed various Jewish institutions gave employment to twenty repatriates who repaired radio and television sets. These people came from Vilnius, where before World War II they had worked at the Elektrit Radiotechnical Society, then the largest privately owned company in the city. According to Libo, this group planned to move to Israel as a collective, which was not a pipe dream: in 1957, seven farmers brought sixty-one cows from Poland to Israel and reestablished their cooperative farm.[70] Libo and his family, including a non-Jewish son-in-law, already lived with packed suitcases, taking private Hebrew lessons three times a week; they came to Israel at the end of 1958.[71]

Although the Soviet-Polish repatriation agreement expired on 31 December 1958, repatriates continued arriving through the entire next year. In the first eight months of 1959, 3,866 Jews came from the Soviet Union, and the total number of Jews who by that time had reached Poland under the repatriation agreement was estimated at 18,700 (there are also higher estimates). About 6,000 of them had in the meantime emigrated from Poland.[72] Judging by the final statistics, 18,743 Jews were repatriated from the Soviet

Union from 1955 to 1959, and approximately 15,000 of them elected not to stay in Poland.[73] It is not clear whether this figure includes, first, non-Jewish members of the repatriates' families and, second, those who did not register with the Jewish organizations that operated in Poland.

There is no clarity whatsoever about the number of former Polish Jews who abstained from repatriation in the 1940s and 1950s and continued to live in the Soviet Union. Some of them had been well integrated into Soviet society. Thus, we don't find among the repatriates Wolf Messing, a magician, hypnotist, and psychic who remains a well-known enigmatic figure in Soviet history.[74] Any number of reasons could stop people from leaving the country. Esther Gessen, grandmother of the Russian and American journalist Masha Gessen, could not apply for repatriation (though she lived in September 1939 in her home city of Białystok) because her divorced husband did not allow her to take their children out of the country.[75]

Concerning those Jews, including the repatriates, who decided, for better or for worse, to stay on in Poland, Boris Smolar distinguished three main rationales for not moving abroad: first, elderly people received state pensions and did not want to change their way of life; second, some people, notably artisans, had found a professional niche that satisfied them; third, mixed families were less inclined to move to Israel, especially as many of them had relatives in the Soviet Union and wanted to maintain family contacts, something that was easier to do from Poland.[76] Still, emigration from Poland did not stop. Thus, in 1961, 990 people left for Israel, 769 of them repatriates from the Soviet Union.[77]

Some of the repatriates arrived in Israel as holders of Soviet passports. At that time, those who emigrated directly from the Soviet Union similarly arrived with Soviet passports in hand. The change would come in February 1967, following a secret decree that made it mandatory to strip of their citizenship all Soviet citizens who emigrated to Israel.[78] Whether the repatriates arrived in Israel with Soviet or Polish passports, the Gomułka Aliyah turned, to some extent, into the Khrushchev Aliyah.

Intellectuals' Emigration

The postwar 1940s saw the "evacuation" from the Soviet Union of scores of surviving Polish Jewish cultural figures, including Yiddish writers, journalists, and actors. By the mid-1950s the majority of them had left Poland and settled in Israel, the USA, France, or elsewhere.[79] Thus, Rachel Korn, a poet who returned to Poland in 1946 and settled in Łódź, went the same year to Stockholm, chosen to represent Polish Yiddish writers at the first postwar congress of PEN International. She did not return to Poland but remained in Sweden until 1948, when she moved to Canada and settled in Montreal. In the Soviet Union, Korn had been a member of the Writers Union and of the Jewish Anti-Fascist Committee. She also had a seat on the city council in prewar Lviv. In all, Korn was one of a score of Polish Yiddish writers who had been well integrated into the Soviet literary milieu. However, the majority of them preferred to leave the Communist zone of Europe at the earliest opportunity and usually developed new, as a rule anti-Soviet, positions in light of their experiences. It meant that even those who survived in the Soviet Union in a relatively privileged position and published works extolling the virtues of the Soviet regime ultimately revised their publicly expressed views in the following years.[80]

In the 1950s the TSKŻ focused its efforts on facilitating the repatriation of Yiddish writers and other cultural figures who still lived in the Soviet Union. Some of them were not directly affected by the repressions, whereas the less fortunate ones had been liberated only after Stalin's death. In addition to the newspaper *Folks-Shtime*, edited by Hersh Smolar, the TSKŻ had at its disposal, directly or indirectly, a literary journal, a publishing house, a theater, clubs, summer camps, and schools. Yet this infrastructure of cultural institutions lacked a sufficient cadre of journalists, writers, editors, actors, and educators. When the new repatriation agreement between the Soviet Union and Poland made Jewish emigration on a small scale possible, Smolar and his associates saw it as a chance to bolster their thinned-out ranks. There can be little doubt that sincere desire to help their colleagues also played a role in these efforts.

Significantly, starting in 1955, when the Soviets simplified and eased their requirements for visits by citizens of satellite countries, thousands of Polish tourists went to the Soviet Union, and many of them were Jewish.[81] As a result, relatives, friends, and colleagues could renew their contacts. Plays for the Yiddish amateur group established in Vilnius were "brought in from Poland, with pages from books first being photographed and diminished to a minimal 9 × 12 cm, for easier hiding in case of searches at the border."[82] Ida Kamińska, the director of the Warsaw State Yiddish Theater, could visit Moscow, where her daughter and granddaughter lived; in November 1947, when Kamińska's daughter, Ruth Turkow Kamińska, and her husband, the popular jazz musician Eddie Rosner, attempted to repatriate to Poland, they wound up in the Gulag.[83] Turkow Kamińska and Rosner's marriage did not survive the prison terms. Ultimately, both left the country—she for Poland and then the United States, he to his native Germany.

Moyshe Broderzon, a poet and playwright, had chosen to stay in Russia rather than repatriate to Poland. In 1946 he had insisted that it was unwise to move to Poland because it was a "snakepit," a country "full of bandits."[84] Following his arrest in 1950 and rehabilitation in September 1955, he established contact with his old friends in Warsaw.[85] In the Polish embassy, Broderzon was encouraged to apply for repatriation, but the process of getting permission took six months. To earn a living he wrote texts for Yiddish variety concerts, which were sanctioned and even encouraged by the authorities. Thus, he and the poet Joseph Kerler, who from 1950 to 1955 served his sentence for "anti-Soviet nationalist activity," prepared the script for performances by the popular Yiddish actor Anna Guzik.[86] Finally, in June 1956, Broderzon and his wife received the necessary papers, and the embassy bought them train tickets to Warsaw. On 17 August 1957, a mere three weeks after arriving in Warsaw, he died of a heart attack.[87] Attempts to bring Kerler, whose wife was a former Polish citizen, had not been successful despite the personal involvement in the case of Tadeusz Gede, the Polish ambassador in Moscow.[88]

Quite possibly Broderzon would later have left Poland. However, his death there meant that his name remained mentionable in Soviet publications.[89] Very different was the Soviets' attitude toward the Yiddish poet Israel Emiot (Goldwasser), who came to Poland soon after Broderzon. The two had been inmates of the same Gulag camp for four years.[90] In 1958 Emiot left Poland for the United States, where he published a series of scathing articles in the *Forverts*, known for its anti-Soviet content. Aron Vergelis attacked him in the *Literaturnaia gazeta*, chastising Emiot as one of the "literary renegades" who survived in the Soviet Union during the war but later, following emigration, began to cast aspersions on the country that had given him a shelter. Vergelis did not mention, of course, that such ungrateful renegades as Emiot had suffered arrest and imprisonment for many years in forced-labor camps.[91]

The year 1956 also saw the repatriation of two actors: Ruth Turkow Kamińska, who finally reunited with her mother, and Abraham Morevski, a star in interwar Poland who headed the Yiddish theater established in Białystok when the city fell under Soviet control in 1939. Morewski later wrote about the turbulent atmosphere that he encountered in Warsaw: "The occurrences in October 1956 in new Poland, the [Suez-Sinai] war in the Middle East, the creative achievements of Yiddish State Theatre . . . on the one side, and, on the other, the emigration movement among the Jewish population."[92]

Mark Rakowski, known for his Yiddish translations in prewar Warsaw—in 1934 he visited Moscow as a guest delegate at the First Congress of Soviet Writers—also repatriated in 1956.[93] Benjamin Nadel, who came to Poland in 1957, specialized in ancient history. Born in Petrograd in 1918 and brought to Vilna as a child, he was accepted on the eve of World War II into the graduate program of the Vilna-based Yiddish research institute, YIVO. In the Soviet Union, he defended his dissertation in 1947, took part in archaeological expeditions in Crimea, and worked as an academic in Leningrad. In Poland, he taught at universities and published two Yiddish monographs on early European Jewish history. He also published articles in *Folks-Shtime*. In May 1962 the Polish government awarded him the Order of Merit. Ultimately, he emigrated to the United States. Earlier, Mark Rakowski, who had stayed put in Poland, was awarded the Knight's Cross of the Polonia Restituta Order for his social and literary work.

Michael Astour (Czernichow), later a professor at Brandeis University, lived in Karaganda, Kazakhstan, after his release from the Gulag in 1950. By pure chance he found out about the repatriation, and after overcoming some red tape he and his wife came to Warsaw in 1956. Before finally reaching the United States he moved to Paris, where he had studied in his youth, thanks to support received from the United States. The Jewish Labor Committee put him on a list of Jewish socialists who wanted neither to remain in Poland nor to immigrate to Israel. French prime minister Guy

Mollet, a socialist, agreed to grant those on the list visas for emigration to France.[94]

Esther Rosenthal-Shneiderman (or Ester Rozental-Szneiderman), who repatriated in 1958, was a highly educated and experienced pedagogue. After moving to the Soviet Union as a political emigrant in 1926, she worked in Kyiv and Birobidzhan. She was the head of the Party organization at the Kyiv-based Institute for Jewish Proletarian Culture, a graduate student and later a research fellow at its Pedagogical Section, and a lecturer at the Kyiv Teachers Training Institute. In the early 1930s she emerged as an editor of children's Yiddish periodicals and an author or coauthor of several textbooks for Yiddish schools. In Israel, where Rosenthal-Shneiderman settled in 1962, she took part in postmortem examination of Soviet Yiddish cultural history. Her books *Oyf vegn un umvegn* (On Main and Circuitous Roads) and *Birobidzhan fun der noent* (Birobidzhan from Close Up), which also came out in Hebrew, intertwine personal memoirs with the results of her research work and provide panoramic, insightful portrayals of Soviet Yiddish academic and cultural circles.

By the end of the 1950s, two more Yiddish writers repatriated from the Soviet Union. One of them, Shloyme (Solomon) Belis-Legis, a member of the Communist-linked Yiddish literary group Yung Vilne (Young Vilna) in the 1930s, worked in the Soviet Lithuanian press. During World War II, Belis-Legis served in the Red Army and then returned to Vilnius, where he took part in the activities around the short-lived Jewish Museum and worked as a journalist. In 1954 his small Polish-language book *Ludzie fabryk Litwy Radzieckiej* (People of factories in Soviet Lithuania) came out in Vilnius. It seems that he was not directly affected during the postwar phase of arrests and remained a member of the Writers Union, but nevertheless decided to move to Poland.[95] His 1964 literary-historical book *Portretn un problemen* (Portraits and problems), published in Warsaw, included chapters on Soviet Yiddish writers.

The poet Naftali Herts Kon endured two imprisonments in the Second Polish Republic for Communist activities and then, after emigrating to the Soviet Union, served two terms in the Gulag following his arrests in 1938 and 1949. In Communist Poland, where Kon and his family repatriated in 1959 thanks to his Polish-born wife (Kon was born in Bukovina, which was part of Romania before World War II), he faced yet another arrest, this one in December 1960. The Polish secret police accused him of having illegal connections with the Israeli embassy and of writing subversive articles. Released in March 1962, he settled in Israel three years later.[96]

It would be an exaggeration to state that the emigration of several cultural activists seriously weakened the Soviet Yiddish cultural milieu. In the 1950s it was still numerically strong. In the Soviet Union, the main problem was not so much the number of still active Yiddish writers, journalists, and actors as the paucity or lack of infrastructure for Jewish creative activity. Meanwhile, the repatriation of the 1940s and 1950s brought to the West and Israel intellectuals who would act as experts on Soviet Jewish life and culture. Their articles and books, mainly in Yiddish but also in other languages, were widely read and cited. For the Western audiences, this multilingual group of authors and scholars played a central role in painting the picture of Jewish life in the Soviet Union.

5

JEWS IN SOVIET SOCIETY

The "Fifth Point"

The "evacuation" to Poland of roughly twenty thousand Jews from 1957 to 1959 further widened the gap between the Jewish population in the west of Belorussia, where the number of Jewish residents had diminished particularly dramatically since 1941, and the eastern provinces of the republic.[1] A similar decline took place in the Jewish population in the areas of Lithuania and Ukraine that had belonged to Poland before September 1939. Otherwise, however, repatriation in the 1950s only slightly affected the size and composition of Soviet Jewry. The 1959 census revealed that the USSR had roughly 2,268,000 Jews or 1.09 percent of the entire Soviet population. It was less than previously expected. In February 1959 Khrushchev told British prime minister Macmillan when the latter asked him about the Jews: "The results of the census would be out soon. Till then it would be difficult to say. Perhaps 3–3 ½ million, perhaps even as many as 5 million."[2]

Soviet Jews did not form "a homogenous entity, sharing uniform perceptions of self and of its non-Jewish environment." Although variations based on old Ashkenazic geographic differences between Litvaks (Lithuanian and Belorussian Jews), Ukrainian Jews, Polish Jews, and other Yiddish speakers had lost most of their meaning for the younger generation, contemporary differences between Jews living in such cities as Moscow, Leningrad, Vilnius, Riga, Kishinev, or Odessa certainly played a role. Even wider and deeper could be the gap between city residents and those who lived in provincial towns. There was also a divide between "old Soviet" Jews and those who became Soviet in 1939 or 1940.[3] This divide was particularly palpable in the areas that had become Soviet in 1939 and 1940 and saw in-migration of population, including Jews, from other parts of the country.

Along with the predominantly Ashkenazic Jews, that is, Yiddish speakers and their descendants, several other ethnoreligious subgroups comprised a minority among Soviet Jewry: Georgian Jews (over thirty-five thousand), Mountain, or Caucasian Jews (over twenty-five thousand), Bukharan, or Central Asian Jews (over twenty thousand), and smaller groups of several thousand Krymchaks, Karaites, and Kurdistan Jews.[4] More often than not there was little in common, apart from a Soviet education and experience, between them and the Ashkenazic Jews whom people in many parts of the country, especially in Russia, Ukraine, Belorussia, Moldavia, Lithuania, and Latvia, knew as neighbors, colleagues, fellow students, or even family members, with their (declining use of) Yiddish, familiar names, and strikingly visible place in various domains of Soviet life, such as medicine, pedagogy, journalism, culture, and science. Contacts between Jews from different subgroups were rare, especially outside the areas of Central Asia and the Caucasus where the majority of the non-Ashkenazic Jews had been living since ancient times and were, as a rule, better known to local people than the Ashkenazic Jews.

Few Jews and non-Jews ever heard anything about the small groups of ethnic Russians, the Subbotniks, who were scattered over the country, including, as we already know, the Jewish Autonomous Region. Such sects appeared more than two centuries earlier, when religious quests led some Christians to embrace the Torah, switching their weekly day of prayer to Saturday (*subbota* in Russian) and adopting circumcision as well as other Jewish practices. While they usually identified themselves as non-Jewish believers, there were also some who considered themselves Jewish and even had this registered in their documents.[5] Presumably, people of the latter group were counted as Jewish during the 1959 census.

Accuracy of census figures on ethnicity, Jewish or non-Jewish, is not perfect, especially as respondents did not have to provide documents proving the veracity of the information given to pollsters. Otherwise, identity papers played paramount roles in Soviet society. The most important mandatory document was the "internal passport," whereas the "foreign passport," needed for traveling abroad, was an abstraction for the overwhelming majority of Soviet citizens who never crossed the borders of the country. The internal passport, on the other hand, was an indispensable element of their life. Introduced in 1932, such identity documents had to be obtained by every urban dweller aged sixteen and older. For many years internal passports were not issued to people living in villages, making it illegal for them to leave the countryside. Without a passport an urban dweller, too, was a nonperson, unable to get a job, to register a civil marriage (the only one valid in the Soviet Union), to mail a parcel, and otherwise legally function in the Soviet environment. Passports contained various details about their holders, including their "nationality," meaning—in Soviet terms—ethnicity.

Starting in 1938, Soviet citizens were restricted in their choice of ethnicity. Henceforth they would be assigned the ethnic identity of their parents. Applied to Jews, this universal rule meant that if both parents were Jewish, their offspring would automatically be categorized as Jewish. Children born to parents of different ethnicities had, at the age of sixteen, a binary choice between the mother's and father's backgrounds. As a result, thoroughly acculturated people born to two Jewish parents lacked a legal path to full bureaucratic assimilation in the form of legal classification as, for instance, Russians, Georgians, or Lithuanians. Importantly, people could not identify themselves as generically "Soviet"; everyone had to have an ethnic label that in some way connoted their status in society.

For the increasing number of Jews with no religious, linguistic, organizational, or territorial attachment to Jewishness, the designation "Jewish" in their passport, along with their family ties, became the principal anchor of their ethnic identity. It was a new kind of Jewish awareness: a more subjective psychological conception of distinctiveness, with a minimal emphasis on overt religious and cultural criteria.[6] There was a clear divide between those who carried *active culture and identity* and those who carried *passive culture and identity*. Jews of the former category were involved in the creation and consumption of various cultural artifacts (books, food, the celebration of holidays, etc.), whereas "passive" Jews' worldview and cultural perspective were "not necessarily consciously ethnic."[7]

For many Soviet Jews their identity was, indeed, to borrow the words of the American historian Arcadius Kahan, "left only as a mythical, almost mystical quality incomprehensive to their environment and one that could become incomprehensible to themselves."[8] In 1965 the future Nobel Peace

Prize winner Elie Wiesel visited the Soviet Union with a fact-finding mission, organized by diplomats in the Israeli Ministry of Foreign Affairs, and wrote a travelogue whose politically expedient title, *The Jews of Silence*, became a widely used byword for Soviet Jews, whose voice could not be heard because of lack of organizations and press outlets, let alone the absence of freedom of speech. One of these Jews, an elderly man, tried to find an answer to the narrator's question "In what way are you a Jew?" He answered: "Apparently you live in a country where Jews can afford the luxury of asking questions. Things are different here. It's enough for a Jew to call himself a Jew. . . . If my son were to ask me one day what a Jew is, I would tell him that a Jew is one who knows when to ask questions and when to give answers . . . and when to do neither."[9]

The writer Vladimir Voinovich maintained that even the word *evrei*, Jew, had in Soviet usage the peculiar status of a term with "a kind of academic meaning, like the Latin word *penis*."[10] Non-Jews would often moderate the perceived offensive nature of *evrei* (Jew) and *evreika* (Jewess) by using the diminutive forms, *evreichik* and *evreiechka*, making it inadvertently more derogatory. The novelist Aleksandr Melikhov opined that the notion of "Soviet Jewish" meant a social role—most notably as a segment of intelligentsia—rather than a nationality.[11]

Indeed, Jewishness increasingly meant belonging to a peculiar Soviet subcommunity. In purely Jewish circles people tended to intimate that such and such person was *nash chelovek* ("one of us") rather than to say that she or he was Jewish. Many Jews preferred another euphemism—*frantsuz*, or Frenchman, probably coined with reference to the guttural ("French-like") pronunciation of the letter *r*, considered to be a peculiarity of specifically Jewish pronunciation. The word *malanets*, also a euphemism, had a limited territorial usage, mainly in Odessa and Moldavia, and may come from the Yiddish *malen*, "to circumcise," thus meaning "the circumcised ones."[12]

> . . . he asked:
>
> "What is it, *malanets*?"
>
> "A Jew."
>
> "But why *malanets*?"
>
> "Well, it's not nice to tell a person [that he is a] Jew."[13]

The internal passport could contain bureaucratically incorrect information, for instance, categorizing its Jewish holder as Russian, Ukrainian, Georgian, and so on. Such records appeared as a result of paying a bribe, of a bureaucratic mistake, of forging identity during the war, or of choosing a different ethnic marker before 1938, when people could pick and choose any background. Mary Leder, an American Jewish teenager whom destiny had delivered to the Soviet Union in the early 1930s, recalled that she even managed to get the categorization "American" in her first Soviet internal passport.[14] From the late 1940s onward, Communists accused of hiding their nationality by claiming a supposedly false ethnicity on official documents or by changing their names to conceal their background could be punished with expulsion from the Party.[15]

A special case was the gross statistical underestimation of the number of Mountain Jews, who were encouraged by some of their leaders and Soviet officialdom to stop thinking of themselves as Jews and instead to identify themselves as Tats, a linguistically and territorially related group. There have been two points of view on this subject: some scholars and laypeople view the Mountain Jews as a separate Jewish ethnic group who historically shared the language and some cultural (but not religious) traditions with the Tats, whereas others view them as the Judaized part of the Tat nation.[16] In Azerbaijan, in 1959, in addition to 10,300 people who declared themselves as Mountain Jews, there were also 5,900 Tats, the majority of whom were, in fact, also Mountain Jews. Moreover, some of the Mountain Jews were "hidden" in the statistics of those who described their ethnicity as simply "Jewish."[17]

For all that, the vast majority of Soviet Jews had been taken into account during the 1959 census. As a rule, Jewish respondents claimed their ethnicity exactly as it figured in their internal passports, in the entry that became popularly known as "the fifth point," widely used as a metonym for "Jewish." In fact, the folklore around "the fifth point" ("handicapped by the fifth point," etc.) stems from the ordinal number of the entry not in passports, but in standard forms used by personnel departments. For Jews, the role of this "point" had become rather different since the late 1940s, though these changes did not appear out of nowhere.

Gennady Kostyrchenko, whose archival research has shed light on many aspects of Soviet Jewish history, traces the origin of the policy of discriminating against Jews to the Personnel Department, established at the Central Committee of the Communist Party in 1939.[18] The department, staffed with young, predominantly Russian and other Slavic functionaries, worked to correct the "abnormal composition of the leading cadres," as Nikita Khrushchev would boast in the 1950s before the Communist leadership of Poland (see chapter 4, p. 102). In fact, the regime was not "blind" at all also earlier, notably in 1937–38 while conducting mass purges, which targeted in particular specific ethnic groups, notably the Poles.[19] Nineteen thirty-nine also can be pointed to as the year when the Soviet regime in many ways lost its ethnic blindness.[20]

The second half of 1942 and especially 1943 saw numerous dismissals of Jews from leading positions in the domains of culture and propaganda.[21] In the sarcastic words of the film director Mikhail Romm, "Until the year 1943, as we know, we had no antisemitism. . . . Somehow, we managed without."[22] Vasily Grossman described the change of status through the thoughts and feelings of Viktor Shtrum, the protagonist of his novel *Life and Fate*:

> Never, before the war, had Viktor thought about the fact that he was a Jew, that his mother was a Jew. Never had his mother spoken to him about it—neither during his childhood, nor during his years as a student. Never while he was at Moscow University had one student, professor or seminar-leader even mentioned it.
>
> Never before the war, either at the Institute or at the Academy of Sciences had he ever heard conversations about it. . . . Point Five. This had been so simple and insignificant before the war; now, however, it was acquiring a particular resonance.[23]

The "fifth point" began to play a powerful or even decisive role in many aspects of life, including choosing and gaining access to professions, some of which—most notably the Party apparatus, security, and foreign relations—had become entirely or almost entirely out of reach to Jews since at least 1951.[24] Jews were as a rule underrepresented or not represented in local soviets (councils) and, with the exception of Lithuania, in the Supreme Soviets (parliaments) of Soviet republics.[25] Given the purely decorative nature of Soviet elections, in which people could vote only for one carefully vetted candidate, the composition of the soviets was determined by the authorities rather than by the choice of the voters or the desire of people to act as elected deputies.

In addition to discrimination in specific fields, informally (in most cases orally, via telephone and closed-door conversations) ordered from the center, the prejudices and overcautiousness of those charged with the selection of appointees, employees, and students often played the dominant role. The restrictions did not necessarily affect existing cadres. Thus, in the Vinnytsia Medical University in 1958, Jewish scholars, doctors of medical sciences, and professors headed the departments of biochemistry, chemistry, pathological physiology, general hygiene, faculty therapy, nerve diseases, skin and venereal diseases, obstetrics and gynecology, psychiatry, and surgery. In two hospitals—nos. 2 and 3—of the city of Vinnytsia, a regional center in Ukraine, among 129 doctors there were 68 Jews, 42 Ukrainians, and 16 Russians.[26]

Younger people, however, faced obstacles usually unfamiliar to their parents. In this climate, Jews could be placed into three groups: first, those who took the glass ceiling as a given and, being unambitious, did not particularly suffer from psychological effects associated with it; second, those who were proud of overcoming the obstacles and gaining what they perceived as an honorable position in society; third, those who can be called "disabled by the fifth point"—people who blamed, rightly or wrongly, their (and their relatives' and friends') underachievement on the nationality recorded in their passports. In different phases of their lives people could move from one group to another.

Meanwhile, the restrictions coupled with change in the prestige rankings of occupations brought changes into the professional structure of the Jewish population. An increasing number of Jews worked in construction and education, while the retail sector was losing its attraction to the younger generation, though in some regions they continued to make up the majority of retail workers.[27] Jews became overrepresented in software engineering, which had emerged as a new niche in the professional landscape. According to a joke, software engineering became "ne spetsial'nost', a natsional'nost'"—"a nationality rather than a profession." Very often these were students of specialized schools or classes, established in the late 1950s and 1960s, who could not get a place at top university departments, notorious for their anti-Jewish sentiment. In the meantime, several second-tier universities opened applied mathematics departments that trained excellent specialists in the field.[28]

Various fields of engineering appealed to Jews even before the emergence of obstacles on their way to getting higher education. Thus, in the summer of 1953, in Dnipropetrovsk (Dnipro after 2016), Ukraine, the number of Jews was high among graduates from local institutes (technical universities): 31 of 330 at the Mining Institute, 22 of 100 at the Engineering-Construction Institute, 22 of 137 at the Chemistry-Technological Institute, and 94 of 387 at the Metallurgical Institute.[29]

Half-Jews whose passports indicated a non-Jewish nationality, most commonly "Russian," encountered fewer educational and career restrictions if any at all. Paradoxically, on the one hand, the authorities made it illegal to change one's nationality, including "Jewish" (connections and money could, however, sometimes smooth things along), but on the other hand an identity change from "Jewish" to, say, "Russian" was quite desirable since it contributed to the statistical decline of the Jewish population.

The situation was different in the bohemian world. In March 1953 the leading figures in the Soviet Writers Union wrote to Khrushchev to inform him inter alia that of the 1,102 writers who were listed as members of the Moscow chapter of the union, 329, or almost 30 percent, were Jewish.[30] Darcy Patrick Reilly, who served as the British ambassador to the Soviet Union from 1957 to 1960, noted that in the Soviet film world, which was a sphere where foreigners, even diplomats, at times could have rewarding and stimulating contacts, the proportion of Jews in the upper reaches of the profession was noticeably high.[31]

Such composers as Arkady (Abraham) Ostrovsky, Eduard Kolmanovsky, Ian Frenkel, Oskar Feltsman, and Mark Fradkin were central figures in Soviet pop culture. In the early 1950s, 239 Jews formed the second-largest group in the Composers Union, after the 435 Russians. The prominence of Jews was especially apparent in some chapters of the Composers Union. Thus, in Moscow there were 174 Russians and 116 Jews, in the Kazakh chapter there were six Kazakhs and six Jews, and in Moldavia eight Jews, five Moldavians, and three Russians.[32] In 1962 the Composers Union convened a congress, the breakdown of whose delegates by nationality showed that, after Russians (165), Jews formed the largest group (91).[33]

The Soviet theater world was populated by many celebrities of Jewish descent. Maya Plisetskaya was known in the ballet world as the exemplary Soviet prima ballerina. After her tours with the Bolshoi Ballet to the United States in 1959 and 1962, she became a cultural emblem of the Soviet Union. Arkady Raikin, director of the Leningrad Theater of Variety and Miniature, led the school of Soviet comedians for half a century. Elina Bystritskaya was known as one of the most beautiful women of the Soviet cinema. If necessary their Jewishness could be instrumentalized by the state, as would happen in March 1970 when Plisetskaya, Raikin, Bystritskaya, and many other "titled" Jews participated in a widely publicized press conference that launched an all-out anti-Israeli and anti-Zionist campaign.[34]

However, in "regular" occupations the administration usually tried to avoid accusations of causing what was called "contamination" (*zasorennost'*) of the personnel. In that climate, only a small fraction of children born in mixed families chose to be identified in their documents as Jewish and carry a recognizably Jewish surname. Soviet researchers offered as a description of this phenomenon such euphemisms as the different "ethnic attractiveness" of various national groups, or "ethnic prevalence."[35] The available statistics show that, on the average nationwide, 19 percent of all children born to Jewish mothers in 1958 had a non-Jewish father. The percentage of such cases was much lower in such republics as Moldavia (7), Georgia (9), and Uzbekistan (10), but in Russia it reached 27 percent. Taking into account that approximately twice as many Jewish men were married to non-Jewish women as were Jewish women to non-Jewish men, in the Russian republic about half of all newborn children with at least one Jewish parent had a non-Jewish other parent.[36]

In many places the proportion of mixed marriages was even higher. Thus, in the Volga city of Ulyanovsk, with a Jewish population of less than two thousand, 156 Jews entered into a marriage with a non-Jewish partner from 1950 to 1961, whereas only 96 Jews formed monoethnic families during the same period.[37] In Estonia, in 1965, 63 percent of Jewish men and 54 percent of Jewish women married non-Jews. In the meantime, among the Georgian, Bukharan, and Mountain Jews intermarriages with non-Jews or Jews from other subgroups remained rare.[38] Despite their prevalence, especially in the Slavic republics, many Jews tended to look askance at mixed marriages. The experience of recruiting Jewish KGB informers for work among Jews had shown that an informer with a non-Jewish wife did not enjoy the same level of confidence within the targeted milieu as an informer with a Jewish wife.[39] Jews preferred to discuss many specific issues privately, among people close to them. An authoritative 1958 book on the anthropology of Soviet peoples noted—four decades after the 1917 revolution—an "ongoing process of gradually eradicating the isolation and insularity that was characteristic of Jewish life before the revolution."[40] Indeed, it was an ongoing, never completely finished process.

In the early 1960s a commission tasked with drafting a new constitution discussed the issue of removing the entry on "nationality" from Soviet documents. Khrushchev welcomed it as a meaningful step toward Communism. However, the entire project was shelved following Khrushchev's involuntary removal from office. The idea of dropping the "nationality" category from personnel documents was raised again later but met resistance at both the union and republican levels.[41]

No other ethnic group in the Soviet Union was as linguistically assimilated as the Jews. By 1959 three out of four Soviet Jews claimed Russian as their first language. This did not mean, though, that the remaining one-quarter did not know Russian; as a rule, they too learned the language. Significantly, Russian was no longer seen as a language imposed by another nation. The history of losing Yiddish and acquiring Russian was water under the bridge for those who had Russian-speaking parents or even grandparents. At the same time, the loss of Yiddish had much more serious consequences in the Soviet Union than in other countries, because the vast majority of Soviet Jews were additionally deprived of other demarcations of national life, which could have facilitated the development of a hybrid Jewish-Soviet identity as an alternative to unattainable full assimilation.

Sovietization usually meant appropriation of the mainstream Soviet Russian culture. Emmanuil Kazakevich toyed with the idea of writing an autobiographical story and "to call it 'Rabinovich'—the surname from a Jewish anecdote [a stereotypical Rabinovich usually figured in Russian anecdotes about Jews]—and to tell the story on behalf of this tragic rather than somehow anecdotal person, who deeply understands and loves Russia and Russians, though they do not always return his love."[42] Characteristically, Bukharan Jews usually could be distinguished from other speakers of Persian or Tajik in Central Asia not by phonetic or morpho-syntactical criteria but by different linguistic behavior, which included an inclination to accept Russian loanwords.[43] Russianisms also made the Georgian language spoken by Georgian Jews recognizably "Jewish."[44] Many Jews became devoted to the Russian language and culture. It is no coincidence, probably, that the linguist Ditmar Rozental, born in Poland into a Jewish family, would become an authority in matters of contemporary Russian orthography and usage. Aleksander Melikhov observed sarcastically that the Russians' attitude toward the Russian language was less careful, because they were the main owners of the language and "do not need the grammar, which is written for some Jews (and by Jews)."[45]

Some Jews, especially of the older generation, spoke a recognizably "Jewish Russian," with insertion of Yiddish words, though this variety of Russian, often described as the "Odessa language," never existed as a uniform ethnolect.[46] Territorial, generational, and social peculiarities determined the nature of Jewishness (or, more often, its absence) in the vocabulary, grammar, and phonology of the speakers' idiolects. For instance, a Moscow or Leningrad Jewish dweller would not normally use the word *nivroku*, the formulas for warding off the evil eye (an equivalent of the Yiddish *keyn ayn hore*), though it was very widespread in Ukraine.[47] Several Yiddish words entered the language of non-Jewish Russian speakers. Thus, the Yiddish word *khokhme*, with the meaning of "wisecrack," settled in Russian as *khokhma* (wisecrack), *khokhmit'* (to wisecrack), and *khokhmach* (prankster).

The Occupations

By the end of the 1950s, a third of Soviet Jews were residents of five cities: Moscow (239,200) and Leningrad (contemporary Saint Petersburg, 168,600) in Russia, Kyiv (153,500), Odessa (108,900), and Kharkiv (81,500) in Ukraine. These cities had housed a third of Soviet Jews since at least the mid-1930s. In the 1950s over 80 percent of Jews lived in the three Slavic republics: Russia, Ukraine, and Belorussia. The Russian republic had the largest Jewish population, 39 percent of Soviet Jews, followed by Ukraine (37), Belorussia (7), and Moldavia (4). Tens of thousands of Jews continued to live in cities in eastern areas of the country, outside the pre-1917 Pale of Jewish Settlement, which had turned into the theater of two world wars as well as the pogrom-ridden civil war in the early years after the revolution. While some Jews settled in the eastern areas before and during World War I or as a result of migrations in the postrevolutionary period, many thousands more came there in the wake of the Nazi attack in June 1941.

When the war came to an end in 1945 or even earlier, after the liberation of the areas that had temporarily fallen under the enemy's control, thousands of Jewish evacuees and demobilized Red Army soldiers did not return to the cities, towns, or villages of their prewar residence. Rather, they decided to stay in the cities untouched by the war's devastation, where they found a new home and gainful employment—whether in the Volga Region, the Urals, Siberia, Central Asia, the Caucasus, or other parts of the vast country. Thus, the Jewish population in Frunze (Bishkek), the capital of Kirgizia (Kyrgyzstan), grew by a factor of six between 1939 and 1945, and it at least doubled in such cities as Tashkent, the capital of Uzbekistan, Kuibyshev (Samara), a city on the Volga, and Sverdlovsk (Yekaterinburg) in the Urals.[48]

Although Jews of Ashkenazic descent prevailed among the wartime Jewish migrants, hundreds of Mountain Jews also fled eastward. Some of them settled in Uzbekistan, where they were welcomed by local Bukharan Jews.[49] Released inmates of labor camps often settled in or close to the places of their incarceration in remote areas of the country. Zalman Shifrin, whose son Efim would become a well-known Russian stand-up comedian and singer, moved from Kolyma, in the northernmost part of Russia's Far East, only in 1966, ten years after his rehabilitation. Thousands of Jews also migrated from the "old" Soviet territories to the areas annexed by the USSR as a result of World War II.

Migration continued in the 1950s and 1960s, despite the heavy restrictions imposed by the state on its citizens, Jewish and non-Jewish alike. The system of mandatory registration of residence (*propiska*) acted as an important and stifling instrument of control. While citizens could travel without restrictions all over the country (apart from entering secret sites or areas close to the borders with foreign countries) to visit their relatives and friends, spend some time at resorts or other places, it was strictly prohibited to settle and get a job without obtaining permission from local authorities in the form of a stamp in the internal passport. A person required a sound reason to get permission to move from place A to place B, such as marrying a local resident, studying at a local educational institution, or being needed professionally. The lack of a real estate market, especially in urban centers where the majority lived in state-owned apartments, made migration even harder. It was particularly desirable—and difficult—to get a *propiska* in such cities as Moscow and Leningrad. Small towns on the outskirts of these cities were easier targets. Beginning in 1958, the insignificant but still existing Jewish rural population, and rural dwellers in general, were gradually allowed to get passports, which some of them used for relocating to an urban setting.[50]

Meanwhile, thousands of young people got permission to stay temporarily at university centers and many Jews used this means to gain access to education unavailable in the locales of their residence. Moscow and Leningrad institutions of higher education had intense appeal to aspiring scholars, actors, artists, and young people generally, who sought to study and perhaps settle in the main cultural and academic centers, which had better job opportunities and where the quality of life was generally more satisfactory than elsewhere. In some cases marriages of convenience were practiced for these purposes.

There was also a special motive for studying in other cities of the Russian republic: while in Ukraine, Belorussia, or Moldavia "positive discrimination" or simply anti-Semitism restricted Jews' access to education, most notably but not exclusively to medical schools, many places in Russia proper did not exhibit strong bias. In 1967, for instance, Novosibirsk University in Siberia admitted seventy-one Jewish students, who constituted after Russians (597) the second most numerous ethnic group.[51] This does not mean that people in Siberia were devoid of anti-Jewish prejudice. Local Jews faced such prejudice in their childhood and youth, but among adult residents open insults and conflicts of an anti-Semitic nature were relatively rare, which pleasantly contrasted with the situation in the areas traditionally populated by Jews.[52] Deservedly or not, Kyiv had a particularly strong reputation as an anti-Semitic city. As the real story (or the anecdote) goes, the preeminent Soviet puppeteer Sergei Obraztsov, who was Russian, said in 1961, addressing Kyiv functionaries: "I don't like to come to your anti-Semitic city."[53]

This helps explain the phenomenon of Jewish youth drain detected by the demographer Mark Tolts: between the 1959 and 1970 censuses, the presence of the 1944–53 birth cohort rose by 12 percent in Russia and fell by 10–11 percent in Ukraine and Belorussia.[54] Young people also migrated after graduating from institutions of higher or vocational education. Education was free and the state even provided modest scholarships, but upon graduation young specialists usually faced obligatory placement (*raspredelenie*) for three years, which could be in any corner of the country. As a result, a seventeen-year-old Jewish graduate from a secondary (high) school in the Moldavian town of Belts could spend five years studying in Tomsk, in West Siberia, and then get placed in Kuibyshev, settle there, and leave the city only in the 1990s, emigrating to Israel or America. The negative experience of searching for a nonprejudicial portal into the system of higher education and, later, employment usually left a memorable impact on young people, reinforcing their Jewish self-awareness.

As early as 1935 Jacob Lestschinsky, a leading Jewish social scientist who at that time lived in Warsaw, noted that, judging by their employment profile, Soviet Jews were beginning to look like a nation of white-collar workers and doctors.[55] Indeed, returns of the 1959 census show a large number of highly educated Jews, including about eighty thousand engineers, sixty thousand doctors, and over fifty-two thousand teachers. However, there were also over fifty thousand sales assistants, hairdressers, and beauticians, as well as tens of thousands of high-skilled factory workers, including ninety thousand metalworkers, machine-builders, and metallurgists. During the war workers (and engineers) of these professions had a higher chance to survive than, for example, textile workers. The former would be more often evacuated together with factories and exempted from military service because their vocational skills were essential to the defense industry. After the war many demobilized men, Jewish and non-Jewish alike, also became highly qualified workers, who often outearned ordinary employees with higher education. This was essential for the family's main breadwinner, whose wife could be a less well-paid teacher or physician. By the end of the 1950s, women made up three-quarters of Jewish medical doctors and teachers and close to half of Jewish lawyers.[56]

Still, the stereotypical Jewish man was a bespectacled holder of a university-level degree, at least. Whereas the average percentage of adults holding university or other higher-education degrees was 3.1 among Russians, 2.1 among Ukrainians, 1.6 among Belorussians, and 0.5 among Moldovanians, the same index for Ashkenazic Jews was 21.8. Judging by the returns of later censuses, the share of highly educated Mountain and Bukharan Jews was lower. As for Georgian Jews, they lagged non-Jewish Georgians in obtaining higher education, especially as the Georgians ranked second after the Jews—7.1 percent of their adults had higher education in 1959. Among Mountain Jews, professions such as pharmacy, medicine, and engineering were quite common, much more so than among Georgian Jews. However, such professionals formed a thin layer in comparison with the comparable stratum among Ashkenazic Jews.[57] Jews living in the Russian republic tended more often to be holders of higher-education degrees: 29.9 percent compared with 16.2 in Ukraine, 12.8 in Belorussia, and 9.9 in Moldavia.[58]

In 1957 there were 260,900 professionally active Jewish graduates of institutions of higher education, almost 10 percent of the total number. In 1966 the number of Jewish graduates rose to 327,800 but now constituted barely 6 percent of the total, reflecting a sharp increase in the number of non-Jewish graduates. The number of Jewish scientific-research workers gives a similar picture. In 1950 they represented the second-largest group, after Russians, with the ratio between them roughly 1:4. Despite the tendency that emerged in the late 1940s to limit the number of Jewish researchers, the Soviet leaders' pragmatic approach prevented their dispensing with the valuable contribution Jewish scientists could make to the development of the technological and hence military potential of the country. As a result, the number of Jewish researchers continued to rise but at a slower pace than the total increase of people in this category.[59]

Higher education meant belonging to the so-called intelligentsia, described in the 1936 Soviet constitution as a social "stratum" rather than a social class. Stalin's rationalization for a Soviet intelligentsia states that "since no ruling class has ever existed without its own intelligentsia, new phases in the rule of the working class in the Soviet Union required the creation of its very own productive-technical intelligentsia."[60] Theoretically, the intelligentsia, serving the ruling proletariat and recruited from both worker and peasant classes, formed a temporary segment in the country aimed ultimately at building a Communist society in which the division of labor into intellectual and nonintellectual, into skilled and unskilled, was supposed to disappear.

Not only higher education but also a white-collar profession (e.g., a teacher or an engineer with a special secondary education) could define one's belonging to the intelligentsia, rather than to the constitutionally recognized two classes in Soviet society: workers and peasants. Even a person without any corresponding schooling could be an "intelligent." For instance, it was rather common for Jews of the older generation to work as accountants even though many of them never underwent proper professional training.

Three major generational groups formed the intelligentsia stratum: the generation that had already reached intellectual maturity before the Bolshevik seizure of power, or at least before the imposition in the 1930s of totalitarian control over Soviet intellectual life; the middle generation, including those who had spent almost all their adult life in the years of Stalin's dictatorship; and finally the group of young men and women who, while largely educated under Stalin, had begun to make their presence felt on the Soviet intellectual scene only under the more clement conditions of post-Stalinist liberalization.[61] There were also Jewish specialists educated before World War II in Poland, Romania, the Baltic states, or even in Western Europe. In all, the Soviet-educated middle and young groups numerically prevailed, especially as the presence of pre-1917 intelligentsia had declined both naturally due to their age and from taking the brunt of Stalinist repressions.

Within the Soviet Jewish intelligentsia there was a separate elite group that occupied high-ranking positions in cultural, academic, and economic life. Such people—including well-established scholars, writers, journalists, actors, composers, heads of enterprises, and influential officeholders—could arrange for their children and protégés access to education and employment that was normally closed to other Jews. Money also talked in some cases.

Belonging to the intelligentsia was particularly important to Soviet Jews, many of whom found in it a form of self-identification more meaningful and attractive than a clearly defined Jewish identity.[62] A journalist recalled:

> "I grew up in the time of Khrushchev's thaw. . . . Back then we—I and my friends—judged other people by their intellect. A wise man is wise, regardless

> of the respective nationality. Idiots remain idiots. That was the central principle of my existence and of my relationships with others." In this ideal world . . . it was insignificant that his passport identified him as "Jewish," insofar as ethnic differences played no decisive role in social inclusion or exclusion, unlike common intellectual interests, level of education, and personal sympathy.[63]

An artist, also of Jewish background, affirmed that "the 1960s was the time of artists and writers," and for him, "nation, ethnicity, or the Jewish question instilled by the authorities were not his concerns; instead his focus was culture and art."[64] The cult of culture, rooted in pre-1917 and Soviet-time social and ideological processes, was especially strong among Jews, who formed a significant portion of the new Soviet intelligentsia. Those who came out of the shtetls wanted to rapidly acquire all the prerequisites to become successful in the new society. It was common among Jews to admire the best representatives of the Russian intelligentsia, and to want to model themselves on them and be included in their circles.[65] They were committed to educating their children at the best schools available, including specialized schools with an emphasis on foreign languages or physics and mathematics.

For the majority of highly educated and well-integrated Jewish city dwellers, the shtetl was something passé, partly cute, but also embarrassing. Jewish urbanites were doing their utmost to distance themselves from *mestechkovost'* (in Russian) or *kleyn-shtetldikayt* (in Yiddish), meaning a shtetl-like, parochial manner of thinking and behaving. The shtetl, typically a market town, belonged to the world that even before the Holocaust lay in ruins; it had no place in a country of workers and peasants. By the late 1920s the shtetl (*mestechko* in Russian), the quintessential habitat of East European Jews, had almost disappeared from the official territorial structure of the Soviet state, getting a status of a town, a village, or an "urban-type settlement" (*poselok gorodskogo tipa*). True, remnants of traditional Jewish life were still very much present behind the new facade.

The Holocaust left very little of the former shtetl, though tens of thousands of Jews—who either survived the wartime occupation, especially in the areas under Romanian control, or returned from evacuation—continued to live scattered over the former Pale of Jewish Settlement, often engaged in artisanal occupations or as part of the local professional class of doctors, dentists, teachers, and others. The situation began to change in the 1960s when many Jews, especially the youth, moved from the former shtetls to regional capitals or other cities.[66]

In the 1960s the Yiddish writer Shmuel Gordon, a master of travel stories first published in *Sovetish Heymland*, emerged as the pioneer of neo-shtetl literature. He formulated his credo of an enthusiast for contemporary topics, asserting inter alia that contemporary Jews preserved their national distinctiveness despite losing their language—Yiddish. Gordon contended that Yiddish writers of his generation had the obligation to portray contemporary life, because they, in contrast to Soviet writers in other languages, had no younger colleagues to fulfill this important mission.

For his part, Gordon revealed a contemporary setting with plenty of Jewish color in the Podolian part of Ukraine, where hundreds of Jewish families returned to the former shtetls and continued to live, preserving, more or less, the prewar mode of life. In one of his travel stories, Gordon finds himself in Medzibezh (or Medzhibozh) among thirty or so Jewish families, people mostly old and ancient. They live out the remainder of their days near the fresh common graves of World War II and the eighteenth-century graves of Hershele Ostropoler, the Jewish jester, and the Ba'al Shem Tov, the founder of Hasidism. The Ba'al Shem Tov's grave appears in Gordon's narrative as a shrine that attracts Jews from all over the country. The pilgrims leave their *kvitlekh*, personal appeals, at the gravestone. Gordon had no qualms about reading a few of them, and was happy to find out (or to invent) that one and all begged the Ba'al Shem Tov to secure peace on earth, thus revealing their exemplary political consciousness.

Medzibezh was a former shtetl skirted by the railway. Such out-of-the-way places tended to be regarded as villages rather than towns. The situation was, however, different in Derazhne (or Derazhnia), a neighboring former shtetl immortalized in Sholem Aleichem's story "The German." According to Sholem Aleichem, Derazhne once was a "small shtetl in the Podolian Province, a really small shtetl," but by 1902, when the story "The German" was written, it had already become "almost a town, with a railway, with a station." In the 1960s, when Gordon visited Derazhne, it still boasted a railway station, which stimulated its industrial development. While Medzibezh was "a half-shtetl-half-village," Derazhne was "a half-shtetl-half-town." True, the Jewish population of Derazhne was also small—thirty-odd households. Nonetheless, the Derazhne Jews' cultural level proved to be higher than that in Medzibezh: some of them read Gordon's works, and the Moscow writer was overwhelmed when a couple of enthusiasts organized an impromptu literary party on the occasion of his visit. (By 1980, when the Yiddish poet Chaim Beider visited Derazhne, its whole Jewish population could easily sit around the dinner table of one of the holdovers.)[67]

Historically, there were no shtetls outside the former Pale of Jewish Settlement. However, there were places populated predominantly by Jews, such as Krasnaia Sloboda, or Red Town, in the northern Azerbaijan city of Quba. In the 1950s and 1960s, about four thousand Mountain Jews continued to live in Krasnaia Sloboda as a community, fully committed to their traditions. Many of them specialized in transporting and selling agricultural products in Russia. This was a risky business that crossed the red lines of legality, so on numerous occasions dwellers of Krasnaia Sloboda would find themselves behind bars and some of them were killed in gang feuds.[68] In Georgia, Kulashi was a predominantly Jewish settlement, known as "Little Jerusalem." Its residents, Georgian Jews, were also heavily involved in the so-called second or shadow economy.

Entrepreneurship at the Margins of Society

Gordon's shtetl stories were highly praised by his colleagues. The writer revealed a soft spot for hardworking simple souls who spoke the idiomatic language of Sholem Aleichem's characters but had the outlook of committed builders of Communism. The authorities certainly did not categorize them as "social parasites," outcasts of society. In his writings, Lenin several times stressed that the precept "Who does not work shall not eat" should become one of the fundamentals of the Soviet moral order. In 1936 this maxim (originally Paul the Apostle's words in the New Testament) appeared in the Soviet Constitution of that year. By the end of the 1930s, workers who were absent from work without excuse or who quit their jobs without authorization were made criminally liable and could be subjected to imprisonment. These measures were repealed only in 1956.

Very soon, however, from 1957 to 1961, decrees issued in Soviet republics provided a legal instrument designed to send loafers to "specially designated places" for a term of several years. In the country that claimed full employment of its able-bodied population, two major forms of parasitism were cited: people who had jobs only "for the sake of appearances" since they actually lived off nonlabor income; and people who carried out "no useful work."[69] In 1961 the maxim "Who does not work shall not eat" appeared in one of the twelve rules of the "Moral Code of the Builder of Communism." The new Party charter, also enacted in 1961, stipulated that all Party organizations should "see to it that each Communist observes in his own life and cultivates among workers the moral principles set forth" in the "Moral Code."[70] The twelve rules applied to all Soviet citizens rather than to Communists only.

In 1964 the poet Joseph Brodsky, a future Nobel Prize laureate, was arrested in Leningrad and put on trial for "social parasitism."

> JUDGE: What is your occupation?
>
> BRODSKY: I write poetry. I translate. I suppose.
>
> JUDGE: None of this "I suppose." Stand straight! Don't lean against the wall! Look at the court! Answer the court properly! . . . Do you have a steady job?
>
> BRODSKY: I thought that this is a steady job.
>
> JUDGE: Give a clear answer!
>
> BRODSKY: I write poetry. I thought that it would be published. I suppose.
>
> JUDGE: We're not interested in what you "suppose." Answer why you didn't work.
>
> BRODSKY: I did work. I wrote poetry.
>
> JUDGE: That doesn't interest us.

The Brodsky case had no direct Jewish context, apart from the fact that both Brodsky and Iakov Lerner, an enthusiastic denouncer and the prime initiator of the prosecution, were Jewish. Brodsky was sentenced to five years of forced labor, a term he did not serve in full: as a reaction to a campaign in the USSR and abroad, the sentence was commuted and the poet was released in the fall of 1965.[71] The state continued to treat him as a pest, but he would not be legally prosecuted in the coming years until his expulsion from the country in 1972.

Brodsky became a random casualty of the antiparasite legislation designed in particular to target people who "lived off nonlabor income." The number of those who operated in the shadow economy increased in the 1950s, and even more so in the 1960s, when, concurrently, the attitude toward material wealth had changed. Many, albeit a minority, belonged to the growing segment of "sated people" who consumed luxury food, wore expensive foreign-made clothing, and came into the possession of a car, an individual apartment and house (including a dacha, or summer cottage), and jewelry. For a broadening circle of people, it became habitual to spend vacations at a Black Sea or Baltic Sea beach.[72]

The high-earners belonged to various cohorts of society and by far not all of them earned their income from underground economic activities. Some were "part-timers," including, for instance, physicians who dabbled in unofficial private practice, or teachers and university lecturers giving private tutorials. Still, really big money would be earned by entrepreneurs operating in the parallel economy, which filled in the niches of socio-economic relations left unattended by the state. Such activity was risky, but there were people ready to take chances, especially since they were not necessarily threatened by a long-term jail sentence, let alone the death penalty. For example, according to criminal legislation, a currency speculator could receive a maximum of three years' imprisonment. The spirit of risk-taking was rather common in some circles. For instance, it was a valued macho attribute in Georgia among Jews and non-Jews alike.[73] Clearly, the entrepreneurial spirit never died among some other Soviet Jews, particularly, but not exclusively, among those who had relatively recently become Soviet.

A 1953 CIA "Information Report" stated inter alia that in Lithuania "British pounds, American dollars, and gold (Tsarist) rubles can be bought from Jewish black market operators."[74] Who needed Western hard currency in a country with hardly any contacts between Soviet citizens and foreigners? Evidently some people did, particularly in Lithuania, where the seaport of Klaipėda became a channel for smuggling various kinds of goods.[75] No doubt, dollars, pounds, and gold appealed to people dealing in the shadow economy and seeking to store private wealth, knowing that the domestic currency and official savings deposits were undependable due to periodic currency devaluations and to strong suspicion that the police kept an eye on bank accounts. A few years later, foreign currency and gold found demand among Jewish and non-Jewish repatriates to Poland or among those who tried to emigrate directly to Israel. In some Jewish families, gold coins and jewelry survived the ravages of the first half of the twentieth century and were kept as family heirlooms.[76]

In 1961 several decrees introduced harsher penalties, including capital punishment, for such crimes as illegal currency transactions and large-scale theft of state and public property.[77] In 1962 eighty-four Soviet citizens were executed for illegal-currency operations, forty-five of them Jewish. Many more, Jews and non-Jews, received prison terms up to the maximum of fifteen years. Among them were eight Jews tried for currency speculation in the Lithuanian capital of Vilnius.[78] While illicit activities often involved groups linked by ethnic or even family lines based on mutual trust and loyalty (hence "Jewish" or other ethnic cases), non-Jewish actors were never completely excluded from them. In the Vilnius case, for instance, a link was found between the Jews and a Lithuanian Catholic priest. According to the Soviet press, all or some of the eight Jews cherished hope that one day they would emigrate and find themselves in the United States, Canada, or Israel.[79] Two of the eight, the Holocaust survivors Basia and Aron Reznitsky, had in 1946 attempted to cross illegally the border with Poland. They could not apply for legal repatriation because before the prewar remapping of Eastern Europe they had been citizens of Lithuania. The couple was caught by Soviet border guards and served several years in Siberian camps. Both were sentenced to death in 1962, but Basia's sentence was commuted to a fifteen-year term. After serving the full sentence she emigrated to Israel.[80]

Without doubt, the 1961 edicts introducing harsher punishments for economic crimes were not specifically anti-Jewish in their intention, but their application, the press coverage and the rumors in the Soviet Union and, to a larger degree, abroad gave them an ethnic coloring.[81] While the foreign press gave overviews with general statistics, which made the picture of anti-Jewish bias look convincing, the Soviet press did not publish any overview articles on the Jewish aspect of the matter. However, the central and local Soviet newspapers did not miss the opportunity to emphasize the Jewishness of the *valutchiki*, or currency speculators. It helped that the culprits more often than not had ethnically marked names. Thus, at the trial in Chernivtsi, Ukraine, the *valutchiki* had such traditional names as Moyshe-Meyer, Alter, and Hersh that would never be given to children born in modern Jewish circles.[82] This was certainly not lost on more attentive Soviet readers.

The names clearly indicated inter alia that the speculators, particularly older people among them, were outliers in Soviet society and did not belong to the acculturated majority of the Jewish population. Rather, many of them were products of the proverbially parasitic shtetl or came from the territories that became Soviet as late as 1939–40. Or else they were people from non-Ashkenazic groups. The press stressed, for instance, that Mordekhai Kakiashvili, an observant Georgian Jew, declined to sign a protocol of interrogation on a Saturday.[83] Some reports skillfully introduced various little details that left no room for doubt of the culprits' Jewishness—money was hidden in the Sacred Scrolls, or a rabbi was involved, or money was embezzled from synagogue funds.[84]

There were truly exotic cases of Jews who left the Soviet Union in the 1930s together with Kazakh nomads and settled in China's Xinjiang Province. In the 1950s they repatriated to the Soviet Union with hands not empty. (Although in the late 1940s and early 1950s the majority of China-based East European Jews moved to Israel or the United states, some of them preferred to settle in the Soviet Union.) As newspapers reported, several arrested recent repatriates smuggled gold into the country, hiding it in nomad tents, hollow frames of bedsteads, and in children's clothing. Apart from gold, their offenses included buying from hunters with the intent to smuggle to China thousands of saiga antelope horns, used in Chinese medicine.[85]

For all that, the case of the three young people with regular names—Ian Rokotov, Vladislav (Vladik) Faibishenko, and Dmitri Iakovlev—received particular media and public attention. Starting from petty trading, their operations quickly grew into a network of scores of street-level dealers and generated a significant fortune. By the late 1950s they became Moscow's preeminent currency speculators. The scale of their business reflected the increase of international contacts. Beginning in the second half of the 1950s, numerous foreign tourists visited the country, while Soviet people also had more opportunities to travel abroad. In 1957 the World Youth and Student Festival brought to Moscow an unprecedented mass of foreigners. It is no coincidence that Rokotov, Faibishenko, and Iakovlev started their black-market activities in that year. They were arrested in 1960 and sentenced to imprisonment, but then, in brazen violation of the fundamental legal principle of *lex prospicit, non respicit* (the law looks forward, not back), they were retried and executed by applying to their case a July 1961 decree that introduced the death penalty for currency speculation.

Although Rokotov and Faibishenko were Jewish (Iakovlev was Russian), the decision to punish them by death had hardly anything to do with their ethnicity or with politics. They were ordinary speculators. However, the press campaign abroad and Khrushchev's involvement in this affair gave the trial a political aspect.[86] Around that time the same legal principle was violated in another case that did not attract international scrutiny. The trial, which took place in Kyiv, involved a group of Soviet POWs who had entered German service, acting as guards in the Treblinka and Sobibor death camps. One of the witnesses of the process was Aleksandr Pecherskii, a Soviet Jewish officer who organized and led in 1943 a well-known uprising in Sobibor, the subject of several books and films.[87] Although strikingly different, the two cases, in Moscow and Kyiv, illustrate how the Soviet judicial system functioned on direct orders from the Kremlin even after Khrushchev's claim of launching a new era of legality.[88]

Currency speculation was not the only economic crime with highly visible involvement of Jews, who faced long-term imprisonment or execution. The shadow economy received a boost from Khrushchev's drive to "decapitalize" completely the Soviet economy by liquidating produce cooperatives, which in the early 1950s employed over 1.8 million people and manufactured goods of various kinds, including, for instance, around 40 percent of knitted goods and furniture as well as many other commodities in high demand. Ideologically, however, the independent, entrepreneurial spirit of successful cooperatives irked dogmatic Marxist-Leninists, who considered such enterprises an obstacle on the road to Communism, which in their utopian vision was just around the corner. As a result, in the second half of the 1950s, the entire system was liquidated and absorbed by the general state economy, where it lost its flexibility and did not leave enough space for people with entrepreneurial spirit.[89]

One of the top figures of the centralized and unwieldy command economy was Veniamin Dymshits, who in 1959 became head of the department of capital construction at the State Planning Committee. In 1961 he was appointed first deputy chairman and, a year later, chairman of the committee. Simultaneously he acted as deputy chairman of the Soviet government, a position he held until 1985. From the 1960s until the beginning of the 1980s, Dymshits was the highest-ranking Jew in the Soviet system. He was also a member of the Soviet Communist Party Central Committee, a deputy to the Supreme Soviet (parliament), and from time to time took part in formulating policy toward Jews.

Meanwhile, illegal production partly compensated for loss of the cooperatives, which had proved to be more effective and more responsive than enterprises in the Byzantine centralized system, especially when it came to manufacturing consumer goods. Because the "command" structure of the economy focused primarily on heavy industry to support the military, the country was characterized by a perpetual imbalance between the limited supply of consumer goods and services and the increasing demand for them due to higher aspirations and expectations of Soviet citizens.

In 1961 a real scandal shook the Kyrgyz republic, whose capital Frunze became an important hub of light industry after several factories had been evacuated there during the war. A group of shadow-economy entrepreneurs ran successful business operations. The organizers knew how to take advantage of the weaknesses of the economic system and of officials' susceptibility to bribery. Operations that were centered on textile factories with workshops, equipped with machinery obtained through unauthorized channels, produced consumer goods of special demand using illegally supplied raw materials. Products such as carpets, artificial silk, underwear, shirts, sheets, handkerchiefs, jumpers, and pullovers were sold through stores controlled by accomplices in the network. Activities appear to have begun as far back as August 1955, and to have survived thanks to a pyramid of minor and top functionaries, including the head of the republican State Planning Committee, a deputy minister, and the head of the Investigative Department of the Prosecutor's Office, kept happy by bribes drawn from a special fund established for that purpose. It is possible that the scale of the illegal network became one of the reasons for Khrushchev's decision to introduce the death penalty for aggravated cases of theft of state property and corruption.[90]

The British Embassy in Moscow reported on 31 July 1962:

> A high proportion of those accused, judging by their names, were of Jewish origin. Of thirty-three defendants listed by *Sovetskaya Kirgiziya* [*Soviet Kirgiziia*, the main newspaper in the republic] on March 25, 1962, fifteen have

> recognizably Jewish names. *Izvestiya*, however, seems deliberately to have concealed from its readers the fact that there was such a large Jewish element among the defendants. Another indication that the authorities found the Jewish aspect of the case a delicate matter for publicity was that the issue of *Sovetskaya Kirgiziya* (that of March 25, 1962) which revealed the Jewish element most clearly was not received by at least three regular subscribers in Moscow (including the British and U.S. Embassies), was missing from the paper's file in the Lenin Library, and was only made available by an obliging assistant from a back-room repository.[91]

Although the press did not emphasize the ethnicity of the convicts, the KGB and the court internally labeled it the "Goldman" (the name of one of the culprits) or "Jewish" case. While eight of those sentenced to capital punishment were Jews, among the executed were more Kyrgyz and Russians. Still, in Western press coverage the Frunze case was described as anti-Semitic.[92]

A pyramid of corruption, which involved predominantly Jewish shadow businessmen and non-Jewish functionaries of various ranks, operated in Lviv, Ukraine. Petr Ovsianko, the Party boss of the city, committed suicide in January 1962 when he faced accusations of providing a cover to illegitimate operations. While the Jewish culprits received severe punishments including the death sentence, the functionaries could get off with being fired.[93]

The argument that the Soviet regime and its legal system were heavily biased against Jews received a strong boost from Evgeniia Evelson, a Soviet lawyer who acted for the defense in a large number of economic trials. In her book, written after emigrating from the Soviet Union, she argued that "the sharp edge of repressions in this case was targeted not so much against the crime as such, but against Jews who committed it." According to her analysis, based on four hundred cases, Jews "with a similar amount of guilt . . . were judged much harsher than Russians," and the sentences "made sharp distinctions between the accused Russians and Jews." Moreover, "high officials who happened to be Russian were freed from responsibility even in cases where they were the direct instigators of criminal activity." In all, a disproportionately large number of Jews were sentenced to death or long prison terms.[94]

One cannot discount, however, that Jews were overrepresented among people with a self-driven entrepreneurial mindset, who—in the face of the widespread antipathy in Soviet culture toward commerce and moneymaking—could not overcome the temptation to use the dysfunctionality of the Soviet economy for making profits.[95] The prominence of Jewish businessmen, including the so-called oligarchs, in the late- and post-Soviet years may serve as an additional retrospective indication of the fact that this mindset was far from being unusual among Soviet Jews. It seems, however, that many people in the Soviet apparatus, including Khrushchev, saw the Jews—probably with the exception of their fully Sovietized, "useful" segment—as an ethnic group posing a threat, and this attitude led to harsher punishments. Significantly, less than ten years had passed since the time when Jews were openly demonized in Soviet propaganda as murderous doctors, spies, bourgeois nationalists, and cosmopolites.

Khrushchev's own opinion on this matter was indirectly disclosed in his reply to Bertrand Russell's appeal concerning the high percentage of Jewish defendants in the "economic trials." In his public answer to the preeminent British philosopher, Khrushchev stated: "The morality of our society is the morality of people of labor. He who does not work, neither shall he eat." The implication probably was that the number of people who sought to live off the labor of others was particularly high among the Jews. According to Khrushchev, the large number of "economic defendants" among Soviet Jews resulted from the persisting negative social traits of that particular minority: "Among which nation there will be more or fewer of a particular type of criminal at any one time—this is not a national question but a social one."[96]

Leonard Shapiro, a British scholar of Soviet politics, suggested the following explanation for the Jewish bias in punishing people involved in economic crimes: "to use the Jews for a 'warning shot'? He [Khrushchev] may reckon, and probably rightly, that to shoot Jews for speculation is less likely to cause widespread resentment than to shoot Russians, or Ukrainians. But at the same time it drives home the useful lesson that the threat to use the firing squad to eradicate those vices which socialism is supposed to have cured long ago is no empty one.[97]

In the mid-1960s a Jewish figure—the Kharkiv-based scholar Evsei Liberman—appeared as a reformer of the tanking Soviet economy. In

February 1965 Liberman's international significance was symbolized by his appearance on the cover of *Time* magazine, captioned "The Communist Flirtation with Profits." The reforms he had advocated—notably, a profit incentive for enterprise managers—were even taken as a sign of the convergence of Communism and capitalism. True, Liberman rushed to explain that "profits cannot become either capital or hoarded treasure in the Soviet Union. They are not, therefore, a social goal or a motive force in production as a whole. The motive force in production under socialism is the satisfaction of the steadily growing material and cultural needs of the population." Finally, however, the reforms came to naught because they met resistance from dogmatic advocates of the existing highly centralized system.[98] In practical terms for the Soviet economy, little or nothing resulted also from Leonid Kantorovich's pioneering mathematical-economic theories, which brought him a Nobel Prize in 1975, or from modern methods suggested by Mikhail Botvinnik, better known as one of the best chess players of the twentieth century.[99]

Following the brief upsurge of "Jewish economic crimes," such cases almost disappeared from public attention. Was it a sign that the majority of risk-taking Jewish shadow dealers and entrepreneurs had been imprisoned or executed? In reality the main reason was the end of the "shooting spree" in the final years of Khrushchev's leadership, though courts continued to sentence people to death. In 1965, for instance, the death sentence was given to Semen Bryskin, accused of large-scale embezzlement and illegal operations with gold coins in Belorusssia.[100] Yet the death sentences were announced sketchily, suggesting perhaps that executions were publicized not so much for deterrence as for giving the malefactors their "just deserts." Even court cases of large-scale economic crime appeared in press reports far less frequently than during the 1961–64 campaign. This did not mean that the problem of the shadow economy had been solved, especially as the state did not provide alternative means to fulfill the functions of the economic crime under attack. As a result, the scale of economic crimes was growing. Although the police continued to prosecute people caught in illegal activities, events associated with the shadow economy, linked with widespread corruption of the state apparatus, had permeated all areas of the economy and turned into a prosaic, largely unsensational part of Soviet life. In addition, the really high-profile cases would soon be in the Caucusus and Uzbekistan, with little if any participation of Jews.[101]

In all, only a small portion of the Jewish population was involved in the shadow economy. The majority received their income as salaries and (probably) bonuses. It was not much, but—coupled with relatively cheap housing, free-of-charge education and medical care, subsidized holidays, and other allowances—usually did not foster a feeling of being destitute, especially on the present-day scale of well-being. Many people moved into new apartments, which were small but with all basic amenities. New gadgets entered their lives, such as TV sets, refrigerators, and gas cookers. And those who had endured the war and the Gulag were simply happy to be alive.

6

A STIFLED TRADITION

In and around the Synagogue

Accusations of economic crimes were also common in cases involving people active in religious communities, including Jewish ones. Rabbis and community leaders were routinely scourged by accusations of embezzling religious funds and using them to lead a "parasitic existence."[1] Charges of misappropriation and speculation figured as an essential part of the campaign against synagogues and often served as an excuse to shut them, as happened for instance in Lviv, Ukraine, where the only synagogue was closed in 1962.[2] Financially, religious communities, strictly limited in their functions by law to conducting religious worship and burial services, had perennially faced existential problems. The only legally permissible mode of fundraising entailed collections from the worshippers and donations from visitors, while other kinds of revenue fell into a risky category, somewhere between permissibility and prohibition.[3] In some cases, indeed, people responsible for running the synagogue had light fingers or were engaged in illegal operations. In Pyatigorsk, a spa resort in Russia's Caucasian Thermal Water region, Rabbi Benzion Gavrilov was sentenced to death (ultimately, following protests abroad, commuted to fifteen years' imprisonment) for his involvement in shady deals with gold.[4]

The Council for the Affairs of Religious Cults (CARC), which was set up in 1944 as a government agency for overseeing religious confessions, used another excuse to close synagogues, namely quarrels and disputes within the congregations. Internecine conflicts of this kind were hardly specific to Soviet settings, but the difference was that in a Soviet city or town each side in a dispute would make attempts to draw in government agencies on which the entire existence of the congregation depended. Deep divisions in the Kyiv and Moscow congregations did not lead to closure of synagogues in those cities, mostly because of the impression this would have made on world public opinion. However, in places less exposed to international scrutiny the disputes often served as a pretext for implementing closures, which usually meant the disappearance of the only enduring local Jewish institution.[5] When the Jewish journalist Ben-Zion Goldberg, who had previously sympathized with the Soviet regime, came to Moscow in 1959, he "found the Soviet Union the only country in the world with no other Jewish address listed but that of the synagogue."[6]

Synagogue attendance saw a short-lived increase after Stalin's death. In Belorussia hundreds of people attended services at the Minsk and Kalinkovichi synagogues, then the only ones officially recognized by the republic's authorities. Some of the Jews were not regular synagogue-goers and in fact came not to pray but to swap the latest news associated with Stalin's death. A woman, who had never been seen at the Minsk synagogue before, shouted: "We are saved!"[7] In the fall of 1953 and 1954, during the Jewish High Holidays, between 700 and 1,200 people gathered at the synagogue in the Siberian city of Omsk, one of the four officially registered synagogues in Siberia. The other three were in Novosibirsk, Irkutsk, and Birobidzhan. The Jewish population of Omsk was about eight thousand and, during the same holidays in 1955, synagogue attendance declined to 300–550. Fewer people would take part in Saturday services too: 100–150 in 1953–54 and 40–50 in 1955.[8] Other factors, including the atmosphere created by repatriation to Poland, could cause a surge in synagogue attendance, for instance, in Vilnius (see p. 99).[9]

In the late 1950s a new tradition began in several cities of young people gathering around synagogues on Simchat Torah. This joyful holiday, which celebrates the conclusion of the annual cycle of public Torah readings, struck many as eminently appropriate for a sort of Jewish "happening." A delegation of British Communists who visited the Soviet Union in October 1956 noted that two thousand Jews came to the Leningrad Synagogue to celebrate Simchat Torah.[10] The number of youths who gathered around synagogues, notably in Moscow and Leningrad, grew from year to year. In 1960 the foreign media estimated that more young people had gathered around Moscow's main synagogue than in the previous year. In 1962 that number was estimated at six thousand. In Leningrad about ten thousand gathered, twenty-five of whom were briefly arrested for obstructing traffic.[11] True, many, if not the majority, of young people would come not because of religious feelings; rather, they wanted to somehow celebrate their Jewishness and to do so at a "Jewish place."

There are no reliable statistics regarding the number of religiously observant Jews in the 1950s and 1960s. The 1937 census, which collected such information, showed that, compared to other religious groups in the country, a remarkably low proportion of Jews defined themselves as of the Jewish faith: about 10 percent of the recorded Jewish population, predominantly the elderly. While in the population as a whole there was approximately the same proportion of religious people aged 16–19 as there were aged 50–59, among the Jews there were 21.5 believers aged 50–59 for each believer aged 16–19.[12] The fact that of all faiths in the Soviet Union Judaism showed the most precipitous decline in recorded adherents reflected the high level of urbanization, secular education, Party membership, involvement in the state apparatus, and, generally, modernization of the Jews. It is highly improbable that the share of observant Jews increased two decades later, following the almost complete devastation of Jewish life in western areas of the country and the passing, including annihilation during the Holocaust, of the older, more traditional generation. Characteristically, in 1962, in the Vinnytsia Province of Ukraine, a third of the residents with Christian background baptized their children and over a quarter of the newlyweds had a church ceremony. However, the local authorities had not registered any analogous rituals among the Jews.[13]

The process of secularization began before the revolution and it was not confined to the lands that became part of the USSR. It is indicative, for instance, that the majority of mass-circulation Yiddish newspapers, edited and read by East European Jewish immigrants in the United States, published editions on Saturdays and Jewish holidays. In 1956, however, Hillel Rogoff, editor-in-chief of the New York *Forverts*, wrote that by that time in the United States the position of religion had become much stronger than before. He listed three contributing factors: (1) many more children attended Jewish day schools; (2) introduction of a five-day workweek made keeping Shabbat much easier; and (3) kosher food could be bought at numerous stores.[14] (For all that, until July 1973 *Forverts* continued to publish on Saturday, the Jewish sabbath.)

In the Soviet Union, where by the 1950s there were no Jewish schools of any kind and kosher food was a rare commodity, a five-day workweek was introduced in March 1967, though the reform did not apply to educational institutions. Most important, still, was the fact that open religiosity was incompatible with life in Soviet society's mainstream. A seven-year-old child would become a member of the children's Communist organization, and then, at age fourteen, of the Young Communist League. An atheist worldview was an important part of the ideological makeup of both organizations as well as of the entire education system. Theoretically, membership in children's and youth organizations was voluntary, but avoiding it meant jeopardizing later educational prospects and career opportunities. Furthermore, card-carrying Communists, who were expected to be militant atheists, had the best career prospects, and Jews, as we have seen, displayed the highest proportion of Party members of any ethnic or religious group. Meanwhile, some people practiced various modified or even grotesque forms of Jewish traditions; for instance, replacing shiva—the weeklong mourning for a first-degree relative—with putting a little earth from the grave into one's socks.[15]

Importantly, while the decline of religiosity was accentuated among Jews of Ashkenazic origin, other Jewish groups remained much less affected by secularization and antireligious measures. In 1956 several American rabbis reported after visiting the Soviet Union that Jews of Georgia "were maintaining their ancient religious customs, hardly touched by the Communist regime." While circumcisions became rare in the Slavic republics, the American visitors witnessed a circumcision rite in a synagogue in Kutaisi, the second-largest city in the Georgian republic, attended by five hundred persons. In Kulashi they found that the majority of local Jewish families celebrated the traditional Feast of Tabernacles, or Sukkot.[16]

Judging by the CARC's 1957 report to the Party Central Committee, at that time 135 synagogues functioned with official permission, only twenty-six of which were in the Russian republic. Moscow had three synagogues and fifty-six small prayer houses. In January 1957 Soviet authorities permitted the opening of a rabbinical seminary, or yeshiva, called Kol Yakov.

Rabbi Solomon Shlifer, chief rabbi of Moscow and organizer of the seminary, died in April 1957. He was succeeded by Rabbi Yehuda Leyb Levin, previously of Dnipropetrovsk.[17] Jewish religious communities in the USSR had no central body or organization to direct, coordinate, or even discuss common affairs. Each Jewish community, organized around a particular synagogue, was a separate unit. As Rabbi Levin said, when asked in 1962: "There is no organization and no center. I am only the rabbi of Moscow and that only of the community near the synagogue."[18]

The seminary was housed in the building of the Great Synagogue. In fact, classes were held in a shed connected to the synagogue, an arrangement uncomfortable for both the synagogue attendees and the yeshiva students. Judging by a letter dated 17 October 1957 and sent to the heads of all regional KGB departments of Ukraine, the secret police were looking for suitable people to work as informants among the students and to groom as reliable religious leaders.[19] We don't know whether they succeeded.

From the start, the yeshiva faced significant financial troubles and survived initially by selling copies of the *Siddur Hashalom* (Prayer Book of Peace), so-called because it included a special prayer for peace composed by Rabbi Shlifer. In 1953 Rabbi Shlifer applied to the CARC for permission to publish the prayer book. Although one reviewer reported that he "did not detect any attacks on the Soviet Union," another reader found "the clear spirit of nationalism" in the text. Despite these problems, three years later, in 1956, the CARC, following correspondence with the Party's Central Committee, authorized the publication of ten thousand copies of the prayer book for distributing in Moscow and other cities. In the same year, not coincidentally, the authorities permitted the Russian Orthodox Church to publish fifty thousand copies of the New Testament.[20]

Of the 2,300 copies of *Siddur Hashalom* sent to 74 communities, 315 went to Kutaisi, 291 to Leningrad, 215 to Tbilisi, 202 to Kyiv, 153 to Riga, 101 each to Odessa and Sverdlovsk, and 60 copies went to Tashkent. Some number of copies was reserved for gifts to foreign visitors. Still, many believers could get the prayer book and were ready to pay up to one thousand rubles (well over an average monthly salary) for a copy. Ideological overseers blocked plans to issue a revised edition in 1961. They also kept reducing the number of copies of the Jewish religious calendar first published after many years in 1955.[21]

Subsequent financing for the yeshiva came from three main sources: (1) Georgian Jews; (2) donations from foreign tourists, who in part transferred funds raised by Jewish groups abroad; and (3) money collected by the Moscow congregation. The majority of students were Georgian Jews. By 1961 only ten students were attending the yeshiva, nine of them from Georgia. In 1962 the authorities brought about the yeshiva's collapse, without closing it officially, by denying Moscow residence permits to the Georgian students. In late 1962 only five students remained at the yeshiva, among them two who had already finished their studies and were serving as kosher butchers in Moscow. In the five years of the yeshiva's existence only two of its students were ever ordained, and they did not serve as rabbis.[22]

Rabbi Levin cut a sympathetic figure to some foreigners. Elie Wiesel wrote a play, *Zalmen*, inspired by his encounter with the Moscow rabbi, "a beautiful man but tired, weak . . . tall, with sad, sad eyes."[23] However, Levin and other rabbis of his age generated little appeal for young Jewish urbanites. Some of them, albeit a very small percentage, preferred to convert to Christianity, a phenomenon particularly of the 1960s. Scores of Jewish intellectuals, most notably Muscovites, took this step, driven mainly by the desire to depart from Soviet ideology rather than to reject Judaism.[24] Immersion or, even more so, professionalization in Russian literature and art might facilitate the conversion. One can speculate that Reform or Conservative Judaism could have appealed to some Jewish urbanites as an alternative to conversion; however, these streams of Judaism did not have a presence in the country.

As a rule, the converts still considered themselves ethnically Jewish, especially as the fact of becoming Christian did not alter their nationality status as recorded in their passports. From the point of view of the state, Jewishness was an ethnic category, detached from Judaism just as Russianness was detached from Orthodox Christianity. Alexander Men, born to Jewish parents, became a charismatic Russian Orthodox priest with a considerable following of Jewish converts. Among them was Melik (Mikhail) Agursky, whose father, Samuel (Sam) Agursky, played a leading role among Jewish Communists in the first two decades after the 1917 revolution. Later, following his emigration to Israel, the younger Agursky returned to the Jewish creed and worked as a scholar in the field of Sovietology at the Hebrew University.[25]

Rabbi Levin was trained in the Misnagdic (counter-Hasidic) tradition, which prevailed in the officially registered Ashkenazic religious communities in the Soviet Union. Shmuel Gordon's mentioning of pilgrims leaving *kvitlekh* at the gravestone of the Ba'al Shem Tov, the founder of Hasidism, did not mean that the CARC permitted such pilgrimages. The CARC most probably did not have a coherent strategy for dealing with Hasidim. The Lubavitch Hasidim preferred to operate underground.[26] Their links with their Russian-born, Brooklyn-based spiritual leader, Rabbi (or Rebbe) Menachem Mendel Schneerson, could not be welcomed by the authorities. In the early 1960s permission was denied for pilgrimages to the grave of Rebbe Israel Dov Ber, buried in 1829 in the village of Veledniki, now in Ukraine's Zhitomir Province.[27] At the same time, the authorities tolerated the activity of Khayim-Zanvl Abramovitsh, known as the Ribnitser Rebbe, in Moldavia, a mystic and healer celebrated by Jews and non-Jews from the region.[28]

In 1965 Elie Wiesel observed people "associated with various Hasidic houses, not just the Lubavitch. And they all pray in the same synagogue, indeed in the same room, each group according to its own liturgical formulas. Standing in the prayer hall you hear the Karlin version with one ear and the Bratslaver with the other. Yet their hearts are united in true brotherhood."

Wiesel understood that there were no more than a few thousand Hasidim scattered throughout the Soviet Union, mostly in large cities.[29]

Scientific Atheism

Khrushchev's time in office saw an effort to decimate religious life. In 1963 a new compulsory course on the "fundamentals of scientific atheism" was introduced at universities and other institutions of higher education. This field, propagandistic in nature though with an academic slant, received a push in 1954, when two decrees formulated a new approach to dealing with the "survivals" of religious mentality. Religion had no place in Communist society of the near future as envisioned by Khrushchev, and atheism, specifically Marxist scientific atheism, was supposed to build a solid dam against it.[30] Introduction of university courses and, generally, intensification of antireligious propaganda can be seen as evidence that five decades of Communist indoctrination in atheism through education and direct action had not succeeded. The Jewish faith was no less affected than other religious groups by the large-scale campaign, which led to the closure of thousands of places of worship across the Soviet Union. The number of registered synagogues fell from 135 in 1958 to 92 in 1964. In Georgia, Jewish religious communities were affected less than their Ashkenazic coreligionists. This was in part due to the special situation prevailing in the Georgian republic, where Jews were historically well treated by the local population, and in part to the stubborn resistance of the Georgian Jews.[31] In addition to synagogue closures, new obstacles were created to importing religious objects from abroad. There were also renewed attacks on Jewish religious practice in the press.[32]

In 1957 the philosopher and propagandist Mark Mitin, born into a Jewish family in the city of Zhitomir, Ukraine, set the tone for the fresh attack on Judaism. A member of the Central Committee of the Communist Party and chairman of the All-Union Society for the Dissemination of Political and Scientific Knowledge (which replaced the League of Militant Atheists in 1947), Mitin wrote that the Jewish religion, as a weapon in the hands of imperialist reaction, "distracts believing Jews from the struggle for a better life here on earth, from the struggle for the building of Communism, and lulls them with sweet hopes of a life of paradise in the 'world to come.' In Israel where Judaism is the state religion, the bourgeoisie uses religion to arouse enmity between toilers of different nationalities."[33]

Moyshe (Moisei) Belenky emerged as the leading figure in the Jewish subfield of scientific atheism. While still a student at the Moscow Teachers Training Institute, which had a Yiddish Department until 1938 and was the alma mater of many university-educated Yiddish literati, he began to teach Marxist-Leninist philosophy to students of the school of the Moscow State Yiddish Theater and then, from 1932 to 1949, he worked as the school's director. Later he combined this position with that of editor-in-chief of the publishing house Der Emes (Truth). Arrested in 1949, he was incarcerated until 1954. Upon his release and legal rehabilitation, Belenky pursued two parallel careers, one in Jewish literary scholarship and one in philosophy (he taught at the prestigious Shchukin Theater School in Moscow), with an emphasis on scientific atheism.

Belenky was well prepared to work in scientific atheism. As early as 1941 he published a Yiddish book entitled *Acosta, Spinoza, and Maimonides.* According to Belenky, Uriel Acosta, "one of the first critics of the Bible, gravitated to materialism," whereas Baruch Spinoza "furthered materialist examination of the world." Maimonides, or Rambam, on the other hand, fought for "the freedom of reason, but in some philosophical issues he slipped to the position of idealism." Belenky emphasized that he based his research on the Marxist methodology because there was no other way to understand fully and correctly the philosophers' worldviews and their roles in the history of human thought.[34]

The Marxist approach also implied a heavily ideological treatment of the subject. In 1959 Belenky stated that "Judaism, like any other religion, represents a conservative, reactionary worldview." Moreover, according to him, "Israeli clerics show solidarity with fascist cannibals, racists."[35] He continued to study the three philosophers, but Spinoza and Acosta were more welcome in the Soviet ideological climate. His 1964 book *Spinoza* came out in the respected and widely read series *Life of Remarkable People.* In 1956 the All-Union Society for the Dissemination of Political and Scientific Knowledge published Belenky's supporting material for lectures on *The Origin and Class Essence of Judaism.* His pamphlet *What Is the Talmud* came out in 1960, and the same title appeared again in 1963 and 1970 on the covers of much weightier tomes.

Belenky was not by any means the only author writing on Judaism. Critiques of Judaism played a significant role in the work of other scientific atheists, including Giler Livshits, a distinguished Minsk-based historian of antiquity and religion. Another important figure in the field was Mikhail Shakhnovich, whose first book *The Social Essence of the Talmud* appeared in 1929. One of the founders of the Museum of History of Religion in Leningrad (Saint Petersburg), Shakhnovich worked as its leading scholar. In his 1960 book entitled *The Reactionary Essence of Judaism*, Shakhnovich argued that Judaism created conditions for spreading ideologies of Zionism and American imperialism, as well as for gender inequality.[36] His monograph *The Decline of Judaism* followed in 1965. Judaism remained, however, a sideline in Shakhnovich's voluminous output. In general, in an imagined competition among scientific atheists dealing with various aspects of Jewish religion, the laurels for the most prolific author would certainly go to Belenky.

In 1960 Belenky's pamphlet *The Talmud in the Light of Science* was released in Moscow. Two years later his edited volume *The Critique of Judaism* came out under the imprimatur of the History Institute at the Academy of Sciences. In his 1966 monograph *Judaism*, he praised the Karaites for becoming a voice of "the latent protest of Jewish masses against the inhuman exploitation justified and defended by the Talmud."[37] He fired his criticism at Rabbi Yehudah Leyb Levin of the Moscow Choral Synagogue for preaching that Jews were provided with *nitzotz Elohim*, the divine spark in the soul that kept them attached to the Jewish faith.[38] Conflating anticlericalism with anti-Zionism, Belenky went on to misinform his readers about the legalities of life in Israel. Thus, according to him, an uncircumcised boy could not become a citizen of the country, and a woman had limited legal rights in many spheres of Israeli life.[39] (Nonetheless, in 1990 he would settle in Rehovot, Israel.)

In 1967 Moscow State University's Department of History and Theory of Atheism accepted Belenky's dissertation on "Critical Analysis of the Dogma, Cult and Ideology of Judaism" and thus effectively certified him as a top specialist. It is highly questionable, though, if his books fulfilled the claimed mission of "firmly shattering the myth of supernatural origin of Jewish religion, holidays, and rites" and "showing the reactionary nature of Judaism."[40] According to Alexander Grushevoi, a historian of antiquity and the Middle East, Belenky's writings on the Talmud have little to do with scholarship. Still, he commends Belenky's work as, at that time, the only widely accessible source of information on this topic.[41]

The lists of books and pamphlets, defined in Soviet bibliographic classification as "antireligious literature" and published between 1959 and 1964, contains 1,847 publications. Of these, 1,176 were directed at religion in general, as a rule also containing criticism of Judaism. Of the remaining 671 titles directed against a particular religion, 8.0 percent targeted the Jewish religion, making the proportion of anti-Judaism titles seven times larger than the proportion of Jews in the population (1.1 percent by the 1959 census). About two and a half million copies of books and pamphlets were published to combat Judaism, not counting the anti-Zionist and anti-Israeli publications that usually also included content about religion.[42] We don't know if this imbalance should be attributed to top-down decision-making or if the authors writing about the harmfulness of Judaism were simply more prolific than their counterparts working in other areas of antireligious propaganda.

We do know, however, that the KGB and the Party propaganda apparatus were in favor of anti-Judaism publications. In September 1959 Ukraine's KGB informed the Party's Central Committee that a group of experts had analyzed Jewish religious books, most notably the Torah, some Talmud tractates, and ten prayer books of various provenance, including the 1956 *Siddur Hashalom*. The anonymous experts, described in the KGB report as "appropriate associates [*sotrudniki*]," had come to the conclusion that all these texts were "imbued with the spirit of militant nationalism and 'spiritual racism', which often develops into biological and political racism." Moreover, such literature "fulfilled anti-Soviet functions," propagating ideas of a worldwide Jewish nation that united Soviet Jews with the Israeli and American communities. Ironically, the *Siddur Hashalom* appeared in the report as "one of the most reactionary prayer books published in the last 100 years." As a result, the KGB suggested increasing the propaganda onslaught on Jewish religion.[43]

In Leningrad the local KGB kept a watchful eye on the synagogue and reported, in August 1964, various breaches of rules, including a secretly practiced ritual of circumcision and having religious classes for children. It was stressed that the synagogue attracted young people, including Komsomol members, many of whom assembled outside it at the time of Jewish holidays. They would "dance, sing Jewish songs, and drink alcohol." Israeli and other foreign tourists had been "spreading nationalist and Zionist literature."[44]

In 1963 a book released in Kyiv under the imprint of the Ukrainian Academy of Sciences, *Judaism without Embellishment* by Trofim Kichko, aroused outrage in the West. In the Soviet Union the book could not attract much public attention, being published in Ukrainian with a rather modest print run of twelve thousand copies. Reflecting the atmosphere of the Soviet drive against "social parasites," Kichko wrote, in particular: "Judaism considers a person to be moral if, not working for the good of society, he devotes all of his free time to prayer and to the performance of religious rites. For Judaism, not work but prayer is the highest manifestation of morality. Furthermore, all of Judaic ideology is impregnated with narrow practicality, with greed, with the love of money and with the spirit of egoism."[45]

Even the Communist editors of *Morgn-Frayhayt* were outraged. On 22 March 1964, the newspaper published an angry editorial, stating inter alia that the illustrations in the book were "reminiscent of the well-known caricatures of Jews in anti-Semitic publications. . . . The blunders in the antireligious drive as well as—or even more so—the serious errors in the restoration of Jewish cultural institutions destroyed during the Stalin cult (more correctly, the non-restoration of these institutions) are matters that disturb many honest people, friends of the Soviet Union."

On 12 April, speaking in New York to a gathering of several thousand people, Paul Novick, editor of *Morgn-Frayhayt*, demanded the author be tried and punished.[46] By that time Novick had certainly read the article published in *Pravda* on 4 April, which criticized Kichko's book:

> A number of the book's erroneous statements and illustrations may offend the feelings of believers and might be interpreted in a spirit of anti-Semitism. . . . The mistaken tenets contained in the book contradict the Party's Leninist policy on questions of religion and nationality and only give our ideological opponents, who are trying to create a so-called "Jewish question" at any cost, food for anti-Soviet insinuations. It is precisely for this reason that the mistaken parts of T. Kichko's book cannot but arouse objections on the part of the Soviet public.[47]

In November 1964 Novick went to the Soviet Union as a guest of *Literaturnaia gazeta*. He spent two months in the country, visiting cities such as Kyiv, Odessa, and Vilnius and meeting many people, including Veniamin Dymshits, Justas Paleckis (chairman of the Presidium of the Supreme Soviet of the Lithuanian Soviet Socialist Republic), and Rabbi Levin. Solomon Rabinovich organized Novick's meeting with a representative of the Office of the Chief Public Prosecutor to discuss such issues as the publication of Kichko's book. Novick was generally happy with the conversation, though by the end of it he stated: "It's necessary to fight against the existing remnants of anti-Semitism. I reckon, Lenin would have taken stricter measures."[48]

Jewish Foodways

At the end of the day, to fight the Jewish religion seemed a useless activity, even a counterproductive one, because some Jews would regard the antireligious literature as an ersatz source of interesting information on history and culture. Synagogues attracted predominantly or even exclusively elderly, often retired people and had little if any appeal to younger people. Forced social engineering had brought radical changes in the worldview of the generations raised under the Communist regime. They perceived the synagogue as a relic of the past, which became valueless or even embarrassing for contemporary life. At best it could serve as a place of gathering on a holiday, the meaning of which might not be clear to them.

The Soviet Yiddish author Tevye Gen, interested in portraying contemporary life, wrote a realistic dialogue between Ita, an elderly Jewish woman, and Volodya, her young Jewish neighbor:

> "Don't you know that today is Passover? Wasn't it even mentioned by your parents?"
>
> Volodia was confused. The old woman kept asking very strange questions, and he came off as a complete ignoramus. How could he know anything about Passover? His father was a scholar, his mother was a doctor, and there was no trace of religiosity in his family.
>
> "I heard about such a holiday. Russians call it Easter, they eat Easter cakes," Volodya tried to demonstrate his knowledge. "And Jews, I think, eat . . . I don't remember how it is called. . . ."
>
> "Matzos," Ita prompted. . . . "Do you think we celebrate only the Passover and Rosh Hashanah?" Ita said, wanting to show her worldliness in case the young man had a one-sided impression about her family. "The First of May [International Workers Day] and the October [Revolution] Anniversary are not less important for me."[49]

The name Volodya, or Vladimir, often associated with Vladimir Lenin, was also a sign of Sovietization. (Granted, the Zionist leader Ze'ev Jabotinsky received at his birth in 1880 the name Vladimir, and Jewish characters called Volodya appear in pre-1917 Yiddish writings, e.g., in David Bergelson's 1909 novella *At the Depot.*) Jewish boys born in the 1950s and

1960s were typically given "neutral" names such as Boris, Mark, Il'ia, Lev, Semen, and Arkady. Mark and Arkady even became, with few possible exceptions, definite signifiers of Jewishness. In the 1960s, in Vitebsk, Belorussia, the name Eduard was chosen only by Jewish parents.[50] Jewish parents mostly shunned certain names, notably Ivan, Peter, and Vasilii, deemed too Slavic. The custom of naming children after deceased relatives was widely preserved, though with modification of names. Thus, Arkady could be associated with Abraham or Aron, while the female names Raisa, Polina, and Anna could be chosen as modernized equivalents for Rachel, Perl, and Hannah.[51]

Ita, an "active" Jewish person, and Volodya, a "passive" one (to use Zvi Gitelman's classification, see p. 113), were Jewish in their own eyes and in the eyes of their neighbors, coworkers, and fellow students. They were commonly recognizable because of their physical features, behavioral patterns, aspirations, and lifestyle, not to mention their passports and other official documents. As a rule, they loved Jewish humor and music and were proud to see so many Jewish names among Soviet celebrities, most notably among scholars, musicians, film directors, actors, and chess players. At the same time, psychological complexes associated with the "fifth point" were also widespread. Although the Holocaust was rarely discussed in the Soviet Union, Jews knew at least something about it. In addition, the authorities, neighbors, and colleagues perceived them as a part of world Jewry. In fact, the "international link" was a perceived Jewish feature, usually more significant for non-Jews, whereas for Jews the "family link" was usually the most important one. They felt that their lifestyle was different in various ways, including some remaining differences in foodways.

Only a small fraction of Soviet Ashkenazic Jews continued to practice kosher foodways. From the Soviet bureaucratic point of view, the legal practice of religion was understood very narrowly as involving ceremonial rites, whereas kosher meat, it was claimed, did not belong to the ritual necessities without which it was impossible to observe any religious obligation. Rather, in the bureaucratic understanding, it was a food preferred to be consumed by a certain portion of the Jewish population.[52] The state, in other words, whose constitution promised to guarantee "freedom of conscience," could claim that it did not carry legal responsibility for facilitating production or import of such food, especially as demand for it was small.

Communists as well as other "politically conscientious" segments of the Jewish population were not supposed to burden themselves with following the "obscurantist" dietary rules, although the regime tried (albeit not always consistently) to show its readiness to tolerate some vestiges of religious traditions, especially if they survived exclusively among the elderly. For purely practical reasons, a nondenominational cuisine simplified catering in the army, children's and youth camps, factories, and other public canteens. Thus, army soldiers' religious or cultural differences did not affect what kind of food they would receive.[53]

This did not mean that Jews would be forced to forget the recipes of their traditional dishes; the dishes simply stopped being kosher. Moreover, the Soviet food mainstream had absorbed some elements of Jewish cuisine, and tzimmes (a sweet stew typically made from carrots and dried fruits such as prunes or raisins) had even enriched the Russian language with the word *tsimes*, meaning "a very good or most important thing."[54] Nonetheless, these never became as important to the pan-Soviet national palate as, for instance, the Caucasian-style *shashlik* (shish kebab) or the Central Asian *plov* (conglomeration of rice, vegetables, and meat bits swimming in fat and oil). In any case, *khala*, or challah, Jewish-style braided bread, could be bought in many Soviet food stores as late as the 1950s or even later.[55] A 1955 textbook for students of food merchandising describes the variety of porkless sausages known as *evreiskaia kolbasa* (Jewish sausage).[56]

Esther Markish, widow of the Soviet Yiddish writer Perets Markish, recalled that in the late 1940s and early 1950s, during the "campaign against the pernicious influence of the West," the "Jewish sausage" was renamed "dry sausage."[57] The poet Lev Druskin felt sorry that *khala* would be sold under a different name, that of *pletenka* or "braid."[58] According to Alice Nakhimovsky, the American scholar of Russian and Jewish literature and culture, "Jewish foods that made it into the public sphere tended to be renamed. Challah was sold in stores in Leningrad and Moscow under the public name *pletenka*, though in some bakeries you could ask for it by its Yiddish name."[59]

No information is available to pinpoint the year when such commodities as challah and "Jewish sausage" disappeared from Soviet store shelves or lost their "ethnic identity." It also remains unclear whether this was a result of a directive formulated from above. Most probably, "Jewish" food products simply became a sore in the vigilant eyes of local functionaries. A parallel can be drawn, for instance, with the tacit and widely violated ban on the public performance of Jewish music, notably at restaurants.[60] The story "And Now Enters the Giant," written by the Soviet Russian writer Konstantin Vorob'ev, illustrates the fact that the word "challah" did not have to vanish completely from usage. The protagonist of the story, a Soviet Russian man of the 1960s or early 1970s, goes to a local store to buy a challah. He does so in 1971, when the story first appeared in the Moscow journal *Nash sovremennik* (no. 9), and continues to do so in numerous later reprints of this work.

Challah may have disappeared, at least temporarily, from bakeries during food shortages in 1962 and 1963, when white bread generally became a rare commodity as a result of a bad harvest and erratic large-scale agricultural experiments.[61] During the same period, which saw an intensive antireligious campaign, organized production of matzo fell under a ban.[62] Earlier, in 1956, a delegation of the Rabbinical Council of America reported that in Moscow and Leningrad a state-run bakery was allowed to bake matzo under rabbinical supervision, while in some other cities people would purchase flour and bring it to the synagogue, where a small bakery had been set up.[63]

In all, the baking of matzo was never categorically prohibited in the Soviet Union. Restrictions depended on a combination of four factors: (1) the attitude toward the Jewish religion in particular at any given time; (2) the availability of flour in particular years; (3) the attitude of the local authorities; and (4) the ability of the congregations to find appropriate channels for the supply of matzo, however partial, to the broader Jewish population. The proportion of religiously observant Jews who did not eat bread during the Passover week was very small, particularly outside the Caucasus and Central Asia. Nevertheless, the demand came not only from them. Quite a few Jews held a festive meal on the first Seder night to commemorate the exodus from Egypt and they strove to have matzo on their table at least for this one night.[64]

Kosher butchers were on hand at some meat markets, including the one in Birobidzhan.[65] The situation was different in some other areas of the Soviet Union, especially among non-Ashkenazic Jews. Thus, the 1956 delegation of the Rabbinical Council of America reported that Georgia was the only place in the Soviet Union where they saw kosher butcher shops.[66] In the 1950s, in Frunze (Bishkek), a state-run *gastronom* (food store) sold kosher meat.[67] In Tajikistan and Uzbekistan, the powers-that-be had chosen not to interfere with Jewish ritual slaughtering.[68]

As Anna Shternshis learned in her oral-history research, a number of her respondents, Jews from the former Soviet Union, mentioned a separate pan for frying pork.[69] This was certainly a very radical addition to—or, most commonly, replacement of—the traditional mandatory separation of *fley-shik* (meat) and *milkhik* (diary) products. There were also other "tricks" to make eating pork "less harmful" —for instance, to eat it on a windowsill without using any cutlery and plates, or to take a piece of the front part rather than from the back, especially as Jews usually did not consume the hindquarters of any animal, even a kosher one.[70] Non-Ashkenazic Soviet Jews, however, seldom ate pork. Importantly, the majority of them lived among Muslims in Central Asia and the Caucasus, whose revulsion to pork remained deeply ingrained during the entire Soviet period.[71]

Even in its nonkosher form, Jewish cuisine tended to differ from that of non-Jews. Apart from cooking Jewish fare, Jews had incorporated numerous non-Jewish dishes but in "Judaized" form. For instance, "Jewish borscht" did not contain pork *salo*, or cured slabs of fatback, an important item in the Ukrainian cuisine. Significantly, meat would be soaked in water before cooking, which was a residue of the traditional process of koshering meat by soaking the blood out of it. On Jewish and general Soviet holidays or birthdays, guests could be fed with such homemade special-occasion dishes as gefilte fish.

Although by the 1950s and 1960s "Jewish food was part of a hidden world,"[72] it certainly was not particularly hidden in such places as the former Ukrainian shtetl of Shargorod, where Jews "formed the most visible and influential group in the town."[73] Weddings, with tables loaded with Jewish dishes, would be organized as public events rather than secret gatherings. The institution of Jewish caterers, known in Yiddish as *sarverns* or *sarverkes*, survived in some areas, notably in Moldova. For all that, the Jewish food tradition had transformed and endured in the Soviet Union by and large in private kitchens rather than in public spaces.

Ancient Studies

While the Soviet book market was inundated with antireligious titles, publications on ethnic history were of particular concern to Soviet ideologists and appeared rarely in bookstores. Peeter Tulviste, an Estonian scholar, wrote that to a significant degree ethnic identity "can be conceived as consisting of various texts which interact with each other. . . . From this point of view, history texts of various kinds interact with each other and many other texts in the formation as well as the functioning of individual identity."[74] A Soviet Jew usually had few, if any, texts on Jewish history for her or his identity-generating interactions. Significantly, vigilant functionaries in the Communist Party's Central Committee routinely blocked publication of scholarly works devoted to the Holocaust, and the term itself did not appear in the vocabulary of Soviet books and periodicals.

Readers interested in Jewish history would look for indirect ways of getting access to information, finding it usually in occasional journalistic coverage of historical topics or in belles-lettres. At the same time, Soviet scholars' studies of the ancient past and history of religion sometimes touched on aspects of Jewish history. Such esoteric topics were obviously considered harmless and incapable of boosting Jewish historical memory. For instance, readers had access to the 1962 book *History of the Khazars* by the archaeologist Mikhail Artamonov, director of the State Hermitage Museum in Leningrad. A decade before its publication, Artamonov had a difficult stretch in his life. In December 1951 he was attacked in *Pravda* for claiming that Khazaria served as a model for Ancient Russia.[75] Rumors ascribed the article, bylined "P. Ivanov," to various people, including Stalin. It was indeed a serious matter in the climate of the time, when agitprop expected validation of Russia's role as a pioneer rather than an imitator. The experience of the early 1950s left an imprint on Artamonov's 1962 book, which claimed inter alia that adoption of the Jewish religion by the ruling class of Khazaria was "a fatal step" because it severed the government from the people, replaced pastoral nomadism and agriculture with mercantile middlemen, and led to the "parasitic enrichment of the ruling elite."[76]

The idea that the Khazar state became parasitic after adopting Judaism found further development in the work of the leading Soviet archaeologist

Svetlana Pletneva.[77] Mikhail Ikhilov, who defended his dissertation on the history and culture of Mountain (or Caucasus) Jews at the Moscow Institute of Ethnography in 1949, wrote about Khazars' involvement in the ethnogenesis of Mountain Jews and did not deal with the issue of "parasitism" ostensibly engendered by Judaism. In his treatment of the subject, some of the Khazars were assimilated by the core group of Jews who had come to the Caucasus from Persia.[78]

The year 1951 saw the revival of the Palestinian Society, whose roots stemmed from the Imperial Orthodox Palestinian Society, established in 1882. Although the revitalized society functioned under the auspices of the Academy of Sciences, its mission was predominantly in the domain of politics. The Palestinian Society's journal, *Palestinskii sbornik* (Palestine Miscellany), became an important outlet for academic publications. No mentioning of the state (or prestate period) of Israel would appear in its pages, but the taboo did not apply to medieval Jewish history and to ancient Israel. Professor Isaac Vinnikov, one of the semitologists who contributed to the journal, headed the Department of Assyrian and Hebrew Studies at Leningrad University's Faculty of Oriental Studies from 1945 to 1949 and returned to the university after a forced hiatus during the late Stalinist years. At the 25th International Congress of Orientalists held in Moscow in August 1960, Vinnikov chaired the session addressed by Yigael Yadin, the former chief of staff of the Israeli army turned well-known archaeologist, one of the twelve members of the Israeli delegation. Vinnikov emphasized the importance of applying materialist methods to biblical studies, which meant looking into the social and economic context of biblical texts through the prism of Marxist theory.[79]

Palestinskii sbornik also published articles by Iulii (Iudel) Solodukho, the well-established scholar of Arabic, Aramaic, and Talmudic studies, whose research focused on the Babylonian Talmud but was officially categorized as focused on ancient Iraq and Iran. The purges miraculously bypassed Solodukho despite the fact that in his youth, before becoming a Soviet Orientalist, he was involved in rather "questionable" activities: he studied at the famed Volozhin Yeshiva, was a delegate to the Fifth Zionist Congress in Switzerland in 1901, and participated in the Hebrew-language movement. According to the American scholar of Judaism Jacob Neusner, Solodukho "made the effort both to preserve the traditions of Talmud learning acquired in his youth and to master and make use of the Marxist hermeneutic which came to dominance in his mature years."[80]

Less fortunate was Iosif Amusin, a specialist in the history of the ancient Near East, who, as a member of a Zionist youth organization, experienced both exile (1926–30) and incarceration (1938–39). Still, he graduated from Leningrad University and served in the army during World War II. After 1945 he taught ancient history at the Leningrad Pedagogical Institute and Leningrad University until he was fired during the campaign against "cosmopolitanism." After a period of unemployment, he found a job at the Pedagogical Institute in the Volga city of Ulyanovsk. Upon returning to Leningrad in 1954, Amusin worked as a research fellow at the Institute of Archaeology and the Institute of Oriental Studies of the Soviet Academy of Sciences and showed great interest in the Dead Sea, or Qumran, Scrolls.[81]

The first Soviet semitologist's article on the Dead Sea Scrolls, written by Amusin's colleague, Klavdiia Starkova, appeared in 1958 in the journal *Vestnik drevnei istorii* (Bulletin of Ancient History). Boris Smolar, editor-in-chief emeritus of the Jewish Telegraphic Agency (in the 1920s he represented the JTA in Moscow and continued to keep a close eye on the situation in the Soviet Union), wrote about Starkova in 1969 after visiting Leningrad: "a Russian woman who has a record in the scholarly world as being dedicated to the study of the history of the Jewish people."[82]

However, semitologists were not the only scholars interested in the Dead Sea Scrolls. Giler Livshits's *The Qumran Scrolls and Their Historical Significance*, the first Russian-language pamphlet-size description of the findings made in the Qumran gorge of the Dead Sea, was published in 1959 under the imprint of the Belorussian State University, where the author worked starting in 1958. In 1967 he put out a much more substantial volume, *The Origin of Christianity in the Light of the Dead Sea Scrolls*. Livshits's 1957 book *Class Struggle in Judea and Uprisings against Rome*, which essentially historicized biblical events and characters, had been a cause of concern to his dogmatic colleagues, who went so far as to insist on destroying the entire print run. Ultimately, the book reached readers thanks to enthusiastic reviews by influential Moscow historians. Still, a chapter on the Jewish diaspora of that time saw publication only a quarter century after Livshits's death.[83]

While scholars turned to studying the Dead Sea Scrolls exclusively, or at least primarily, for purely academic interest, the Soviet ideological watchdogs welcomed such studies for a completely different reason, highlighted, for instance, in a review of the 1960 book *Scrolls of the Dead Sea* by history popularizer Anatoli Varshavsky. Scientific atheists could use the dating (long before Jesus), provenance, and content of the scrolls for arguing that the official history of Christianity and, by extension, of other religions represented "an enormous falsification."[84] As a result, Varshavsky's book came out in fifty thousand copies under the imprint of Molodaia gvardiia (Young [Communist] Guard), one of the biggest Moscow publishing houses. Also in 1960, the Moscow Publishing House of Political Literature released *Finds in the Judean Desert* coauthored by Sergei Kovalev, director of the Museum of Religion and Atheism, and Mikhail Kublanov, a historian of religion. This book had a print run of fifty-five thousand. Its revised edition, released in 1964, had an even bigger one of sixty-eight thousand.

Kovalev and Kublanov, as well as some other Soviet historians, impugned one of the previously unquestionable postulates of Soviet historiography of early Christianity, namely that the birthplace of the new religion was located outside Palestine. The postulate originated from Friedrich Engels's statement: "The legend that Christianity arose ready and complete out of Judaism and, starting from Palestine, conquered the world with its dogma already defined in the main and its morals . . . can continue to vegetate only in the theological faculties and with people who wish 'to keep religion alive for the people' even at the expense of science."[85] Alexander Kazhdan, a Soviet Byzantinologist who had been publishing studies on the Dead Sea Scrolls since the 1950s, argued that the whole massive tradition of Marxist scholars' assertion that Christianity was born in Asia Minor, not in Palestine, stemmed from misinterpretations of Engels's original writings. Kazhdan, who consequently emigrated from the Soviet Union and worked as an academic in the United States, also came to the cautiously phrased conclusion that Jesus was a historical person.[86]

Although Starkova, who pioneered the study of Qumran in the Soviet Union, continued to publish on this theme, Amusin's works would dominate the Soviet book market. His book *The Dead Sea Scrolls* came out in Moscow in two editions, in 1960 and 1961. In 1962 it appeared in a Slovak translation; translations into Polish and Romanian followed in 1963.[87] In

1965 Amusin was awarded a doctorate for this research. At the award ceremony he concluded his speech with a quote in Hebrew from *Pirkei Avot*, a tractate that contains sayings and ethical teachings of the rabbinic sages: "You are not expected to finish the job, but you cannot shirk the obligation to undertake it."[88] In the same year the Moscow publishing house Nauka (Science) put out sixty thousand copies of Amusin's new book *Finds at the Dead Sea*, edited by Vasily Struve, the founder of the Soviet school of historical research on the ancient Orient. In his introduction, one of his last written works, Struve referred to Engels's recommendation to study the historical conditions that led to the rise of Christianity. In other words, he emphasized that Amusin's work was useful from the point of view of Marxist scholarship.

Amusin's books continued to appear in the coming years, even after 1967, when a vigilant eye might deem the topic of Qumran ideologically harmful, too proximate, at least geographically, to Zionism. His paper, prepared for the 27th International Congress of Orientalists held in Ann Arbor in August 1967, was circulated and reviewed though he did not attend the event. The Soviets, as well as Czechoslovaks, Bulgarians, and East Germans had decided to withdraw at the last moment in light of the current international situation—the war in Vietnam and the tensions in the Middle East—which made the time inopportune for cultural and scholarly exchange.[89] Significantly, from the official point of view, Amusin, Starkova, and other semitologists were not categorized as scholars working directly in the domain of *Jewish* studies; Jewish scholarship and culture continued to be associated predominantly with Yiddish.

7

THE CULTURAL LANDSCAPE

The Return of the Yiddish Word and Song

Categorized as the language of Jewish toilers, Yiddish prospered in the Soviet Union in the first two decades after the revolution. In Belorussia, in the Jewish Autonomous Region, and in the five Jewish National Districts in the European part of the country it had the status of an official language. It was the main language of instruction in hundreds of educational institutions at all levels, from kindergartens to university departments. Yiddish speakers had access to theaters, radio programs, books, and periodicals. This rich and variegated infrastructure was curtailed in the late 1930s and then destroyed in the final years of Stalin's life. Officially, however, Yiddish remained the only "legitimate" language of Ashkenazic Jewish culture, and some forms of Yiddish cultural expression began to be slowly resuscitated in the 1950s.

We have no information on when and how the Soviet apparatus allowed Yiddish actors to perform in groups, duets, or solo. It might appear that the general atmosphere of de-Stalinization rather than an explicit decision by the Kremlin made Yiddish concerts a reality of the second half of the 1950s. Yet, in the strictly subordinated Soviet system such concerts would not have happened without the permission, or some kind of blessing, coming from the Kremlin, whose denizens felt pressure from foreign organizations, including Communist parties, to take steps in that direction, especially as Yiddish enjoyed state support in Poland and Romania, Soviet satellites, and had thousands of devotees in pro-Soviet circles in many other countries.[1] As a result, according to the British embassy,

> by 1955 there were a few, a very few, Jewish musical-literary evenings. These were enormously popular, and in the present year their numbers have grown. They have included the singer Lyubimov, who is said to have been arrested in 1948–9 and released only very recently. The folk-singer Anna Gruzik gave four concerts in Moscow, and she was advertised as giving three in Leningrad in May 1956. Four concerts were given in Moscow in the same month by Klara Waga, of Riga. Four more are advertised at the moment, to be given by Mikhail Epelbaum. At nearly all of these, there are readings from Yiddish classics, notably from Scholom [*sic*] Aleichem. An evening wholly devoted to him, in connection with the fortieth anniversary of his death [in 1956], was held on 12th May and was sympathetically reported in the newspapers, but the other events do not seem to be either advertised or reviewed in the press, though they appear on posters in the Moscow streets.
>
> A member of the Embassy attended one of these musical-literary evenings, in the company of a secretary of the Israeli Embassy. The hall was packed, as apparently it always is on such occasions. There were a great many young people. The audience listened to the readings and the songs with rapt attention, and gave the impression that they derived the keenest pleasure from the mere fact of attending a Jewish function. These concerts are the only permitted purely Jewish activity of a secular kind, and so satisfy a deep craving among the audience. From the first announcement to the last, not a word of anything but Yiddish was spoken from the stage. Only one "Soviet" song was sung, and politely applauded. All the rest of the programme was traditional.[2]

On 9 September 1956, a special commission appointed by the Ministry of Culture of the Russian republic had submitted for approval a detailed project of (re)establishing a Yiddish state theater in Moscow and naming it after Sholem Aleichem. Numerous cultural events were dedicated to the classic Yiddish writer's jubilee, including a gala under the auspices of the Writers Union. The literary part of the event was followed by performances of Yiddish singers as well as several scenes presented by a group of actors from the defunct State Yiddish Theater.

Four members of the commission were active in pre-1948 Yiddish cultural life: the omnipresent Moyshe Belenky; the experienced theater directors Moyshe Goldblat and Efraim Loyter; and the composer Leyb Pulver, who for many years served as the musical director of the Moscow State

Yiddish Theater. Their project envisaged a theater situated in the heart of Moscow, with a company of thirty actors and a school for ten young actors.

It was seen as a certainty that the inaugural performance of the new troupe would take place in May 1957.[3] However, in the end this did not happen. Three months after the scheduled opening date, during the Moscow Youth and Student Festival, Pulver told Israeli delegates that many actors were still hoping that the efforts to set up a theater would soon bear fruit, especially as the authorities had explained that there was no ideological opposition to such an undertaking. Rather, the opening had been held up for lack of a suitable building.[4] Finally, however, the project never got off the ground, which indicated that the reasons were more complicated than simply a lack of suitable premises.

For the time being, concerts represented the sole public sphere made available by the government for Yiddish cultural activities after a period of virtually complete devastation. It seems that at best only one group of Yiddish actors performed in the early 1950s: the Chernivtsi Philharmonic Society continued to employ Sidi Tal, a popular Yiddish singer and actress, and two other actors, even after the closure of the local Yiddish theater in February 1950, which chronologically was the last Yiddish theater to close during the assault on Yiddish culture.[5] No doubt, this was not just a quirk of the Philharmonic Society to keep a Yiddish ensemble under its patronage. "Miraculous" decisions of this kind could be made only in Kyiv or even in Moscow. Tal wrote later:

> I remained one of the few who continued to perform in Yiddish. How did it happen? I don't think that it was because I was so talented and unique. I simply lived in a rather unusual city. Always—under Austria-Hungary [until 1918], Romania [until 1940], and Soviet rule—Chernivtsi was unique as regards the "Jewish question." Of course, in Chernivtsi, like in the entire country, synagogues would be closed down, turned into clubs and storehouses. The Yiddish theater was closed down, too. Nonetheless, somehow miraculously the unique Jewish spirit continued to live, Yiddish continued to be spoken, and Jews felt themselves somewhat freer. This was the reason, perhaps, why after the war many Jews began moving to Chernivtsi from other areas of the Soviet Union and the local Jewish population increased rapidly, nearing the prewar figure.[6]

For all that, according to other information, there was a period of time when she also was not allowed to perform in Yiddish at all and had no choice but to struggle with preparing a program in Russian, the language that Tal knew only poorly.[7] She became a Soviet citizen as late as 1940, when the Soviet Union annexed Chernivtsi and other areas previously belonging to Romania.

On 16 August 1955, Tal gave a concert at the Pushkin Theater in Moscow. This was the beginning of a new phase in her—and, to a degree, generally Jewish—artistic life.[8] Earlier, in March 1954, Yiddish songs were performed in a Moscow theater hall by the popular non-Jewish singer Irma Jaunzem, whose repertoire included folk songs in many languages.[9] Since 1954 and even more so since 1955 authorities had allowed the renewal of Yiddish entertainment programs. The concerts provided some earnings also to writers whose works, usually poems, sometimes specially written, would be sung or recited at such concerts. Soon a score of Yiddish professional groups were touring under the auspices of Rosestrada, the central organization in the Russian Federation for variety, concert, and recitation enterprises. The largest of these was Anna Guzik's troupe of twelve. During the years when Yiddish was banned from the Soviet stage, Guzik continued to give concerts, albeit in Russian and predominantly in provincial places. As early as December 1953, her concerts took place in Leningrad and probably contained Yiddish songs.[10]

Yiddish concert programs were put on by such artists as Shaul Lyubimov, Marina Gordon, Mikhail Epelbaum (Applebaum), and Isaac Rakitin. Epelbaum, the "Jewish Chaliapin"[11] as his admirers called him, enjoyed an unprecedented popularity among Soviet Jews. In 1937 he received the title of the Meritorious Artist of the Russian Federation, but in 1949 the state treated him differently, sending him to labor camps and confiscating his personal property. He was accused of "using ethnic prejudices for the incitement of national discord" and of "anti-Soviet agitation" during his concert tours.[12] Released from the Gulag in 1954 (Lyubimov was freed in the same year), poor in health, Epelbaum was one of the first Yiddish singers to resume touring the country. He died in 1957.[13]

In 1954 Rakhmil (later known as Emil) Gorovets prepared a program called "Freylekhs" (Joy)—this was the title of one of the last plays in the repertoire of the Moscow State Yiddish Theater. Gorovets, a graduate of the theater's school, had had a leading role in the play, so his concert program was a nostalgic "joy." In 1955 he began to work with the jazz band directed by Eddie Rosner, whose orchestra became a launching pad for Gorovets's successful career as a Soviet pop singer renowned for several widely successful hits. His concerts usually included a couple of Yiddish songs, but his last full Yiddish concert in the Soviet Union took place in Moscow in 1963.[14]

In the first seven months of 1956, Yiddish performers gave 121 concerts that attracted sixty-five thousand spectators. For instance, on 30 January 1956, Marina Gordon, a soloist of the State Radio Committee (together with the Birobidzhan-affiliated actress Leah Kolina) gave a concert of Yiddish songs to a sellout crowd at the Moscow Mossovet Theater. On 2 April 1956, several Yiddish folk songs, performed by Lyubimov, were broadcast on Moscow radio. From 1957 onward, the popular singer Zinovii (Zalman) Shulman renewed his Yiddish concert tours, interrupted by his arrest in 1949. Given the previous Jewish cultural vacuum, the concert groups did not have to struggle for an audience: in 1957 the Soviet Ministry of Culture reported about three thousand Yiddish concerts with three million tickets sold. Although the profile of the audience was predominantly elderly, many relatively young people, some of them army officers, were among those who came to a Moscow concert by Sidi Tal in 1958.[15] Moscow, however, was not the main stronghold of Yiddish. Harry Schwartz, a *New York Times* journalist who visited Minsk in 1955, wrote: "Yiddish is still a living language among Jewish adults here, and unlike Moscow it can be heard frequently on the streets."[16]

Numerous records of Yiddish songs became available in Soviet stores. Thus, the 1966 catalog of Melodiia, the major Soviet record company, contains thirty-four Yiddish records. The year 1956, for instance, saw the release of at least four records by Anna Guzik and three by Sidi Tal.[17]

Yiddish cultural life such as amateur theater groups sponsored by trade-union organizations emerged not exclusively in places that came under Soviet control in 1939 or 1940. In 1958 the Warsaw *Folks-Shtime* reported about an amateur Yiddish theater collective formed in Leningrad. It debuted on 1 April in the club of the papermaking factory Svetoch.[18] Faivish Arones, formerly an actor and director at various Yiddish theaters, most notably in Minsk, Kharkiv, and Birobidzhan (where he was arrested in

October 1949), was the central figure in the Leningrad theater group, which included several people with an experience of working in Yiddish troupes. Arones also dabbled in literary pursuits, the best-known of which was his translation into Yiddish of Samuil Marshak's satirical antiracist and—even more—anti-American poem *Mister Twister*, a fixture in the canon of Soviet children's literature.

In the summer of 1955 Arones came to Leningrad after seven years in the Gulag. In 1957 and 1958 he took charge of the group, which called itself the Leningrad Yiddish Music and Drama Ensemble. Raphael Skliarski, a former music teacher at the Moscow Yiddish Theater School, became the ensemble's musical director. They made unsuccessful attempts to gain official status as a "people's theater." Introduced in 1959 for successful amateur troupes, this status as a semiprofessional collective opened access to financial and other support from the state. However, the Leningrad Department of Culture criticized the ensemble for "not touching on contemporary themes" and characterized its performance as "quite raw and unpolished." At the same time, the department did not "fundamentally oppose the possibility of establishing an interesting Jewish national ensemble."

Boris Geft, a Meritorious Artist of the Russian republic who was a member of the commission that discussed the issue of the Jewish ensemble, made the problem clear: "One must say that with Jewish art we face an absolutely confusing conundrum. It is known that Jews want a Jewish theater. It is known also that even bad actors attract an audience. No doubt this [Leningrad Yiddish] troupe will attract an audience and will be profitable. But we encounter a perplexing phenomenon. Whereas the culture of any ethnicity living in the Soviet Union does not raise any question, there is some unexplainable resistance toward Jewish musical culture."

All endeavors at "legalizing" the troupe led nowhere and were ultimately blocked by the Culture Ministry. Local authorities permitted a concert performance, prepared by Arones and his fellow artists, on the premises of one of the theaters. The two permitted performances were "closed," that is, denied permission to print playbills. Finally, Arones and his wife Bella (Bertha), a singer, moved to Riga, where they gave Jewish concerts under the umbrella of the Latvian Philharmonic Society and then, in 1972, emigrated to Israel.[19]

The Leningrad amateur troupe continued its activity after Arones's departure. Skliarski remained its leader, and several new people joined the collective. Among them were David Stiskin, the cantor of the Leningrad Choral Synagogue who earned his bread as an engineer, and Naum Agranov, a singer in the synagogue choir. The participation of Agranov, a hairdresser, turned the troupe's fortune. Thanks to him, the amateur actors found an official umbrella and a source for modest financial support at the culture department of the trade union of workers of local industry and utilities. Most importantly, the ensemble gained the status of an amateur troupe of the hairdressers' branch of the trade union. A milestone in the history of the ensemble came on 11 April 1958, the day of the debut concert of its new program, which was prepared with active participation of Zalman Kagan (also known as Zinovy Baev), an experienced Yiddish man of letters who previously worked at the Yiddish theater in Minsk.

There was a plan to organize Yiddish classes at the state-run foreign-language courses, with Kagan and one more person, Asher Blank, as teachers. However, this plan had the misfortune of attracting the interest of an Israeli journalist who was making a documentary about Soviet Jews. Her involvement scared the potential Yiddish teachers and, of course, those who were responsible for the foreign-language courses. Blank nonetheless taught Yiddis; for lack of a textbook, he had to construct an alphabet using letters cut from copies of the *Folks-Shtime*.

The short history of the ensemble ended in 1960. The timing was not coincidental: the relatively liberal period that followed the 20th Party Congress had come to an end and the culture department of the trade union was told to stop the "Jewish bazaar."[20] In 1974 Fedor Miasnikov, then a KGB officer with the rank of captain (he would steadily rise in the ranks to become a general, deputy chairman of the KGB, and in the early 1990s an official at the Russian embassy in Israel), shared his experience of recruiting agents among Jewish activists:

> In the 1950s, the state security organs began receiving signals that a group of individuals of Jewish nationality were making attempts to establish in Leningrad a Jewish people's theater. The group was organized by engineer Pinsker [most probably not his real name]. In the process of investigating Pinsker, it was confirmed that he had no hostile intentions. Rather, he simply knew well

> and loved Jewish culture and wanted other people to have access to it. In a conversation with a [KGB] operative Pinsker stated that he disapproved of nationalism and was ready to fight it. On that ground, Pinsker had been recruited [as an informant] and for twenty years actively helped the state security organs to fight with Jewish nationalists and foreign Zionists. . . . A person with a literary bent, Pinsker wrote for many foreign Jewish newspapers and journals, widely promoting abroad the real situation of Jews in the Soviet Union.[21]

In 1962 the Moscow Jewish Dramatic Ensemble was established, whose first director was Veniamin Shvartser, the only Soviet Yiddish actor who once played the role of Lenin. The troupe had no premises of its own and performed in Moscow only rarely. The *New York Times* described its first performance in the capital in February 1963:

> At the first of four Moscow performances yesterday, 800 persons cheered a truncated stage version of "Tevye, the Milkman," based on stories of Sholem Aleichem, the classic Yiddish writer.
>
> The five-character playlet, in three scenes lasting an hour and a half, has been brought to the Soviet capital by a traveling troupe after a two-month tryout in the Ukraine and Central Asia. . . .
>
> As if to express appreciation for the gradual relaxation, a woman member of the troupe stepped in front of the curtain before yesterday's performance in the Young Spectators Theater and launched into an impassioned speech about the Soviet Union, its size, its diverse peoples and their successes as "builders and creators of communism."
>
> A seemingly dutiful round of applause rose on the playlet, in which Mr. Shvartser, in the title role, was the most professional participant. The audience laughed appreciatively at the slightest humor. There was often buzzing conversation after applause, as those more fluent in Yiddish explained a point to neighbors.
>
> In the second half of the evening, members of the troupe doubled as reciters of Yiddish verse, monologists and singers. . . .
>
> In a monologue from the play "Milk and Honey," by Emmanuil Kazakevich, an actress impersonated a Jewish milkmaid who told of having been elected Deputy to the Supreme Soviet (Parliament) from the Jewish autonomous region of Birobidzhan.[22]

The repertoire of the Leningrad, Moscow, and all other Yiddish troupes remained stuck in the past. Their performances were nostalgic trips both for the actors and their audiences. In fact, for many or even the majority of them Yiddish itself was a language of their past; in their daily life they spoke Russian. Plays by Soviet Yiddish authors set in the 1920s and 1930s became irrelevant in the 1950s and 1960s. As a result, Yiddish theater directors preferred time warps to the shtetl.

On the Outskirts of the USSR

Vilnius witnessed many Yiddish concerts. In the beginning of 1956, Anna Guzik, Isaac Rakitin, Klara Vaga, Mikhail Epelbaum, and Sidi Tal performed for the local audience. In March and April 1956, Kaunas and Vilnius saw the first performances of Nehama Lifshitz (Lifshitzaite). A young singer (she was twenty-nine at the time), Lifshitz grew up in a Yiddish-speaking family, though her parents sent her—before 1940—to a Hebrew school. In May, Mark (Meir) Broido, an experienced actor and director, formed a troupe with Lifshitz, who previously appeared under the Russian name of Nadezhda, and two other actors. His attempts to establish a Yiddish theater troupe for the three Baltic republics were unsuccessful. In 1958 Lifshitz won an all-Soviet competition of variety artists. In 1959 the troupe changed, for one year only, its affiliation to the Leningrad Philharmonic Society, which broadened the geographic diversity of their tours.[23]

In Vilnius and in Lithuania in general, the authorities displayed relative tolerance of Yiddish cultural activities. To an extent this had to do with the attitude of top officials. Characteristically, Justas Paleckis, chairman of the Presidium of the Supreme Soviet of Lithuania until 1967, was an ethnic Lithuanian but a fluent Yiddish speaker.[24] Personal sympathies, however, did not stop him and other officials from closing all Jewish cultural and educational institutions in the republic when such orders came from Moscow. More importantly, though, in Lithuania two national minorities, Jews and Poles, demanded their cultural rights. It would therefore have been strange to ban Jewish groups while permitting Polish ones, and discrimination against the Poles would have provoked protests from neighboring Communist Poland. This made the situation in Lithuania a peculiar one.[25]

In Vilnius a Yiddish section was opened at one of the town's libraries in the summer of 1956. Yakov Yossade (Jokūbas Josadė), who in the late 1940s briefly headed the Vilnius branch of the Moscow Yiddish publishing house Der Emes and later worked as a Lithuanian man of letters, held seminars for enthusiasts of Yiddish literature in the library. The local Yiddish chorus, along with dramatic and dancing groups, occupied particularly important positions in Vilnius Jewish life. The three amateur collectives performed for the first time in December 1956. Although the authorities allowed them to exist, from time to time the activists of Yiddish culture encountered problems. One of the core activists, Berl Cesark, a veteran of World War II and long-standing member of the Communist movement, complained to Party leaders in Vilnius and Moscow. In one of his letters he described the following incident:

> In October 1958, with the approval of the department of culture of the Republic Council of Trade Unions of the Lithuanian SSR, a children's choir participated in a festive program for the forty-first anniversary of the Great October Revolution. The children's choir performed songs in Russian, Lithuanian, and Yiddish.
>
> Several days after the festive concert, the secretary of the Vilnius town council said to me that singing in Yiddish and the study of the Yiddish language lead to isolation, that the Jews should assimilate. . . . I was immediately ordered to disband the children's group, it being stressed that this had been agreed upon with the Central Committee of the Communist Party of Lithuania.[26]

Nonetheless, eight years later, some two hundred people were involved in the Vilnius amateur collective led by the Lithuanian Republic's Honored Worker of Arts Leonid Lurie, who used to work as Mikhoels's assistant. Such Jewish Communists as Cesark and Yossade, veterans of the Sixteenth Lithuanian Division of the Red Army during World War II, formed an influential pressure group, able to break the bureaucratic resistance. The collective, affiliated with the House of Culture of the Lithuanian Republic's Central Council of Trade Unions, had received the status of a "people's theater." The amateur and professional Vilnius actors had their public: according to the returns of the 1959 census, almost 70 percent of Lithuania's Jews (17,025 out of 24,672) declared Yiddish as their first language. This was the highest percentage of Yiddish speakers in any Soviet republic.[27] Paul Novick wrote in his 1964 travelogue after visiting Lithuania: "Very few cities in the Soviet Union have what Vilna [Vilnius] does in respect to Yiddish culture. In Kovno [Kaunas] there is a Yiddish drama group and a chorus, on a smaller scale, the entire Jewish population being only 5,000."[28] The Vilnius and Kaunas amateur actors were allowed to perform in the Estonian capital, Tallinn, where local activists also formed a Yiddish drama group.[29]

The Vilnius experience became an inspiration for enthusiasts of Yiddish culture in other parts of the country. Genia Lev and Boris Landau worked before the war as actors at the Kharkiv Yiddish Theater, which after its evacuation merged with the Odessa Yiddish Theater, and functioned in Central Asia until 1947. The couple moved to Vilnius but in 1956 returned to Tashkent, capital of Soviet Uzbekistan, and formed there a Jewish theater ensemble. In the 1970s they once again moved to Vilnius and performed there with the local Yiddish troupe.[30]

As in Vilnius, Riga enthusiasts of Yiddish culture periodically met resistance from local Party functionaries, who promoted the idea of assimilating Jews. Still, in 1957 a Yiddish chorus was affiliated to a local trade-union club, and a Yiddish section was opened at one of the libraries. There was also a drama group that consisted of twenty amateurs led by former Yiddish actor Joseph Garfunkel. The group decided to choose two plays, or playlets, written by Sholem Aleichem, *Mentshn* (People) and *A dokter* (A Doctor). We don't know what determined the choice of the repertoire: Was it a desire to have an idiomatically rich text, which contained much traditional Jewish humor and a gallery of Jewish types from the past? Or was Sholem Aleichem considered acceptable by censors? In any case, the authorities gave permission for both plays, which could be performed in one evening. Sarah Fegin (who later founded a music school in Holon, Israel) composed the music for both plays. At every performance several seats were provided with earphones so that the play could be heard simultaneously in Latvian and Russian. In the spring of 1962 the drama group gave eight performances of both plays. The audience consisted almost entirely of Jews who were very enthusiastic.

Although the authorities had capped the number of performances at eight, the troupe was allowed to choose a new play. The choice fell on a play about the life of Baruch Spinoza, written by Chaim Sloves. As it turned out,

Sholem Aleichem was indeed a safer choice than a contemporary Parisian author. In September 1962 the authorities banned the play's staging and disbanded the group under the excuse that Jews should "assimilate and not look back to Jewish culture."[31] The chorus, however, continued to function. In 1959, the Parisian *Naye Prese* reported that the chorus, under the baton of Israel Abramis, had one hundred participants. Although publicity was very limited and none of the announcements mentioned that the program was in Yiddish, every performance was sold out.[32]

In Daugavpils (also known as Dvinsk, its official name from 1893 to 1920), the second-largest Latvian city after Riga, a Yiddish dramatic circle was formed as early as 1955. In fact, a group of enthusiasts, led by Leyb Brukhis, revived a well-established tradition. In 1940–41, when Daugavpils became Soviet, there were plans to transform the successful local amateur troupe into a state Yiddish theater. In November 1946 surviving members of the prewar troupe and several new amateur actors gave their first postwar performance and continued to give performances without interruption until the spring of 1952.[33]

In December 1965 an amateur Yiddish dramatic circle emerged in Birobidzhan. It is not clear if that had happened thanks to a grassroots initiative or to the authorities' decision to have such a cultural institution in the JAR. Mikhail Bengelsdorf, the new troupe's director, worked at the Birobidzhan State Yiddish Theater until its liquidation in 1949. In 1967 the troupe received the status of people's theater. Grigory Gurevich, a Leningrad theater director who specialized in training directors of people's theaters, spent some time in Birobidzhan and gave a report on his impression of the Yiddish troupe. He praised the older actors, who—in Gurevich's opinion—were "almost professional." As for the younger generation, whose Yiddish was rusty at best, he found them "helpless, like barely literate amateurs."[34]

In Kishinev (Chişinău), whose 42,900 thousand Jews made up a fifth of the city's population in 1959, a Yiddish dramatic troupe emerged in November 1966 and became recognized as a people's theater in 1968. Its director, Ruvim Levin, and his wife Khana were students of the Moscow Yiddish Theater School, which was closed in 1949. Among the troupe's roughly one hundred participants were several professional actors. They also found support among local Yiddish literati. Thus, Motl Saktsier wrote the first play in its repertoire, *New Kasrilovka*, based—once again!—on Sholem Aleichem's stories. Saktsier was a poet and playwright who experienced eight years of imprisonment in both waves of repressions, in the 1930s and 1940s, but after his release continued to work with Yiddish actors, notably Sidi Tal. His *New Kasrilevka* featured an array of shtetl characters coming onstage to tell their stories. The troupe had its own chorus and dance ensemble, and a production team drawn from the elite of Kishinev's music and theater scene. The Levins were in contact with Moyshe Belenky, who knew them as students at the Moscow theater school.

Like virtually everywhere, the Kishinev troupe had a short life. The phasing out of the Thaw, the anti-Zionist campaign launched after the 1967 war in the Middle East, and the emigration to Israel cut short Yiddish amateur activities. In the new climate, the group was deprived of its permanent stage and moved to the outskirts of Kishinev. Its performances were routinely canceled for invented reasons. A tragedy contributed to the decline of the troupe: Levin, who had applied to emigrate, died following a traffic incident—regarded by some as an assassination—in December 1971.[35]

Meanwhile, recordings of the American Yiddish singers Claire and Mina Bagelman, better known as the Barry Sisters, were gaining in popularity following their August 1959 performance in an American variety show, produced in conjunction with the American National Exhibition in Moscow. Known also as "Queens of Schmaltz," the Barry Sisters injected swing into their songs, which appealed to the younger generation, often left unimpressed by traditional performances of Yiddish repertoire.[36] A 1967 review in the newspaper *Sovetskaia kultura* (Soviet Culture) mentioned their influence on the musical bands that performed in summer resorts on the Gulf of Riga.[37] These resorts attracted many Jewish visitors, not only from Latvia but also from Moscow and Leningrad. The Baltic seaside had a reputation as "almost West European" and appealed to members of the intelligentsia who turned up their noses at the "plebeian" Black Sea beaches.

In the 1960s a Mountain Jewish people's theater operated in the town of Derbent, Dagestan, an autonomous republic in the northern Caucasus. Interestingly, the theater with over thirty actors was established thanks to the initiative and sponsorship of three Derbent-based collective farms. Their initiative found support from the Dagestan government. The collective farms were remnants of the campaign in the 1920s and 1930s, when Jews were encouraged to work on land. The campaign was rather successful among Mountain Jews, many of whom were involved in farming, particularly in viticulture, also earlier. By the end of the 1930s, such farms had lost their definition as Jewish ones but remained, by the composition of their members, essentially Jewish collectives.[38]

Jewish Bookshelves

Concerts of ethnic songs, dances, and recitals would routinely be held outside a given ethnic group's territory, so Yiddish concerts in the Baltics, Ukraine, and elsewhere did not undermine the Birobidzhan-centered, "normal" model of Soviet Jewish life. Rather, to use Soviet parlance, they "met the Jewish population's cultural demands" and, not less importantly, served to prove that Soviet cultural politics was devoid of bias against Jews.

As for the Jews' reading supply, its specifically national component remained very limited. True, there is no information available on how many Jews sought to get this "component" and in which form—and language—they wished to consume it. There is little doubt that only a small minority of Soviet Jews dreamt of Yiddish schools, periodicals, and books. While translations of Soviet Yiddish authors, most of them justly or unjustly forgotten now, would find a place on some bookshelves, translations of such works as Lion Feuchtwanger's *Judean Wars* and Thomas Mann's *Joseph and His Brothers* were much more popular among acculturated Jewish and non-Jewish urbanites. Only one of the two, Feuchtwanger, was Jewish, but both left Germany after the Nazi Party's rise to power. Feuchtwanger, the most broadly published German-language fiction writer in the Soviet Union, was particularly widely read. Judging by Soviet statistical data up to and including 1957, his books came out in sixty editions, translated into eight Soviet languages, with a total print run of over 2.6 million copies.[39] Literary historian and translator Shimon Markish, Perets Markish's older son, wrote about the Feuchtwanger phenomenon:

> In the second half of the 1950s and in the 1960s his works were published in the USSR many times. All of his novels with the exception of *Jephthas Tochter* (Jephtha's Daughter) were published or republished within this fifteen-year period, and his collected works in twelve volumes were published in an edition

> of 300,000 copies. In all, this comprised a kind of compendium of Jewish history from the beginning of the Christian era to the Nazi persecutions. Most Jews of my generation and of the generation after mine experienced the fascination of Feuchtwanger, if not always as a writer at least as a Jew. As for myself, to this day I take pride in the fact that I translated his last novel about Josephus and compiled the notes to the whole trilogy about him. While doing this work, for the first time in my life I felt the true meaning of the lofty words which have been so perverted by ideology and propaganda: to labor for one's people.[40]

In the 1960s Moscow publishers had released four books of Russian translations of Israeli authors (see chapter 11). In 1966 the Moscow publishing house Khudozhestvennaia literatura (Belles-Lettres) produced a volume of Sholem Asch's selected stories, translated from Yiddish into Russian. The book had a respectable print run of fifty thousand. The title story, "People and Gods," portrays two poor widows, the Jewish Golda and the Polish Antonia, who live together in a little hovel where "two gods are glimmering—little Sabbath candles on the table and a little icon-lamp."[41] Asch, one of the best-known Yiddish writers in the West, was considered to be a friend of the Soviet Union thanks to his support for it during World War II. Soviet ideologists' relatively warm attitude toward Asch survived despite his decision to cut all links to pro-Soviet circles in the West following the repressions of Yiddish writers and other intellectuals during the late Stalin era.

The initiative to publish Asch's book came from Moyshe Belenky, who after returning from the Gulag prepared a never-realized program of over one hundred volumes of Russian translations of Jewish literature. In 1962 Belenky submitted a proposal to publish a two-volume edition of Asch's works; however, one of the volumes—the novella *America*—appeared only in 2008, when the Moscow publishing house Tekst (Text) used the manuscript of a translation done in the 1960s. Belenky's proposal found support from two veterans of the Soviet Yiddish cultural world: the philologist Eli Falkovich and the prose writer Joseph Rabin. Falkovich maintained that it would be good for Soviet readers to be introduced to the "well-established writer on social themes, master of [portraying] landscapes, still lifes, and genre scenes; a realist writer in a romantic wrapping, who fought for the right of people, including those at the bottom of the social scale, to live happily." Rabin characterized Asch as a person who "was not always stable in his views, and in politics, too, he was a man of moods." Rabin also stressed that his literary legacy contained "many progressive works, which educated ordinary, working people and portrayed their strength, their humanity and their protest against God in heaven and the wealthy on earth." Rabin recalled that during the 1905 Russian Revolution Asch "was radically disposed" and even "took the liberty of speaking against circumcision, which invited the rage of reactionaries and philistines." (In fact, Asch wrote about circumcision in 1908.) Thus, Asch's writings, at least some of them, had been qualified for access to the Soviet reader.[42]

The attitude toward the novelist Howard Fast differed completely. Soviet propagandists found themselves in a bind of having to castigate the man they used to describe as an exemplary American intellectual. By the mid-1950s over twenty million copies of Fast's books had been sold throughout the world, most notably in the Soviet Union, where his works were studied in secondary schools and universities and literary scholars wrote dissertations on his life and oeuvre. His Soviet royalties measured in the hundreds of thousands of dollars. At the same time, Fast's novels on Jewish topics, including his 1948 *My Glorious Brothers* (a popular Hanukkah gift in the USA), did not appear in Soviet translations. The winner of the Stalin International Peace Prize in 1953, Fast was the leading intellectual voice of American Communists. However, on 1 February 1957, the *New York Times* featured on its front page an article entitled "Reds Renounced by Howard Fast." The editorial writer Harry Schwartz broke the news about Fast's departure from the Communist Party, mentioning Khrushchev's de-Stalinization speech and the April 1956 *Folks-Shtime* article about the repression of Soviet Yiddish writers as the main reasons for his ideological metamorphosis. In August 1957 *Literaturnaia gazeta* informed its readership that Fast had become "a deserter under fire" and an author of "anti-Soviet slander."[43] As a result, his works stopped appearing in Soviet print.

Very popular, especially among teenagers, was Aleksandra Brushtein's autobiographical trilogy *Doroga ukhodit v dal'* . . . (The Road Goes Off into the Distance . . .), written and issued in the second half of the 1950s. Previously known as a prolific playwright for the children's stage, Brushtein wrote an autobiographical narrative about a Jewish girl from the time she enters school until she graduates. The action takes place in Vilna at the end of the nineteenth century. The prototype for the novel's hero, the girl's father, is Brushtein's father Jakub Wygodzki, a prominent physician and public leader, murdered by the Nazis in the early days of the occupation. The book, which refers to many subjects that the Soviets half forbade or relegated to silence, served young Soviet Jews as a source of information about the Pale of Settlement, the numerus clausus, preparations for Passover and the Passover Seder, and the identity of such people as Alfred Dreyfus and the revolutionary Hirsh Lekert.[44]

Brushtein's book passed through Soviet censorship because its references to the anti-Jewish social climate and state policies targeted the prerevolutionary period and the Nazi occupation. In fact, she wrote about it also earlier. In an article published in September 1939, when Poland had been occupied and partitioned by Germany and the Soviet Union, Brushtein recalled her visit to interwar Vilna, where she had grown up. In her words, the trip left her with an impression that "a crazy projectionist drove the film tape in reverse—backward, to czarist Russia." For Brushtein it was also a déjà vu of what she used to experience as a Jew: "At the very moment of crossing the [Soviet-Polish] border, I experienced the return of the long-forgotten 'feeling of my nose,' that is, an almost physical sensation of having several extra millimeters in its length. In Soviet territory, no one pays attention to these extra millimeters, but here they play the same role as medieval *peyes* [sidelocks] and a *lapserdak* [long frock coat], they are a kind of a stigma that shouts: 'Look—this is a pariah, an outcast walking—tally-ho! Hit him!'"[45]

In the 1950s several aging writers, whose childhood had passed in a less assimilated or simply in a traditional Jewish environment, published their recollections and autobiographies. Literary critics looked on such writings with favor, finding in them an educational tool for introducing the younger generation to wrongs and injustices of the prerevolutionary past. In this context, some nostalgic notes were also acceptable. In his memoir *People, Years, Life*, Ehrenburg mentioned that his parents resorted to Yiddish only when they did not want the children to understand. He recalled how his mother used to kindle the candles before Yom Kippur: "My mother never forgot Yom Kippur in the heavens or the pogrom on earth." Ehrenburg warmly portrayed his Orthodox grandfather's house in Kyiv, where he learned the meaning of the Sabbath and Jewish tradition.[46] In October 1960 a fragment from Ehrenburg's memoir appeared in *Literaturnaia gazeta* under the title "Kyiv." The reader learned that, as Ehrenburg was growing up, "many Jews" lived in Kyiv and that his cousin once drew his attention to a bespectacled man with long hair. It was Sholem Aleichem, in whose writings Kyiv was called Egupets, and people of Egupets populated the Yiddish writer's books.[47]

Shimon Markish, Perets Markish's son and a significant literary scholar in his own right, maintained that Ehrenburg "was the only significant and exceptionally popular [Soviet Russian] writer who regularly repeated, reminding his reader: I am Jewish. . . . Ehrenburg's stubborn reminders helped sustain the weak national glimmer in the common layperson, in the masses, in the people." For the Jews of post-Stalinist Soviet society, Ehrenburg's writings, particularly *People, Years, Life*, as well as such literary sources as numerous publications of Lion Feuchtwanger's novels, became "effective textbooks" for making Soviet Jews more nationally aware.[48]

Novyi mir published recollections of Samuil Marshak, a leading children's poet and translator, who entered literary society as a poet writing in Russian about Jewish topics for Jewish audiences. In his memoirs he dwelled on his grandparents' house in Vitebsk, where a private teacher tutored him in Hebrew and the Bible. Shmuel Halkin's memoir came out in a collection entitled *Soviet Writers* and edited by Bertha Breinin. His parents were poor in means but rich in spirit. The spiritual legacy they gave him included a great love for the Hasidic nigunim (religious songs or tunes), for wise folk humor, and for the folktale. As a child he did not even attend a heder, a religious school, for lack of money to pay the fee. It was his elder brother who taught him Hebrew, Bible, and religious law and introduced him to the world of Aggadah and Kabbalah. Zalman Wendroff's collection of stories *On the Threshold of Life* marked sixty years of his literary activities. The stories reflect the life of Russian Jews at the turn of the twentieth century.[49]

Colorful stories of Jewish Odessa became available to readers of a collection of works by Isaac Babel, the main creator of the Russian (and Ukrainian) myth of Odessa, of specific Odessa humor and music. Leonid Utesov (Leyzer Vaysbeyn), the famous jazz singer, provided an additional underpinning to this partly mythological, partly realistic portrait of the "Jewish" city. In Yiddish this myth hardly existed, although many Yiddish writers used to live in Odessa. Funny and exotic was not so much the "regular"

Jewish life in Odessa as its Russian-Jewish hybridization, including the local Russian vernacular spiced up with elements of Yiddish. For Yiddish authors such places as Warsaw, Vilna, and Berdichev played a more important role as main habitats of urban Jewish culture. After 1917 Warsaw and Vilna remained abroad, and Berdichev was too provincial. Meanwhile, Odessa was increasingly reputed to be the Jewish capital as well as the capital of Russian humor, and the city's name became a signifier for "Jewish."[50]

Russian translations of Yiddish writers' books usually did not belong to the category of popular literature. Significantly, it is hard to get adequate information about a Soviet-published book's real popularity or lack of it. The criterion for publishing a book was the "need" for it recognized by some decision-making experts, rather than actual reader "demand." Readers were not regarded as independent subjects of culture but only as objects whose taste had to be cultivated in specific directions.[51] Occasionally, however, "need" and "demand" overlapped. With a few exceptions, translations from Yiddish transcended the linguistic rather than ethnic boundaries, reaching mostly Jewish readers but—as a rule—not becoming a particularly popular read also among them. Russian renditions of poems by Leyb Kvitko occupied a prominent place in Soviet children's literature, but the fact that they had been written in Yiddish was never emphasized. Similarly, outside the Soviet Union, only three Yiddish authors, Sholem Aleichem, Sholem Asch, and later (mainly after winning a Nobel Prize in 1978) Isaac Bashevis Singer became relatively well-known to non-Yiddish readers.

In the Soviet Union, Yiddish literature was perceived to a significant degree—if perceived at all—as the literature of one author: Sholem Aleichem. This was fitting for a lower-tier position in the Soviet literary hierarchy, which effectively placed Yiddish in the category of literatures with one representative on the all-Soviet scene, such as the Avar-language poet Rasul Gamzatov and the Chukchi-language prose writer Yuri Rytkheu. Moreover, the Yiddish literary tradition represented by Sholem Aleichem, who died in 1916, appeared moribund, whereas Gamzatov and Rytkheu were contemporary writers.

Sholem Aleichem

A mini-industry of Sholem Aleichem scholarship, publications, and jubilee extravagances had emerged in the 1920s, matured in the 1930s and 1940s, and continued to function during the last Soviet decades. Isaac Bashevis Singer tried to explain the motivations for keeping the Jewish classic author in the Soviet canon: "Among Sholem Aleichem's characters, there are neither villains nor saints. . . . The worries and difficulties connected with making a living, generally overlooked or ignored in world literature, are his main topic. This is perhaps the reason for the Marxists' special fondness for his work. Despite all the twists and turns of Soviet attitudes towards writers, he has always remained *kosher*."[52]

In fact, Singer, an attentive observer of Jewish life, had missed the point this time. In order to occupy a place in the Soviet literary canon, the Yiddish writer had to be seen as more than a harmless humorist. Just laughing was not enough to qualify as a classic. The writer had to be a sharp critic of exploiters. Irme Druker, a writer and literary scholar, played a particularly important role in the "Sovietization" of Sholem Aleichem. In the 1930s he suggested an ideologically acceptable understanding of the classic Yiddish writer's satire. He argued that both the "vulgar sociologist critics" (as dogmatic simplifiers of Marxism were called in Soviet parlance) and "bourgeois nationalist critics" wrongly described Sholem Aleichem as a "good-natured" humorist. The former criticized his good nature, whereas the latter praised him for it. According to Druker, Sholem Aleichem was "good-natured" only toward the toiling masses but was a sharp critic of exploiters.[53]

This was exactly what Alexander Fadeev, then head of the Writers Union, emphasized in his speech during the celebration of Sholem Aleichem's eightieth birthday in 1939: "Sholem Aleichem found scathing words, full of disdain and sarcasm, aimed at the bourgeoisie and plutocracy." As a result, Soviet ideologists could embrace him. In addition, Sholem Aleichem was born and lived mainly in Ukraine, was Russian-schooled, wrote some of his stories in Russian, and—significantly—wanted to be buried in his home country (this did not happen when he died in America in May 1916; World War I and the ensuing revolution in Russia made the realization of his will impossible). No less important was his admiration for Maxim Gorky, the guru of the Soviet literary world, and Taras Shevchenko, the Ukrainian national poet.[54]

In 1956 numerous cultural events were dedicated to the fortieth anniversary of Sholem Aleichem's death.[55] In March a literary gala marking the anniversary took place at the Central House of Writers—a nineteenth-century art nouveau mansion that housed the headquarters of the Writers Union.[56] During the break viewers were able to purchase the April issue of the Russian-language Polish magazine *Pol'sha* (Poland), which contained an article on the Warsaw Yiddish theater. A telegram with greetings from the Social-Cultural Association of Jews in Poland and the presence of the Birobidzhan writer Buzi Miller, who had been recently released from prison, underlined the international and all-Union significance of the event.

The year 1956 saw publication of three collections of Sholem Aleichem's stories translated into Russian. They came out in Moscow with a total print run of close to half a million copies. In general, in the 1950s and later Soviet publishing houses printed scores of Sholem Aleichem's writings in translation into various languages. Thus, by the mid-1960s, forty-two Ukrainian translations came out with a total print run of over seven hundred thousand copies.[57] By that time the combined list of all books by Sholem Aleichem published in the Soviet Union contained over five hundred titles in twenty languages with a total print run of over six million copies.[58]

Riva Rubina, who in the 1930s lectured on the history of Yiddish literature at the Minsk Pedagogical Institute and, from 1934, at the Moscow Pedagogical Institute, was reputed to be a leading scholar on Sholem Aleichem. Following the closure of the Yiddish Department at the Moscow institute in 1938, she established herself as a compiler of and commentator on Russian translations of Sholem Aleichem's writings. In the 1950s she continued her activity, which began in 1940, when the State Publishing House produced her edited collection of stories by the classic writer. Nineteen fifty-six saw the publication of his stories for children edited by Rubina for the Publishing House of Children's Literature. In 1957 the State Publishing House brought out a seven-hundred-page volume of Sholem Aleichem's prose with Rubina's introduction. In 1959, the year of Sholem Aleichem's centenary, a smaller collection of his writings, also produced by the State Publishing House, carried Rubina's introduction. Her biographical-overview article opened the first volume of the collection of Sholem Aleichem's works, whose publication, with a quarter-million print run for each of its six volumes, marked the writer's centenary. Belenky played a particularly significant role in the production of books by and on Sholem Aleichem. He was the main person appointed to carry responsibility for compiling and editing the six-volume centenary edition.

The Soviet ideological apparatus saw the Sholem Aleichem centenary as a public relations opportunity to show the world that Jewish culture enjoyed full state support. In this climate, Israel Serebriani, who worked in the 1930s as a Yiddish literary scholar in Minsk, had a chance to publish in Russian his book *Sholem Aleichem and Folk Creativity*. In 1959 the Foreign Language Publishing House distributed an English translation of Sholem Aleichem's *The Bewitched Tailor*. Central, regional, and professional periodicals published articles about Sholem Aleichem. The Ministry of Communications issued a postage stamp with his portrait.[59] Boris Sandler, a Yiddish writer of the post–World War II generation, recalled how a street in his Bessarabian hometown Belts was named after Sholem Aleichem in 1959.[60]

Still, some functionaries had chosen to abstain from celebrating Sholem Aleichem's centenary. For instance, party officials in the Ukrainian city of Dnipropetrovsk banned a literary gala organized by the local branch of the Writers Union. When a Dnipropetrovsk Jewish resident wrote about it to the Central Committee of the Communist Party, he lost his job as history teacher and could not continue freelancing for newspapers published in the city.[61] Such episodes, however, usually remained invisible to foreign observers.

The centenary celebrations of Sholem Aleichem's birthday reached their climax on 2 April, when the main event took place in the Moscow Hall of Trade Unions. Russian writers, such as Aleksei Surkov, Boris Polevoy, and Vasily Azhaev, were central figures in the gala event, whereas Yiddish writers appeared as a literary garnish: Noah Lurie spoke in Yiddish about Sholem Aleichem; the poets Halkin and Vergelis recited their poems. There were also American guests: Paul Novick and the African American bass vocalist Paul Robeson, who sang a couple of Yiddish songs. Among the performers were young singers Nehama Lifshitz and Emil Gorovets.

A reasonably visible effect was made on foreign audiences by sending abroad a group of Yiddish artists. According to Mikhail Aleksandrovich,

French Communists asked Khrushchev to send the artists. Apart from Aleksandrovich, a Latvian Conservatory alumnus and singer whose recordings sold millions of copies in the Soviet Union, the group included his younger colleagues Lifshitz, thirty-one, and Gorovets, thirty-five, as well as two veteran performers, Meritorious Artists of the Russian Republic: Naum Valter, a pianist, and Emmanuil Kaminka, a reciter (whose Yiddish was rather rusty). Boris Vladimirskii, director of the All-Union Studio of Gramophone Records, headed this cultural delegation.

A few days before their departure, the group was summoned to the Central Committee to receive instructions on how to behave abroad: to avoid excessive contacts with foreigners, to restrain themselves from openly admiring what they were going to see during the tour, to walk only in a group, and to "dispel the myth" that Yiddish culture had been wiped out in the Soviet Union.[62] Lifshitz, who began to be seen as a symbol of the Jewish cultural awakening in the Soviet Union, stood out as the only Soviet artist in this group who did not perform a single item in Russian or a Yiddish version of a Russian song. She also appeared in Vienna in May 1959, and again in Paris, as well as in Brussels and Antwerp, in February 1960.[63] Ultimately, Lifshitz, Aleksandrovich, and Goroverts emigrated from the Soviet Union.

On 14 January 1960, Vergelis's article in *Literaturnaia gazeta* summed up the results of celebrating Sholem Aleichem's centenary in Moscow, Paris, and Tel Aviv. Clearly, Vergelis was au courant with the foreign non-Communist Yiddish press, which was normally inaccessible to his fellow writers. Predictably, in his judgment, the Moscow gatherings and publications were the grandest. The anniversary gala occasion in Paris, organized by the progressive Jewish organization Union, also became a significant event thanks to Soviet Yiddish actors: "When the Soviet artists Aleksandrovich, Kaminka, Lifshitzaite, Valter and Gorovets appeared on the stage, there was no end to the rejoicing. The Jewish workers sitting in the audience acclaimed this manifestation of cultural exchange between the countries." Vergelis, however, ridiculed the jubilee evening in the Habima Theater in Tel Aviv, where there were no representatives of Yiddish literature, and even worse, "efforts . . . were made to artificially unite Sholem Aleichem's centenary with the 25th anniversary of the poet H. N. Bialik's death." Vergelis quoted Mordechai Tsanin (Canin), editor of the Tel Aviv daily *Di Letste*

Nayes (Latest News): "It would have been possible, on the whole, to forget that Sholem Aleichem had ever lived in this world, if not for Moscow's decision to mark his centenary."[64]

The publication of the Sholem Aleichem volume opened a new—and final—page in the history of Yiddish publishing in the Soviet Union. This was a direct result of Anastas Mikoyan's American 1959 visit (see pp. 79–81), when on numerous occasions he had to find evasive answers to questions concerning the state of Jewish culture and religious life in the Soviet Union, including the fact that throughout the country, including Birobidzhan, there was not a single Jewish school nor even one class where Yiddish or Hebrew was taught.[65] The first Yiddish book in the post-Stalinist period, a collection of stories by Sholem Aleichem, came out in Moscow with remarkable speed, just over two weeks (compared to the usual five or six months in Soviet book production) for all stages from manuscript to appearing in Moscow bookstores in time for the classic writer's one hundredth birthday on 2 March 1959, printed on high-quality paper and bound in a nice dust jacket.[66] After the 1959 volume no other books by Sholem Aleichem appeared in the Soviet Union in Yiddish.

The *Jewish Chronicle* wrote:

> Although the preparations for the Sholem Aleichem Centenary celebrations were completed some time ago, the Soviet authorities have taken unprecedented pains to give the event the widest publicity, especially abroad. Bookshops in Israel and the United States were informed by cable that the Sholem Aleichem volume in Yiddish, of which 30,000 copies have been printed, would be supplied to them for sale shortly.
>
> At the same time the Russian Embassies in London, New York, Paris, and several other capitals have distributed a special article by . . . Aron Vergelis, on Sholem Aleichem's influence in Russia, and describing how much his works are appreciated all over the Soviet Union. . . .
>
> Like most activities in the Soviet Union, the publication of a volume in Yiddish and the widespread nature of the celebrations are not without political meaning. The Soviet authorities are by now fully aware of the apprehension felt by Jews all over the world at the discrimination shown against the Jewish minority in the USSR. . . . This issue was the subject of a conference recently between Mr. Mikoyan and American Jewish leaders.[67]

Boris Gershman, a former proofreader at the publishing house Der Emes, helped to find Yiddish typesetting equipment. He recalled bits and pieces of conversations heard years before indicating that, after the Yiddish publishing house had been closed down, some equipment had survived at the printshop of the newspaper *Isvestiia.* Indeed, it was stored there in a cellar.[68]

The publishing house Khudozhestvennaia literatura (Belles-Lettres), which brought out the Sholem Aleichem book, produced during the same year similar volumes of works by two other classic Yiddish writers—Mendele Moykher-Sforim and Yitskhok Leybush Peretz. However, Yiddish works by Soviet writers still did not have access to printing presses. An interview with Vergelis shows that in the fall of 1959, following Sholem Aleichem's jubilee, the Soviet poet did not know yet if the authorities were ready to allow publication of Yiddish books by contemporary writers.

> If it were proved, he [Vergelis] said, that there is demand for Yiddish, it would be "more than likely that other books in that language would be published in Russia." He would not predict the date, but he was confident. The demand for Yiddish, he maintained, would create a possibility for the rebirth of Yiddish culture which, he stressed, had "never ceased to exist but was only interrupted for a period." But, he said, the "Yiddish reading public has shrunk." The young Jews no longer understand the language and the older ones are also gradually changing over to Russian. This, he said, is a natural form of "positive assimilation"; this is the reason . . . why so many Yiddish authors are translated into Russian. . . .
>
> "Don't you feel rather humiliated." I asked, "that while writing in Yiddish you cannot have your works published in the language you yourself speak and dream in." "No." he replied firmly. "I feel it to be an honor and a recognition that my work is being made accessible to a wider public. This is a mark of respect not only for me and other Yiddish writers . . . but it is also a mark of respect for my people. . . ."[69]

Vergelis obviously lied, which was customary and even obligatory for a Soviet person interviewed by a foreign journalist. Frankness in formal conversations was, in general, a rare commodity in a society whose members were supposed to think and to talk, especially face-to-face with foreigners, in accord with the current official Party and government line. In reality, Vergelis, like all Yiddish literati, hoped, no doubt, to get a Soviet outlet for his works.

8

SOVIET HOMELAND

The Yiddish Cadre

By the end of the 1950s, the Writers Union had among its 4,800 thousand members about seventy writers, critics, and translators associated with Yiddish literature. About thirty of them lived in Moscow or its suburbs. Over ten lived in Kyiv, and there were smaller groups in Chernivtsi, Odessa, Vilnius, Kishinev, Birobidzhan, and Minsk. Many of the writers had had a full and thorough Yiddish education, including a degree in Yiddish linguistics and literature from a university-level pedagogical institute in Moscow, Kyiv, Minsk, or Odessa. The majority of them were products of prewar Soviet schooling. Their ranks were reinforced by literati who lived in the Baltic countries, Poland, or Romania and had become Soviet citizens only in 1939 or 1940. Culturally and ideologically, these "westerners" were often a world away from their homegrown Soviet colleagues.

Rehabilitation returned former Gulag inmates to "normal" life, reinstating them in the Party (if they were members) and in the Writers Union. Those surviving Yiddish writers who did not experience the Gulag usually endured their portion of hardship in the form of psychological stress and threadbare existence. Some of them had to fight for reinstating their membership in the Writers Union because in the late 1940s and early 1950s their ostensible creative passivity was used as a reason for purging Yiddish authors. In Minsk this reasoning led to the expulsion of Hirsh Reles, a poet.[1] The Kishinev writer Ikhil Shraybman, similarly expelled, remembered it as the most tragic day in his life. This brought psychological torment, forcing him to spend several months in a psychiatric hospital.[2]

A number of the professional Yiddish literati were recruits of the campaigns of the late 1920s and early 1930s, when young workers with signs of literary talent were stimulated to move from the "machine tool" to literature because the builders of Soviet culture believed that only writers belonging to the proletariat could become a reliable exponent of its interests. Such "proletarian talents" often remained dependent on "ghostwriters," or editors who would virtually rewrite their works. Ritalii Zaslavskii, a Ukrainian poet and translator who knew several Yiddish proletarian talents, wrote about them: "This type of individual was formed in the ideological and social conditions of that time . . . I sometimes wondered whether these people would have become writers in another, non-Soviet society. Most likely not. The thought of devoting themselves to such a strange activity would have never crossed their minds."[3]

Meanwhile, publications in Yiddish remained only a hope, because party ideologists clearly gave the green light to the plan according to which Yiddish writers could continue to work in their language but their prose and poetry would appear in print only in translations. The possibility to publish translations certainly improved the status and financial security of the writers. For Shraybman, for instance, it meant the restoration of his position in the Writers Union. His children's book was recommended for publication and appeared in Moldovan translation in 1955, his book of novellas appeared in 1957, also in Moldovan, and his two books came out in Russian in 1959 and 1960. These events, though they certainly revived his career as a writer, did not revive Shraybman as a Yiddish writer.[4]

The Moscow publishing house Sovetskii pisatel (Soviet Writer) played the central role in producing translations from Yiddish. By 1963 it had brought out sixty-three books by Yiddish writers, initially giving preference to works by murdered authors.[5] Sofia Fray, a veteran Yiddish journalist and later, after her liberation from the Gulag (her husband, Vulf Nodel, a journalist, was executed in 1938), a lecturer in economics at the Moscow Institute of Foreign Languages, wrote in 1959: "It may seem paradoxical at first glance, but the mass publication of Yiddish writings in Russian translation has resulted in broadening the circle of Jewish readers, because the Russian language long ago became their mother tongue."[6]

The model of write-in-Yiddish-but-publish-in-translation actually dated from the late 1930s, but the annexation in 1939 and 1940 of new territories, densely populated by Yiddish-speaking Jews, saved Soviet Yiddish literature temporarily and staved off the eventual termination of Yiddish publishing until after the war.[7] In the 1950s, however, the American historian Leon Shapiro, who closely monitored the situation in the Soviet Union, came to the conclusion that for Soviet authors almost the only possibility for publication in Yiddish—a very limited one—was in Poland, particularly in the newspaper *Folks-Shtime*.[8]

Initially, Hersh Smolar, editor of *Folks-Shtime*, failed to establish contacts with his Soviet colleagues. Emmanuil Kazakevich, a friend from Smolar's youth, rejected his invitation to publish something in the Warsaw newspaper. An attempt to engage Iakov Rives, a veteran Communist writer, also came to nothing.[9] Gradually, however, Soviet authors began to send their works for publication in Warsaw in the pages of *Folks-Shtime* and the Warsaw literary journal *Yidishe Shriftn* (Yiddish Writings), especially as—apart from the obscure *Birobidzhaner Shtern*—they had no other outlet for their poems, stories, and essays. In some cases a publication in *Folks-Shtime* was the first sign of life received from a survivor of Stalinism. For Yiddish writers, publication in the foreign Communist press became a source of income—the Sovinformburo, responsible for cultural export, paid them honoraria.[10] It seems, though, that some publications, especially those that the authors sent directly to the newspapers, did not bring any financial gains. Zalman Wendroff, for instance, asked Novick, editor of *Morgn-Frayhayt*, to send him, as a substitute for royalties, a suit or, at least, a couple of white shirts and a tie.[11] Such publications could also cause problems for their authors. In 1960 the Chernivtsi-based poet Meir Kharats faced blistering criticism for publishing "ideologically deficient" works in the Polish Yiddish press. True, this time Kharats was not sent back to labor camps, where he had spent five years. Rather, he soon received an apartment and lived there until his emigration to Israel in 1972.[12]

The press distribution agency Soyuzpechat, which operated as a monopoly under the Soviet Ministry of Communications, did not include foreign Jewish periodicals in its catalogs, even if they were, like *Folks-Shtime*, Communist outlets. Nevertheless, according to an American Communist Yiddish journalist who met with his Warsaw colleagues in the summer of 1956, close to two thousand copies of each of the paper's four weekly issues would go to the Soviet Union.[13] Apart from some "difficult" periods, censors regarded *Folks-Shtime* as a periodical that a Soviet citizen could receive by mail. As a result, the newspaper's editorial office became inundated with letters from Soviet Jews asking for the paper. There was no way to pay for the subscription in unconvertible Soviet rubles, hence the editors would receive parcels with salami, dried fruit, and caviar mailed as barter payment by readers hungry for the Yiddish word. The paper's editorial staff sponsored subscriptions for a number of their Soviet colleagues, and many Poland-based readers participated in raising funds to cover the expenses incurred from printing additional copies and mailing them to the Soviet Union. The most significant contribution came from the American Federation of Polish Jews.[14] An additional readership was important for the survival of the Warsaw newspaper, too. Interestingly, a Leningrad-based Zionist group, formed in the late 1950s, disseminated literature received through the Israeli embassy as well as letters from Israel, and articles from *Folks-Shtime*.[15]

In 1959 Itsik Kipnis, a recently rehabilitated Gulag inmate, serialized in the Warsaw newspaper his autobiographical novel *Mayn shtetl Sloveshne* (My Shtetl Sloveshne). In 1961 the Warsaw publishing house Yidish Bukh brought out a collection of stories, *33 noveln* (33 Novellas), by Shira Gorshman, and next year a children's book by Kipnis, *Zeks epl; di kluge binen* (Six Apples; The Wise Bees), came out under the same imprint.

In the summer of 1957, *Folks-Shtime* dispatched to Moscow its journalist, and later its editor, Abraham (Adam) Kwaterko, to report about the International Youth and Student Festival, which aimed to show the world that the post-Stalinist USSR was open to international contacts. Indeed, the festival left a lasting impact on Soviet society, introducing such things as jeans and rock 'n' roll. It also brought additional worries for Soviet ideologues. In particular, it was disappointing to observe that Soviet Jews demonstrated enthusiasm for Israel in their meetings with the two hundred delegates selected to represent the Jewish state. In fact, there were two Israeli delegations—half of them represented the Communist movement, another half came as delegates of the Zionist movement.[16]

Kwaterko wrote about a remarkable meeting, in mid-August 1957, that was a by-product of an earlier meeting with a group of Soviet writers, in which Aleksei Surkov, head of the Writers Union, was forced to admit openly his mistake of not inviting any Yiddish colleagues. To rectify his mistake, he promised to convene a separate roundtable conference for delegates interested in Yiddish literature. Among those who came to the hastily organized gathering, conducted in Yiddish, were left-wing activists from Argentina, Uruguay, Brazil, Chile, France, and Poland, as well as journalists and writers from England, Israel, and Germany. The meeting was chaired by Zalman Wendroff, the elder among the Yiddish writers. Addressing the meeting, Wendroff declared that irrespective of what had taken place in the days of Stalin's terror, Jewish cultural life in the country had not been completely uprooted.

Nokhem Oyslender, a literary critic and scholar, also one of the oldest among the Yiddish litterateurs, was the key speaker at the meeting. He tried to sidestep the thorny question of the absence of outlets for Yiddish publications and instead focused the audience's attention on the "miracle" of Soviet Yiddish literature's transformation "from rejected literature to great literature" (*fun oys-literatur tsu groys-literatur*). To all appearances it was a popular catchphrase among Soviet Yiddish writers.[17] Oyslender revealed the "secret" of his fellow writers' postcomatose creative survival: the opportunity to be translated into Russian became a powerful incentive for them to continue writing in Yiddish. The roots of this phenomenon he saw in a 1909 letter by Sholem Aleichem, in which the classic Yiddish writer expressed his dream of becoming "a drop in the ocean of Russian literature."[18] Oyslender conceded, though, that without outlets for publishing their works in the original, this stimulus would eventually run out.

The prose writer Joseph Rabin, who had already experienced imprisonment (arrested in December 1937 in Birobidzhan) and fought in the war, noted, however, that a Russian translation often "had no taste," Rokhl Boymvol, a poet, quipped that the river of Soviet Yiddish literature might feed into the Russian ocean only if it could flow, whereas now only a few "spoonfuls" were being transfused. Still, she ended her speech by reassuring the guests that "we write and we hope that tomorrow will bring us good news." The last speaker was Ziama (Zinovii) Telesin, Boymvol's husband and a poet in his own right, who also ended on a note of hope: "The day will come when Yiddish books will appear again in Russia, and we shall be able to dispatch them to Jewish communities all over the world."[19] The Moscow festival closed on 11 August 1957. On the next day, which was the fifth anniversary of the execution of the thirteen people secretly tried in the case of the Jewish Anti-Fascist Committee, some of the participants went to visit widows of the murdered Yiddish writers.[20]

Since 1955 the apparatus of the Writers Union had had a Yiddish expert: Aron Vergelis worked at the union's Foreign Commission, chaired by Boris Polevoy, one of the best-known Soviet novelists. From a bureaucratic point of view, Vergelis, a young literary functionary without Gulag experience, apparently was a better pick for the leading Yiddish-literature-related role than a more venerable surviving member of the Soviet Yiddish literary guild. In addition, the regalia of "the first poet of Birobidzhan" and "the Great Patriotic War veteran," which adorned Vergelis's biography, doubtless played a role in choosing him. By the strictest criteria, Kazakevich rather than Vergelis was the first poet of Birobidzhan, but his "defection" to Russian literature (some Yiddish writers did indeed see him as a deserter) left the Birobidzhan Yiddish poetic throne vacant.

In 1955 Vergelis's poems began to appear in prestigious Russian literary journals. Twenty-two poets translated poems for his 1956 Russian book *Zhazhda* (Thirst). A shrewd opportunist, Vergelis knew the ideological importance of Birobidzhan. In his poem "Exotic Taiga," Vergelis himself emerged as an excellent product of Birobidzhan-based Soviet Jewish nation building—a determined, aggressive man from the Far Eastern frontier rather than a milksop from a Belorussian or Ukrainian shtetl:

> Nu yo, kh'bin avade der yung der farshayter,
> vos opgelebt hob ikh a lebn bam shayter,
> bam shayter gegesn, in tayge gezesn,
> in valdbrukh gekrokhn—di fis nit farshtokhn,
> geshpayzt zikh mit feygl—ot ersht fun der shure,
> geblozt, vi af milkh, af di khayishe shpurn,
> gegangen af mesers: der tiger—a vikher,
> un ikh gey af zikher—mit mole-retsikhe,
> mit altn farshtand un mit khokhme mit nayer:
> nit zayn ba di khayes a tsar-balekhayim.[21]

> Well, I am indeed the young daredevil,
> who spent his life at a campfire,
> at a campfire I ate, in the taiga I sat,

in the thicket I climbed, but didn't prick my legs,
I lived on wildfowl—straight from the flock,
I knew how to follow the wild animal's trail,
and I went with a knife: the tiger was like a whirlwind,
but I took no chances—with fury,
with old cleverness and with new wit:
not to show any pity to wild animals.

Such derring-do was unusual even for a Jewish toughie in Birobidzhan, where hunting on the taiga was regarded as a Gentile pastime.[22] Yet Vergelis apparently liked to be seen as a young Communist barbarian and cultivated this image even decades later by telling stories of his fortitude. In any case, he looked like the right man to deal with those meddlesome foreign guests, who came to Moscow trying to understand and influence the Soviet leaders' attitude toward the Jews.

On 14 September 1956, the Secretariat of the Central Committee gave the green light to the Writers Union to publish Yiddish books and a literary quarterly with a print run of five thousand. This resolution was, however, soon shelved, and *Morgn-Frayhayt* informed its readers that—due to a divergence of views among Soviet officials—the Kremlin had reneged on promises to renew Yiddish cultural activities.[23] Arguably, Khrushchev was the only man who could overrule the secretariat's resolution. Judging by his pronouncements, the Soviet leader was not in disagreement with those functionaries who, at least from the late 1940s, began to see Jews, especially unassimilated ones, as unreliable elements. With this frame of mind, it was easy to regard the fostering of Jewish culture as misguided at best. Indeed, in 1957, Maurice Thorez, leader of the French Communist Party, learned from his Soviet colleagues that they regarded Jews as the weakest link in society and that reviving Yiddish culture would only reinforce Jewish nationalism.[24]

On 31 January 1957, Vergelis and Elena Romanova, a functionary of the Writers Union, shared with Polevoy their frustration. During their meetings with foreign guests they had spoken about a number of Yiddish-related projects, feeding the visitors with the information they had received from the leaders of the Writers Union, but now they were at a loss, did not know what they could and should write in response to the letters that kept arriving from abroad. They also had to decline invitations, including one from the Argentinian Jewish Cultural Association, a left-wing organization. Vergelis and Romanova argued that lack of contact and information had a damaging effect on progressive foreign Jewish organizations and contributed to the rise of a new wave of anti-Soviet propaganda.[25]

Polevoy, who "seemed to have become a kind of cultural plenipotentiary,"[26] played an important role in creating post-Stalinist outlets for Yiddish letters. Thanks to his numerous trips abroad, he was acquainted firsthand with the state of opinion among foreign left-wingers and, generally, did not see any harm in allowing Yiddish writers to publish their works. Simple human empathy also could play a role in Polevoy's and some other writers' willingness to help their Yiddish colleagues, some of whom were, or used to be, their neighbors or even friends. Not to mention that high-ranking literati might feel remorse over being involved in the Yiddish writers' arrests, because—according to the Stalinist system of collective responsibility—such arrests had to be "sanctioned" by the leadership of the Writers Union. In December 1957 Moyshe Broderzon's widow published in the Parisian Bundist newspaper *Unzer Shtime* (Our Voice) a number of articles devoted to the tragedy of Soviet Yiddish culture. In particular, she wrote—and later repeated in her 1960 book—how her husband told her about seeing an appendix to his indictment signed by the renowned writer Konstantin Simonov.[27] As the Russian poet Anna Akhmatova wrote in 1956, "Two Russias are eyeball to eyeball—those who were imprisoned and those who put them there."

Polevoy complained to the Central Committee that he and his colleagues in the Writers Union found themselves in an embarrassing position: they had promised to revive Yiddish cultural activities, but now were unable to reply to inquiries by foreign activists because there was no clarity with regard to the decision taken by the Soviet leadership. Polevoy issued his criticism of Soviet policies mainly through the words of French poet and novelist Louis Aragon, a highly respected and valued figure in the Soviet Union:

> One can say that each and every Western writer who comes to visit [the Soviet Union] in some form reveals an interest in this [i.e., the Jewish] question. It is well known that this issue was one of the reasons for Howard Fast's leaving the

[American Communist] Party and his later [ideological] transformation. The delay in solving this question hinders the return to the circle of our friends Carlo Levi and Alberto Moravia and destabilizes the position of Vercors [Jean Bruller]. The English writer Doris Lessing, who left the Communist Party, writes about the same issue. The list of names is endless, even in the domain of literature only.

The other day we had an in-depth conversation with Louis Aragon and Elsa Triolet [born Ella Kagan in Moscow in 1896], who are visiting the Soviet Union [in May 1957]. They were and remain loyal friends of the Soviet Union, who did not dither even in the sharpest moments at the end of the last year [during the Soviet military suppression of the uprising against Communism in Hungary].

"It's hard to understand why you persist in this issue," said Aragon. "Among people who know little about the Soviet Union this immediately causes suspicion, they question your internationalism. Whatever the quality of Yiddish literature and whatever one's attitude to it, we have to admit that it is being published in every country of the Western world that has a Jewish population. No arguments can prove convincingly that Yiddish literature or Yiddish culture are not needed in your country, which has written on its banner the slogan of internationalism. Given the fact that, as a rule, Yiddish newspapers published in various countries are being read all over the world, this problem constantly has an international resonance, it turns into an unhealing sore, which your enemies will never stop picking at. It will be your Achilles' heel, which they will attack. On the contrary, if you establish a Yiddish newspaper, a Yiddish almanac, publish a series of books by Yiddish writers, which will also find distribution all over the world, in every country, you'll be able to use all these for disseminating your ideas, your facts, and your arguments. Why are you depriving yourselves of this possibility?"

After quoting and thereby endorsing Aragon's call for showing more political acumen in dealing with Yiddish literature (even if Aragon clearly considered it subpar), Polevoy added that the problem of Yiddish culture in the Soviet Union was particularly important for foreign writers and journalists of Jewish origin. "No doubt, for them we'll never find a sufficiently convincing reasoning for not having Jewish culture and arts in our country. I think that the situation has become so sharp in recent months that it can seriously undermine the prestige of our culture in the West and that this issue is ripe for serious and urgent consideration."[28]

The Birth Pangs

In the Moscow circle of Yiddish literati, two people, Moyshe Belenky and Aron Vergelis, competed for leadership of the reemerging Jewish cultural establishment. Although not a member of the Writers Union, Belenky, who found his métier in atheism and literary criticism, aspired to lead the Yiddish literary community. Nonetheless, it was Vergelis, born in 1918 and eight years Belenky's junior but already an experienced literary functionary without a Gulag past, who gradually took on this role.

In May 1960 Vergelis wrote to Khrushchev, claiming that it was imperative to establish a Soviet Yiddish forum for literature and propaganda.[29] It is clear that somebody gave him the signal to write this letter. Assuming that Khrushchev dealt personally with this issue, his reaction was tardy. Among the Yiddish literati, Shmuel Halkin, physically broken after six years of imprisonment—rather than Vergelis, two decades younger and in good health—was widely seen as the best choice for the position of editor-in-chief of the new Yiddish periodical. Although it would be naive to suggest that functionaries of the Central Committee and the Writers Union coordinated their plans with Halkin's expected demise, rumor had it that Vergelis and his supporters intentionally delayed the journal's launching because they knew that Halkin's days were numbered. He died in September 1960 and was the only Yiddish writer buried at the prestigious Novodevichy Cemetery in Moscow.

In fact, the delay in launching the journal had to do with the resistance of two top functionaries in the Central Committee: Leonid Ilyichev, head of the Propaganda and Agitation Department, and Dmitri Polikarpov, head of the Culture Department. On 20 July 1960, they suggested rejecting Vergelis's proposal, arguing that it sufficed to publish Yiddish books. It seems, however, that on the eve of the 22nd Communist Party Congress, scheduled for October 1961, at which the program of building Communism as the next phase in the development of Soviet society was to be announced, Khrushchev decided to approve the proposed journal as a kind of gift to foreign Communists and pro-Soviet liberals. A number of factors—incessant international pressure, the findings of the 1959 Soviet census (which reported over four hundred thousand claimants of Yiddish as mother tongue, a figure that contradicted the official Soviet line that Jews had been fully acculturated),[30] a potential worldwide readership, and the support of several influential Russian writers—may have played a role in convincing Khrushchev to sanction a new Yiddish literary journal.[31]

On 11 February 1961, the secretariat of the governing board of the Writers Union actualized the decision of the Central Committee to start publishing (in the second half of the year) a Yiddish journal to be entitled *Sovetish Heymland*, with a print run of twenty-five thousand copies. The title, meaning "Soviet homeland," made clear its ideological commitment and, at the same time, referred back to the Moscow-based Yiddish literary periodicals *Sovetish* (1934–41) and *Heymland* (1947–48). Characteristically, *Vatan Sovetimu*, the title of the annual literary publication in the Tat language, effectively a Jewish periodical for Mountain Jews published from 1955, had the same meaning.

The main objective of the new periodical was defined as follows: "to publish the best works of Soviet writers, which reflect the achievements of the Soviet people in building Communism and developing the economy and culture, and which contribute to the education of toilers in the spirit of Soviet patriotism, proletarian internationalism and peoples' friendship." The secretariat appointed Vergelis as editor-in-chief and allocated funds for nineteen salaried staff members as well as for royalties and production of the journal. Even with the planned but never-achieved target of twenty-five thousand copies sold through subscription and single-copy sales, the Sovetskii pisatel publishing house had to cover at least half of the expenses.[32] Initially, the editorial staff of the new journal occupied several desks at the office of the *Literaturnaia gazeta*, but it later moved to more spacious quarters at 17 Kirova (from 1991, Miasnitskaia) Street. The journal was launched as a bimonthly (the first issue came out in August 1961) and in 1965 doubled its periodicity from six to twelve issues in a year.

Over time, *Sovetish Heymland* became the state-sponsored central forum of Soviet Yiddish culture. In addition, it controlled the publication of the majority of Yiddish books, which, from 1965 onward, were as a rule reprints of poetry and prose works by active writers that had previously appeared in *Sovetish Heymland*. Based in Moscow, the journal effectively undermined the Birobidzhan-centered model of Soviet Jewry. Whereas domestic factors had shaped Soviet policy toward the Jews in the 1920s and 1930s, post-Stalinist Soviet leaders paid more attention to international factors.[33] By the 1960s a Moscow journal was deemed a more marketable Cold War propaganda tool than the failed Jewish colonization project in a remote area eight times zones away in Russia's Far East.

Indeed, *Sovetish Heymland*, "the most discussable literary journal in the history of Yiddish literature,"[34] came to be a significant political phenomenon. The appearance of the expensive and handsomely printed periodical was reported around the world. Its initial print run was unprecedented in the history of Yiddish literary periodicals. (The exact circulation of the flagship Yiddish literary periodical in the post-Holocaust period, the Tel Aviv–based journal *Di goldene keyt*, remains a sealed secret, but it barely exceeded a few thousand copies.) In addition, *Sovetish Heymland* boasted the largest and youngest pool of contributors; in 1961 alone more than one hundred people formed its creative milieu.[35] In August 1961 an article in the *New York Times* noted that "the Yiddish language [has] won a round in the struggle with the Kremlin." Indeed, the status of Yiddish as an officially recognized national language of Soviet Jews was restored and placed beyond dispute. Any attempts to question the status of Yiddish would be met with rebuffs on the part of *Sovetish Heymland*, whose editors regarded themselves as custodians of the language.[36] However, this did not mean that Yiddish had won in the struggle with the Kremlin. Rather, at that juncture, the Kremlin had decided to use Yiddish and Yiddish culture in such a manner.

Sovetish Heymland never had its own bank account or other markers of financial or administrative independence. In fact, it was a department of Sovetskii pisatel and was wholly dependent on subsidies of the publisher, one of the most successful monopolies of the Soviet book market. A single Moscow printing shop (no. 7, Iskra revoliutsii) was responsible for the entire process of typesetting and printing. Until the end of 1991, linotypes belonging to this printing house also produced almost all of the secular and religious books in Yiddish and Hebrew for the Soviet Union. Subscription and distribution were functions of other centralized organizations: Soyuzpechat (Soviet Union Press), a unit in the Ministry of Communications, for Soviet readers, and the foreign-trade organization Mezhdunarodnaya kniga (International Book) for readers living outside the Soviet Union. In terms of ideology, *Sovetish Heymland* was guided by the dictates of the Central Committee of the Communist Party. Like any Soviet institution, *Sovetish Heymland* had a "triangle" (*treugol'nik*) or troika of management (editor) and two elected functionaries: the Party secretary and the trade-union organizer.

Of the initial 1961 print run of twenty-five thousand copies, about eight thousand went to domestic subscribers (via Soyuzpechat) and seven thousand to foreign subscribers (via Mezhdunarodnaya kniga); some copies—though less than the remaining ten thousand—were sold in kiosks. According to the annual *Pechat' v SSSR* (Periodicals in the USSR), in 1966 the number of printed copies fell to sixteen thousand and continued to decline in the following years.[37] During the first fifteen months of its existence, the journal published works by ninety-five authors, fifty-six of whom were members of the Writers Union, thirty-seven had participated in World War II, and twenty-two were Party members.

While some people in the West, notably in the camp of Soviet sympathizers, were happy that Soviet Yiddish authors now had an opportunity to gain access to their readership, Jewish activists of more dominant ideological segments saw a Yiddish literary periodical as a gimmick rather than an adequate solution to the needs of Soviet Jews. Foreign Jewish activists' greatest concerns were associated with restrictions on religious freedom and overtly antireligious propaganda. The ban on the baking of matzo in bakeries met with particular indignation. In addition, there was concern about the high percentage of Jews among people executed for committing large-scale economic crimes. Finally, there was the nearly wholesale ban on emigration. Problems encountered by Jewish applicants to top universities also caused a ripple in the American press but did not figure as a particularly serious concern, probably because of still-fresh memories of similar restrictions in American elite educational institutions.[38]

Things looked rather different from the vantage point of Soviet Jews. Issues of religion usually did not particularly, if at all, worry the Soviet-reared Ashkenazi Jewish majority, whereas anxieties about access to higher education and desirable occupations were pervasive among them.[39] Especially worrying, however, were numerous general, non–specifically Jewish problems. Although the reforms of the Thaw period had improved standards of living, many aspects of daily life remained difficult and became especially acute in 1963, when the poor harvest and large-scale experiments with cultivating corn caused inadequate food supply, with long lines for buying bread and other basic commodities.[40]

Meanwhile, media information about Jewish problems in the Soviet Union gnawed at the conscience of Jews in the United States, Israel, and many other countries, especially as many of them had guilt feelings that they or the older generation had failed to do enough to prevent the Holocaust. American Jews also had other motives: to prove their loyalty to Israel despite very weak emigration from the USA to the Jewish state, and to avert accusations of Communist sympathy.[41] The general atmosphere of the 1960s, full of mass demonstrations and protests, certainly contributed to the rise of grassroots initiatives. In 1963, in Cleveland, several members of a men's study group from Beth Israel–The West Temple, a decade-old religious center for Reform Jews, were alarmed by press reports and founded a committee that heralded the initiation of a transnational movement. The group had four cochairmen, representing the Jewish, Catholic, and Protestant activists and the Cleveland City Council. Initially called the Cleveland Committee on Soviet Anti-Semitism, the organization later changed its name to the Cleveland Council on Soviet Anti-Semitism as similarly named councils sprang up in other cities.[42]

The grassroots groups in the United States demanded more effective actions, on a national scale, by existing Jewish organizations as well as the establishment of a new centralized agency devoted exclusively to the cause of Soviet Jewry. The existing organizations working on behalf of Soviet Jews were distinctly unenthusiastic about the prospect of a new entity on their operational and fundraising turf.[43] Still, in the fall of 1963, a conference on the status of Soviet Jews led to the establishment the following year of the American Jewish Conference on Soviet Jewry. In the words of Solomon Andhil Fineberg, an executive of the conference, "After that there was no longer pressure brought within any Jewish circles, except the tiny pro-Communist element, to stop American Jews from pleading the cause of Soviet Jewry."[44]

Like the vast majority of Soviet people, domestic readers of *Sovetish Heymland* usually had no idea about the turmoil associated with the formation of the movement aimed at helping Jews in the USSR. The Soviet media, meanwhile, informed readers of "rampant anti-Semitism" in the USA.[45] America was also accused of sheltering Nazi criminals, including those who had participated in murdering Jews.[46] While in the 1960s admiration of America was widespread among the Soviet intelligentsia, especially its young portion, it was also the norm to have a sense of superiority over the capitalist system and a strong belief that Soviet-style socialism would ultimately prevail. Communists generally saw the whole world as prospective areas for expansion. In 1960 Emmanuil Kazakevich visited Rome and noted there in his diary:

> When [socialist] revolution takes place in Italy, we'll start sending there, at least for 10 days, every worker in turn—Russian workers and peasants. Pushkin once dreamt of going there. Gogol spent a few years there. Now we'll send workers there. We'll show them everything. I think that Italians will keep the Pope, because some of them will remain believers. They will not force him to become a member of the Party and trade union. The number of monks will decline, but several monasteries will remain.[47]

Aron Vergelis

Vergelis, five years younger than Kazakevich, was of a similar ideological mold. Born in 1918 in a Ukrainian Jewish shtetl, Vergelis grew up in the Jewish Autonomous Region. Like the majority of the re-settlers, the Vergelises moved to the Far East primarily for economic rather than ideological reasons. Aron became known as a local poetic talent and was sent to Moscow, where education in the Yiddish Department of the Teachers Training Institute became his and many other Yiddish literati's pathway to professional success. In 1940 three young Birobidzhan Yiddish writers, Vergelis, Kazakevich, and Buzi Miller, a 1936 alumnus of the same Teachers Training Institute, were accepted as members of the Writers Union. By that time Kazakevich and Vergelis already lived in Moscow; Miller, on the other hand, settled in Birobidzhan for good, not counting the years in Gulag.

After his postwar demobilization from the army, Vergelis occupied prominent positions in the Yiddish literary hierarchy, but was stuck in a dangerous and unemployed limbo during the last years of Stalin's life, when many of his literary peers faced execution or imprisonment. At the same time, Vergelis appeared on a list of 213 individuals "stored up" for future arrest in the event of a witch hunt against Jewish intellectuals. In February 1953 he came close to losing his status as a Communist Party candidate member; Stalin's death the following month cut short the process of his expulsion.[48]

Many of Vergelis's literary colleagues scoffed at him as an arrogant upstart and impugned his professional and personal integrity. Writers who spent years in prisons and camps generally looked down at those who remained untouched by repressions. The heavy burden of traumatic experiences and old personal scores added venom to the commonplace conflicts within this group, which had always been far from united and never spoke in one voice. For his part, Vergelis, a boisterous but humorless man, failed or perhaps never tried to find a route to the hearts of his fellow writers. He often distrusted or despised them, whereas they feared or at best grudgingly respected him but rarely liked him. In the absence of an alternative outlet for Yiddish literary works, conflicts with Vergelis were particularly consequential. Writers usually did not consider the low-circulation provincial newspaper *Birobidzhaner Shtern*, the only other Soviet Yiddish periodical, as a serious option. *Sovetish Heymland* enjoyed a much broader readership, paid relatively high royalties, and had a strong say in defining the program of book publications, in Yiddish and in Russian translation.

In November 1961 two abrasive characters, Vergelis and Smolar, his Warsaw counterpart, had a confrontation when Smolar came to Moscow and visited the office of the journal. They knew each other from the time when both were associated with the Jewish Anti-Fascist Committee. Smolar knew all or almost all the participants at the meeting; he had worked with some of them in the 1920s. During this "friendly" meeting, with many fine words said about *Folks-Shtime*'s role in "saving" Soviet Yiddish literary culture, Vergelis and several other Moscow writers sharply rebuked Smolar for "indiscriminately" publishing materials without approval from the Moscow-based Yiddish editors. For example, Irme Druker incurred their displeasure by writing in *Folks-Shtime* that Shmuel Halkin had passed the baton to veteran writer Joseph Rabin.[49] This was a particularly sensitive issue for Vergelis and his supporters whose opponents maintained that the launch of *Sovietish Heymland* had been purposefully delayed in expectation of Halkin's death.

From the very beginning, Vergelis kept a jealous eye on authors who were in a "nonexclusive relationship" with his journal. He sought to reestablish the conditions of the 1940s when no direct contacts existed between Soviet authors and non-Soviet Communist periodicals. Manuscripts would be sent only through such official channels as the Sovinformburo, succeeded by the Novosti Press Agency. For his part, Smolar saw himself as a custodian of *real* Leninism and an "elder brother" of the surviving Soviet Yiddish literati. He was thirteen years older than Vergelis and, like many Soviet Yiddish writers, saw him as an insolent upstart. Smolar met separately with those writers who opposed Vergelis. The alternative meeting took place at the apartment of Vergelis's archenemy, Moyshe Belenky. The latter enjoyed support among the opposition group and, it seems, remained convinced that he, rather than Vergelis, deserved to edit the Moscow journal. Smolar promised the writers that he would publish their works, disregarding Vergelis's complaints.[50] Ironically, the Warsaw newspaper became a kind of "dissident periodical"—not, of course, in terms of Communist ideology but vis-à-vis Vergelis's "domestic policy."

In November 1962 Konstantin Fedin, a prominent Russian novelist and the head of the Writers Union from 1959 to 1971, convened a meeting to discuss a letter that was signed by seventeen Yiddish writers. The spokesman of the dissenting group was the poet Joseph Kerler, who in the coming years would become known as a vociferous refusenik, or a person refused permission to emigrate. In his presentation, he argued that the majority in his circle were deeply worried about the appointment of Aron Vergelis as editor-in-chief. "Even before the appointment of this individual [*lichnost'*] as editor of *Sovetish Heymland*, a significant number of writers met with . . . secretaries of the Writers Union. We warned them then that comrade Vergelis was an utterly inappropriate candidate to edit a journal, especially one with international rather than exclusively Soviet significance. Vergelis is a neurotic man who maniacally overestimates his creative powers and stature."

In Kerler's words, Vergelis was "an opportunist willing to do anything for his career." Himself a former Gulag inmate, Kerler said that there was a time when Vergelis "was a terrifying figure," hinting at the latter's alleged complicity in the Stalinist repression of Yiddish writers. At the same time, Vergelis had his supporters. One of them, the prosaist Tevye Gen, said: "I think that in our literary milieu, comrade Vergelis is the most suitable person to be editor. He is a man of principle and a good organizer."

In his own response to the criticism, Vergelis switched the topic and spoke about his understanding of the concept of contemporary Soviet Yiddish literature.[51] This was Vergelis's hobbyhorse: to stress that contemporary themes and settings dominated in Soviet Yiddish literature, whereas the foreign Yiddish authors preferred to write about the past. (Later in that year, during a soul-searching meeting of the journal's editors and writers, Kerler was full of ridicule: "We are fortunate that the journal is a bimonthly rather than a weekly. Otherwise we would be obliged to write not only about a man of the 1960s, but about a Wednesday-at-thirty-five-minutes-past-five man.")[52]

Fedin, to all appearances, understood his mission as giving the displeased writers a chance to let off steam rather than making any organizational changes. Vergelis clearly remained the favorite of literary and party functionaries. Fedin summed up the discussion by admitting that Vergelis obviously had his faults, but referred to Jesus's words "Let him who is without sin cast the first stone." He added that "a fight is unavoidable in literary life" and appealed to the writers to follow the example of Sholem Aleichem, of his collaborative instincts and his love of his people.[53]

Letters denouncing Vergelis for various misdeeds continued to punctuate his career. An undated report (probably from the first half of 1967) reflects the work of a commission established to respond to a letter signed by "a group of Yiddish writers" whose names do not appear in the report. The screenwriter and critic Vladimir Sutyrin, who chaired the commission, was Russian and Communist through and through, though he was targeted as a "rootless cosmopolitan" in the late 1940s and early 1950s.[54] At the time of writing the report, Sutyrin headed the Party organization of the Writers Union's Moscow branch. The "group" had made three charges against Vergelis: first, his adherence to the theory of the "golden chain" in Yiddish literature—from religious texts to contemporary Soviet writings—qualified him as a Zionist and nationalist; second, his "flirtation" with foreign reactionaries undermined the journal's ideological standing; third, he had turned the journal into his personal fiefdom.[55]

Vergelis's adversaries knew that the timeless "golden chain" of the Jewish literary tradition, stretching from biblical texts to contemporary works, could annoy a dogmatic Communist ideologue, especially as Vergelis's "chain" contained links for such ideologically questionable writers as Hayim Nahman Bialik and Sholem Asch. Granted, Maxim Gorky, the guru of the Soviet literary world, had praised both writers, which made Vergelis's "brave" statements much less risky. He had also wisely excluded from the "chain" the entire "reactionary" American Yiddish literature, which he claimed had become so weak that it could not be "seriously taken into account." Jacob Glatstein, a Yiddish poet and essayist, was the only representative of the "right-wing" writers who had, with some reservations, earned a place in Vergelis's canon.[56]

The Sutyrin Commission, none of whose members could read Yiddish, had not detected nationalism or Zionism in Vergelis's writings available in Russian translations. Rather, it had concluded that Vergelis's ambitions seemed to outstrip his capacity. Thus, his theoretical articles reflected "the stark difference between his knowledge and the complex problems that he quite arrogantly had undertaken to solve." A bigger problem was the divisiveness of Vergelis's personality. This was the commission's main argument for finding a new editor for the journal. However, this recommendation was not acted on. Influential officials kept faith with Vergelis or simply did not see a person able to replace him. To a significant degree, it was Vergelis's international career that shored up his position.

The American Visit

Vergelis became known to a broad international public at the end of 1963, when he visited the USA as a member of a delegation of Soviet intellectuals whose official mission was to mark the thirtieth anniversary of establishing diplomatic relations between the USA and the USSR. The State Department, however, made a point of not celebrating this event and regarded the group as tourists because their visit was not part of any official cultural-exchange program. Rather, it was sponsored by the Institute of Soviet-American Relations, a body established in Moscow in 1961 as a so-called "public" or ostensibly nongovernmental organization.[57]

The voyage launched Vergelis's quarter-century career as globe-trotting Cold War propagandist. Previously, or at least since 1956, such international assignments, which were rare and therefore particularly estimable in the insulated Soviet society, remained a prerogative of the most highly decorated Jewish war veteran—the two-time Hero of the Soviet Union, General David Dragunsky.[58] Yet a general did not fit into the group of writers, journalists, and scholars. Importantly, Vergelis was a war veteran too, although he had served as a sergeant rather than a tank-brigade commander. *Morgn-Frayhayt* ran an adulatory piece about Vergelis, based on a reprint of a 1941 article describing his wartime exploits.[59]

Vergelis's visit to the USA was the first by a Soviet Jewish cultural figure since the famous 1943 tour by Solomon Mikhoels and the Yiddish poet Itsik Fefer as leaders of the Jewish Anti-Fascist Committee. Significantly, Vergelis announced that he did not come as a representative of Soviet Jews.[60] Indeed, he was seen instead as a mouthpiece of the Kremlin's policy toward Jews. As such he garnered a brighter spotlight than all the other members of the delegation. This was paradoxical because on the Soviet scale he was, in fact, a big fish in a small pond compared with such people in the delegation as the popular young poet Robert Rozhdestvensky, or Boris Polevoy, the classic socialist-realist writer with clout in the Kremlin and editor of the mass-readership journal *Iunost'* (Youth). The *New York Times* remarked that Vergelis's appearance in the United States was "of interest against the background of American allegations about limitations of Jewish culture in Russia."[61] Characteristically, upon the group's arrival, American customs officers decided, from what they heard from journalists, that not Nikolai Blokhin, president of the Medical Academy, but Vergelis was the headman.[62]

Gabriel Reiner, the owner of the New York–based Cosmos Travel Bureau and a pioneer of American tourism in the post-Stalinist Soviet Union, was wrong when he assured Vergelis that America would show him warm hospitality.[63] The largely hostile reception given to Vergelis and his cotravelers had partly to do with the political strain caused by the concurrent arrest in Moscow of the Yale professor Frederick C. Barghoorn, who used to work there in the American embassy in the 1940s and later participated in a program of interviewing former Soviet citizens in West Germany. The KGB picked Barghoorn as a candidate to trade for Soviet spies arrested in the United States.[64] The assassination of President John Kennedy in

November 1963 also affected the delegation's program; several of the previously planned engagements had to be canceled.

Meanwhile, Jewish organizations orchestrated a broad boycott aimed specifically at Vergelis. It seemed, apparently, expedient to select a figure who would personify Soviet policy toward the Jews, and to attack this policy by discrediting its personification. No doubt, a writer was a more cogent target than Dragunsky, a transparently heroic even if rigidly dogmatic Communist figure. Vergelis's opponents had a strong argument against him: he not only survived but was not even arrested. It is known that Vergelis once asked to compile a list of Yiddish writers who, like him, had not experienced incarceration—to show that his case was not unique by any means. This tally appeared in some publications: of the 140 Soviet Yiddish literati active in the 1960s, 80 remained untouched by the arrests.[65]

The British historian Max Beloff, at that time an Oxford professor, fired one of the first salvos. His letter, published in the London *Jewish Chronicle* on 22 November 1963, aimed at character assassination. Beloff, born into a family of Jewish immigrants from Russia, warned American Jews that the Moscow Yiddish editor's name was "associated in a circumstantial way with the purge of the Soviet Jewish intelligentsia between 1948 and 1953, of which he is one of the few survivors."[66] On the same day as the publication of Beloff's letter, the *New York Times* introduced Vergelis as "the Soviet Government's leading spokesman on Jewish affairs," who "had survived in the Soviet Union because he had made an accommodation with Stalin when other Jews were being murdered by the regime."[67] In his extended remarks made for the *Congressional Record*, Seymour Halpern, a Republican congressman, berated Vergelis for calling "himself a Jewish poet" and being "the puppet who edits the Soviet Union's only Yiddish-language magazine . . . a blatant propaganda instrument which operates against true Jewish interests."[68] The Synagogue Council of America, founded in 1926 to bridge the three primary religious movements within Judaism in the United States—Orthodox, Conservative, and Reform—cautioned American Jews "not to fall into the trap" of one of the "architects of the destruction of Judaism" in the Soviet Union. The Jewish Labor Committee and the daily *Forverts* joined the boycott. Both organizations were consistent in their anti-Sovietism, having similarly boycotted the 1943 delegation of the Jewish Anti-Fascist Committee.

The characterization of Vergelis as a member of the Soviet secret police[69] shaped Elie Wiesel's attitude toward the Moscow editor. In 1965, when Wiesel visited the Soviet Union with a fact-finding mission organized by Israel's Liaison Bureau, he "would not appear at the editorial offices of *Sovetish Heimland.* Whatever Aron Vergelis and his comrades were prepared to tell me they had already repeated countless times before to visitors from the United States, France, and Israel."[70] In 1976, addressing in Brussels the Second World Conference on Soviet Jewry, Wiesel was ready to forgive all Soviet Jewish public figures' anti-Zionism, presenting Vergelis as the only object of special loathing: "He, I believe, is an enemy of the Jewish people and should be treated as such."[71] In his 1981 novel *The Testament*, devoted to the tragedy of Yiddish culture in the Soviet Union, Wiesel included an ad hominem satire of Vergelis: "Among the Jewish writers one alone infuriated me: a young poet, redheaded, arrogant, opportunistic, who signed his poems Arke Gelis. . . . He took part, uninvited, in conversations. He was not trusted: voices dropped the moment he appeared." Moreover, during the war Gelis wore the uniform of a secret-police major.[72]

Sober voices among American Jewish journalists suggested easing off the media overdrive. Jack Fishbein, editor and publisher of the Chicago Jewish weekly *The Sentinel*, who met Vergelis in Moscow in 1961 and found him ignorant about virtually all aspects of American life, took the view that the boycott was counterproductive: "We see nothing wrong with permitting him to tour our great Jewish institutions such as our hospitals, old people's homes, etc., and to see the manifold contributions we have made to American culture. What are we afraid of? Nothing he can say or do is going to subvert us or weaken our determination to protest the treatment of Soviet Jews."[73]

The poet and literary critic Jacob Glatstein wrote that the Moscow editor was in an impossible situation, quoting Proverbs 18:21 to make his point: "The tongue has the power of life and death." Vergelis had to control his tongue, which meant that he simply could not provide truthful answers to many difficult questions.[74] As a result, even the editor of *Jewish Currents*, a Communist-leaning journal, admitted that Vergelis "left many questions unanswered (for instance, about the blood-libels against Soviet Jews in five places in three years and about anti-Semitic features of anti-religious propaganda)."[75]

Nahum Goldmann, chair of both the World Zionist Organization and the World Jewish Congress, characterized the boycott of Vergelis as "stupidity" (*narishkayt*). He also said that he had no proof to support the allegations of Vergelis's complicity in Stalinist suppressions.[76] Goldmann believed that "quiet diplomacy" could be more productive than noisy protests organized by grassroots organizations. On 28 October 1959, the Parisian *Le Monde* quoted his words in an article title: "We do not wish to make the Jewish problem in the USSR an element of the Cold War." According to Zachariah Shuster, director of the American Jewish Committee's European office, Goldmann followed "his own policy with regard to the USSR, a policy of dignified pleading rather than vigorous protest."[77] In Cleveland the Soviet delegation was hosted by Cyrus Eaton, a powerful financier and an advocate of rapprochement with the Soviet Union. Still, "progressive" (as Communists and Communist sympathizers preferred to call themselves) activists, whose enthusiasm for *Sovetish Heymland* was strongest, gave Vergelis a particularly hearty welcome in the USA.[78] They were glad to listen to his words that "forced assimilation was a crime" and that he and his like did not believe that assimilation among Soviet Jews was so far advanced that there was no future for Jewish culture.[79] Vergelis implicitly rebuked earlier statements by General Dragunsky that Soviet Jews faced full natural assimilation.[80] In the spring of 1961 Vergelis committed to paper his understanding, which at least partly reflected reality, of the contemporary Soviet Jew's hyphenated—or Jewish-spiced—spiritual world: the opera *Eugene Onegin* and the Jewish folk song; an anniversary celebration of Sholem Aleichem, and the latest works of Mikhail Sholokhov or the Kazakh writer Mukhtar Auezov.[81]

Novick and the circle around his newspaper organized for Vergelis an intensive program of meetings and sightseeing. Like many other Yiddish activists on the political left, Novick regarded *Sovetish Heymland* as a journal "obtained by [his] pleading and sobbing."[82] Hundreds of *Morgn-Frayhayt* readers formed the main contingent of the Moscow journal's subscribers in the United States. However, despite the efforts of Vergelis's "progressive" friends, the trip turned into a grueling experience. During a press conference held at the Soviet embassy, Vergelis "compared himself to another Yiddish writer [he clearly meant Sholem Aleichem] who had been accused of anti-Semitism for 'truthfully reflecting the life of Jewish people.'"[83] Virtually unembarrassable, he laughed off the criticism piled on him, arguing that he did not care about it because his experience of spending time in the Birobidzhan taiga had trained him to feel his face being beaten with tree branches.[84] Although he never visited Birobidzhan after the late 1940s, he never missed mentioning his adolescence there as a school of endurance and resilience. Now, thousands of miles from the taiga, Vergelis turned to whataboutism, chastising the negatives of capitalist societies instead of explaining the faults of Soviet policy and life.[85]

From Obscurity to Notoriety

Ironically, the anti-Vergelis campaign counterproductively and disproportionally raised the profile of the editor whose journal's readership did not amount even to 1 percent of the Soviet Jewish population. Many Soviet Jews had never heard of the journal or of Vergelis. The few thousand copies of the journal that arrived in America and other countries also could not exert any tangible impact on public opinion, especially as its issues, in the 1960s at least, carried mainly literary rather than overtly political works, none of which was destined to make a big splash in the world of letters. In fact, only Vergelis's travel notes, many times revised (with deletion of the names of former "friends" turned "renegades") and reprinted in Russian under the title *Sixteen Countries, Including Monaco*, had a high number of readers.[86] Foreign travelogues were a popular read among people without prospects of traveling abroad.

In his report to the Central Committee, Vergelis analyzed the reaction of the American press to his trip. He tried to validate development of Soviet Yiddish cultural activities, arguing that this would be an effective answer to Zionist propaganda. In particular, he suggested increasing the annual number of issues of *Sovetish Heymland*, establishing in Moscow a Yiddish theater, and publishing more books in Yiddish. Indeed, in 1965 *Sovetish Heymland*, initially published six times a year, turned into a monthly, and the Moscow publisher Sovetskii pisatel began to produce Yiddish books by contemporary authors whereas previously its program had focused on posthumous publication.

Vergelis also considered it important to relax control over Jewish religious communities and to intensify cultural exchange with foreign Jewish organizations.[87] In the beginning of 1964, Gabriel Reiner conveyed the Soviet authorities' decision to admit parcels of matzo mailed from abroad.[88] It is not clear, however, whether Vergelis's report had any influence on the decision to relax the ban on production of matzo and on obtaining it from other countries. More likely, it was "atonement" for publication of Trofim Kichko's 1963 pamphlet *Judaism without Embellishment* (see pp. 151–52). Ironically, since the state controlled the entire publishing industry, the state also was responsible for dealing with embarrassing glitches that occurred in the published books and periodicals.

From America Vergelis went (or, better, was sent) to Paris, where he did not face a boycott. Rather, a reception given in his honor was attended by top figures in the Jewish community, including Admiral Louis Kahn, president of Israelite Central Consistory, and André Blumel, former president of the French Zionist Organization.[89] He had an extensive meeting with Armand Kaplan, the head of the French section of the World Jewish Congress who reported the results to Nahum Goldmann.[90] In his report to the Central Committee, Vergelis suggested inviting Goldmann to visit the Soviet Union, underlining the latter's rejection of rabid anti-Sovietism and critique of Israeli prime minister Ben-Gurion.[91] This recommendation, however, did not find support in the corridors of power.

A year after his first foreign trip, Vergelis again became newsworthy, this time in association with Bertrand Russell. In May 1964 the British philosopher received through the Israeli Liaison Bureau, or Nativ, a letter from a Soviet Jewish war veteran asking him "to look into the problem of the forced assimilation of Jews that is taking place in the Soviet Union."[92] In a postscript, the writer of the letter, whose name was withheld, asked that Russell address all questions concerning this problem to *Sovetish Heymland*. Russell complied with this advice and wrote a letter to Vergelis, voicing his concern about the Jews' "right to full cultural life in the Soviet Union." A year earlier, in February 1963, Russell had written to—and received a widely publicized reply from—Khrushchev about "the official encouragement of anti-Semitism" in the Soviet Union.[93] This might seem as if Russell and the Nativ were trying to put Vergelis on a par with the Soviet top leader. This reflected a bizarre phenomenon: both the Soviet and Israeli agitprop had anointed a cultural-cum-propagandist figure of modest influence and stature to play a central political role on the Jewish periphery of the political theater of the Cold War. No doubt, Vergelis was happy with his role on the political proscenium because it helped him shed the reputation of an upstart. Now, with the clout of an internationally known (and notorious) cold warrior, he was head and shoulders above the rest of his colleagues.

In his retort to Russell, published in the September-October 1964 issue of *Sovetish Heymland*, Vergelis put on airs and pounced on the sad state of Yiddish culture in England. Then he expatiated about a new type of Soviet Jew, one who was "a full and equal member of the great, friendly workers' collective," and argued that "the actual needs of Soviet Jewry with respect to Jewish culture are being satisfied." In sum, Vergelis contended that Russell was being exploited by people who used the campaign about "the allegedly unsolved Jewish problem in the Soviet Union" as a smokescreen for diverting "attention from the virulent racism and anti-Semitism" in the West.[94]

Racism and anti-Semitism in the Western countries and the "slander" about discrimination against Soviet Jews formed the agenda of a roundtable discussion presented in *Sovetish Heymland*'s final issue for 1963. Still, during the first decade of the journal's existence Vergelis, presumably following official instructions, sought to underline its exclusively literary nature.[95] The roundtable material, the letter to Russell, and a remark by David Dragunsky, in issue no. 1 in 1962, about the "cutthroat aggression against Egypt" were rare examples of political polemics in the 1960s. An American critic, discussing the first decade of the journal's existence, stressed its "sedate tone" in comparison with Soviet Yiddish periodicals published before and after World War II.[96]

In December 1966 Vergelis visited Britain. The *Guardian* remarked: "All the signs are that (he) will get as cold a shoulder from British Jews . . . as he did from their American cousins on a recent trip to the U.S. Vergelis, here on a Society for Cultural Relations visit, is a minor poet from Birobidzhan and just about the only official Jew allowed west of the Iron Curtain. With good reason. He's a slavish follower of the Kremlin line on Soviet Jewry."

Indeed, as in the United States, he was mainly boycotted by British Jewish organizations.[97]

Yiddish Scholarship

Despite the devastating losses endured by Yiddish literary circles during World War II and the postwar Stalinist repression, *Sovetish Heymland* could always rely on scores of contributors, including literary scholars. In one of his first interviews, Vergelis stated: "We are allotting much space in our magazine to problems of literary theory and criticism."[98] Initially, Nokhem Oyslender, a central figure in Soviet Yiddish literary life from its early days, acted as the doyen of the critical guild heading the journal's literary-criticism section. However, a year after the journal was launched, he died.

Hersh (Grigory) Remenik, Oyslender's replacement, belonged to the generation schooled during the Soviet period. He graduated from the Yiddish Department of the Odessa Pedagogical Institute and worked as a teacher in an old Jewish agricultural colony in Ukraine. In 1934 the Yiddish Department of the Moscow Pedagogical Institute admitted him as a graduate student, and in 1937, after defending his dissertation on Sholem Aleichem's novellas, he received the academic title of candidate of philological sciences. (The advanced academic degrees of "candidate" and "doctor" were introduced in the Soviet Union in 1934.) Two years later, however, Remenik was arrested. Following his liberation and legal rehabilitation, around 1955, he taught Russian literature at the pedagogical institute in Yaroslavl, an old Russian city.

Remenik was not the only Yiddish literary scholar who had to rebrand himself as a specialist in another field and find a job at a provincial institution of higher education. His fellow student, Moyshe Notovich, also a recipient of the degree of candidate of philological sciences, settled in Kazan and built a reputation as a specialist in the field of teaching Russian at Tatar schools. He was arrested in January 1953, but in the summer of that year released "owing to the unproven nature of the charges." Stalin's death in March 1953 made the charges no longer relevant.

After moving to Moscow to replace Oyslender as head of the literary-criticism section, Remenik played an important role in shaping the literary-critical politics of the journal and engaging other literary specialists. In *Sovetish Heymland*'s "pale of literary settlement," critics and historians could analyze works by authors who were of no interest to the rest of Soviet academia. Outside the "pale," the list of Yiddish writers usually ended up where it started: Sholem Aleichem. In 1966 *Sovetish Heymland* reported that in December 1965 Remenik had organized a "scientific session" devoted to Y. L. Peretz, marking the fiftieth anniversary of the classic writer's death.

Hillel Aleksandrov, who came to the "session" from Leningrad, began his academic career in Minsk as a specialist in social-demographic aspects of Jewish life, but in 1933 he settled in Leningrad and worked there as a professor at the Institute of History, Philosophy, and Linguistics. Arrested in 1937, he was not rehabilitated until 1956 and then taught at the Oriental Faculty of Leningrad University. He wrote in *Sovetish Heymland* about his archival findings, most notably about the legacy of Israel Tsinberg, the preeminent historian of Jewish literature whose death he witnessed in the Gulag.[99]

Khatskl Nadel and Oyzer Holdes (born Holdesheym) came to the Peretz conference from Kharkiv. They were holdovers from the time, until 1934, when the city was the capital of Soviet Ukraine and, as such, housed Jewish cultural, educational, and publishing organizations. Both were arrested in 1951 and were able to return to Kharkiv only after several years in the Gulag. Holdes was reinstated as a member of the Writers Union, whereas Nadel renewed his work as a bibliographer, hailed as the founder of the local academic tradition in the field of bibliography.[100] Irme Druker, who came to the conference from Odessa, was also incarcerated from 1950 to 1956. His book on Mendele Moykher-Sforim, *The Grandfather Mendele*, appeared in Yiddish in Warsaw in 1964.

De-Stalinization was a personal topic for Remenik. In his article for the *Concise Literary Encyclopedia*, he wrote about the heavy blow dealt to Yiddish literature "during the period of Stalin's personality cult."[101] In the January 1965 issue of *Sovetish Heymland*, he pointed to two "wrong" approaches to Stalinism: advocates of the first approach argued that there was no need to return to this topic because the Party had successfully eradicated the mistakes of that time, whereas advocates of the second approach did not believe that the de-Stalinization campaign could last long and therefore were leery of participating in it. Remenik insisted on a serious attitude toward de-Stalinization and welcomed the first attempts by journal contributors Shira Gorshman, Hirsh Dobin, Note Lurie, and Riva (Rivke) Rubina to write on this topic.[102] In 1965 it was still possible to mention the "victims of the personality cult" of Stalin. Soon, however, neither Remenik nor other writers would return to this theme, which became taboo in the Brezhnev era. As a result, for instance, the anti-Stalinist novel *In yenem yor* (In That Year), set in 1937, remained unpublished until 1988, though Joseph Rabin (1900–1987), himself a former Gulag prisoner, finished writing it toward the end of Khrushchev's Thaw.

A 1966 letter by Vladimir Semichastnyi, head of the KGB, illustrates the situation in the mid-1960s. Semichastnyi wrote to the Ideological Commission of the Central Committee about several evenings held at the Moscow-based Central House of Writers, dedicated to the memory of Jewish men of letters who had suffered Stalinist repression. At the Markish evening, on 8 December 1965, a telegram was read from Ilya Ehrenburg, who asserted that "one must not kill singing birds and poets." At the evening in memory of Kvitko, on 5 January 1966, "a poem was read by the Jewish nationalist writer Iosif [Joseph] Kerler, who for a long period has been requesting an exit visa to Israel. It ended with the words: 'How could the traitors take aim at his face? Who raised them? Where are they from?' Many present, including those on the panel, were in tears. These evenings were attended by personnel of the Israeli embassy in Moscow, who went to great lengths to receive invitations to the Central House of Writers."[103]

This poem, which appeared in the April 1965 issue of *Sovetish Heymland*, was Kerler's last publication in the journal. Soon he was dismissed from the Writers Union, though not for the Kvitko poem but for his request to emigrate to Israel. Needless to say, the KGB's reaction mirrored the Kremlin's negative attitude toward gatherings and writings devoted to the perished writers.

The Jewish academic centers established by the early Soviet state functioned almost exclusively in Yiddish and had eclipsed or subdued the remnants of Jewish studies pursued by independent organizations of the pre-1917 period. In Kyiv the most vigorous of the new centers developed ultimately into the Institute of Jewish Proletarian Culture (IJPC), a structural unit of the Ukrainian Academy of Sciences. By 1934 the IJPC had on its payroll over seventy people in academic and administrative roles. Two years later, however, Stalin's purges consumed the IJPC and sent many of its employees to prison to be later sentenced to death or the Gulag.[104] In

Minsk the authorities similarly destroyed the academic Institute of National Minorities, which mainly dealt with Jewish-related research.[105]

The Kyiv IJPC had something of an afterlife: in the fall of 1936 the authorities permitted the formation of a small academic unit called the Bureau (*kabinet*) for Research on Jewish Literature, Language, and Folklore. The Bureau endured until 1949, when it fell victim to a campaign that targeted the remaining Jewish institutions. In the same year, the authorities closed the Lithuanian Jewish Museum, which was established in Vilnius soon after the city's liberation from the Germans.[106] The year 1950 saw the closing of the Department of Assyrian and Hebrew studies at the Oriental Faculty of Leningrad University.[107] In Tbilisi the Historical and Ethnographic Museum of Georgian Jews survived longer, but its turn to be phased out came in 1952.[108] In the post-Stalinist Soviet Union, no institutions or programs for studying Jews and Judaism were in existence, apart from small-scale Hebrew courses and Oriental studies at universities and research centers in Moscow, Leningrad, and Tbilisi.

The bulk of the output produced by Yiddish-language academic institutions from the 1920s to the 1940s later became irrelevant to the radically changed societal, linguistic, and ideological environment of Jewish life. The emphasis in the research was on serving the needs of the then existing network for Yiddish culture and education. With the liquidation of the network, the research results remained largely ignored. However, this does not apply to the legacy of the momentous works in the field of Jewish ethnomusicology left by Moisei (Moyshe) Beregovski.

In 1927 Beregovski initiated the establishment of the Commission for Jewish Folk Music Research at the Department of Jewish Culture of the Ukrainian Academy of Sciences, and, from 1929, he headed research on musical folklore at the IJPC and—after its dismantling—at the Bureau. The purges of the 1930s spared him, but he did not avoid incarceration in the 1950s. Released from the Gulag in 1955, Beregovski returned to Kyiv and, until his death, prepared his collections for publication. Although Soviet musicology generally shunned Jewish themes, the attitude toward folk music was different.[109] As a result, Beregovski's two books posthumously saw publication: in 1962 the Moscow publishing house Sovetskii kompozitor (Soviet Composer) produced his *Jewish Folk Songs*, edited by composer and music critic Sergei Aksiuk, formerly editor-in-chief of Sovetskii kompozitor, and in 1987, the same publisher put out *Jewish Folk Instrumental Music*, edited by ethnomusicologist Max Goldin, who taught at the Conservatory of Riga.

Meanwhile, *Sovetish Heymland* began to play the supplementary role of an outlet, often the only one available, for publications of popular and, increasingly over the years, serious academic essays, most notably on various aspects of Yiddish philology. Abraham Brumberg, the first editor of the journal *Problems of Communism*, characterized Vergelis as "the most quixotic of all the figures on the contemporary Soviet Yiddish literary scene" and as a person whose endeavors counteracted rather than encouraged the process of assimilation.[110] Indeed, Vergelis aimed, mainly in vain, at expanding his operation into an umbrella organization for Yiddish culture. He and his colleagues seriously considered themselves keepers of the fire of Yiddish culture and either stubbornly ignored the fact that their work appealed to a declining number of people or sincerely believed that all was not lost, that younger people would come to warm themselves at the fire.[111] True, in this sense they had much in common with Yiddish writers and cultural activists in other countries. The journal formed a small "pale of Jewish cultural settlement," whose internal life remained little visible even to Soviet Jews, the prevalent majority of whom could not or would not read it. Yet the journal acted as an umbrella for various projects, including the preparation of a Russian-Yiddish dictionary.

In 1948 the Kyiv Bureau's dictionary manuscript, the product of many years of work, was already in the hands of the Moscow Jewish publishing house Der Emes. However, in November of that same year the publishing house stopped operating, as it was closed down concurrently with the liquidation of the Jewish Anti-Fascist Committee. In January 1949 the secret police arrested Elye Spivak, the Bureau's director and editor-in-chief of the dictionary, and transported him to a prison in Moscow, where he would die. Two months later Chaim Loytsker, a senior scholar, was also arrested and received a sentence of fifteen years of hard labor. The year 1951 saw the arrest of two other dictionary compilers, Moyshe Maidansky and Ruven Lerner, both sentenced to ten years' incarceration. The logic of the selection of targets for persecution often escaped contemporaries and remains a puzzle for historians. In any case, Moyshe Shapiro, the leading linguist of the Bureau, was never arrested. He left Kyiv to teach Russian philology at the pedagogical institute in the city of Tiraspol in Moldavia (the breakaway Transnistria territory in contemporary Moldova).

In the early 1960s Vergelis enthusiastically supported the idea of reviving the dictionary project and allocated office space for Shapiro, who had moved to Moscow after retiring from teaching in Tiraspol. Shapiro and other surviving linguists began revising and refocusing the dictionary, which, in its original design, was intended for users with a good knowledge of Yiddish. By the mid-1960s it had to address a different audience, including people who wanted to learn the language or lacked the means to express the realities of modern life. In addition, it was necessary to take into account new Yiddish dictionaries published outside the Soviet Union by that time. In 1965 a reworked version was submitted to the publishing house Sovetskaia Entsiklopedia (Soviet Encyclopedia).

Shapiro and other linguists associated with *Sovetish Heymland* rejected the militant purism practiced by some of their American colleagues, who were always on the warpath against etymologically "unacceptable" words. According to Shapiro, the German, Hebrew, or Slavic origin of a word was of less importance than its authenticity (i.e., longevity and naturalness), stylistic adequacy, and clarity. Although *Sovetish Heymland* toed the official Soviet line of rejecting the notion of a worldwide Jewish nation, the journal, a publication with a cultural-diplomatic mission, sought to attract foreign readers. Therefore, it did not try to erect an artificial wall between the Soviet and non-Soviet varieties of Yiddish. Shapiro even doubted the value of the notion of Soviet Yiddish. He wrote: "This definition never had nor could have any terminological meaning, since it never meant a new quality of a literary language different from the literary Yiddish outside the borders of the Soviet Union. In fact, there were only a few peculiarities which could justify speaking (even conditionally) of a specific Soviet Yiddish style."[112] Significantly, although the journal and other Moscow Yiddish publications did not reintroduce the traditional spelling of Hebrew words, the final consonant letters characteristic of Hebrew and non-Soviet Yiddish reappeared in the journal after three decades of abandoning them as a result of radical orthographic reform.[113]

The compilers hoped the dictionary would come out in 1967. In June 1966 *Soviet Weekly*, the Soviet embassy's information journal in Britain, informed readers that an academic Russian-Yiddish dictionary was to be published "shortly." In July *Folks-Shtime* carried a report from its correspondent in Kyiv that a contract for its publication had been signed in June. In the event, the publisher's guidelines demanded serious, time-consuming improvements.

At some stage, the text incorporated a clandestine epitaph to the leading figures in the Anti-Fascist Committee executed on 12 August 1952: the combination of words "on the twelfth of August" illustrated the usage of "twelfth," although examples of usage did not accompany any other ordinal numbers. The dictionary, which finally appeared in 1984, was, in a sense, a memorial to the Soviet Yiddish linguists of the IJPC and the Bureau. None of them lived to see this publication completed by Moyshe (Moyni) Shulman, a retired senior editor of *Sovetish Heymland*.[114]

9

MEMORY OF WAR

The Treatment of the Holocaust

Prior to 1961, when the journal *Sovetish Heymland* began to appear in Moscow, discussions of Holocaust-related writings took place in the pages of Warsaw Yiddish periodicals, the newspaper *Folks-Shtime* and the journal *Yidishe Shriftn*. Some Soviet writers attempted to instruct their Polish counterparts how to treat war-related topics. In 1956 Motl Grubyan, a Moscow poet, published in *Folks-Shtime* a poem in which he persuaded his fellow literati "not to bathe in grief / not to fill the sail with hatred."[1] In the same year, the Chernivtsi-based poet Hirsh Bloshtein, a frequent contributor to the *Folks-Shtime* literary section, criticized his Warsaw colleagues for their pessimism, which, he said, found expression in the continuous mourning for victims of the Holocaust.[2] David Sfard, the Party-appointed leader of Yiddish writers in Communist Poland, responded that it was not the editors' mission to dictate the degree of pessimism or optimism, especially as Jewish writers had valid reasons to be pessimistic.[3]

Soviet writers, however, were supposed to be optimists, which meant focusing their work on contemporary, postwar topics. The very first issue of *Sovetish Heymland* featured a poem by Joseph (Yosl) Lerner calling for enjoying the bright present: "Enough wailing already! Enough wailing already! / The dawns are so wonderful . . . / You cannot revive the dear martyrs!" In 1962 this poem was reprinted as the lyrics of a song written by Vladimir Shainskii, later one of the most popular Soviet song composers. That same 1962 issue also featured an article, "Where Is the Pulse Beating?," by veteran literary critic Oyzer Holdes, who argued that the works published in the journal had to express "the spirit of the time." In other words, the Soviet writers were encouraged to focus on contemporary topics.

Alexander Pomerantz, an American commentator, formerly a Communist Yiddish poet and scholar himself (he defended a dissertation during his stint, 1933–35, in Kyiv at the Institute of Proletarian Jewish Culture), attempted to categorize the contents of the first two issues of *Sovetish Heymland.* According to him, 17 of the 85 poems and 5 of the 24 stories were "purely ideological." Among the remaining 68 "nonideological" poems Pomerantz found 13 devoted to the Holocaust, 16 love poems, and 39 poems focused on such topics as landscape descriptions and daily occurrences. Among the 19 "nonideological" prosaic texts, 6 were about the Holocaust, 4 were love stories, and 9 portrayed daily Jewish life.[4]

There is no point in even looking for the word Holocaust in the vocabulary of official Soviet discourse. While generally rarely used in the 1950s and 1960s,[5] this term remained ideologically impermissible in the Soviet Union. Such a distinct designation emphasized that the Nazis considered Jews their prime targets, whereas, according to the official line, Jewish suffering was no more than part of the common Soviet wartime agonies. Jews simply *happened to be* the first in line. Boris Rosenthal, the protagonist of Vasily Grossman's 1943 story "The Old Teacher," one of the first works of fiction about the Holocaust in any language, spelled out the Soviet official stance:

> The Fascists have created an all-European system of forced labor and, to keep the prisoners obedient, they have constructed a huge ladder of oppression. The Dutch are worse off than the Danes, the French are worse off than the Dutch, the Czechs are worse off than the French. Things are still worse for the Greeks and the Serbs, worse still for the Poles, and last of all come the Ukrainians and Russians. These are the rungs of the ladder of forced labor. . . . And then, at the very bottom of this huge, many-storied prison is the abyss to which the Germans have condemned the Jews. Their fate has to terrify all the forced laborers of Europe, so that even the most terrible fate will seem happiness in comparison with that of the Jews.[6]

That reflected, also, the ideology-shapers' apprehension that intense Holocaust narratives might generate or reinforce among Soviet Jews undesirable religious, Zionist, and other "nationalist" sentiments and intentions. Notoriously, for instance, the authorities of Belorussia did not want to recognize that the young member of a clandestine group, hanged by the Nazis in Minsk in June 1941, was a Jewish woman named Masha Bruskina, a niece of Zair Azgur, one of the most celebrated artists in Belorussia. Photos of that first public execution in the occupied Soviet territories became important symbols of the population's resistance, and during the entire Soviet period Party functionaries preferred to describe the heroine as an "Unknown Girl."[7] The enormous loss of life in the Soviet Union, reaching twenty million in the official underestimates of the 1960s,[8] made the task of minimizing Jewish victimhood easier.

Significantly, a Soviet citizen, who usually did not have access to overarching descriptions of the Holocaust, often perceived it as a series of *local events*. In a Jewish family circle, for instance, the focus was on the tragedy that took place in a particular town or city, where relatives or otherwise close people had been murdered by the Nazis and their collaborators. In this picture, the Jewish aspect of the war, on a broader scale of six million victims, caused associations predominantly with the Nazi atrocities in Poland or Western Europe rather than in the Soviet Union.

The estimate of six million Jewish victims first appeared in Ilya Ehrenburg's article published in *Pravda* on 17 December 1944.[9] Earlier that year, in April, Ehrenburg wrote: "We [the Soviet people] want to make sure that the Germans will never fight again. Not only the followers of Hitler, but the rebellious generals of the Reichswehr [German army], who hope to be able in 1964 to correct the mistakes of 1944."[10] A decade later, following the USA's decision to sponsor the formation of the Bundeswehr (West German army), Clifton Daniel, the *New York Times*'s Moscow correspondent, reported that the "menace of German militarism" and its damage to the prospect of peaceful coexistence dominated the Soviet discussion of international relations. Daniel referred, in particular, to Ehrenburg, who compared the American government's move to buying a revolver in an attempt to solve mutual problems, whereas it would be more adequate to put coffee or a bottle of wine on the table.[11] Like many other Soviet writers, Ehrenburg, by that time an important figure in Moscow-sponsored peace campaigns, stressed that the Soviet people, more than any other, knew the horrors of war from personal experience and hated it more than any other.[12]

Meanwhile, the Soviet media instrumentalized the Holocaust topic in publications aiming to show how former military officers and functionaries of the Nazi regime had not been brought to justice. This happened allegedly, and in many cases clearly, because of the negligence, manipulation, or protection of state institutions and authorities in Western countries, most notably the German Federal Republic. Soviet periodicals published accounts, sometimes detailed, as irrefutable evidence of the atrocities committed by the individuals in question. Thus, paradoxically, an anti-Western critique led, collaterally, to the appearance of Holocaust-related material in newspapers, including the central Party and state dailies *Pravda* and *Izvestiia*, read by millions in the Soviet Union.

In some cases Holocaust themes appeared in Soviet media and cultural products in coordination with East German (GDR) propagandists. The latter saw Adolf Eichmann's 1961 trial in Jerusalem as a valuable gift for their ideological campaigns at a time when economic and ideological discontent drove hundreds of thousands of East Germans to move to the West. This was relatively easy to do before 12 August 1961, when the Berlin Wall sealed the border. Former Nazi officials remained the principal target of the East German propaganda campaigns and their reflection in Soviet reporting also before 1961. Show trials were one of the methods used in the ideological offensive.

The first show trial, in 1960, in absentia, was against Theodor Oberländer, a member of the Bundestag and the federal minister for displaced persons, refugees, and victims of war. While Oberländer attracted close attention in the Soviet press, Jews were rarely mentioned as victims of the Nachtigall and Bergmann Battalions, which had been formed from local collaborators and operated under his command. In addition to the press assault, a documentary entitled *You Are a Criminal, Mr. Oberländer!* (*Vy prestupnik, Oberlender!*) was released in Moscow in 1960. The Ukrainian troops of the Nachtigall Battalion were accused of murdering civilians, including Jews, notably in Lviv. Oberländer served also as commandant of Nalchik, the capital city of the Kabardino-Balkar Autonomous Republic in the northern Caucasus.[13] Much was written later that Oberländer, certainly a disciplined Nazi, appeared nevertheless as the person who effectively saved many Mountain Jews by convincing SS officers that this non-Ashkenazic group only practiced Judaism, but in terms of their race—a cornerstone of Nazi ideology—had nothing to do with Jews and therefore were not legitimate targets for the program of racial purification.[14]

In the beginning of 1963, the Soviet press decried the unwillingness of German authorities to allow Berta Gindelevich and Lazar Goldin, survivors of Nazi persecution, to participate as witnesses in a trial in the West German city of Koblenz. Among the war criminals in the dock was Georg Heuser, head of the Gestapo in occupied Minsk.[15] In August of the same year, *Izvestiia* wrote about Aleksandr Ermolchik, a Belorussian, who deserted the Red Army and collaborated with the Nazis as a policeman, an active and brutal participant in executions, including of Jews. After the war Ermolchik settled in the German town of Celle. The West German authorities rejected Soviet demands to extradite him.[16]

Friedrich Karl Vialon, secretary of state in the Federal Ministry of Economic Cooperation in Bonn, was another high-profile target of condemnation. Vialon served as registrar of Jewish property in the German administration in Riga from 1942 to 1944. His instructions regulated how to appropriate the assets of murdered Jews. According to *Izvestiia*, on 24 September 1943 he wrote to the heads of German occupation forces in Riga, Tallinn, Kaunas, and Minsk, calling on them to collect and keep for further use such things as clothing and shoes. He stressed that special attention should be paid to golden and silver items. They had to be counted, registered, and delivered at the disposal of Vialon's department.[17]

The case of Erwin Schüle, a top prosecutor, turned into an embarrassment for the West German justice system when the GDR made public documents showing Schüle's role as a Nazi Party member and a member of the SA, the so-called Nazi storm troops.[18] Efim Uchitel, a former war cameraman, directed a 1965 documentary, *The Case of Erwin Schüle* (*Delo Ervina Shiule*), based on a script by Lev Ginzburg. A Russian Jewish journalist and translator of German poetry, Ginzburg followed closely the events in Germany and wrote numerous articles on former Nazis. In 1961 he criticized the appointment of Adolf Heusinger to the position of chairman of the NATO Military Committee. Heusinger was wanted by the Soviet Union for war crimes committed in various Soviet localities, including Babi Yar in Kyiv.[19]

Soviet Trials

Soviet officials did not show clemency to those who committed crimes against Jews on Soviet territory. However, in the open trials of the 1940s, the perpetrators were predominantly foreign citizens and, in the press reports, the Jewish victims usually appeared as de-ethnicized "Soviet citizens." The collaborators, categorized as *posobniki* or accomplices, faced trials that were closed to the public, often based on insufficient investigations. As a result, there were cases in which even notorious murderers could be seen as relatively minor war criminals and released after serving about ten years in the Gulag. In the 1960s open trials of collaborators became much more common. Among those in the dock appeared also some of the released "minor" criminals, including those who had participated in murdering Jews. They would be retried and convicted, receiving new sentences, including death. Still, the majority of those punished in the 1960s had previously avoided retribution, often by taking a new identity and moving after the war to a distant area of the country. Some of them had even served in the army in the final stages of the war and enjoyed the status of war veterans. In 1961 six of such criminals faced a public thirteen-day-long trial in Mineralnye Vody, a spa town in southern Russia. In addition to other crimes, they were accused of participating in murdering almost ten thousand Jews in September 1942. Five of them were sentenced to death and one received a fifteen-year sentence.[20]

While the Soviet regime pursued justice for murdered Jews as an aim in and of itself, the propaganda apparatus simultaneously utilized the Jewish wartime fate for broader goals, in particular as prosecutorial evidence against the "remnants of the capitalist West" in the Baltic republics, where the armed struggle against Soviet rule spanned from 1940 to the mid-1950s. Several trials of Nazi collaborators took place in the Soviet Union in March 1961, just a few weeks before the beginning of the Eichmann trial on 11 April 1961. Jewish victims were frequently mentioned in reports of the trials in the Baltic republics.[21]

The first of the Soviet trials was that of three Estonians. A Soviet court accused Ain Erwin Mere (in absentia), Ralf Gerrets, and Jan Vijk of ordering and participating in the murder of inmates at a place called Kalevi-Liiva, not far from the Jägala concentration camp in Estonia. SS

Obersturmführer Aleksandr Laak, commandant of the Jägala camp, fled to Canada after the war and lived in Winnipeg. He committed suicide when information of his atrocities appeared in the press. Mere, the head of the Security Police (Sicherheitspolizei) in Estonia following its creation in 1942, denied all the charges. He lived in Britain, which refused to extradite him.

On 27 February 1961, Ilmar Reidi, a correspondent for *Pravda*, wrote from Tallinn that the victims of the mass executions in 1942 and 1943 were "about six thousand citizens of Czechoslovakia, Poland, Germany and the Soviet Union." The article mentions Mere's words addressed to other Estonian collaborators that they had "the honor to fulfill Hitler's order of liquidating the lowest races, including Jews."[22] A week later *Pravda* was more specific about the victims of the executions—they appeared as "Jews . . . brought from Czechoslovakia, Poland, Germany, and other European countries." The newspaper apparently considered it unnecessary to inform its readers that the majority of the Jägala inmates were Jews from Lithuania. The court sentenced all three collaborators to death by shooting, arguing that they not only were culpable for bringing death to thousands of people at the Jägala camp but had also committed "crimes against all mankind."[23] After the end of the trial, the *Literaturnaia gazeta* published an article by Uno Laht, an Estonian writer, who made clear that the accused were responsible for the shooting of people "whose only guilt was to have been born Jews."[24]

A second trial was held in Latvia and involved a group of Latvian and Belorussian collaborators charged with killing Jews among others. The West was censured for giving asylum to two individuals identified in the trial as "war criminals"—Riblis and Ertsams. The newspaper *Sovetskaia Latvia* (Soviet Latvia) commented on one of the charges: "Old men, women, infants were first driven into the local synagogue, then taken to the wood and bestially killed."[25]

A third trial took place in Lithuania. According to a report, published on 1 March in the daily of the All-Union Council of Trade Unions, *Trud* (Labor), the Lithuanian collaborators were charged with torture of Jews in the town of Alytus and the extermination of two thousand Jewish citizens. At about the same time, Soviet sources accused another man of Baltic descent, the Lithuanian Mečys Paškevičius, resident of Chicago at the time, of having been a policeman who helped plan and participated in massacres in the Ukmerge District in Lithuania.[26] In a long article on Mečys Paškevičius, who changed his name to Mike Paker, *Izvestiia* applied the method of "Jews last in the pecking order," stating that Paškevičius participated in murdering "Lithuanians, Russians, Poles, and Jews."[27]

The Warsaw Ghetto Uprising

Even though universalization of the Jewish tragedy—by subsuming it in the suffering of all victims of Nazism—remained a cornerstone of Soviet strategy, Holocaust-related narratives set outside Soviet territory could have an easier time with censorship. Thus, the 1957 collection of Russian translations of poetry by the Yiddish poet Itsik Fefer contained a fragment from the poem "The Shadows of the Warsaw Ghetto," while the play *The Uprising in the [Warsaw] Ghetto* by the Yiddish poet and playwright Shmuel Halkin found a place in the latter's 1958 collection.[28] To be sure, Soviet ideological overseers did not consider the Warsaw Ghetto uprising a taboo topic in the Soviet Union. At the same time, on the scale of notable events of World War II, the uprising was categorized as a relatively minor episode. This scale found its reflection, for instance, in the story "A Night in Warsaw" by Lev Slavin, a Russian-language (Jewish) prose and script writer, who built a plot around the 1944 Warsaw uprising. A fragment of the story appeared in December 1947 in the Moscow weekly journal *Ogonek*. The Warsaw Ghetto uprising is mentioned in Slavin's narrative simply as a "Jewish mutiny" (*evreiskii miatezh*).[29]

Still, the uprising would be mentioned from time to time in the press. Thus, on 11 September 1954, the newspaper *Literaturnaia gazeta* featured an article, "An Ominous Amnesty," which told, in particular, about the acquittal of twenty members of the police force tried in Dortmund on charges of murdering Jews in the Warsaw Ghetto.[30] The Warsaw Ghetto could appear in a Soviet newspaper also without using the words Jew and Jewish or otherwise mentioning that it had anything to do with Jews. Thus, on 14 September 1955, an article ("A City Risen from Ruins") in the Moscow newspaper *Gudok* described the successful reconstruction of the Polish capital, particularly its Muranow District, which was

> built on the place where, during the occupation, the German fascists established a ghetto. The history of this neighborhood is full of tragedy. SS men herded hundreds of thousands of people to this walled and barbwired part of the city and regularly sent from there transports of the condemned to annihilation in the ovens of Majdanek and Auschwitz. Brought to despair, people decided to die in battle. In April 1943 they started an uprising. The Hitlerites, in their turn, used aviation and artillery to raze to the ground the area of two square kilometers. 600 thousand people perished there. Now, there is here a memorial to heroes of the ghetto, and new buildings raised as if to symbolize the unstoppable force of life.[31]

A short, illustrated travelogue by Aleksandr Zhitomirskii, artist-in-chief of the glossy propaganda journal *Soviet Union* (which appeared in dozens of languages), is another example of "universalization." Published in the Moscow weekly *Sovetskaia kultura*, it mentions the Warsaw Ghetto memorial to "people" murdered by the fascists. As in other cases, we don't know if Zhitomirskii (who was Jewish) decided to avoid using the word Jewish or his editors decided for him. His travelogue appeared in October 1958, the year of the fifteenth anniversary of the uprising.[32]

This was also the year when, for the first time, a Soviet delegation came to Warsaw to participate in the ceremonies marking the anniversary. The delegation included three people: General David Dragunsky, poet Evgeni Dolmatovsky, and writer (and Hero of the Soviet Union) Vladimir Pavlov, who was not Jewish.[33] Characteristically, the choice had fallen on a poet, who was Jewish and a war veteran but wrote in Russian, rather than on one of the Yiddish authors. Although the most prominent Yiddish writers were executed or died in prisons and camps during the Stalinist repressions of 1948–53, scores of established poets and prose writers survived or remained untouched directly by the repression. Many of them were also war veterans.

It seems that the Soviet press had received an instruction to mark the twentieth anniversary of the Warsaw Ghetto uprising. Moreover, judging by the *Daily News Bulletin of the Jewish Telegraphic Agency* (23 April 1963), the Moscow Synagogue also received a similar instruction—about 1,500 Moscow Jews observed the anniversary. Among those attending was Yosef Tekoah, Israel's ambassador to the Soviet Union. On 18 April 1963, *Izvestiia* carried a long article entitled "Ashes Tear at the Heart" and bylined by someone named A. Panfilov. His article did not follow the example of the 1955 *Gudok* description of the uprising as an act of despair. Indeed, it could not be characterized as such because of its claimed Communist leadership. "The uprising in the ghetto was not merely an act of despair. The rebels wanted to contribute to the struggle against Hitlerism." Of course, the obligatory ideological context was added. First: "The hope of the ghetto prisoners for freedom came true thanks to the heroic exploits of the Soviet army [still called the Red Army during the war], which smashed the Hitlerite hordes and saved mankind from fascism." Second: "The people of People's Poland realize that the past should not be forgotten today. The tragic experience of the war has made them especially sensitive to all manifestations of fascism, which is rearing its head again today in West Germany."[34]

Some fifty pages of the March-April 1963 issue of *Sovetish Heymland* were devoted to the twentieth anniversary of the uprising. It was important to define the Jewish uprising's role as an episode, even if a momentous one, in the general Soviet-led struggle against Hitlerism. Hersh Remenik, the head of the criticism section of *Sovetish Heymland*, explained in his article on Soviet Yiddish writings devoted to the Warsaw Ghetto uprising: "The Warsaw Ghetto uprising has to be seen as an important contribution of the Jewish masses to the international struggle of the progressive sectors of all peoples, led by the Soviet Union, against fascism and imperialist reaction. Indeed, in such light this topic has found creative embodiment in Yiddish Soviet literature."[35]

The special issue of the journal included a few pieces by Polish Yiddish writers, including an article by Hersh Smolar, who stressed once again the leading role of the Communist underground. The same trope was central to Perets Markish's novel *Trot fun doyres* (Footsteps of the generations), the most monumental Soviet literary treatment of the topic. The March-April issue contained a fragment from Markish's prose canvas. The novel's manuscript survived although Markish was executed in August 1952.

Despite the resistance of some vigilant functionaries who sniffed out nationalism in Markish's novel, it was published in 1966 by Sovetskii pisatel, the main outlet for Yiddish literature in the post-Stalinist Soviet Union. No doubt the manuscript was edited in the process of its preparation for publication, but the number and nature of those changes remains unknown.

The book could not appear in a Russian translation because ideological overseers in the Communist Party's Central Committee were generally reluctant to allow any publication devoted to the Warsaw Ghetto uprising. Various excuses would be used to prevent the appearance of monographs written by Ber Mark (his book on the Warsaw Ghetto uprising never came out in Russian) and the Soviet historian Valentin Alekseev, whose work would see the light of day only in 1998.[36]

A laconic "universalized" note in *Pravda* (19 April 1968) marked the twenty-fifth anniversary of the uprising: "The public of People's Poland is marking the 25th anniversary of the uprising in the Warsaw ghetto. Today representatives of the central and Warsaw organizations of the National Unity Front and the Union of Fighters for Freedom and Democracy laid a wreath and flowers at the monument to the heroes of the Warsaw Ghetto. In connection with the memorable date, a ceremonial meeting was held in the Hall of Congresses of the Palace of Culture and Science."[37]

By that time the content and tone of Jewish-related publications had undergone significant changes. After the June 1967 war in the Middle East and, as a concomitant, the disruption of diplomatic relations between the Soviet Union and Israel, Soviet propagandists felt unleashed to openly advance theories that Zionism was a prime enemy of the Soviet people, that it was rooted in anti-Communism and bellicose nationalism, and had a long history of collaboration with various reactionary movements, including Hitler's followers. From time to time they referred to personalities or events associated with the Warsaw Ghetto. Evgeni Evseev (Yevseev), one of the most notorious among the Israel-hating authors, wrote in his article "Flunky at Their Beck and Call," published on 4 October 1967 in the daily *Komsomolskaia pravda* targeting young readers: "In the years of fascism's heyday the Zionists actively cooperated with the Nazi leaders and were their outright accomplices in a number of cases." For an example, he referred to the case of Alfred Nossig, a sculptor, poet, and journalist who, indeed, once was a Zionist activist and whom the Jewish Combat Organization executed in February 1943 for collaborating with the Nazis.[38]

Heroism of Jewish soldiers, officers, and partisans rather than the Holocaust was the dominant theme of Soviet Yiddish writings on World War II. Some writers, most notably the war veterans Misha Lev and Ikhil Falikman, specialized in writing novels set in wartime. Instrumentalization of the Holocaust, a characteristic feature of Soviet propaganda, was less pronounced in *Sovetish Heymland*, though it also published writings by—as a rule less extreme, middle-of-the-road—authors specializing in anti-Zionism. The dominant agenda differed from that of the Russian-language press, as did the scale: the uprising was not a minor episode at all. The Yiddish journal continued to put a "nationalist" emphasis on the heroism of the ghetto fighters, doing effectively what the Jewish Anti-Fascist Committee's *Eynikayt* was accused of doing in the 1940s. Writing about his impression of visiting the site of the Warsaw Ghetto, Vergelis drew a parallel between the main bunker of the Jewish Combat Organization and Pavlov's House, a symbol of the Battle of Stalingrad.[39] The Yiddish journal continued to publish material on the uprising, usually in its April issues, combining such commemorative material with obligatory sections devoted to Lenin's birthday (22 April). In 1968 the twenty-fifth anniversary was marked, in particular, by printing fragments from Ber Mark's book *Der ufshtand fun Varshever geto* (The Warsaw Ghetto uprising) and from the book *Pusta Woda* (Empty water) by Krystyna Żywulska (Zofia Landau).

The 1949 Yiddish-language textbook *College Yiddish* by Uriel Weinreich contains, inter alia, the author's insightful observations about contemporary Jewish life. In one of the texts we read about the New York press: "An English newspaper writes little about Jews. But in a Yiddish newspaper one can read about Jews living in all countries."[40] Indeed, Jewish-related topics tended to occupy only a marginal place in non-Jewish periodicals. It is no coincidence, for instance, that during World War II even the *New York Times*, with its high proportion of Jewish contributors and readers, did not give much prominence to materials on the Nazi persecution and killing of Jews.[41] The "division of labor" between the Jewish and non-Jewish press remained characteristic also of the postwar media. In Communist Poland, the Yiddish and partly Polish newspaper *Folks-Shtime* played an important role as an outlet for articles and literary works on the Holocaust. Significantly, from 1956 the Warsaw newspaper was published under the auspices of the Social-Cultural Association of Jews in Poland. Thus, notwithstanding all the ideological restrictions under the Communist regime, it was a publication of a *Jewish* organization.

In the Soviet Union, on the other hand, the authorities did not allow the establishment of any Jewish organizations apart from the strictly controlled local religious bodies, which had no access to the printing press. The journal *Sovetish Heymland*, an organ of the Soviet Writers Union, boasted of focusing predominantly on contemporary topics rather than "digging in the past." For all that, the Moscow journal did, even if with some qualms, publish essays, memoirs, prose and poetic works devoted to various aspects of the Holocaust. It seems that, taking into the account the journal's narrow readership and its international circulation, the ideological overseers took a lenient view of this.

Anne Frank

Wartime events taking place in faraway Amsterdam might have been rendered ideologically innocuous. In reality, however, the tragic story of Anne Frank came to Soviet readers through drastic filters of editing and censorship, including self-censorship.

In March 1956 the well-established journalist and literary translator Boris Izakov praised the production of Frances Goodrich and Albert Hackett's play *The Diary of Anne Frank* at Broadway's Cort Theater, favorably comparing it with Tennessee Williams's *A Streetcar Named Desire*. He disliked the latter for demonstrating "a whole gamut of base passions" and including a scene of rape, shown "in revoltingly naturalist detail." Izakov's life experience, especially during the anticosmopolitan campaign in Stalin's final years, had taught him—the son of a Saint Petersburg Jewish pharmacist—to be careful with Jewish topics. In any case, his article in the Ministry of Culture's weekly *Sovetskaia kultura* obfuscated Anne Frank's Jewish identity. Instead, she appeared as "a girl, who was hiding in Holland during the Hitlerite occupation and perished in Buchenwald."

We can only surmise whether Izakov was really unaware that Anne expired in Bergen-Belsen from typhus, or Buchenwald sounded to him less associated with the Holocaust.[42] Anne appeared as a de-Judaized teenager also in a May 1956 issue of the Moscow illustrated weekly magazine *Ogonek* when it printed a few approving words about the same theater production.[43] Although Goodrich and Hackett had downplayed the Jewish aspect of the story, drawing the audience's attention to the themes of adolescent development and a more general concern with death,[44] the Soviet commentators' silence could hardly have stemmed from a failure to understand why the Franks went into hiding. Significantly, we don't have access to the articles' original texts to compare them with the ultimate products of editorial intervention. It does not mean that the words Jew and Jewish were entirely taboo. A February 1957 article in *Sovetskaia kultura* did not shy away from describing the Franks as "Jewish refugees" and welcomed a coordinated venture of eight theaters in West and East Germany, as well as in Vienna and Zurich, to perform *The Diary of Anne Frank* on the same day.[45]

A March 1957 article in *Literaturnaia gazeta* made only a passing reference to the Jewishness of the play's characters. Bylined "V.Z.," the piece, entitled "The Past That Has Not Turned into History," most probably came from the pen of Valentin Zorin, then a rising star of political journalism. Later a major television commentator, Zorin was one of those Soviet public personalities who preferred to "keep as discreet a silence as possible about one or the other of their parents being *Jewish*."[46] In V.Z.'s grotesque description, Goodrich and Hackett told "a phenomenal, almost fantasy story" about a group "of antifascists" who had gone into hiding in order to save themselves from deportation to concentration camps. The article emphasized that, in Germany, the play's success reflected opposition to "Bonn's policy of creating a new Wehrmacht [the name of the armed forces of Nazi Germany] of former SS troops, who are being camouflaged in an American-style uniform for fulfilling the same 'great national,' i.e., aggressive, tasks."[47]

In the same year, 1957, the Moscow publishing house Iskusstvo (Art) put out a Russian translation of Goodrich and Hackett's play with a print run of fifteen thousand. Victor Louis, one of the two translators, cut a notorious figure in Moscow intellectual circles, a cross between a journalist and a KGB agent.[48] In the summer of 1958, Goodrich and Hackett visited Moscow and came back wary of the chances for their play to reach the stage in the Soviet Union.[49] In reality, the play's status remained open to interpretation: it was neither forbidden nor listed as allowed to be performed. The central authorities simply did not have the capacity to spell out policy on all specific questions of cultural production.

Some theaters availed themselves of the loophole. In 1960 the State Theater for Young Spectators in the Latvian capital of Riga included *The Diary of Anne Frank* in its repertoire and Leningrad television broadcast scenes from that production.[50] The Student Theater at Moscow University, a popular cultural institution, was the first to do the play in the capital. Its production premiered in the 1960–61 season and was performed, by one count, more than sixty times.[51] Although the Leningrad-based Theater for Young Spectators failed to get permission to stage the play, the Leningrad Theater of Drama and Comedy (known also as the Theater on Liteinyi [Avenue]) included it in its repertoire.[52] In 1964 *The Diary of Anne Frank* premiered at the Russian Theater in the Georgian capital of Tbilisi.[53] In 1970 the Tallinn amateur drama troupe staged the play in their own Yiddish translation.[54]

A cinematic version followed the international success of the play. In January 1959 the Moscow journal *Iskusstvo kino* (Film art) informed its readers that 20th Century Fox had released a film "based on the eponymous antifascist play."[55] The film would win numerous awards, including three Oscars in 1960. In August 1959 it was shown "out of competition" at the first Moscow Film Festival. The State Department originally decided to boycott the entire festival, but later changed its mind and in the end sent *The Diary of Anne Frank* as the sole American entry. Perhaps in retaliation for getting information about the Americans' decision at the last moment, the festival organizers ran the American film only once, at eleven p.m. on 5 August. About a thousand viewers, mostly the upper crust of Moscow society, were leaving the Kremlin Theater, one of the festival's locations, after two o'clock in the morning.[56] It seems that the State Department's posture was driven by the belief that the Soviets had arranged the festival specifically to divert attention from the American National Exhibition in the Moscow park Sokolniki, a cultural diplomatic event of great significance in Soviet-Western relations.[57]

The term "cultural diplomacy" was introduced by Robert H. Thayer, special assistant to the US secretary of state, in a speech he delivered in August 1959, several weeks after Richard Nixon, then vice president in the Eisenhower administration, went to open the exhibition.[58] In the same year, as part of Soviet cultural diplomacy, the newly published collection of Sholem Aleichem's stories, heralding a new start for Yiddish publishing in the Soviet Union, was displayed at the 1959 Soviet National Exhibition, which ran in New York following the Soviet-American agreement on organizing such fairs in both countries.[59]

To make the impact of the exhibition stronger, a group of American performers assembled by the CBS television star Ed Sullivan gave concerts in Moscow and Leningrad. Among them, as we already know, were the Barry Sisters, whose recordings would gain wide popularity in the Soviet Union.[60] The selection of *The Diary of Anne Frank* and the inclusion of the Barry Sisters in the show clearly indicates that the State Department decided to play the Jewish card, especially as conditions of Jewish life in the Soviet Union had been a high-profile issue, triggered partly by unsubstantiated rumors about plans to force the Jews to resettle in Birobidzhan in the Far East of Russia. Significantly, Yiddish books formed part of the library shown at the American National Exhibition. So did English-language books on Jewish topics, though Soviet censors had removed some of them, most notably Israel-related titles.[61] Hyman Bloom's painting *Younger Jew with Torah* found a place in the fine-art section of the exhibition.[62]

In the meantime, the Moscow press commended the film *The Diary of Anne Frank* as a talented work, but at the same time panned it for not showing any spiritual resistance by the protagonist and other characters. Lazar Lazarev (Shindel), literary critic and war veteran, wrote that, by his standards, they deserved only pity rather than respect.[63] In one of its editorials, *Literaturnaia gazeta* compared *The Diary of Anne Frank* with the Soviet film *Fate of a Man* (*Sud'ba cheloveka*), based on Mikhail Sholokhov's story, whose protagonist, Andrei Sokolov, a Soviet POW, never lost hope and fought on bravely.[64] Sergei Bondarchuk, who directed the film, which became a Soviet classic, and played Sokolov, argued that the striking difference between the foreign and Soviet concepts had confirmed once again the superiority of socialist realism.[65]

In the Soviet press reviews of the film Anne Frank initially appeared as a "girl" without mentioning that she and other people in the secret annex were actually Jewish. Finally, however, *Pravda* printed an article by Peter Reni, a Hungarian critic, allowing him to reveal "the secret." Reni wrote about the centrality of themes of World War II in the program of the film festival and gave as an example *The Diary of Anne Frank*, "devoted to the fate of the hunted [*gonimykh*] Jews in Amsterdam."[66] Nor did Laert Vagarshian, an Armenian film director, make a secret of Anne Frank's Jewishness in his Yerevan-published notes on the Moscow festival.[67]

The festival program included one more film associated with Anne Frank's diary. This was the documentary *Ein Tagebuch für Anne Frank*, produced in East Germany and premiered there in February 1959. Anne Frank's story formed a backdrop for achieving the main purpose of making the documentary: to show that the West German government of Konrad Adenauer had been sheltering Nazis from receiving condign punishment for crimes committed during the war.[68] "The camera shows how the Bonn chancellor Adenauer protects criminals, how they walk with impunity in the streets of cities in the German Federal Republic, and how they enjoy comfort in their villas. There they are, the brazen faces of the criminals, who remain unpunished by the justice system and are patronized by their new minders."[69]

Nineteen fifty-nine was also the year when work began on a Russian version of the book *The Diary of Anne Frank*. No doubt, in the Soviet capital there were people able to translate the original Dutch text of the diary, but it was nevertheless commissioned to Rita Rait-Kovaleva, an accomplished and prolific literary translator from English, German, and French, "one of the translators who shaped the literary horizon for several generations of Soviet people."[70] Around the same time she worked on her Russian rendition of J. D. Salinger's *The Catcher in the Rye*. The text of her version of *The Diary of Anne Frank* carries clear signs of consulting a previous German translation.[71]

The introduction to the book, written by Ehrenburg, touched on the question of the nature of hatred toward Jews: "Why had the fascists vented their fury primarily on the Jews? Thick books were written about this, offering elaborate explanations, but they explained nothing at all. Numerous age-old prejudices, legends that were more like bad anecdotes, superstitions built up into a philosophical system, envy, blockheadedness, the necessity to find a scapegoat—all this wove itself into a single net that cut Anne off from her little Dutch girlfriends and six million people from their neighbors and countrymen."[72]

Shrewdly, Ehrenburg did not mention anti-Semitism in contemporary Soviet society. A year later this would be done by the poet Evgeni Evtushenko in his poem "Babi Yar," thus immediately provoking an angry response. It was safe, however, to write about anti-Semitism in pre-1917 Russia or in contemporary capitalist countries, especially as none other than the Soviet leader, Nikita Khrushchev, spoke in January 1960 about "acts of anti-Semitism that took place in many cities of Western Europe" and characterized such acts as "a telling sign of the strengthening of the forces of reaction."[73]

Ehrenburg also commented on a burning contemporary issue: "The law of 'racial purity' during Hitler's time was drawn up by Hans Globke. Six million innocent victims are on his conscience. Six million perished—and Dr. Hans Globke, Chancellor Adenauer's right hand, distributes money for propaganda."[74] Hans Josef Maria Globke, a powerful political figure during Adenauer's long administration, was secretary of state and chief of staff of the German Chancellery from 1953 to 1963. He authored, in particular, the much-discussed, albeit unsuccessful, "Globke Plan" of normalizing relations between West and East Germany.[75] For the Soviet press, however, Globke, a man tainted by his past, served as a perfect target for severe and just censure. Most notoriously, although he was not a member of the Nazi Party, he had taken part in the preparation and execution of the Nuremberg Laws, depriving Jews of most rights in Nazi Germany. The Soviet and the (often pronouncedly anti-Soviet) Western press echoed each other in their critiques of whitewashing the Nazi past. Thus, Philip Slomovitz, editor of the *Detroit Jewish News*, wrote: "The fact remains that Globke was responsible for the device of having Jewish passports stamped with the letter 'J,' so that no escape was possible for their bearers, and that he publicly remarked of the cases [with] which he dealt that 'they should have chosen their parents more carefully.'"[76]

In 1963 Globke was tried and symbolically convicted in absentia in East Berlin, in a publicized legal action with participation of Soviet legal specialists. *Pravda* stated that the indictment revealed "Globke's role in the preparation and implementation of anti-Semitic measures and laws, aimed at persecuting and annihilating Jews."[77] The tone-setting newspaper also stressed that Globke "had on him the death of over six million Jewish citizens."[78]

In 1960 *The Diary of Anne Frank* came out under the imprint of the Moscow publishing house Inostrannaia Literatura (Foreign literature) and, unlike the vast majority of books published in the Soviet Union, did not carry any information about its print run. Yet, no doubt, the diary, sold out in a matter of days, had many thousands of readers.[79] It seems that press publications about the play and film based on Anne Frank's diary had expanded her name recognition in the Soviet Union even prior to the book's publication. A newspaper article published in May 1960, when the book still remained in a production phase, listed the diary among other heroic documents of World War II.[80]

Claims of Anne's passivity in resisting Nazi persecution quickly faded in Soviet discourse. In an essay written in 1961, Vladimir Sappak, an influential television critic, shared his thoughts about worthy role models for the Soviet public: "Very much needed are exemplary people [*liudi-primery*] like the Communist with a crystal soul Julius Fučik, like the strong young woman Anne Frank . . . and like the man who achieved the 'feat of the century,' Yuri Gagarin."[81] Lev Ginzburg included in his 1962 book *The Price of Ash* an essay in which he contrasted the tragedy of Anne Frank's short life with Globke's deplorably successful post-1945 career.[82]

It was during the year of the Moscow publication of the diary that the Yiddish poet Moyshe Teif, a war veteran and twice a prisoner of the Gulag, wrote "A Ballad about Anne Frank." In the absence of Soviet outlets for Yiddish writing—not counting the newspaper *Birobidzhaner Shtern*—Teif published the poem in the Warsaw *Folks-Shtime*.[83] In 1964 the ballad came out in the poet's collection of Russian translations by Yunna Morits, known at that time as a literary frondeur.[84] (In 1963 the artist Elza Khokhlovkina painted Morits sitting against the backdrop of a wall with Anne Frank's portrait on it.)[85] The book, printed in ten thousand copies, attracted the attention of composers. One of the poems, "Kikhelekh un zemelekh" (Cookies and rolls; the Russian title: "Near a bakery in Gorky Street"), written to the memory of the poet's son perished in the Holocaust, was set to music by Maxim Dunaevsky. Alexander Vustin wrote music to three other poems, including "A Ballad about Anne Frank."[86] In 1969 Vustin's former teacher Grigori Frid—who in 1965 founded the Moscow Youth Music Club, which acted as an important center of musical life and also a meeting place for composers who did not conform with officialdom—wrote the mono-opera *The Diary of Anne Frank*, widely performed since the 1970s particularly in the West.[87]

In April 1963 *The Diary of Anne Frank* was performed on the stage of the Moscow Maly Theater by Compagnia Italiana Dei Giovani. According to the *New York Times*, the Italian troupe succeeded in including the play in their repertoire only after considerable negotiation with Soviet authorities. Permission was obtained to present it only twice, while other plays of their repertoire were performed five times.[88] A review article in the journal *Teatr* (Theater), an organ of the Writers Union and the Ministry of Culture, praised the performance but did not speak directly about its Jewish aspect. Rather, the reviewer hinted at it by mentioning the "tragedy of the ghetto" and that Peter, a boy who hid with the Frank family, was not destined to become a new Albert Einstein or Jascha Heifetz.[89]

In December 1963 the Soviet press reported that investigators had identified and found the Nazi officer, Karl Silberbauer, who, in August 1944, had commanded the group dispatched to arrest Anne Frank and seven other fugitives hiding in the secret annex. In the end, Silberbauer did not face any penalties and could return to his work as a police officer in Vienna. Such an outcome provided Soviet propagandists with a perfect opportunity to show how the Western justice system gave preferential treatment to former Nazis.[90] The fact that Wilhelm Harster, head of the Nazi Security Police in the Netherlands, had received a relatively lenient punishment also did not escape the attention of Soviet publicists.[91]

Mariia Rolnikaite

The years when Anne Frank's diary was inching its way to the Soviet public coincided with the years when Yiddish printing struggled to revive in Moscow after its full devastation in 1948. In fact, these two developments did not simply coincide but rather became interwoven into the fabric of the Thaw period, when, despite the lack of comprehensive reforms, many previously unacceptable things loosened up.

In 1962 the Yiddish singer Nehama Lifshitz (Lifshitzaite)—who, after winning the 1958 all-Soviet competition of variety artists, had been touring the country and, in 1959 and 1960, performed abroad—brought to *Sovetish Heymland* a few excepts from a diary of her friend, Masha Rolnik (Mariia Rolnikaite), a survivor of the Vilnius (Vilna) Ghetto. Rolnikaite worked at that time in Vilnius at the Philharmonic Society. Neither of the two knew that the Yiddish editors had already chosen the Riga Ghetto memoir of the sculptor Elmar Rivosh (Elmārs Rivošs) to be their first significant

Holocaust publication. As a result, the journal rejected Rolnikaite's manuscript, apparently being wary of overemphasizing the Jewish tragedy by publishing two ghetto diaries in a row. The editors, some of them former inmates of the Gulag, painfully remembered the accusations of nationalism piled, in the 1940s, on the newspaper *Eynikayt*. Small wonder that they took pains to preserve what seemed to them a safe and proper balance between "Jewish" and "Soviet." The editorial reply included an invitation to submit something written on contemporaneous topics. Rolnikaite felt deeply offended and never worked with the journal.[92]

Rivosh, the only survivor in his family, escaped from the ghetto and spent over two years in hiding, helped by Russian and Latvian friends. In 1945 his diary, written in Russian, was selected for the *Black Book*, which the Jewish Anti-Fascist Committee planned to publish about the Nazi atrocities against the Jews. Vasily Grossman and Rakhil (Rose) Kovnator, a writer and a veteran of the Bolshevik Revolution, prepared Rivosh's diary for publication, but, ultimately, the Soviet authorities blocked the release of the *Black Book*.[93] In 1961 a Latvian translation of short fragments from the diary came out posthumously (Rivosh died in 1957) in the journal *Padomju Latvijas Sieviete* (Soviet Latvian woman).

Now the diary came out translated into Yiddish by the poet Avrom Gontar, head of the poetry department of *Sovetish Heymland*, with an introduction by Misha Lev, managing editor of the journal.[94] The latter, a war veteran and an author of novels, mainly autobiographical, set during the war, played the key role in publishing the diary.[95] (This did not hurt, however, the cordial friendship between Lev and Rolnikaite.) Yet Rivosh's diary did not draw particular attention at the time of its publication, which, no doubt, at least partly had to do with the nature of *Sovetish Heymland*, a niche periodical. Furthermore, the journal had a reputation as a front for Soviet propaganda. It was generally characteristic of works published in the Yiddish journal that they, with very few exceptions, did not make a noticeable impact, even after being translated into Russian and published with a large print run. Most importantly, Rivosh's diary went unnoticed by Soviet propagandists.

Things turned out differently for Rolnikaite's *I Must Tell*, written—in Yiddish, then in Lithuanian, and finally in Russian—as a diary (and to some unknown extent really based on Rolnikaite's original diary) of a teenage girl incarcerated in the ghetto and, later, in concentration camps in Strasdenhof (Latvia) and Stutthof (Poland). The agitprop had discovered in Rolnikaite and her book a Soviet answer to Anne Frank and her diary. Importantly, also, Vilnius became part of the Soviet Union shortly before June 1941, when the German army crossed the Soviet border. Thus, the city was one of the semiexternalized settings where the population had not been fully Sovietized. This gave writers and editors more freedom in reflecting on collaboration or passivity on the part of real and fictionalized characters.

Whether for propaganda reasons or not, Jewish and Jewish-related cultural projects often had a better chance to be realized in Lithuania than in other parts of the country.[96] In 1961 Grigorijus Kanovičius (Grigori Kanovich), later known as an acclaimed Russian-language novelist on Jewish themes, and Vytautas Žalakevičius, a Lithuanian film director and writer, wrote a screenplay entitled *Gott mit uns* (the slogan "God with us" was used by the German military). The story was about a Roman Catholic priest who hid a Jewish boy and a Soviet partisan during the Nazi occupation. After long deliberations with the authorities in Vilnius and Moscow, the screenplay was not accepted for production despite considerable rewriting to meet the demands of the censors, like minimizing the Jewish aspect, inserting a critique of the church, and adding a story line about the Soviet partisans. Meanwhile, the screenplay appeared in the main Soviet Lithuanian literary journal *Pergalė* (Victory).[97]

Rolnikaite's father, Hirsh Rolnik, who participated in drafting the constitution of Soviet Lithuania, was an officer in the Sixteenth Lithuanian Rifle Division, which had a uniquely high percentage of Jewish troops in its ranks.[98] After the war, veterans of the division and the partisan movement formed a network of personal relations that could help overcome bureaucratic hurdles, especially as many of the former comrades in arms worked in the Party and state apparatus of the Lithuanian Soviet republic. Characteristically, from 1945 to 1970, Genrikas Zimanas, a onetime Yiddish journalist and veteran of the Communist underground, edited *Tiesa* (Truth), the main Lithuanian-language newspaper in the republic. Rolnikaite had a high opinion of Antanas Sniečkus, the first secretary of the Communist Party of Lithuania, Justas Paleckis, chairman of the Presidium of the Supreme Soviet of the republic, and Juozas Banaitis, the minister of culture, and praised them for having a fair attitude toward the Jews.[99] Such an environment made it easier to publish the Lithuanian version of Rolnikaite's book in 1963.[100] In December of that year, a countrywide broadcast on Soviet television featured Rolnikaite's story.[101] For all that, an international political factor played arguably the decisive role in the publishing story of the Russian version of Rolnikaite's book.

The factor in question had to do with West Germany's twenty-year statute of limitations for murder, which was set to put a halt on 8 May 1965 to the criminal prosecution of former Nazis.[102] Worldwide protests ensued. A statement of the Soviet government charged that "thousands of Nazi criminals are still at large and go unpunished in the Federal Republic of Germany. Furthermore, many prominent Hitlerites today hold high posts in the state machine, are active in the Bundeswehr, the police, the judiciary and the prosecutors' officers."[103] In that context, Soviet agitprop endorsed the publication of works documenting atrocities against the Jewish population among others. For instance, a documentary collection on *The Crimes of the German-Fascist Occupiers in Belorussia*, which came out in Minsk in 1965, made numerous references to the fate of the Jews.[104] The same year saw the publication in Vilnius of the first part of a two-volume collection of documents, *Mass Murders in Lithuania*, "that made extremely clear who the Nazis' primary victims were."[105]

Also in 1965, the documentary film *Ordinary Fascism* (or *Triumph over Violence*), directed by Mikhail Romm, reached Soviet audiences after gaining the approval of Communist leaders in East Germany and winning a prize at a festival in Leipzig. The Soviet film spoke relatively openly about the Holocaust.[106] According to Alexander Solzhenitsyn, the Moscow intelligentsia considered Romm—who stood out for his openly Jewish stance—their second most prominent spokesman after Ehrenburg.[107] A renowned film director, Romm enjoyed state support throughout his career but was allowed to make the film *Ordinary Fascism* only on the condition that the word Jew would be omitted. Nevertheless, this word is mentioned in the film.[108]

It is thus no coincidence, given the USSR's ideologically driven publication policy, that the Russian version of Rolnikaite's book, entitled *Ia dolzhna rasskazat'* (I must tell), went through three editions in one year, 1965. First it was serialized in two issues of the Leningrad-based journal *Zvezda* (Star) with a circulation of over 75,000, and then in book form in Moscow

(280,000 copies) and Vilnius (10,000 copies). It is quite possible that the publication in *Zvezda* reflected the desire to have a "Soviet Anne Frank" and had nothing to do with the German twenty-year statute of limitations, whereas her books appeared as a result of an afterthought by policymakers. Echoing Ehrenburg's introduction to *The Diary of Anne Frank*, the Lithuanian poet Eduardas Mieželaitis, who wrote the introduction to the Russian version of *I Must Tell*, stressed that many former Nazis continued to live carefree lives in the West.

Rolnikaite's books were followed in 1966 by Anatoli Kuznetsov's *Babi Yar*, serialized in the Moscow journal *Iunost'* (Youth), and two other Holocaust-related books in Russian: Ilya Konstantinovsky's *Srok davnosti* (Statute of limitations) and Icchokas Meras's *Na chem derzhitsia mir* (What the world rests on). The latter, a novel originally written in Lithuanian, was Meras's second book translated into Russian. Previously, in 1963, *Zheltyi loskut* (The yellow patch) appeared in Moscow under the rubric of books for middle- and high school students. In Yiddish, Perets Markish's last novel *Trot fun doyres* (Footsteps of generations), with chapters devoted to the Warsaw Ghetto uprising, was released by the Moscow publishing house Sovetskii pisatel also in 1966.

The Soviet press praised Rolnikaite's book, though usually—as in the review by the Latvian author Dagnia Zigmonte—refrained from using the words Jew or Jewish.[109] In December 1965 Rolnikaite's status rose noticeably after her expedient acceptance into the Writers Union. The Novosti Press Agency, or APN, arranged to publish her book abroad. In 1965 the Yiddish version came out under a joint imprint of APN and the Warsaw publishing house Yidish Bukh. Its title carried her Jewish name: Masha Rolnik. Concurrently, there was discussion of publishing a Yiddish version of *The Black Book*, but it did not gain traction.[110] At the APN, Solomon Rabinovich dealt with organizing the joint-publication venture and, in the meantime, authored a propaganda pamphlet *Jews in the USSR*, released by the APN in 1965 in Russian, English, Hebrew, Yiddish, and French. It is hard to tell how many of the ten thousand copies of *I Must Tell* (*Ikh muz dertseyln* in Yiddish), printed in Warsaw (apparently, the highest print run in the practice of Yidish Bukh), reached Soviet readers.[111] Most of them probably either stayed in Poland or went to other European countries, Israel, and America.

The APN made arrangements with publishers in other countries. In 1966 translations of *I Must Tell* came out, for instance, as new releases of a Finnish and German-Austrian-Swiss publishers. In France Éditeurs Français Réunis, one of the main Communist publishing houses in the country, produced the book in the same year. Its translator, Gastor Laroche (pseudonym of Boris Matline), was a prominent veteran of the anti-Nazi Resistance and played a distinguished role in the French Communist Party.[112] Ehrenburg wrote a preface to the Parisian edition. Rolnikaite met the renowned writer almost by happenstance and received from him strong encouragement to prepare a Russian version of her book manuscript, which he then read, praised, and sent to Paris, the city where he had numerous friends.[113]

Significantly, 1965 was a turning point in the memorialization of the war in the Soviet Union, the year when Victory Day (9 May) gained the status of a nonworking national holiday. For many Jews, 9 May became by extension the day of memory of their relatives and friends murdered by the Nazis and their collaborators. There were numerous instances after 1965 when on that day Jews would visit—often traveling from afar—the gravesites, even if they knew the exact date of the actual killing.[114] In literature, however, Soviet Jews had to be shown not simply as defenseless people murdered by the fascists and buried in mass graves, but as fighters. On 6 May 1965, *Pravda* published an ethnic breakdown of those who had been awarded the title Hero of the Soviet Union for extraordinary bravery shown during World War II. Jews appeared in fifth place, behind (in absolute numbers) only the Russians, Ukrainians, Belorussians, and Tatars.[115] The Jewish heroes' "overrepresentation" (compared to the population) was a boost to many Jews' pride, but most probably did not convince those who belittled the Jewish contribution to the war effort.

Like any Soviet author whose work wound up in the hands of a publisher, Rolnikaite was, ideologically speaking, a captive. At the phase of preparing the manuscript of the first edition, in Lithuanian, she was told to introduce ideologically motivated changes, including to portray the resistance of ghetto inmates led by Communists, even if such things were not etched in her memory. As a reviewer put it, the manuscript was not "a work written in the perilous years of fascism, like Anne Frank's diary. It has been written in our days, so it has to be written in a contemporaneous way, correctly, from Marxist positions."[116]

It seems that the changes had the desirable effect on some readers. S. J. Goldsmith, a London-based journalist who contributed to a range of Jewish periodicals, wrote in his review of the Yiddish version of the book: "Those who argue that there was little resistance on the part of the Jews may have second thoughts as the facts of defiance and resistance are brought to life."[117] A more inquisitive reader, Lucy Dawidowicz, an American-Jewish historian and writer, however, felt that something did not add up in Rolnikaite's book: "Even if the diary is an authentic document, it has unmistakably been doctored. For instance, accounts about the resistance movement that the diarist could never have known at the time are set down."[118] Most probably Dawidowicz's skepticism had nothing to do with it, but Rolnikaite's book, available, notably thanks to the APN, in eighteen languages, remains virtually unknown in the English-speaking world.[119] Publishers of books in languages of Soviet people generally did not—and, apparently, were not instructed to—show interest in translating *I Must Tell*. It did come out, though, in 1966 in Latvian, the language in which *The Diary of Anne Frank* was published in 1963.

The diaries of Anne Frank and Masha Rolnikaite appeared in print in the Soviet Union predominantly as a corollary of foreign policy considerations, though the climate of the Thaw and the involvement of Ehrenburg, a central figure of the period, also were contributing factors.

The two diaries played rather different roles in the Soviet cultural sphere. Anne Frank's diary would be read and referred to as an important antifascist narrative with distant relevance to the wartime events in the Soviet Union. Parallels can be drawn between the Soviet images of Anne Frank, a "Dutch girl," and Janusz Korczak, a "Polish writer, pedagogue, and physician." As Olga Gershenson notes about the Soviet memorialization of Korczak, the Jewish side of his story was underplayed, making him "a universal humanist hero. The Holocaust in this case was both externalized and universalized."[120] Much the same is true about how Frank's image was packaged for the Soviet public. Characteristically, non-Jewish teenage diarists could also get the moniker "the Soviet Anne Frank."[121]

To a considerable degree, the publication of the diary with Ehrenburg's introduction paved the way for the Russian version of *I Must Tell*, which clearly met the expectations of agitprop pundits. Characteristically, a 1981 documentary history of the Soviet Union included an excerpt from Rolnikaite's book that does not mention the word Jew.[122] In fact, the entire book, or what was left of it after editorial interventions, did not make the Jewish aspect too ostentatious. It was even characterized as "un-Jewish" and "inauthentic."[123] Nonetheless, Rolnikaite was—especially after Icchokas Meras emigrated to Israel in 1972 and thus became a nonperson in the Soviet Union—arguably the only widely published belletrist author writing on the Holocaust, the "Soviet Anne Frank," or at least the most important of them. Her first book, and her later prose works dedicated to Holocaust themes, continued to be read and translated in various languages. A radio dramatization of *I Must Tell* premiered on 26 May 1967.[124] In the same year Rolnikaite appeared in sequences shot for the propaganda documentary *Land of Our Birth* (*My zdes' rodilis'*), produced by the APN as a counter-propaganda reaction to the Western campaign on behalf of Soviet Jews.[125]

Theoretically, Rolnikaite could be branded as a Soviet answer to Elie Wiesel, especially as his *Night* and her *I Must Tell* had Yiddish palimpsests. Indeed, Anja Tippner, an attentive student of Rolnikaite's writings, suggested classifying her book as a text situated at the border of adult and young-adult fiction, which is also widely read by grown-ups and falls within the same group of texts as Elie Wiesel's *Night*.[126] However, Rolnikaite and Wiesel belonged to ideologically incompatible worlds. In the 1950s Wiesel was associated with the intensely anti-Soviet New York Yiddish daily *Forverts* and the Israeli daily *Yediot Aharonot*, and then, after visiting the Soviet Union in 1965, wrote *The Jews of Silence: A Personal Report on Soviet Jewry*, which placed him in the forefront of the Cold War. Rolnikaite, on the other hand, filled to a great degree the niche of Holocaust literature allocated in the socialist-realist cultural landscape of the 1960s. At the same time, she never really went on to become a household literary name in the Soviet Union, let alone abroad. Despite (and thanks to) lack of support from the powerful agitprop machinery, "Babi Yar," a short poem by Evtushenko published in September 1961 in *Literaturnaia gazeta*, had generated incomparably more lasting international attention and recognition than *I Must Tell*.

10

"BABI YAR"

The 1960s Generation

The term *shestidesiatniki*—plural for *shestidesiatnik*, a derivative from the Russian *shest'desiat*, meaning "sixty"—is one of the keywords of the period under our discussion. In fact, the name of Evgeni Evtushenko, the protagonist of this chapter, is also a keyword for the time around 1961, when the events under analysis took place. As a signifier of Soviet intellectuals of "the 1960s generation," *shestidesiatniki* first appeared in a 1960 essay by the literary and film critic Stanislav Rassadin, who wrote about a reborn intelligentsia distinguished by its "ability and desire to think, to reflect about life and its complexities."[1] Rassadin repurposed the word *shestidesiatniki*, coined a century earlier to describe followers of the Russian revolutionary thinker Nikolai Chernyshevsky, author of the highly influential novel *What Is to Be Done?* The *shestidesiatniki* of the 1960s also read this 1863 work as part of the mandatory school curriculum, but usually had different literary heroes. Still, literature, and poetry in particular, was a bridge that linked the two "60s." As in the 1860s, the Soviet *shestidesiatniki* widely read, loved, and discussed poetry, although the audience for poetry always remained a relatively elite and, compared with the audience for novels, small one.[2]

The *shestidesiatniki*, who appeared center stage during the Thaw, belonged to a broad and disparate cross-section of the intelligentsia, particularly of its literati and artistic segment in Moscow and Leningrad. At the same time, they developed a unifying generational identity. Born mostly in the 1930s, often with fathers lost in combat or in Stalin's purges, they experienced hardship as young children during World War II and the immediate postwar years. Later they witnessed drastic improvement in living standards from privation to a kind of normalcy and even relative prosperity. This, coupled with a rigid, ideologically insulated upbringing, typically filled them with belief in Soviet values and exuberantly optimistic views of the future, fueled by the USSR's impressive technological, scientific, and cultural achievements. As the bard-*shestidesiatnik* Vladimir Vysotsky sang: "But we make rockets, / And have dammed off the Yenisei River, / And also in the domain of ballet / We are ahead of the entire planet."

Loyal to the Soviet order though they usually were, *shestidesiatniki* did not consider it faultless. They saw themselves as uncorrupted by Stalinism, whose cult had been dismantled and mass repressions condemned, often half-heartedly, following Khrushchev's revelatory speech at the Communist Party's 20th congress in February 1956. Significantly, the Thaw shaped an environment that conceded some space for "permitted dissent"[3] in literature and arts.

In the literary landscape of the time, the newspaper *Literaturnaia gazeta*, the central organ of the Soviet Writers Union, became one of the main strongholds of the "liberal" camp, whereas the "conservative" (meaning usually Stalinist-nostalgic) camp controlled several other periodicals, including *Literatura i zhizn'* (Literature and Life), which was produced by the Writers Union of the Russian Soviet Federative Socialist Republic dominated by Russian ethnonationalists.[4] *Literatura i zhizn'*, dubbed by the "liberals" as "*LiZhi*" (meaning "to lick" in Russian) for its servility to the party's agitprop, was a loss-making periodical with a circulation of sixty thousand, or just one-fifth of *Literaturnaia gazeta's*. In addition to subscribers, both newspapers were available at many newsstands and libraries, so people could read it in various corners of the country.

Evgeni Evtushenko (1932–2017, also spelled Yevgeni Yevtushenko) was one of the best-known poets of the period. In addition to calling himself a *shestidesiatnik*, he described himself as one of the "children of the Party's 20th congress." Andrei Voznesensky, also a cult figure among poets of the time, characterized Evtushenko as a "poet-tribune" and a master of "poetic journalism."[5] "A poet in Russia is more than a poet" is arguably the most quotable of Evtushenko's lines (from his poem "The Bratsk Power

Station"). Admitted to the Writers Union at the age of twenty and thus becoming the youngest member of this venerable body, Evtushenko had gained a reputation as a voice of the young generation. He found himself considered a troublemaker and, as such, was expelled from the elite Maxim Gorky Literary Institute in 1957. It came as a surprise to foreign observers that the expulsion did not stop editors of leading literary journals from publishing Evtushenko's poems.[6]

In January 1960 the British journalist Edward Crankshaw came to the conclusion that one poem by Evtushenko contained more "basic criticism" of the Soviet system than all "rather pretentious posturing" of the dissident Soviet Russian writer and literary critic Andrei Sinyavsky, whose works came out abroad under the Jewish-sounding pseudonym Abram Tertz. Crankshaw was, arguably, the first to define Evtushenko and other poets of his cohort as "angry young men" or "angry young poets," similar to the sobriquets used for contemporaneous antiestablishment British writers such as John Osborne and Kingsley Amis.[7]

In reality, Evtushenko was not a dissident poet and never became one. According to Moisei Kogan, a philosopher and culturologist, the *shestidesiatniki* tended to fill the clearance between the dissidents and orthodox Communists.[8] Evtushenko would not question the political system as such but rather highlighted some of its negative aspects, and, according to Richard Sheldon, had an almost uncanny ability to sense the limits to which he could go in challenging the official position.[9] This attitude evidently suited the authorities. As a result, Evtushenko faced criticism, sometime intense, but it rolled off him, and his works continued to appear in Soviet periodicals and books. Crucially, the authorities would allow him to travel abroad. In a country with thoroughly sealed borders, this privilege signified a high estimation of his usefulness and reliability. As early as 1960 he visited the United States with a group of writers.

Media and audiences welcomed him in Europe and America, though he was not universally liked. After attending his gala reading, Mirra Ginsburg, an American translator of Russian and Yiddish literature, wrote to the Soviet children's writer and translator Kornei Chukovsky (Ze'ev Jabotinsky's close friend in their youth in Odessa) that the poet was "unacceptably rude and provocative toward the audience, which was absolutely friendly to him, came to be charmed by him, and left being charmed."[10] The "enchantment" was associated primarily with Evtushenko's poem "Babi Yar," published on 19 September 1961 in *Literaturnaia gazeta*.

In his overview of the Soviet Russian literary scene in 1961, Peter Rudy, an American Russian-language and literary scholar, noted about the poetic harvest during a year of "mild permafrost thaw" that if any of the poems were "remembered five years hence," certainly Evtushenko's poem would be among them, "not because of its quality, but because of the reaction it provoked."[11] Vasily Grossman (manuscripts of his novel *Life and Fate* with a strong Jewish slant were confiscated at the beginning of 1961) commented: "At last a Russian person has written that anti-Semitism exists in our country. It's not much of a poem, but this is beside the point; the main thing is the deed—a wonderful and even a brave one."[12]

One can draw a parallel between Ehrenburg's novel *The Thaw* and Evtushenko's poem: hardly literary masterpieces, they nevertheless caused quite a stir in the USSR and abroad. Babi Yar, the site of a Holocaust massacre, triggered the poet's muse, and his "Babi Yar" triggered a broad public discussion of the treatment of Jews by the state and society. The reaction to this poem will be discussed in this chapter using various sources, including readers' correspondence preserved at the Yad Vashem Archives and the Russian State Archive of Literature and Art (RGALI). Letters offer a broad range of views, discussing sometimes related, sometimes unrelated questions of politics, history, and culture. Many readers injected their own life experience into the Babi Yar debate. The political-ideological language of newspapers and textbooks also made its way into the letters. Whether their authors supported Evtushenko or viewed his poem as a calumny, they revealed the mindset shaped by Soviet ideology.

Spelling Out Anti-Semitism

The poem "Babi Yar" was a product of what was supposed to be a rather prosaic trip to Kyiv in August 1961. The newspaper *Pravda Ukrainy* (The truth of Ukraine) informed its readers that "the prominent Russian poet" Evtushenko had come to Kyiv after his recent journey to Cuba as a special correspondent for *Pravda*. Two appearances were scheduled for Evtushenko: on television and at a high-attendance poetry reading.[13]

It so happened that Evtushenko also visited the place where the massacre of Kyiv Jews had taken place twenty years earlier. Anatoli Kuznetsov, with whom Evtushenko had studied at the Literary Institute, brought him to Babi Yar (Babyn Yar in Ukrainian), the ravine that was the unmarked site of mass executions, particularly on 29 and 30 September 1941 when a special team of German SS troops supported by other German units and Ukrainian collaborators systematically shot dead by machine-gun fire over thirty-three thousand local Jews. Kuznetsov grew up in the vicinity of Babi Yar and survived the war as a non-Jewish teenager in Kyiv.

Evtushenko had probably already heard about the Babi Yar massacre and he certainly knew generally about the tragedy of Jews during World War II, especially as the Soviet media concurrently covered, not without bias, the Eichmann trial.[14] Significantly, many people in his literary circle were Jewish. In the 1950s he translated Yiddish poems by Aron Vergelis. Evtushenko also may have seen the American movie *The Diary of Anne Frank*, shown at the first Moscow Film Festival in August 1959, and apparently read the Russian translation of the diary published in 1960. Thus when he wrote in his "Babi Yar": "I seem to myself like Anne Frank, / to be transparent as an April sprig / and that I am in love,"[15] he expected his readers to understand the allusion.

By publishing Evtushenko's "Babi Yar," *Literaturnaia gazeta* returned to the theme first broached in October 1959 in the article "Why Has It Not Been Done?" Its author, the Russian resident of Kyiv Viktor Nekrasov, later a dissident and an émigré, was at that time a well-established prose writer. A World War II veteran, he won a Stalin Prize in 1947 for his novel *Front-Line Stalingrad*, with a Jewish protagonist named Farber, a frontline officer. In 1956 Farber appeared on the cinematic screen, memorably played by the Russian actor Innokentii Smoktunovskii (a son-in-law of the Yiddish writer Shira Gorshman), in the film *Soldiers*, based on Nekrasov's novel and film script.

Only people in the know could understand Nekrasov's hint in his 1959 article that the place, Babi Yar, had something to do with the annihilation of Kyiv's Jews: "a large ravine, whose name is known to the entire world" situated "behind an old Jewish cemetery." (The cemetery would be bulldozed several years later to make way for the construction of a television tower.)[16] According to Nekrasov, the tragedy that took place there affected in some way the entire city population: "There is no person in Kyiv whose father, son, relative, friend, or acquaintance is not laid to rest (no, a different word is needed here) in this place, Babi Yar. . . ." The writer described as deplorable the decision to shelve the monument project.[17]

Nekrasov was referring to the monument proposed shortly after the war. On 4 April 1945, *Pravda* printed its Kyiv correspondent's short article devoid of any Jewish context:

> Babi Yar is known to the entire world. Many thousands of Kyiv residents received their death at the hands of Hitlerite beasts.
>
> According to the decision of the government of the Ukrainian Soviet Socialist Republic, a monument to the victims of the German barbarians will be erected in Babi Yar. . . . The surface of the monument will carry the engraved report of the State Extraordinary Commission for the investigation of the atrocities of the German occupiers. A white marble bas-relief depicts a mother holding a murdered child in her hands.
>
> A museum will be situated in the basement of the monument.[18]

On the following day, *Pravda* once again, in an article describing the Nazi atrocities in Latvia, turned to the project of a Babi Yar memorial and explained its educational goal: "Let future generations know the danger faced by peoples in the grim hour of world history, and the catastrophe from which the Red Army and the Soviet people saved their Homeland and all of mankind."[19] Clearly, ideological supervisors of the memorialization project were reluctant to highlight the Jewishness of the majority of the victims, thus following what Zvi Gitelman describes as the consistent "party-line" on the Holocaust: passing over it in silence or blurring it "by universalizing it."[20]

Miriam Aizenshtadt (Zheleznova), the author of an article in the Moscow Yiddish newspaper *Eynikayt*, emphasized that the memorial would be dedicated to "the 140,000 Kyiv residents, predominantly Jewish—women, old people, and children."[21] However, this clarification regarding Jews appeared in a marginal periodical and by no means changed the *all-Soviet* character of the approved monument. Still, people interpreted the official announcement of the memorial project as a signal that the authorities had sanctioned the theme of Babi Yar. It is no surprise then, for instance, that

Dmitry Klebanov, a successful composer of Jewish origin, wrote a symphony entitled *Babi Yar*. In the 1940s Klebanov headed the Kharkiv organization of Soviet composers and took part in composing the anthem of the Ukrainian Soviet Socialist Republic.

The 1945 memorial project was not destined to come to fruition. The Soviet leadership generally did not hurry to build memorials to heroes and victims of the war. The complex commemorating the Battle of Stalingrad, a central event of the war, was unveiled as late as 1967, and the opening ceremony for the Khatyn memorial, a tribute to the millions of wartime victims in Belorussia, was held two year later. Numerous Holocaust obelisks were put up, as a rule in provincial places and thanks to private initiatives of Jewish survivors. Under Soviet conditions these decentralized, atomized initiatives could not develop into an organized movement. Arkadi Zeltser's analysis shows how the realization of the initiators' plans fully depended on the local authorities. Significantly, it usually remained unknown to the broader public that, despite the encountered difficulties, there were at least 733 cities, towns, or villages in the territory of the Soviet Union where, prior to 1991, Jews themselves had established one or more monuments to those killed in the Holocaust. As a result, it was common among Jews, most of whom had never been to sites where Jews had been shot, to think that there was a ban on memorializing Holocaust victims. The presumed total silencing of the subject of the Holocaust upset them as a manifestation of Soviet anti-Semitism.[22]

The situation in the capital of the second-largest Soviet republic differed from other, less visible places, especially as it was not a *purely* Holocaust site—thousands of non-Jews were also executed at Babi Yar. Ideological campaigns and repressions conducted in the last years of Stalin's life against various groups of Jewish intellectuals made implementation of a Babi Yar project altogether impossible at that time. In this climate, Klebanov's musical memorial was censured as a work "permeated by the spirit of bourgeois nationalism and cosmopolitanism." The Ukrainian poet Andrii Malyshko accused the composer of forgetting "about the friendship and brotherhood of the Soviet peoples" and developing "the idea of complete isolation of the Soviet peoples tortured to death by the Germans at Babi Yar."[23]

Nekrasov's 1959 article in *Literaturnaia gazeta* had been written or edited to voice his concern about *universal* memorialization of a wartime tragedy rather than specifically of the place where Kyiv's Jews were slaughtered in 1941. In any case, the writer was outraged to learn that the city's architectural department had proffered a radically new plan, namely to fill up the ravine for building a park and a stadium on that location. Nekrasov wrote: "Is it really taking place? In whose head could this idea have come—to fill the 30-meter-deep ravine, and to frolic and play on the place of the greatest tragedy? No, this can't be allowed to happen!"[24] It seems that André Blumel, a well-known activist in French socialist and Jewish circles and a top figure in the France-USSR Friendship Society, also tried to dissuade Soviet authorities from taking such a step.[25]

In December 1959 *Literaturnaia gazeta* printed a letter signed by a group of war veterans who supported—or, characteristically for the time, most likely had received instructions to show their support for—the idea of leveling the ravine and providing the new residential area with a park, which would also house a memorial to victims of fascism.[26] The letter was supposed to demonstrate the public's approval of the plan. In a short note, placed in the newspaper on 3 March 1960, a deputy of the Kyiv city council pointed to "the generally poor state of the area" as the only reason why a memorial had not been built so far. He reassured readers that the situation was going to change shortly, following landscaping work on the slopes of Babi Yar, and that, according to the decision of the Ukrainian government taken in December 1959, a monument, erected in the center of the new park, would carry "a memorial plaque to Soviet citizens slaughtered by the Hitlerites in 1941." Indeed, as a way to "improve" the area's topography, pulp from a nearby brick-works began to be used to fill the ravine. The authorities greenlighted this faulty engineering project, whose implementation led, on 13 March 1961, to the bursting of a nearby dam, causing massive flood damage and loss of life.[27]

Six months later the scene made a ghastly impression on Evtushenko, who wrote: "Over Babi Yar / there are no memorials. / A steep hillside, like a rough inscription. / I am terrified."[28] Nonetheless, the poet was not afraid to invoke anti-Semitism when describing the conditions of the site where the mass execution had taken place. Evtushenko later explained that he "had long wanted to write a poem on anti-Semitism" but only after visiting Babi Yar did the poetic form come to him.[29] He wrote that "foul hands" of anti-Semites had "rattle[d] . . . the clean name" of Russians who, by their nature, were internationalists.[30]

Earlier, in 1960, during his first visit to the United States, he had written a poem, known in English as "Talk," which later would sometimes be wrongly cited as an afterthought to writing "Babi Yar." He contended that the younger generation, "our children," would look back and be ashamed that in "so strange a time / common integrity could look like courage."[31] Yet the editors of *Literaturnaia gazeta* certainly manifested courage by publishing "Babi Yar," even if they buried it on the last page, behind a smokescreen of two other, ideologically impeccable Evtushenko poems devoted to Fidel Castro's Cuba. They certainly could not have predicted the scale of the tumult that lay ahead.

In Evtushenko's own account of the events, Valerii Kosolapov, editor-in-chief of *Literaturnaia gazeta*, had a long conversation with his wife that led to the couple's joint resolve to send the poem to print. It remains unclear what role the censors played in this regard. "Kosolapov was not reckless at all, neither was I," Evtushenko later wrote. The editor "never was a dissident concerning the ideals of socialism," but his ideals were "incompatible with a 'witch hunt' and cowardly aggression of the bureaucracy against normal human freedom of the mind."[32] Leonid Ilyichev, then the top party ideologue, wrote that the publication of Evtushenko's poem "contributed to vitalizing the unhealthy sentiments around the Jewish question in our country and was widely used by bourgeois propaganda for purposes of defamation against the Soviet Union."[33]

In the end, nothing terrible happened to Kosolapov. Although he was reprimanded and then forced to vacate the position of editor in 1962, it was hardly a severe career blow given his new high-ranking appointment as head of the publishing house Khudozhestvennaia literatura and later of the monthly literary journal *Novyi mir*.

The Conservatives' Outrage

Much has been written about the reaction of conservative literati grouped around *Literatura i zhizn'* who ranged themselves against Evtushenko, considering his poem an affront to their Soviet beliefs. It would be simplistic to label them all anti-Semites, especially as among them were also Jews. Rather, they continued to operate within ideological categories of the 1940s and early 1950s, including "cosmopolitanism," which deemed intellectuals unreliable if they showed signs of what was called "kowtowing to the West." Evtushenko, whose mother was Russian and paternal ancestors were German, conveyed to the conservatives an impression of a "cosmopolite," an intermediary to the West. His father's surname, Gangnus, would sometimes be falsely interpreted as a sign of concealed Jewishness.

On 24 September 1961, five days after the publication of "Babi Yar," *Literatura i zhizn'* featured Aleksei Markov's poem "My Answer." The poetic retort starts with the line "What kind of a Russian are you . . . ?," goes on to accuse Evtushenko of neglecting the heroism of the millions of Russians who died fighting fascism, and uses the loaded word "cosmopolite."[34] Markov, twelve years older than Evtushenko, with whom he was well acquainted, and a World War II veteran, graduated from the Literary Institute in 1951. Significantly, he was hardly a Kremlin court poet. In 1958 Markov had refused to chastise Boris Pasternak for publishing abroad the novel *Doctor Zhivago*, and a decade later he would protest against the Soviet invasion of Czechoslovakia. By 1961 his list of book publications was longer than Evtushenko's, but this did not propel him to popularity on the scale enjoyed by his younger poetic counterpart. Aleksander Bezymenski, a Soviet literary celebrity, mocked Markov's poetry in his 1961 *Book of Satire*.[35]

We can only surmise what Markov's motifs were for writing his anti–"Babi Yar" poem. Was it driven by Russian nationalism, anti-Semitism (incidentally, his wife, the daughter of a high-ranking public prosecutor executed in 1937, was Jewish), or a personal grudge against his more successful colleague? In any case, while Evtushenko's "Babi Yar" brought him lifelong worldwide popularity, Markov found vigorous support in conservative quarters of Soviet society but otherwise faced strong opprobrium. Moreover, wary of public humiliation, Markov canceled his poetic recitations.[36] His later work has been consigned to obscurity.

Meanwhile, on 27 September 1961, *Literatura i zhizn'* featured an article by the literary critic Dmitri Starikov. It aimed, but failed, to reduce the intensity of Markov's harsh, line-crossing critical attack, which caused concern even among the editors of the newspaper. A resignation from the editorial board came from Lev Kassil, whose books, including *Konduit* and *Shvambrania*, had become a staple in the canon of Soviet literature.[37] Illuminating is the letter of the poet Konstantin Pozdniaev, deputy editor of *Literatura i zhizn'*; he would be appointed the first editor of *Literaturnaia Rossiia* (Literary Russia), the new incarnation of *Literatura i zhizn'*, after the latter stopped being published at the end of 1962. Pozdniaev, who was absent at the time of the explosive poems' publication, wrote to the (Jewish) literary scholar Aleksandr Dymshits, one of those who had approved Starikov's article: "Evtushenko's poem consolidated around itself a scum of various kinds from the camp of those who hate bitterly the Russian people, the Soviet people in general, whereas Markov's poem became a call to arms for Black Hundredists."[38]

Starikov, whose father-in-law Anatoli Sofronov was—in Evgeny Dobrenko's words—"one of the most horrible literary hangmen of the Stalin epoch,"[39] worked as a staff critic of *Literaturnaia gazeta* in the late 1950s. Many people in literary circles knew that Starikov's mother was Jewish. As a point of reference, he had chosen Ehrenburg's poem "Babi Yar," underlining that the timing for publishing such a work, in the January 1945 issue of *Novyi mir*, would have been justified by the still-raging war. Now, seventeen years later, Starikov could not see any sound reason for visiting this topic, especially from the perspective chosen by Evtushenko.

> Has he [Evtushenko] remembered Babi Yar to put the world on its guard against Fascism? Or have the hysterical howls of the West German revanchist curs prevented him from keeping silent? Or did he want to remind some of his contemporaries of the heroism, exploits, glory and great sacrifices of the fathers?
>
> Nothing of the kind! Standing above the steep precipice of Babi Yar, the only inspiration the young Soviet writer found were verses on anti-Semitism! And thinking today of those who perished . . . the only fact he recalled was that they were Jews. This to him seemed the most significant, the most vital point.[40]

Starikov insisted that the Nazis hated all East European peoples equally and that anti-Semitism was only part of their murderous policy; therefore it was insulting to other peoples who had suffered under the Nazis to read a poem that focused exclusively on the Jewish tragedy. Markov and Starikov voiced the opinion of an influential group of Soviet writers, and their Party overseers. No doubt, such views were also held by people of various walks of life, particularly among those convinced that Jews were underrepresented on the front lines of the war but were overrepresented among bureaucratic figures and black-market dealers in safe rear areas.

The Voice of the Authorities

Ehrenburg was in Rome during those September days, but a letter from the poet Boris Slutsky kept him in touch with what was going on in Moscow. On 3 October Ehrenburg mailed a short note intended for publication in *Literaturnaia gazeta*, pointing to Starikov's misuse of quotes from his writings. However, this time Kosolapov acted cautiously and did not send the note to print. Upon his return to Moscow, Ehrenburg wrote to Khrushchev, informing him that Markov's poem and Starikov's article had engendered a widespread negative response in the Italian press. He also complained about the misquotes in Starikov's text. This letter reached Khrushchev thanks to Vladimir Lebedev, arguably the most liberal and intellectually sophisticated among Khrushchev's advisers. (Evtushenko characterized him later as a "romantic schemer.")[41] As a result, *Literaturnaia gazeta* published it on 14 October, three days before the opening day of the 22nd Party Congress, which approved the unattainable plan of building Communism in twenty years. The congress also authorized the removal of Stalin's remains from the Red Square Mausoleum, and the renaming of cities and other toponyms, as well as factories, educational institutions, and many other bodies that carried the name of Stalin.[42]

Although the Party and state apparatus suspected Jews of potentially or actually bearing loyalty to Israel and to their brethren in the capitalist world, the same apparatus would censure what was deemed an open manifestation of anti-Jewish attitudes. Saving face before the West, including Western Communists, remained an important, if not prevailing, factor in determining the tactics for dealing with the "Jewish question." In the official narrative, anti-Semitism was an ideological infection brought by non-Soviet, most notably Nazi, propaganda. On 17 December 1962, during a meeting of Khrushchev and other Party functionaries with the creative intelligentsia,

Leonid Ilyichev, the notoriously dogmatic top Party ideologist, turned to the question of anti-Semitism:

> In the Party, comrades, there are not two opinions: anti-Semitism is a repulsive phenomenon, and the Party has been fighting with elements of anti-Semitism. However, is it the right time to raise this question as the sharpest and most urgent one? . . . We know that the appearance of poems, which condemn anti-Semitism and are essentially correct ones, has provoked a reverse reaction. Is it appropriate to raise this question in the conditions of our country, which has lost 20 million lives of Soviet people, representatives of all peoples of the great Soviet Union?[43]

Khrushchev, who consistently blocked the implementation of Babi Yar memorial projects,[44] also made off-the-cuff remarks on this issue:

> When I worked in Ukraine I visited Babi Yar. Many people were murdered there. However, comrade Evtushenko, not only Jews died there, there were many others. Hitler exterminated Jews, exterminated Gypsies, but his next plan was to exterminate Slavs, we know that he also exterminated many Slavs. If we now calculate arithmetically, how many exterminated people were Jews and how many Slavs, then those who spoke about anti-Semitism would have seen that more Slavs had been killed, their number is higher than that of Jews. It's correct. So, what is the purpose of separating, of sowing discord? What aims have those who do it, who raise this issue? Who needs it? I think it's wrong.[45]

For all that, Kremlin agitprop gave the foreign media a bit of fodder to repudiate charges of silencing information about Nazi extermination of the Jews. Thus, in 1962 an attentive observer of Soviet Jewish life could not miss a remark by Oleksandr Korniychuk (in Russian, Aleksandr Korneychuk), who combined the roles of foremost Ukrainian playwright and top functionary—chairman of the Supreme Soviet (parliament) of the Ukrainian republic. In April of that year, speaking in Moscow during a session of the Soviet parliament, he charged that the West was overlooking Nazi Germany's murderous policy and, in that context, mentioned the Jews among principal victims. He noted that Jews had been slaughtered not only at concentration camps but also in Babi Yar. In the foreign press, Korniychuk's remarks, buried in his long speech and mainly overlooked by the Soviet public, appeared in newspaper headlines and were linked, deservedly or not, directly to the publication of Evtushenko's poem.[46]

Meanwhile, Evtushenko incurred the wrath of the conservative segment of the literary community and the ideological apparatus. In March 1963, at a plenary meeting of the Writers Union's governing board, much critical attention was devoted to Evtushenko's writings and pronouncements. The poet chose to admit his faults. Moreover, he highlighted his dislike of Ehrenburg's definition of the current era as a "Thaw," because, he argued, they had been living in "spring, in the years of flourishing of the country."[47] Nevertheless, Evtushenko continued receiving rebukes from his peers. The Ukrainian poet Dmytro Pavlychko, only three years older than Evtushenko and also considered to be a *shestidesiatnik*, contended that "Evtushenko and his like long ago should have undergone amputation of their conceit, the most cancerous tumor of talent."[48]

Nonetheless, and notwithstanding the criticism leveled against him, Evtushenko retained the backing of influential people in the Central Committee of the Communist Party and his status as a *vyezdnoi* (authorized to travel abroad) literary celebrity remained in force. As Robert Conquest put it, "He had earned what is not a right but a privilege."[49] The same (probably) people did not allow him, however, to accept an invitation to visit Israel, where his poem had created a particularly strong stir.[50]

The phenomenal popularity of "Babi Yar" in the West certainly contributed to Evtushenko's standing in the eyes of policy advisers and makers responsible for shaping the international public perception of the Soviet Union. Characteristically, on 8 March 1963, during another meeting with the creative intelligentsia, Khrushchev stressed that "there was nothing counterrevolutionary" in Evtushenko's "Babi Yar." Rather, it was a result of his failing to understand that real foes of the Soviet Union had pushed him to fight anti-Semitism in order to "revive the nationalist Zionist rat."[51] Khrushchev argued that the poet did not "show political maturity" and, therefore, represented "things as if only Jews [had been] victims of fascist atrocities, whereas, of course, many Russians, Ukrainians, and Soviet people of other nationalities [had been] murdered by the Hitlerite butchers."

Setting an example of a balanced approach, the Soviet leader spoke about a certain Kogan, a former low-ranking functionary in the Kiev apparatus of the Young Communist League, who was captured along with German soldiers during the Stalingrad battle. Kogan, who was an interpreter with Field Marshal von Paulus's staff, exemplified a Jewish traitor.[52] (The entire "Kogan affair" turned out to be pure fiction.)[53] By contrast, Khrushchev praised a Jewish war hero—the political officer Leonid Vinokur, who played the central role in capturing the same von Paulus.[54]

Letters

The publication of "Babi Yar" increased the number of people with a strong opinion about Evtushenko, even if previously his persona and poetry left them unmoved. In his "A Precocious Autobiography," published in the American magazine *Saturday Evening Post* in August 1963, Evtushenko wrote that he was "showered with letters" from all over the country as soon as the poem appeared in print and that general readers—as distinct from government and Party officials—had shown overwhelming approval of the poem.[55] People addressed their letters also to *Literaturnaia gazeta*, Ehrenburg, Khrushchev, and others.

Meanwhile, some readers developed a loathing for the poet. A woman wrote that she used to "do her best to defend" Evtushenko, but now, after his "betraying the Russians," he should forget about her support. A man who signed his letter "A. Gerasimenko" asked rhetorically: "How could you, a Soviet poet, insult and slander, in this way, the Russian people, whose unparalleled bravery inspired admiration by the world? You speak about Jews who perished in Babi Yar. And the entire time, in each line [of your poem] you insinuate that the perpetrators were Russian. But this is slander!"

Aleksandr Egorov, who wrote "on behalf of a group of genuine Russian people," supported Markov, arguing that Evtushenko's poetry carried a message of international Zionism. "Evtushenko writes in his poem that in his 'blood there is no Jewish blood'. It seems that this statement has to be checked. Someone, among his mother's ancestors, must be a 'cosmopolite.'"

Among the letters there is a postcard, signed "Genuine Russian," with harsh invective against Evtushenko:

> When you were writing the poem "Babi Yar," you imagined you were a Hebrew, a Jew, Anne Frank, and many other things.
>
> Answer, please, through *Literaturnaia gazeta*: Did you not imagine also that you were Fanny Kaplan, Gregori Zinoviev, Leon Trotsky, and many other representatives of the Jewish people, who figure regularly in satirical articles and criminal trials dealing with cases of all possible fraud offenses?[56]

While Kaplan, who shot and wounded Lenin in 1921, and Trotsky certainly remained in the category of evil, Zinoviev had been partly publicly rehabilitated following the publication of Emmanuil Kazakevich's story "The Blue Notebook." The story appeared in the April 1961 issue of the literary journal *Oktiabr'* (October) thanks to the intervention of the same Khrushchev's adviser, Lebedev, who helped Ehrenburg publish his letter criticizing Starikov's article.[57] Kazakevich showed Lenin and Zinoviev in late summer 1917, when they were hiding together to evade arrest. "Genuine Russian" either did not know this or kept his own list of enemies, probably remembering the "Trotskyist-Zinoviev conspiracies" fabricated in the 1930s to form a basis for persecuting people during the mass repressions. Clearly, outlandish charges of Stalin's years had mixed in Genuine Russian's propaganda-created worldview with press reports on economic crimes, whose culprits often had distinct Jewish names.[58]

Benedikt Sarnov, a literary critic at *Literaturnaia gazeta* who was known for his dislike of Evtushenko's poetry, remembered that the writer Leonid Likhodeev, also a member of the newspaper's staff (both were Jewish), had told him sarcastically on the day of publication of "Babi Yar": "You, rebbe, can say what you want, but today he [Evtushenko] put all the twelve million Jews in his waistcoat pocket."[59] In the event, though, Jews were also present among authors who criticized Evtushenko. One such letter came from Kustanay (after 1997 Kostanay), Kazakhstan, written by a V. Girshovich, a student at the local pedagogical institute: "I am Jewish by nationality and must admit honestly that I used to like this poem. However, after reading B. Russell's letter to N. S. Khrushchev [on the situation of the Jews in the Soviet Union] I have realized into whose hands the authors of such works are playing, willingly or not. Thanks to them, the sensation-hungry bourgeois press uses it as an excuse to spread lies about our country."[60]

A similar thought is expressed in the letter of Iakov M. Lerner, who worked in the Donbas region of Ukraine at a project institute, was a member of the Communist Party from 1942, and headed a volunteer citizens' patrol (*narodnaia druzhina*). He committed his thoughts to paper after reading Khrushchev's speech on 8 March 1963. Lerner's father was "Jewish, but his entire life was a worker." By using "but" he emphasized that it was considered uncommon for a Jews to be a worker. He was unhappy that "some scoundrels once again (apparently for their own good) raise[d] the so-called 'Jewish question.'"

> I understand that they get support from American and British moneybags, who pretend to crusade for the "suppressed Jewish question," though they were, in fact, mainly responsible for the mass annihilation of Jews, Ukrainians, Russians, Belorussians, and other peoples during the years of the war against fascism. . . .
>
> I admit that there are certain silly jerks who being drunk can call someone in a tram "*zhidovskaia morda*" [Yid mug]. But do they represent a majority? They are few and far between. They can call anyone they want a "mug."
>
> I've decided to write to you because I can't agree with what I hear many Jews mumble following your speech.
>
> They say: "Evtushenko is brave, he is not afraid of Khrushchev."
>
> "Evtushenko is the first who inveighs against anti-Semites."
>
> A cult of Evtushenko is being built. However, the builders of this cult are not the Jews who together with all peoples of our country fought for its honor and independence, but those who strive to blow the so-called "Jewish question" out of proportion.
>
> After your speech, Evtushenko gets the halo of a "martyr for the Jewish people."[61]

In Dnipropetrovsk, a KGB informer reported that Semen Erlikhman, a journalist of the Kyiv daily *Pravda Ukrainy*, who wrote under the improbable pseudonym Akhmatov, had extinguished the enthusiasm of Samuil Ortenberg, a fifty-eight-year-old teacher. The latter had initially believed that the poem's publication in a Moscow newspaper coupled with the launching of *Sovetish Heymland* heralded a change in policy toward Jews. Erlikhman, six years younger than the teacher, had told him that he could not understand why all Jews were singing the praises of "Babi Yar." He was convinced that its publication was nothing more than an attempt to placate public opinion abroad.[62]

L. Semenova (nothing else is known about her) reacted to Khrushchev's speech in a completely different way:

> You accuse the author of writing that only Jews had been ostensibly executed in Babi Yar, whereas people of other nationalities had been executed there as well. . . . The thing is that representatives of other nationalities usually would be put to death for fighting against the Hitlerites. It was different for the Jews. . . . Those who had survived the war in the occupied areas came out from this experience with a broken and debased soul. Therefore, the author had a moral right to focus on this category of the murdered, especially as Babi Yar is widely associated with the massacre of Jews.

Anti-Semitism, "penetrating from time to time into the life of society," was a burning issue for Semenova, who most probably was Jewish. Limitations faced by Jews applying to study at top universities caused increasing anxieties. Although the situation had improved compared with the last years of Stalin's life, Semenova maintained that it was "[too] early to say: 'We don't have a Jewish question.' The absence of pogroms and the [presence of] equal voting rights do not amount to a great achievement for a socialist country."[63]

Markov's rhymed attack on Evtushenko prompted particularly strong responses. The historian and bibliographer Daniil Al'shits stated that he was not "an admirer of E. Evtushenko's poetic manner" and did not "belong to Jewish nationalists. The latter would certainly consider me a very bad Jew—I don't even know any Yiddish at all." At the same time, he was "deeply outraged by Mr. Markov's response to Evtushenko's 'Babi Yar.'"[64] M. (only the initial is known) Vaisman, a Tartu-based correspondent of the newspaper *Sovetskaia Estoniia* (Soviet Estonia), saw a similarity between Markov the Soviet poet and Nikolai Markov, a leader of the 1905-established chauvinist Union of the Russian People, who—in Lenin's words cited by Vaisman—was ill-famed for his "harassing non-Russians and [propagating] a pogrom ethos."[65] Another letter writer, E. D. Movshenzon, also labeled Markov a follower of the infamous Black Hundreds: "Markov! The name rings a bell. Did he not . . . shout: 'Beat the Yids, save Russia'?"

According to Ilya Shtivelman of Vinnytsia, Ukraine, Starikov, for his part, had "hurt people's innermost feelings, opened the deepest wounds, and cynically laughed at them." A veteran of the war, Shtivelman found it particularly painful to realize that the critic sought to trivialize the tragedy of the Jewish people, to present it as a topic of little import. He saw a similarity between Starikov's article and critical attacks during the Stalin era against the Soviet Ukrainian poet Volodymyr Sosiura (whose poem devoted to the Babi Yar tragedy, albeit without mentioning the Jews, came out in December 1943). Sosiura faced opprobrium for his 1944 poem "Love Ukraine!," in which he stated that a Ukrainian could not respect other nations "unless you love Ukraine and hold her high."[66] All in all, Shtivelman concluded that Starikov, without realizing it, "did a great service to Evtushenko. Respect for the young, talented and sincere poet has increased exponentially."[67]

In April 1962, when Vladlen Izmozik, later a well-established historian, wrote his letter, he worked as a teacher in Priozersk, Leningrad Province. Fifty-five years later he would publish an analysis of the issue of anti-Semitism in letters sent to authorities.[68] Back then, in 1962, he chose to share his thoughts with Ehrenburg, whom many Jews regarded as a figure of moral authority. (I. B. Mints, an elderly person, wrote to Ehrenburg that, since reading "Babi Yar" and the scathing responses in *Literatura i zhizn'*, he had been feeling a need for consolation. Ehrenburg replied: "I understand and share your pain.")[69] In Izmozik's judgement, the poem was "imperfect stylistically" but had been "written by a genuine Soviet Russian patriot and internationalist." He praised the "great strophe that 'The Internationale' [the Communist anthem] will thunder when the last anti-Semite on earth dies," and focused his criticism on Markov and Starikov:

> Markov heaps vulgar insult on Evtushenko ("cosmopolite," "mercenary creature") in the language of revelry of the Black Hundreds, shrouding it with flowery words about the heroism of the Russian people.
>
> But who is questioning this heroism? Who can forget that the Jewish people had been saved from complete annihilation thanks to the heroism of the *entire*

> *Soviet* nation, the heroism of ordinary Russians. However, the Jewish people, together with all peoples of the Soviet Union, participated heroically in this fight.

After World War II the slander that Jews were shirking military service or showing cowardice continued to circulate among the population. The phrase "Jews fought in Tashkent," that is, thousands of miles from the front lines, gained currency in various quarters of society.[70] As a reaction, many Jews had developed a syndrome of devoting obsessive attention to collecting facts and statistics that showed the heroic reality of Jewish participation in the war. The "counter-Tashkent syndrome" revealed itself also in Izmozik's letter:

> Expressions "They battled for Tashkent in the rear" and "They are all such" (about a gang of profiteers with many Jews among them) circulate rather widely and make a nonnegligible impact on the education of children and young people. I've learned from my own experience that pupils of the sixth, seventh, eighth, and ninth grades know very little about the persecution of Jews by the fascists and the fight of Jews, together with other peoples, against fascism. (There is not even a memorial in Babi Yar. What can one read about the Warsaw Ghetto uprising apart from Falikman's *Vosstanie obrechennykh*, which is next to impossible to find? How many years has the book *Avengers of the Ghetto* [*Mstiteli getto*], about the Minsk ghetto, remained out of print?) Accordingly, we have anti-Semitic incidents, abuse, and derogatory nicknames.

Starikov's article also received bitter criticism. A reader who signed his letter E. Tartakovskii censured the critic for doing harm "to the brotherly commonwealth of Soviet peoples, especially on the eve of the 22nd congress [of the Communist Party], which has to approve the program of building a communist society." And he added: "Incidentally, it would not be bad to erect a memorial in Babi Yar, one for tens of thousands of victims." Nathan S. Krulevetskii, of the South Sakhalin Province, echoed this sentiment in his letter, noting "the atmosphere of concealment of the horrific disaster that befell my people."[71]

Vladimir Chestnokov, a People's Artist of the USSR whose stature as a Communist was above reproach (he was a delegate to the 22nd Party Congress), made his cinematographic debut in 1938 in the film *Professor Mamlock*. Based on a play by the German Jewish Communist writer Friedrich Wolf, it portrayed persecution of Jews in Nazi Germany. Chestnokov's letter took the form of an (unpublished) article entitled "What I Am Concerned About." In particular, he wrote:

> I had three sleepless nights, so incensed was I by his [Starikov's] article, so disturbed by its content and tone. Evtushenko, a young talented poet, has written a poem, whose main and only thought boils down to the following: anti-Semitism still exists on earth and, as long as this phenomenon exists, we have to fight it, like progressive people of all times and generations used to do. . . . Any compassionate, clearheaded person cannot get any other thoughts from reading the poem "Babi Yar." D. Starikov, however, managed to do so. I read the poem again and again. No, it certainly does not contain what Starikov writes is in it.

Judging by the letter signed with the name N. A. Soboleva, its author sincerely believed that her country was, as the propaganda claimed, a stronghold of internationalism:

> I am Russian, a citizen of multi-national Russia, where—I believe—very soon the question concerning nationality will disappear in the profile forms of personnel departments . . . , where we choose friends without asking them about purity of their Slavic blood. I am a citizen of Soviet Russia, the only country in history that has succeeded (or will succeed) in ending the chronicle of History's uprooted scapegoat—the Jewish people, who for the first time have found [in Russia] their proper homeland.

S. Kuznetsova, a Russian woman who apparently saw around her only well-acculturated Jews, wrote:

> In one sense Starikov is right. There is no Jewish nation. There are Soviet Jews or, as Starikov puts it, Russian Jews with the mark of "Jew" in their passport. The hitherto harassed, homeless people have found their proper homeland in

> the Soviet Union. However, let Starikov and Markov not delude themselves: sons and daughters of the Jewish population of Russia earned their homeland by fighting with guns in their hands, side by side with their Russian class brothers and sisters.

Other letter writers, who introduced themselves as non-Jewish Soviet citizens, expressed their sympathy for Jews. Evgeni Raskov, "a Russian man," agreed that anti-Semitism, "in a rude, but well-concealed form," existed in the Soviet Union, although "nobody speaks about it openly, nor are there any publications about it." L. Deriabina, who wrote that she felt offended by Markov's poem and expected to see a riposte in *Literaturnaia gazeta*, shared her experience as a teacher of Russian language and literature somewhere in the Russian provinces. She felt sorry for her Jewish student:

> I looked at pale-faced Misha Gershovich, and at that moment he seemed to me somewhat similar to a Negro in the American southern states. This is certainly an exaggeration, because Misha has been studying as an equal with all other students, without being subjected to rude, racist harassment. However, we are heading to communism, therefore it is long overdue to make our newspapers free from any remnants of anti-Semitism.[72]

The Trace Left Behind

In the coming years, Evtushenko would calibrate and recalibrate the meaning of his words. In the version used in Dmitri Shostakovich's Thirteenth Symphony, with a segment based on "Babi Yar," Evtushenko made two principal additions: "Here together with Russians and Ukrainians lie Jews," and "I am proud of Russia which stood in the path of the bandits."[73] This did not save the symphony from being banned by the authorities.[74] The journal *Sovetish Heymland* ignored "Babi Yar." This was particularly striking and telling because Aron Vergelis, the Yiddish journal's editor, eagerly translated Russian poetry. He explained, however, that the poem was "not well thought through" by Evtushenko.[75] Meanwhile, at least five Yiddish and ten Hebrew translations of the poem came out abroad.[76]

Anastas Mikoyan during his meeting with John F. Kennedy. Photo Credit: Abbie Rowe, National Park Service / John F. Kennedy Presidential Library and Museum.

Soviet Grandmaster Mikhail Botvinnik playing simultaneous chess. Photo Credit: BNA Photographic / Alamy Stock Photo.

The memorial at the site of the murder of Jewish men in the town of Nevel, with inscriptions in Yiddish and Russian, and the Hebrew abbreviation *peh nun* (abbreviation for "here lies") inscribed inside the five-pointed star. The monument was erected in the late 1940s. Photographer: Alexander Frenkel. Courtesy of photographer.

Poster for the Yiddish People's Theater show in Vilnius. Photo Credit: From Milan Khersonskii personal archive.

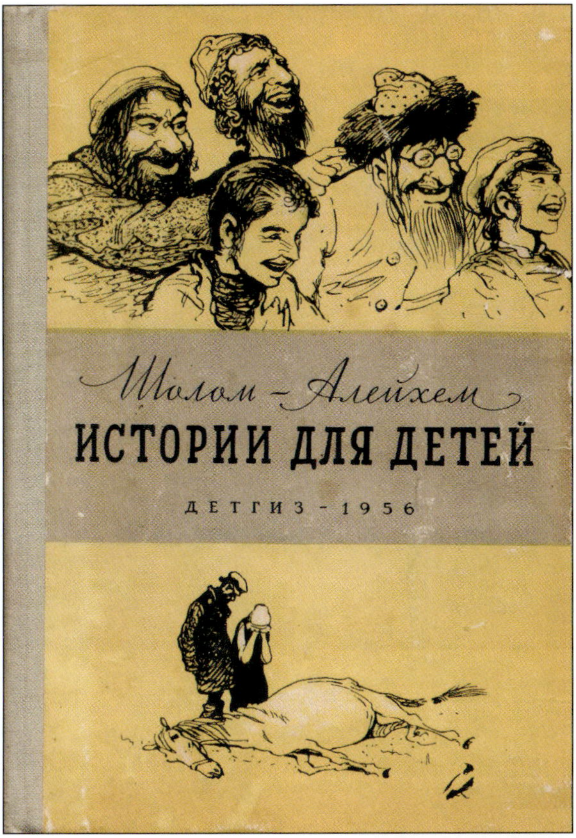

Sholem Aleichem's 1956 book *Stories for Children*. Photo Credit: Courtesy of Alexander Frenkel.

The Leningrad Yiddish actors Yakov Klebanov and Esther Roitman performing in the 1960s. Photo Credit: Courtesy of Alexander Klebanov.

Ilya Ehrenburg photographed by Ida Kar. Photo Credit: © National Portrait Gallery, London / Art Resource, NY.

Three members of a Soviet visiting group of intellectuals at a news conference at the Soviet Mission to the United Nations in New York, November 1963. They are Aron Vergelis (left), editor of the Moscow Yiddish literary journal *Sovetish Heymland* (Soviet Homeland); Boris Polevoy (center), editor of the Moscow Russian-language literary journal *Iunost'* (Youth); and Professor Nikolai Mostovets (right) of the Economics Institute of the Soviet Academy of Sciences. Photo Credit: AP Photo / John Rooney.

A family portrait of David Stavitsky, his wife, and their daughter. Photo Credit: Courtesy of Inna Stavitsky.

A Jewish family enjoying a summer day in a country house in Pushcha-Voditsa, a subdistrict of Kyiv. Many residents of big cities would spend the summer at *daches*, homes in suburban or rural areas. Photo Credit: Courtesy of Gennady Estraikh.

Group of rabbis in Moscow, 1958: Eli Sandler (first on right), Solomon Shlifer (third on right), Yehuda Leyb Levin (fourth on right). Photo Credit: Courtesy of Leonid Sandler.

Evgeni Evtushenko on the podium reading his poems to public. Photo by Gerhard Rauchwetter / picture alliance via Getty Images.

Joseph Stalin's funeral. The coffin of Stalin is carried out the House of Trade Unions by Soviet political leaders. Photo Credit: Hulton Archive / Getty Images.

Soviet poet and translator Samuil Marshak. Photo by Leonid Lazarev / Hulton Archive / Getty Images.

Boris Pasternak outside his house at the writer's colony located near Moscow. Photo by Jerry Cooke / Corbis Historical via Getty Images.

Comedian Arkady Raikin on his arrival at London Airport. Photo by WATFORD / Mirrorpix via Getty Images.

Leonid Utesov performing with his jazz band. Photo by Sovfoto / Universal Images Group via Getty Images.

A scene from *200,000*, a play by Sholem Aleichem, performed by the Moscow Yiddish Drama Ensemble, created in 1962. Photo Credit: Jewish Museum and Tolerance Center.

The first Russian edition of Anne Frank's diary, published in the USSR in 1960. Photo Credit: Courtesy of Ludmila Gordon.

Judaism without Embellishment by Trofim Kichko. Photo Credit: Memorial International Library.

Yiddish theater poster for Sholem Aleichem's play *200,000*. Photo Credit: Courtesy of the Museum of Jewish History in Russia.

Postcard of Elina Bystritskaya, a Soviet theater and cinema actress of Jewish descent. Photo Credit: Courtesy of the Museum of Jewish History in Russia.

Vatan Sovetimu (*Soviet Homeland*) journal. Photo Credit: Courtesy of the Museum of Jewish History in Russia.

An autographed photo of Grigory Novak, a Soviet weightlifter of Jewish descent who won a world title in 1946 and a silver medal at the 1952 Summer Olympics. Photo Credit: Courtesy of the Museum of Jewish History in Russia.

Sidi Tal, a Yiddish actress, reading at home. Photo Credit: Courtesy of the Museum of Jewish History in Russia.

Klavdiia Starkova. Photo Credit: Institute of Oriental Manuscripts, Russian Academy of Sciences, St. Petersburg.

The postage stamp honoring the Sholem Aleichem Centenary issued in the USSR in 1959. Photo Credit: Alamy.

Nehama Lifshitz performing on stage. Photo Credit: Courtesy of Roza Litay.

The Leningrad Philharmonia poster announcing Nehama Lifshitz's concert. Photo Credit: Courtesy of Roza Litay.

Iosif Amusin. Photo Credit: Institute of Oriental Manuscripts, Russian Academy of Sciences, St. Petersburg.

The Lenin monument in the city of Birobidzhan. Photo Credit: Courtesy of Valery Gurevich.

Jewish families gathered for a commemoration by the monument erected in memory of the murdered Jews in the town of Diatlovo in 1958. The note on the photo reads: "3,000 Jews were brutally murdered by German invaders in Diatlovo in 1942. Photo by the gravestone." Photo Credit: Yad Vashem Photo Archives.

Interior of the Kutaisi synagogue. Photographer: Yulia Oreshina. Courtesy of photographer.

In 1962, during his visit to Britain, Evtushenko declared that both foreign journalists and dogmatic Soviet ideologues missed the point, interpreting the poem as his indictment of Russian anti-Semitism. In reality, he argued unconvincingly, he did not mean that, but rather sought to draw a clear line between the Russian people and anti-Semitism.[77] Speaking with a correspondent of the Israeli Communist newspaper *Kol ha-Am*, he said that Russian hearts did not carry anti-Jewish feelings before World War II, but the war had left anti-Semitism as its legacy.[78]

In 1966 Anatoli Kuznetzov's documentary story, also entitled "Babi Yar," came out in the mass-circulation Moscow monthly journal *Iunost'*. Heavily censored at the time of the publication, its full text saw the light of day after Kuznetsov's emigration in 1969.[79] Yet the fact itself of making this work available in two million copies of *Iunost'* and then, in 1967, in 150,000 copies of the resulting book, brought out by the Moscow publishing house Molodaia gvardiia (Young Guard), shows that Babi Yar was not a completely taboo topic. Several Soviet Yiddish writers dedicated their works to Babi Yar.[80]

Evtushenko's "Babi Yar," however, would not be reprinted, quoted, or mentioned in any Soviet publications, and had some circulation in the Soviet Union only in unofficial duplicates. On 29 September 1969, Vitalii Nikitchenko, chairman of Ukraine's KGB, wrote to the Central Committee of Ukraine's Communist Party:

> On 28 September 1969, 175 documents were mailed from Kiev to addresses of individuals of Jewish nationality, Kyiv residents, containing an inserted text, which started with the words: "Remember! Exactly 28 years ago thousands of your brothers and sisters were savagely murdered." This was followed by an epigraph—Julius Fučík's words: "People, be vigilant!"—and then an abridged text of Evgeny Evtushenko's "Babi Yar."
>
> The inserted text was typographically printed. . . .
>
> Measures have been taken to find the author and distributor of this document.[81]

As late as 1983, "Babi Yar" finally made an appearance in Evtushenko's three-volume collection of writings, but it had to be accompanied by an author's note:

> Babi Yar—a ravine on the outskirts of Kyiv, where the Hitlerites annihilated several tens of thousands of Soviet people, including Jews, Ukrainians, Russians and other inhabitants of Kyiv. When this poem was written, there was as yet no monument at Babi Yar. Now there is a monument to the victims of fascism.
>
> Fascism inflicted on the Jewish people a policy of genocide. Now, through a tragic paradox of history, the Israeli Government has inflicted a policy of genocide on the Palestinians, who have been forcibly deprived of their land.[82]

Thus, the link, established earlier in Starikov's article between the issue of Babi Yar memorialization and various Israel-related issues, most notably of emigration of Soviet Jews, lingered in the logic of ideological watchdogs. After all, virtually anything that had to do with Jews in the Soviet Union had to be considered in the context of the struggle against international Zionism.

In the meantime, "Babi Yar," translated and published in numerous languages, made Evtushenko a household name outside the Soviet Union. His first volume in English, containing twenty-two poems, came out under the imprints of E. P. Dutton and Penguin with a print run of 12,500, whereas the usual first printing of an American poet was often fewer than a thousand copies.[83] On 13 April 1962, Evtushenko's portrait against a backdrop of an early spring landscape appeared on the cover of *Time* magazine. American Jews held him in particularly high esteem. The journal *Commentary*, published by the American Jewish Committee, wrote in 1963: "Yevtushenko needs no introduction to Western readers. He burst into national [i.e., Soviet] and world renown after September 19, 1961. . . . He remains today a significant, if erratic and somewhat ambitious, spokesman of the younger Soviet intelligentsia."[84] True, in 1968 his reputation seemed not impeccable enough to give him a chance, for instance, to be elected as Oxford's professor of poetry.[85]

While "Babi Yar" gained Evtushenko worldwide attention and acclaim, in the Soviet Union the effect of the poem, concealed from the readers' eyes, might appear less significant or, at least, less abiding than Kuznetsov's mass-printed work. There is no way to quantify the impact of the two literary works by Russian writers. Still, Evtushenko's poem and the discourse around it left a tangible, if unmeasurable, trace in the Soviet public, particularly its Jewish conscience. Thanks to the publication of the poem, "for the first time the Jewish theme appeared openly in an official publication, with a positive connotation, with compassion toward Jews, and with condemnation of anti-Semitism, indirectly recognizing its existence in the Soviet Union." And a hope emerged that this theme would continue to be discussed, thereby improving the Jews' situation.[86] Although this did not happen, the publication in *Literaturnaia gazeta* engendered discussion of the problem at least in the letters sent to Evtushenko and various officeholders, including Nikita Khrushchev. The official reaction to "Babi Yar" had shaped, or at least reinforced, the strategy of a "balanced approach" to subject matters associated with World War II: negative Jewish characters had to balance out the presence of non-Jewish traitors and collaborators, while positive non-Jewish characters should underscore people's friendship. This ideological prescription was practiced in the writings that appeared in *Sovetish Heymland*.[87]

Twenty years later, the same socialist-realist formula made possible the appearance in print of the novel *Heavy Sand* by Anatoly Rybakov, which concludes with an unveiling of a monument on the site of a communal grave: "A large slab of black granite had been erected above the grave, and on it was engraved, in Russian: 'To the eternal memory of the victims of the German Fascist invaders.' Below it was an inscription in Hebrew." A foundation stone would be placed in Babi Yar in 1966, and a memorial proper would be erected a decade later. The 1976 monument had only one inscription, in Russian: "Soviet citizens, POWs, soldiers and officers of the Red Amy, were shot here in Babi Yar by German Fascists." Against this backdrop of half-truths, Evtushenko's poem remained an effective Soviet-era literary monument to the tragedy of Kyiv's—and only Kyiv's—Jews.

11

FIGHTING ZIONISM

Culture, Scholarship, and Propaganda

In February 1953 the Soviet legation in Tel Aviv was bombed by a terrorist group protesting the "doctors' plot" case. One diplomat and the wives of two others were injured by the blast of explosives in the garden, and the building was damaged. This led the Soviet government to break off diplomatic relations with Israel. In July 1953 diplomatic relations between the two countries were reestablished, while the Israeli side promised to find and punish the bombers. The Soviet press greatly reduced anti-Zionist publications and, in August 1954, the diplomatic missions were upgraded on both sides from legations to embassies. The Soviet government had done the same thing several months before with Egypt, trying thus to maintain the appearance of balance in its policy toward Israel and the Arab states.

The upgrade did not mean, however, that Soviet-Israeli relations had become particularly close or friendly. The 1956 Suez War brought new tensions. An article headlined "The Way to Suicide: Where Is the Reckless Policy of the Ruling Circles in Israel Leading?," published in *Izvestiia*, accused Israel of seeking *Lebensraum* just as Hitler had and cast Zionist leaders as war criminals. The Soviet press called the Israeli government a clique and hardened its anti-Israeli propaganda.[1] Although a particularly assiduous anti-Zionist campaign would begin around 1970, the late 1950s also saw a heavy propaganda onslaught. On 3 October 1957, the Presidium of the Communist Party's Central Committee launched a media campaign "to reveal the Zionist propaganda against the USSR and the reactionary nature of Israel's internal and foreign policy."[2] This was, at least in part, also the agitprop reaction to the emigration of thousands of Soviet Jews, who had left the country in 1957–59 as repatriates to Poland but sooner or later wound up in Israel.

Later too, as the effects of the Suez Crisis and repatriation waned, Soviet journalists pictured Israel as an essentially racist country where the Arab minority played the role of the indigenous population, like Indians in America, Aborigines in Australia, or—a rather frequently used analogy—the Black population in South Africa, equating Israeli policies with apartheid. A separate problem concerned Israeli tourists coming to the Soviet Union; they were usually portrayed as bearers of disinformation and propagandists for emigration to the Jewish state.[3] Much attention was also paid to persistent complications with water supply in the Middle East.

By the 1960s relations between the two countries had improved, which made it possible to develop such cultural projects as publication of four books of Israeli authors in Russian translation. The 1963 volume, edited by the poet Boris Slutsky, was entitled *Poets of Israel* and contained works written originally in Hebrew, Arabic, and Yiddish. The 1965 collection, *Stories of Israeli Writers*, with an introduction by Vergelis, confined itself to works by Jewish (Hebrew and Yiddish) authors. The same year saw the publication of a collection of poems by Alexander Penn, *The Heart on the Road*, comprising his original Russian poems and translations of his Hebrew ones.[4] The poet David Samoilov had edited the translations, himself translated several poems, and authored an introduction to this volume. Penn was a Communist and the literary editor of the Israeli Communist Party newspaper *Kol ha-Am*. The 1966 collection of novellas, written originally in Hebrew, Arabic, and Yiddish, carried the title *Searchers of Pearls*. It came out under the editorship of Lev (Arye Chaim Leyb) Vilsker, who worked at the Public Library as a specialist in Semitic studies after graduating from Leningrad University in 1950. Vilsker did numerous literary translations from Hebrew, signing them "Vilsker-Shumsky"; Shumsk—now a town in the Ternopol region of Ukraine—was his birthplace. (In the 1980s Vilsker would publish his valuable research articles in *Sovetish Heymland*, most notably on unknown poems of Yehuda Halevi.)

The choice of the editors—two Russian-language poets, a Yiddish poet, and a semitologist—highlights the fact that neither Soviet academia nor its literary milieu had a recognized specialist in modern Hebrew literature. By their own choice or the decision of policy-makers, Leningrad semitologists were scarcely involved in Israel-related studies or cultural projects. They also did not take part in training specialists with knowledge of Hebrew for the Ministry of Foreign Affairs and other Soviet agencies. The selection of a Hebrew-language teacher was rather random, especially as among Moscow Jews there were people who had lived in Palestine and for various reasons had moved to the Soviet Union or who had lived in Poland or the Baltic states and studied or taught at Hebrew day schools before they were closed by the Soviet authorities in 1939 or 1940. Nonetheless, Joseph Braginsky, a well-known Soviet Orientalist, encouraged Feliks (Fayvl) Shapiro to work as a teacher of Hebrew. The choice was determined seemingly only by the fact that he knew Shapiro because many years ago, in the early 1920s, their fathers had taught at the same Jewish school in Baku. Shapiro also had experience of teaching Hebrew, but later changed his profession. Now, retired, he was happy to return to Hebrew, the more so as it filled his life with interest and brought additional income. There is little doubt that Shapiro's candidacy had to pass a KGB background test.

In 1954, on his own initiative, Shapiro threw himself body and soul into preparing a Hebrew-Russian dictionary. Israeli radio programs helped him incorporate contemporary language usage. For the same purpose, he asked Shmuel Mikunis, the head of the Communist Party of Israel, who visited Shapiro at home, to send him a Hebrew newspaper, the Communist Party's *Kol ha-Am* (Voice of the people). Shapiro's death in 1961 delayed the publication of the dictionary, however. Two people played decisive roles in preparing the publication afterward: Abraham Rubinshtein, a former Jewish actor and later a lecturer of Hebrew at various Moscow universities, and Bentsion Grande, a leading Soviet semitologist. Grande wrote an overview of Hebrew grammar for this edition.[5]

In large part thanks to this dictionary, the word *ivrit* (Hebrew) increasingly appeared in Soviet publications. Clearly, the term *drevneevreiskii iazyk* (literally "the ancient Jewish language"), used in Russian-language literature to designate Hebrew, could no longer be used to denote the Hebrew spoken in contemporary Israel.[6] Shapiro's dictionary, published with a print run of twenty-five thousand, was almost immediately sold out. In the 1970s the same dictionary was reprinted in Israel in a paperback edition and was smuggled into the Soviet Union. Thus, ironically, a Moscow-produced lexicographical work turned into an illegal publication.

Diplomatic relations between the Soviet Union and Israel made possible cultural and academic contacts not only through Israeli Communists. In January 1962 Armand Volkov, the Jerusalem-based representative of the Palestinian Society, affiliated with the Soviet Academy of Sciences and himself an Orientalist scholar, visited the Central Rabbinical Library of Israel. He promised to organize an exchange of publications and said that there was room for visits to the Soviet Union by Israeli academics.[7] In June 1962 Zvi Harkavy, director of the Central Rabbinical Library, returned from a visit, lasting several weeks, to libraries of Moscow and Leningrad. It was a visit to the country where Harkavy had been born and spent the first two decades of his life. He brought an agreement with the Leningrad State Public Library (since 1992 the National Library of Russia) permitting Israeli researchers to receive copies of Hebrew manuscripts.[8]

In 1964 Tbilisi hosted the First Conference on Semitic Languages, with papers on ancient and modern Hebrew. The choice of the place was not random: Tbilisi University had a Department of Semitic Studies at the Faculty of Oriental Studies. In 1960 the founder and head of the department, the distinguished Orientalist Giorgi V. Tsereteli, was allowed to establish the Institute of Oriental Studies at the university. Shapiro and Rubinshtein took part in the Tbilisi conference with papers on the contemporary lexis of Hebrew. Michael Zand, a Moscow Orientalist whose main expertise was in the Persian and Tajik languages and cultures, spoke on Yiddish as a substrate of contemporary Hebrew.[9] A decade later Zand's struggle for emigration to Israel won the support of academicians in the Unites States and other countries.

In Moscow the academic Institute of Oriental Studies had scholars specializing in Israel studies. In 1953 one of them, Galina Nikitina, defended a candidate dissertation, on the basis of which she wrote her 1956 book *The Suez Canal: The National Asset of the Egyptian People*. The idea that Israel had revealed itself as an aggressive outpost of the USA was central to her 1958 article "Israel and American Imperialism."[10] Economic and political expansion of Israel in Africa, a popular topic in the Soviet press, was also discussed in academic publications, notably in Nikitina's 1963 article in the scholarly journal *Peoples of Asia and Africa*.[11] Judging by her publications, she could not read Hebrew sources and relied on translations and English-language publications.

The late 1950s saw the establishment of the school of Soviet anti-Zionist propagandists with a Marxist approach to history and contemporary developments in the Middle East. Nikitina's 1968 book *The State of Israel: A Historical Economic and Political Study* (which also came out in Polish and English and shaped her 1977 doctoral dissertation—the first Soviet doctoral dissertation on Israel) would set the tone for academic-cum-propagandist endeavors in this field.[12] At no time did she ever use the word Palestinian, but rather referred to that section of the Israeli population as "Arabs."[13] Also, in Vergelis's introduction to the 1965 collection of *Stories of Israeli Writers*, the word Palestinian is reserved for the pre–state of Israel period. There is nothing unusual about this; the notion of a distinctly "Palestinian" people, as opposed to "Arabs," became common throughout the world only after 1967.

Nikitina's book stressed militarization of the Israeli state and its heavy dependence on foreign capital, particularly from the United States and West Germany. It also questioned the socialist nature of kibbutzim and the Histradut, Israel's nationwide trade union. Some contemporary authors find parallels between Nikitina's analysis and the later theories of the Israeli "new historians" and "critical sociologists," particularly in rejecting the claims that Jewish-Israeli history represented a continuous national history, starting with the biblical era and going on unbroken until the establishment of the state of Israel.[14]

Like other books on Israel, as well as anti-Zionist journalism, Nikitina's work, whose print run was twenty-five thousand, found a place on the bookshelves of thousands of Jewish families; they were the keenest readers of such literature. Some of them took everything at face value, while the majority "separated the wheat from the chaff," filtering out what they believed was propaganda.

Sovetish Heymland for the time being eschewed political discussions concerning Israel and the Arab world. Nor did Israelis and Arabs appear in the homegrown literary works published in the journal. Those of its Soviet contributors who had once lived in Palestine, most notably Shira Gorshman and Liuba Vasserman, or visited it (Zalman Wendroff) were careful to avoid this topic. Therefore, the only alternative was to use literary imports. In fact, the vast majority of the Israel-related texts published in Soviet periodicals were produced by recycling foreign publications. For instance, the Kishinev-based Russian daily *Sovetskaia Moldaviia* (Soviet Moldova) had on its staff a regular reader of the Parisian Communist Yiddish daily *Naye Prese*. In one article reprinted from the Parisian paper called "A Victim of Fanaticism and Nationalism" (on 16 May 1964), *Sovetskaia Moldaviia* reported the tragedy of an Israeli girl killed by her relatives who could not forgive her love affair with an Arab.

In 1963 a significant part of the fourth issue of the *Sovetish Heymland* was dedicated to "Works of Progressive Writers of Israel." The bulk of the selection had been translated into Yiddish by Pesakh Binetski, a former Polish left-winger who survived World War II in the Soviet Union and later—using repatriation to Poland in 1946 as a means—settled in Israel in 1949. Among the seven progressive writers, Hanna Ibrahim, with her story "Smugglers," represented Israeli Arab literature. The story described how an innocent Arab woman and her old father were killed on the Israeli-Jordanian border because they were suspected of being spies. At the same time, the writer underlined the idea that Jews and Arabs could live peacefully if only their leaders did not create an atmosphere of mutual distrust and hatred. Jewish-Arab friendship in left-wing Israeli circles was exemplified by the poem "To My Friends—the Arabs," written by Akhiem Noyf. Binetski, too, had written poems about the Arabs, about the lot of all disadvantaged Israeli citizens. Two such sonnets, called "Ibrahim," had been translated into Russian and published in the journal *Aziia i Afrika Segodnia* (Asia and Africa Today, issue 10, 1963). *Sovetish Heymland*, however, published other poems by Binetski.

In issue 4, 1963, the journal finally published its own Arab-related production—the poem "An Arab in Moscow," written by Ziama Telesin and dedicated to Tawfiq Toubi, a member of the Knesset and a leading member of the Israeli Communist Party. Telesin's poem is a typical example of lyrics written to order. The poet, who knew very little about Arabs in general and his hero in particular, employed clichés of popular imagination: "a white kerchief [kaffiyeh]" and a "black woven hoop" on the Arab's head, and the

"Muslim awe" (Toubi was born in a Christian family) that the Communist guest felt when he approached Lenin's mausoleum. Of course, the poet did not forget that "his brother" was a "dark-skinned Semite" and that they both boasted the same origins. A striking stereotype emerges in the poetic lines: "He is going uphill to the old Kremlin . . . / And suddenly it seems to me for an instant / That I'm seeing him sitting on a tall camel / Swaying on the sands of the Negev."[15]

(Six years later, in 1969, Telesin's only son, Iulius, a dissident activist, applied for emigration to Israel. Ziama Telesin and his wife, Rokhl Boymvol, also a Yiddish poet, decided to follow him. This triggered a slanderous attack upon them in 1971 in *Sovetish Heymland.* To ridicule them, the journal reprinted samples of their Soviet patriotic poetry, while the poet Motl Grubyan alleged that the couple had collaborated with the secret police during the Stalinist repressions. The journal published the minutes of the two poets' meetings with functionaries of the Writers Union, quoting Telesin who—already deprived of his Party membership—promised that in Israel he would continue to defend Communist positions.)[16]

Soviet journalists rarely visited Israel. But even when they did and then wrote about it, Arabs, the alleged allies of the Soviet Union, appeared rarely if at all. For instance, in 1964 the highbrow *Literaturnaia gazeta* published "A Trip to Israel: Journey in the Year 5724" by V. Komissarzhevskii (probably Viktor Komissarzhevskii, a theater and film director and critic). The author went to Israel as a member of a Soviet delegation, dispatched to a congress of the friendship movement "Israel-USSR." (Characteristically, this Communist-controlled association did not have a Soviet counterpart.) Such delegations usually either did not include any Jewish members at all or had only one Jew. A non- or minimal-Jewish composition of the delegations underlined the fact that they represented all the Soviet peoples and came to Israel as friends of all its peoples. For all that, Komissarzhevskii mentions only the names of Jewish intellectuals with whom the delegation met in Israel, while Arab Israelis figure mainly in the form of "shapely Arab women with jugs on their heads."

The years 1964 to 1966 formed a period of fruitful cultural ties between Israel and the USSR.[17] Significantly, in 1964, the Soviet Union and Israel reached an agreement that divided up ownership of the Russian Compound in Jerusalem. The buildings were constructed in the nineteenth century by the Imperial Orthodox Palestinian Society for Russian pilgrims. In what became known as the "Orange Deal" (*Iskat Hatapuzim),* Israel paid for the property partly in oranges.[18]

In March 1966 David Oistrakh gave fourteen concerts in Israel. Another Soviet violinist, Leonid Kogan, also enjoyed colossal success.[19] The high point of all the performances by Israelis was the tour of singer Geula Gil, mimic Yaacov (Juki) Arkin, and two guitarists in summer 1966. In their concerts in Moscow, Riga, Vilnius, and Leningrad the audience wildly applauded the Israeli and Yiddish songs. Local and central Soviet newspapers published positive reviews of the Israeli artists' performances.[20] At the same time, in Riga, the combined frustration and exhilaration of the city's Jewish youth led to a fracas with the police at the end of the performance. Given the mass enthusiasm that these concerts aroused, the Soviet authorities first postponed and then canceled a visit by the Israel Philharmonic.[21]

In 1966 a Jewish journalist—Solomon Rabinovich—eventually visited Israel. He came there together with the Moscow soccer team Spartak, which played a couple of friendly matches with Israeli teams. *Sovetish Heymland* (issue 6, 1966) published Rabinovich's travel log "Moscow–Tel Aviv." Characteristically, his patronizing depiction of the country left the reader with the impression that the writer had not met any Arabs at all. No doubt, such a disregard for the Arab population had nothing to do with the experienced journalist's sense of observation. Rabinovich knew what was what politically and his "blindness" clearly illuminates that in the pre–Six Day War period Palestinian Arabs were, in his understanding at least, not an issue for the Novosti Press Agency.

In the same year, 1966, when the Israeli writer Shmuel Yosef Agnon received the Nobel Prize, *Literaturnaia gazeta* ran a warm commentary. Interestingly, Vergelis *happened to be* in London when Agnon stopped there on his way from Stockholm, and he and Agnon had a friendly conversation. Four of Agnon's stories appeared in the April 1966 issue of *Sovietish Heymland.* In the mid-1960s Vergelis corresponded with Abraham Sutzkever, editor of the Tel Aviv Yiddish literary journal *Di goldene keyt,* about a "guest issue" of *Sovetish Heymland,* that is, an entire issue of the journal devoted to new works by Soviet Yiddish writers. A literary event was devoted to the work of the Israeli poet Avraham Shlonsky at the Mayakovsky House in

Leningrad in October 1966. It was one in a series of programs on foreign writers. The event was not announced or reported in the Soviet press, but large numbers of Jews attended.[22]

The Six-Day War in June 1967 terminated cultural exchange. Lev Frukhtman, a translator from Yiddish, tried to find a place for his Russian rendition of Agnon's stories, but the outbreak of the war made this task impossible.[23] Moreover, even pseudobiblical literary settings began to be regarded as serving contemporary Israeli ideology: characteristically, Moyshe Altman's play *Yiftokhs shpil* (Jephthah's Game), based on a biblical legend, was typeset in 1967 but appeared only twenty-three years later in the May 1990 issue of *Sovetish Heymland.* Also, the post–June 1967 climate blocked the release of Aleksandr Askoldov's film *Commissar*, based on Vasily Grossman's story "In the Town of Berdichev," with a sympathetic portrayal of a Jewish family.[24]

Emigration

In the 1950s Soviet emigration to Israel was not yet a significant factor, though in various cities of the country there were people interested in learning Hebrew and having access to literature about Israel. Some people, both religious and secular, dreamed of living in the Jewish state. However, in the period from 1954 to 1957, only 750 Soviet Jews were permitted to leave the country, which was still progress compared with only eighteen during the last five years of Stalin's rule.[25] This figure does not include those who came to Israel via Poland (see chapter 4).

Importantly, in the 1950s, the Kremlin did not feel pressure to allow Jews to emigrate. In fact, quite the opposite was true. In Israel and in the West, many believed that Soviet Jews had been assimilated or were moving toward complete assimilation within the larger Soviet population, perhaps with the exception of those who had become Soviet citizens relatively recently, during World War II. Therefore, the vast majority of Soviet Jews seemed to be "less promising" as potential emigrants to Israel than Hungarian, Polish, or Romanian Jews.[26] In addition, according to a May 1953 "Department of State Position Paper," the American government did not consider Israel "a viable state" without receiving outside, mainly American, financial assistance and had concerns about "immigration into Israel of an additional mass of Jewish people from the communist countries." The foreign policy strategists felt that "chaos would be created in Israel and the Arab states by the sudden influx into Israel of any appreciable number of immigrants" and that "the release of a large number of persons from the USSR should be treated as an international problem which would require the settlement of the majority in countries other than Israel."[27]

Judging by a 1956 KGB training manual, the Soviet security agency knew that the Israeli Ministry of Foreign Affairs had a special department—the Liaison Bureau—dealing with issues of emigration from the Soviet Union to Israel and that the department was headed by a professional intelligence officer. It was also known that some of the diplomats working in the Soviet Union were, in fact, intelligence officers, whose task was, in particular, to collect information about Jews, mainly in the Baltic republics, and to use it "for establishing contacts with Jewish nationalist elements and inducing them to betray their homeland." The Liaison Bureau (neither this name nor its other name, Nativ, appeared in the KGB material) also launched a clandestine campaign, financed and operated by the Joint Distribution Committee, of sending parcels to the Soviet Union.[28]

Nativ representatives appeared in Moscow, though the ambassador, Shmuel Eliashiv, did not approve their activity. He claimed that the activity of the Liaison Bureau's operatives was unhelpful and endangering the very existence of the embassy. Yosef Avidar, who replaced Eliashiv in 1955, was more supportive of the Liaison Bureau's cause. By 1960 all of Israel's emissaries at the Moscow embassy, with the exception of the ambassador, were the Liaison Bureau's officials. While the KGB monitored the sentiment of Soviet Jews and equated any expression of serious interest in Israel with "security risk," Israeli diplomats were regarded as spies and agents of the CIA. The KGB followed the Liaison Bureau's operatives, from time to time expelling them from the country as persona non grata and arresting their local contacts.[29]

Meanwhile, Khrushchev and his ideologists remained categorically opposed to direct emigration of Jews, allowing only a trickle of people to move to Israel and only if the move facilitated the reunification of families.[30] In 1958, in the same interview that left a bad taste in broad circles, especially among Jews, Khrushchev spoke about his attitude toward Israel:

> We Communists feel very sorry for the Jews who emigrated to Israel. The letters which we receive from them in fact move us by their number and their sadness. Over there there is a housing shortage, there is a lack of success in accustoming people to agricultural work. Exiles arriving from so many different backgrounds experience difficulties of mutual understanding. What are all those Jews there going to do? They were conscious of the return to the land of their fathers' fathers; this is not sufficient for living side by side nor for forging a true nation.
>
> Israel has not adopted auspicious positions for the Jewish people. The USSR voted for Israel at the United Nations. She supported this state at its birth—in an extremely effective way. Israel has shown herself ungrateful and unfortunate in her choices. This nation plays the game of the imperialists and the enemies of socialist countries. All we buy from Israel are a few oranges. And we can make do without them.[31]

Two years later he stated: "There are no files at our Ministry of the Interior with applications from persons of Jewish nationality or other nationalities who wish to emigrate to Israel. On the contrary, we have many letters from Jews in Israel, applying to us with the request to permit them to return from Israel to their homeland, the Soviet Union."[32]

Virtually all those who were allowed to emigrate in the 1950s were pensioners reuniting with their children in Israel. Occasionally, women in their thirties and forties (presumably widows or divorcees) were allowed to leave with their children. Although most of these emigrants came from the territories that became Soviet in 1939 and 1940, some of them were from other places, including Frunze, Alma-Ata, Samarkand, and Tashkent.[33]

On 14 December 1954, the British embassy in Israel and the Jewish Telegraphic Agency reported that six Soviet Jews, the largest single group of Soviet emigrants to reach Israel since the establishment of the state, had arrived by air to join members of their families already there. The British report stressed that "none of these families will be able to support the new arrivals who will, therefore, fall as a charge upon the State. All six of the immigrants are said to be of the semi-illiterate peasant class; all are over 50 . . . and none is capable of doing any productive work. . . . All six travelled via Vienna." According to Israeli papers, a further three emigrants from the Soviet Union had reached Vienna and were en route to Israel.[34]

Among those who came to Israel in the second half of the 1950s was Maria Weizmann, the sister of the first Israeli president, Chaim Weizmann. Arrested in February 1953 in retaliation for the bombing of the Soviet legation in Tel Aviv, she—a physician—and her husband were kept in prison for six months.[35]

In the USA, the prospects of mass emigration of Soviet Jews to Israel continued to cause alarm. George V. Allen, assistant secretary of state for Near Eastern, South Asian, and African Affairs, noted in March 1957:

> Internal United States policy statements have expressed the United States objective of convincing Israel leaders that continued emphasis on large-scale immigration increases area tensions. Arab leaders are fond of claiming that further immigration into Israel's small territory can only lead to an explosion and further Israel territorial expansion. Mr. Henry A. Byroade [Allen's predecessor], speaking as Assistant Secretary of State for NEA in Philadelphia in May 1954, expressed publicly the view that Israel should de-emphasize immigration in the interest of area peace and stability. The official Israel reaction to such suggestions on the part of the United States has been quite violent. It has been stated that immigration is a matter completely within Israel's sovereignty and that one of the primary aspects of Israel's mission on earth is the "ingathering of the exiles." It is doubtful that Israel will ever alter its official position on this question. Israel has, however, quietly but effectively controlled immigration in the past, by limiting the funds to purchase passage for immigrants. The present ruling class in Israel comes almost entirely from Eastern European stock and can be expected to exert every effort to encourage and absorb immigrants from behind the Iron Curtain.
>
> It is believed that United States policies of failing to favor large-scale immigration into Israel have become sufficiently known to the Israelis. United States failure to increase its economic aid to Israel on the basis of increased immigration has probably been the most effective way of making our point with the Israelis.[36]

We don't know if the Soviet government's decision to allow thousands of Jews to move to Poland in the 1950s had anything to do with an attempt to destabilize the situation in the Middle East or was based on the mistaken assumption that the bulk of Jewish repatriates would settle in Poland.

Khrushchev claimed later, probably to cover up the miscalculation, that the Soviet authorities had known beforehand that after leaving the Soviet Union some of the repatriates would make their way to Israel, especially as on 1 January 1955 Poland reopened emigration to the Jewish state and thus provided the highest number of European Jewish emigrants.[37]

The repatriation of Polish Jews in the second half of the 1950s had a domino effect, energizing many other Jews in the Soviet Union. Most importantly, it showed that emigration was possible. Accordingly, several Jewish residents of Chernivtsi and Kishinev approached the Romanian embassy with the hope, which remained unfulfilled, that Romania and the Soviet Union would also forge a new repatriation agreement.[38] While there were immigrants who did not find the Jewish state attractive, the majority integrated successfully, and letters from them stirred up their relatives' and friends' interest in Israel. As a consequence, Jewish emigration became an issue on the agenda of Soviet decision-makers, who instructed agitprop to adapt its media and other products to the new situation. The Soviet press habitually denounced synagogues as spy centers, describing them as places used by Israelis for recruiting agents and encouraging people to apply for emigration.

The *Pravda* journalist David Zaslavskii, formerly a prominent Jewish socialist, used an anti-Semitic slur comparing Israeli diplomats, most notably the cultural attaché Eliahu Hazan, with con artists from the black market at Lilienblum Street in Tel Aviv.[39] In fact, Hazan was a representative of the Liaison Bureau. The KGB sought to stop these kinds of activities, especially after the World Festival of Youth and Students, convened in Moscow in July and August 1957, when many Soviet Jews demonstrated enthusiasm for Israel in their meetings with the two hundred delegates from the Jewish state. Hazan's detention on 7 September 1957 was interpreted as a warning to Soviet Jews and to Israel. This minor clash between the KGB and the Liaison Bureau could have intensified into a serious diplomatic scandal, but it did not.[40]

In October 1957 *Literaturnaia gazeta* published Lev Sheinin's article "The Tragedy of the Deceived," which explained: "The Soviet Union fought for the right of the population of Palestine to live in an independent state. In May 1948 Israel was created in a part of the Palestinian territory. In this new state, Jewish bourgeois nationalists-Zionists came to power. They determined the foreign and domestic politics of the new state, turning it into a weapon of Anglo-American imperialism." Sheinin went on to cite letters of emigrants from the Soviet Union who wanted to go back to their home country.[41] To all appearances, Sheinin used real correspondence of recent immigrants who had arrived in Israel either directly from the Soviet Union or as double repatriates via Poland.[42] It is known that, disillusioned with what they found in Israel, some of the recent immigrants tried to decamp back to Poland or, in a number of cases, the Soviet Union.[43] Around the same time, hundreds of Spaniards who had repatriated to Spain in the mid-1950s got permission to return to the Soviet Union. In 1958 the Central Committee considered in tandem the consequences of emigration to Israel and repatriation to Spain, urging measures to reduce the migration of the two groups and encourage both to return to the Soviet Union.[44]

The year 1958 saw the publication of Konstantin Ivanov and Zinovii Sheinis's *The State of Israel: Its Situation and Policy*, the first book-length piece of Soviet anti-Zionist propaganda. A revised edition of the book came out in 1959. According to the authors: "The majority of new immigrants, having arrived in Israel from the countries of the socialist camp, begin on virtually the next day to think about how to get out of this country." The Soviet embassy is mentioned as one of the places where hundreds of disillusioned people attempt to obtain passage back to their home country.[45] In other words, the book confirmed the phenomenon of Soviet Jewish emigration to Israel. Similarly, the Soviet press admitted that some of the emigrants arrived in Israel via Poland. Thus, the Warsaw-born Soviet citizen Nusim Kosovich, the protagonist of one of the stories covered by the Soviet press, moved first, in 1957, to Poland and then, in 1959, to Israel, whence he returned to the Soviet Union in 1962.[46]

The journalist Rostislav Iyul'skii—whose article "Hell in the Israeli 'Paradise'" appeared in the weekly *Sovetskaia kul'tura* in March 1958—painted a horrifying picture of life in the Jewish state: "Engineers, physicians, musicians are happy if they get a job emptying cesspools. People forty or older are fated to live in poverty." According to Iyul'skii, immigrants faced particularly grave problems because Israeli society treated a former Soviet citizen as a leper, painting a black cross on the door of his or her shanty house (*khalupa*) as a warning sign for indigenous Israelis. Adding the final flourish to his portrayal, the Soviet propagandist informed his readers (and many of them certainly took this at face value) that immigrant women should be ready to turn to prostitution as a way of earning bread for their families.[47]

As part of the new propaganda drive, Soviet Jewish tourists were dispatched to Israel in the summer of 1958. The composition of the group reveals a careful selection: "The visitors from Russia, whose ages ranged between 40 and 60, came from Moscow, Leningrad, Kiev and Minsk. Six of them were engineers and the others included a poet, a professor of Botany at Leningrad University, a professor of Domestic Economics at the Moscow Institute, a journalist and the dean of the Kiev Polytechnic School. All of them spoke Yiddish; three of them could speak English and several said they knew a little Hebrew. The trip to Israel, they said, cost them 4,000 rubles each."[48] The "professor of Domestic Economics" was in fact Sofia (Sonia) Fray, a veteran Communist and an experienced Yiddish journalist, who returned to Moscow in 1956 after many years in the Gulag. (In 1961 she appeared as a member of the editorial board of *Sovetish Heymland*.)

Without a doubt, none of the "tourists" paid for the trip because they came to Israel following a decision of the Soviet Communist Party's Central Committee "to send to Israel for 10 to 12 days . . . a specially selected group of Jewish tourists consisting of 15 to 20 people, whose expenses will be covered by hard-currency allocations included in the budget for tourist trips to capitalist countries in 1958." The Soviet Ministry of Foreign Affairs received instructions "to prepare a program for the group's stay in Israel so that the participants can convincingly refute fabrications about the allegedly difficult position of Jews in the USSR and, on their return to the Soviet Union, carry out analogous work among the Jewish population to clarify the true situation in Israel." Selection of people for the "tourist group" was entrusted to the Moscow, Leningrad, Kyiv, and Minsk provincial Party committees.[49]

One of the "tourists," the Ukrainian-language poet Grigorii Plotkin, published several newspaper articles and, later, a short book entitled *Journey to Israel: Travel Notes*. He described the suffering of new immigrants, who supposedly formed long lines in front of the Soviet embassy trying to arrange for their return. The Israeli press interpreted the fact of sending the "tourists" to Israel and publishing Plotkin's report as indicating that Soviet Jews' desire to immigrate to Israel remained undiminished.[50] Plotkin also wrote a play, *The Promised Land*, an excerpt from which appeared in the Kyiv daily *Radians'ka Ukraina* (Soviet Ukraine) on 10 January 1960. The play's protagonist, Monia, a young Jewish man from Ukraine who feels like a complete stranger in Israel, shouts out: "I can't stand it anymore. Even if they make me president, god or devil here, I can't stand it. Every person must know where his promised land is and love this land [the USSR], kiss every clod of its soil and not look for another."[51]

The Soviet propaganda machinery had an additional stimulus for publishing material on anti-Jewish Nazi atrocities, namely anti-Zionist propaganda. The press carried articles whose leitmotif was: shame on you, Israelis, for having close relations with the German Federal Republic, where former Nazis play an important role in the government, army, and industry. In 1959 *Izvestiia* bemoaned the decision of the Israeli government to sell 250,000 grenade launchers to Germany, describing it as "arms sales to German militarists whose hands are steeped in blood of six million Jews, murdered by fascist pogromists in the years of World War II."[52]

The 1961 trial of Adolf Eichmann in Jerusalem engendered numerous articles and editorials targeting "militarist Germany" and "Zionist Israel." The primary value of the trial for Soviet ideologists consisted in its possible indictment of West German officials, but Israel was not willing to comply with Soviet wishes. After Israeli prime minister Ben-Gurion publicly gave assurances that Israeli-German relations would not be involved in the trial, *Pravda* wrote: "In its desire to oblige West German ruling circles, the Israeli government has decided to have an understanding with the revanchists and is trying to shield the Hitlerite criminals from exposure. . . . Soviet public opinion hopes and believes that the wider public in all countries, including Israel, will find the necessary ways and means to prevent turning the Eichmann trial simply into a farce serving the interests of sinister forces of revanchism."[53]

Meanwhile, Soviet moral posturing on Israel took a new form: instead of shame on you, Israelis, for having close relations with West Germany, the Soviet propaganda began to find similarities between Israel and Nazi Germany. In 1965 the Soviets used the UN rostrum to draw a parallel between Zionism and Nazism.[54] After 1967 this parallel would become commonplace in Soviet propaganda.

"Unification of families" was the only motive for emigration to Israel officially recognized by the Soviet authorities. Some Soviet Jews appealed directly to top Soviet leaders for permission to emigrate. In 1963 an appeal to Khrushchev led to issuing a passport and exit visa to Rachel Margolina, who helped Feliks Shapiro in his work on the Hebrew-Russian dictionary. Eli (Ilya) Sandler, eighty-seven, once rabbi of the Arbat Synagogue in Moscow (closed in 1950) who later taught at the Kol Yaakov Yeshiva, wrote to Mikoyan, by that time chairman of the Presidium of the Supreme Soviet, explaining that he would like to die in the Holy Land. He received permission to leave in the fall of 1966.

In order to emigrate, one had to have an invitation from a related Israeli citizen (*vyzov*) to move to Israel as a permanent resident. This invitation had to be notarized and confirmed by the Israeli Ministry of Foreign Affairs. In the 1950s the responsibility for confirming the invitations and accompanying documents was transferred to the Liaison Bureau, which often resorted to some trickery for people who had no relatives in Israel. The Liaison Bureau implemented a system of fake invitations, having them signed by Israeli citizens who preferably had the same last name as the Soviet Jews who requested the documents. A whole system of collecting such invitations was organized, which did not contain the statement on family relation, giving instead a blank space for invention. In this way, the whole system of invitations was primarily one of falsification.[55] While in the 1950s Israel tried to keep a distance from the campaigns organized by American and other Western Jewish organizations on behalf of Soviet Jewry, by the early 1960s the Israelis began to feel that they had nothing to lose by coming out into the open, especially since the Soviets made it clear that they already suspected Israel of being behind many of the public campaigns as well as behind-the-scenes diplomatic intercessions.[56]

The change in the modus operandi was reflected in a number of incidents. In July 1960 the first secretary of the Israeli embassy in Moscow, Yaakov Sharett, the son of the former Israeli prime minister, was expelled from the Soviet Union on charges of espionage. According to *Pravda*, Sharett was caught red-handed while attempting to obtain secret documents. His expulsion was seen as an answer to the judicial proceedings undertaken in Israel against two convicted spies working on behalf of the Soviet Union, directly or via its satellites. Particularly damaging to Israeli interests had been the career of Israel Beer, a personal aide to Ben-Gurion who gained access to high-level meetings on military strategy.[57]

There were several other episodes in which Israeli diplomats were accused of organizing spy rings and Soviet citizens were imprisoned for allegedly associating with Israeli diplomats. In the beginning of 1967, the Soviet press announced that a certain Solomon Dolnik, a retired engineer, had been arrested for spying for Israel.[58] It seems that Dolnik did in fact have contacts with the Israeli embassy, but there was no evidence of spying.[59] Rather, he was involved in attempts to facilitate emigration by arranging invitations and by distributing educational or other literature meant to foster the cultural "awakening" of Soviet Jews. Whereas initially the idea of emigrating to Israel appealed predominantly to traditional elements in the Jewish population, in the 1960s they were increasingly joined by younger people, often from assimilated families, whose "awakening" could be directly or indirectly stimulated by the activities of Israeli diplomats. Developments in Soviet society at large also undoubtedly had an effect on the revival of Jewish national sentiments. Various groups of people had started using appeals and petitions as a means of protest as early as the mid-1960s. The imprisonment and trial of Andrei Sinyavsky and Yuli Daniel, usually seen as the catalyst of the dissident movement, caused a wave of written public protests. A number of Jewish intellectuals, who later became active in the circles demanding freedom of emigration, were among those who signed various petitions.[60]

A push factor for emigration to Israel could be the glass ceiling faced by Jews in society, limiting their educational, social, and professional mobility. As Mikhail (or Michael, as he later became known) Zand wrote soon after arriving in Israel, "Every [Soviet] Jew, except the genius, knows there are certain positions he can never occupy and that he cannot hope to rise to the top."[61] Significantly, Zand sought to work in Jewish studies, so Israeli academia could—and did—provide an enabling environment for him. However, emigration to Israel, which at that time was not famed as a country of advanced science and technology, had a limited appeal to specialists in other fields, even if their career aspirations looked uncertain in the Soviet Union. To all appearances, in the period described and analyzed in this book, Jewish factors—religious, cultural, and ideological (Zionist)—were central in the gamut of motivations that drove people to apply for emigration. At play were also other factors, notably the desire to unite with other members of the family who already lived in Israel, and the general disillusionment with the Soviet system.

Meanwhile, Soviet leaders changed somewhat the tone of their pronouncements about emigration. In 1966, with a deposed Khrushchev living in a kind of exile outside Moscow, Aleksei Kosygin, the prime minister, said at a press conference in Paris—its transcript appeared in *Pravda* on 5 December 1966—that "if some families want to meet or want to leave the Soviet Union, the road is open to them, and no problem exists here."[62] Earlier that year the Soviet Union signed the United Nations International Convention on the Elimination of All Forms of Racial Discrimination. One of its articles required signatories to guarantee the "right to leave any country, including one's own, and to return to one's country." Whereas only between one and two hundred a year were permitted to leave for Israel between 1960 and 1962, and the number grew to 388 and 539, respectively, in 1963 and 1964, it reached the unprecedented heights (except for the period of the Polish repatriation) of 1,444 in 1965, 1,892 in 1966, and 1,162 in the first six months of 1967.[63]

For all that, though, emigration to Israel remained highly problematic and not necessarily achievable. A series of articles in the Soviet press strongly discouraging applications suggested that the initial interpretation of Kosygin's remarks in Paris had been overoptimistic. The campaign began in *Sovetskaia Moldavia* on 18 January 1967 with a long description of the frightful conditions awaiting Jews who emigrated to Israel. *Sovetskaia Latvia* on 1 February 1967 spoke of those who bitterly regretted their great error in going there—"they found themselves in a society where men are like wolves to one another, where brutal capitalist laws are in force: either you will eat others, or they will eat you"—and summed up: "The USSR is a socialist country, a country building Communism. Israel is a capitalist country. Anyone choosing the latter is not simply travelling to join his relatives. Such a person at the same time consciously chooses mankind's yesterday, with all its consequences. Such a person cannot arouse compassion."[64]

Effectively contradicting the recently signed convention, on 17 February 1967 a secret decree was issued on stripping emigrants to Israel of Soviet citizenship.[65] This meant, in particular, that a "family unification" (sometimes with an unknown Israeli citizen or a never-seen second cousin) would most probably mean never again seeing one's actual relatives in the Soviet Union.

There was an anecdote that reflected the atmosphere among Soviet Jews: a man comes up to a group of strangers saying "I don't know what you are talking about, but I agree with you—we all have to leave [this country]." However, this atmosphere became prevalent only later, mainly after the Six-Day War in 1967. Meanwhile, by the mid-1960s, the idea that "we all have to leave" had been conceived but still had not sunk in among the Soviet Jews. On the scale known to them, their life was not bad at all; Israel appeared too provincial, too religious, too shtetl-like to be appealing to the vast majority of them, especially dwellers in big cities; and emigration to the United States or other countries was not yet an option. It would take some time, years or even decades, until an increasing number of people, especially the younger generation who felt more palpably the effects of the glass ceiling, realized that the "fifth point" could give them, paradoxically, an advantage compared to almost all other Soviet citizens: a chance to leave.

Although Soviet ideologists continued to postulate that Jews did not form a worldwide nation, the authorities nevertheless treated Jews as a constituent of world Jewry who, on that account, could easily fall under the influence of Zionist and imperialist propaganda. At the same time, virtually nothing had been done to forge a meaningful Soviet Jewish identity. The remote Potemkin village of Birobidzhan and the small oases of Yiddish culture in the form of *Sovetish Heymland* and occasional concerts did not appeal to the vast majority of people categorized as "Jewish." Meanwhile, the notion itself of Jewish culture in Russian, the dominant language of Soviet Jews, remained strictly anathematized. The fear of reinforcing nationalism among Jews by allowing them to establish clubs or some other nonreligious organizations led to cocooning Jewish life in family-and-friends circles, which turned into loosely interconnected miniclubs in whose midst Jews were not afraid to talk about their grievances and to share rumors, ideas, and plans, including thoughts about emigration.

The 1967 war and ensuing severance of diplomatic relations with Israel delineate the end of the period surveyed in this book. The events of 1967 strongly contributed, on the one hand, to national awakening among many Soviet Jews and, on the other hand, to new restrictions on various aspects of their life. The authorities continued the policy of not allowing the establishment of any Jewish organizations, apart from the strictly controlled local religious bodies. Even the Anti-Zionist Committee, formed in the final Soviet decade, in 1983, was shaped by the agitprop as an organization that represented, ostensibly, the "Soviet public" rather than the most ideologically conscientious, reliable segment of the Jewish population. In the amorphous structure of Jewish life, ideas percolated at different speeds and not necessarily from one source. Dissatisfaction with what they had in Soviet life and often overblown expectations of living better lives elsewhere generated and reproduced a spirit of emigration in various social and geographic segments of Soviet Jewry, including people whose passports carried a "fifth point" of their non-Jewish parent. While many sought to make their Jewishness more meaningful, albeit preferably keeping it secular, there was also a small minority who considered emigration a way to get rid of their "fifth point" completely, similar to what Ehrenburg claimed he would do if he were destined to live in a society devoid of anti-Semitism.

It would be wrong to overstate the role of prevalently or exclusively "Jewish factors," including Zionism and religion, in the motivations for emigration. It is no coincidence that, from the 1970s onward, Moscow, Leningrad, Kyiv, Odessa, and Kharkiv, the five cities with the highest concentration of Jewish urbanites, gave the highest proportion of applicants for emigration to Israel who, after crossing the Soviet border, made clear—to the frustration of many Israeli and Western officials and activists—that they really desired to move to North America.[66] Prospects of living in a technologically and otherwise distinctly advanced society appealed to them more than the idea of settling in the Jewish state.

The spirit of emigration imbued many people's life with meaning and purpose, but at the same time often strained or even poisoned their relations with those—still the majority—who, at least at that juncture, planned to stay put, feeling comfortable, congenial, and secure in Soviet society. Such people had achieved respectable positions thanks to their hard work and top qualifications. Some of them had a strong feeling of belonging to the elite of a local, regional, or national level, or even of playing some roles at all the levels. Well-placed and well-connected Jews usually did not feel, or felt less, the pressure of the Jewish glass ceiling in their life and often could pass on their status and well-being to their children.

It is illuminating that the percentage of card-carrying Communists among Jews aged twenty and over continued to grow, remaining more than twice higher than the average in the country: 15 percent in 1961, 19 percent in 1966, 21 percent in 1972, 22 percent in 1989.[67] This does not mean that the Party members necessarily believed in Communist ideals, but they certainly saw their future in Soviet society and had earned categorization as trustworthy, useful citizens. In any case, such people represented a category among Soviet Jews who did not feel, or did not yet feel, that their ethnic status or their increasing level of general dissatisfaction had affected their lives strongly enough to overcome the fear of extracting themselves from their existing way of living and moving to the unknown.

ACKNOWLEDGMENTS

This book is a product of several years of work, but it also incorporates what I have learned during decades of my research in the field of Soviet Jewish studies. Although academic research tends to be a lonely endeavor, it cannot be done without drawing on the work of others or collaborating with fellow scholars. This means that the list of people to whom I owe gratitude is a very long one. Here are just a few names out of many.

In late Soviet Moscow, the Historical and Ethnographical Commission, whose members acted unofficially but wholeheartedly (most notably Mikhail Chlenov, Igor Krupnik, Rashid Kaplanov, and Mark Kupovetsky), and the circle around the Yiddish journal Sovetish Heymland (Aron Vergelis, Chaim Beider, Velvel Chernin, and many others) played important roles in my transformation from a computer engineer into a student in humanities. Later, in the Oxford phase of my life, Howard Spier, Mikhail Krutikov, Arkadi Zeltser, Joseph Sherman, Graham Nelson, Dovid Katz, Dov-Ber Kerler, Antony Polonsky, and Ken Frieden had a stimulating influence on my research and academic publishing activities. Encounters with Mordecai Altshuler, Chone Shmeruk, Shimen Abramsky, and John Klier left a lasting impact on me and my work. Joachim Schlör's hospitality made it possible for me to spend fruitful months in Berlin.

Mikhail Krutikov, Arkadi Zeltser, Viktor Kelner, Efim Melamed, Boris Sandler, Hasia Diner, Harriet Murav, Mark Kupovetsky, Michael Aronov, Iosif Brener, Hillel Kazovsky, and Mark Tolts endured hours and hours discussing topics of interest to me, and provided insight and encouragement.

This book—and the Eugene Shvidler Project for the History of the Jews in the Soviet Union at New York University—would not have come about without Lawrence Schiffman and David Engel, my colleagues at the

Department of Hebrew and Judaic Studies. The creative and friendly atmosphere at the department has contributed enormously to my work and life. In some way, all participants of the project, especially David Engel, Benjamin Nathans, Arkadi Zeltser, Zvi Gitelman, Anna Shternshis, Oleg Budnitskii, Elissa Bemporad, Deborah Yalen, Vadim Altskan, Efim Melamed, David Fishman, Jeffrey Veidlinger, Alexander Frenkel, and Alexander Ivanov, helped shape my research and its textual representation. Lawrence Schiffman, among many other things, turned my attention to Judaic studies in the Soviet Union. Ludmila Gordon was instrumental in finding images to illustrate the text.

Ellen Chodosh, Jennifer Hammer, Martin Coleman, and other staff members of NYU Press showed immense patience and skill in working with me and other authors. A lot of understanding and support came from Eugene Shvidler. I am at a loss to find the right words for describing the patience of my wife, Elena.

All in all, working on the book and getting support from many people was a very rewarding experience for me.

NOTES

1. THE THAW

1 Burton, "Soviet Medical Attestation," 1221.
2 Dumitru, "Jewish Social Mobility," 991.
3 See, e.g., Kichelewski, "Imagining 'the Jew,'" 505–22.
4 Zelenina, "'Otravlennaia vata' i 'privitaia gipertoniia'."
5 Barnai, "Jews in Soviet Lithuania," 435.
6 Grüner, "Anti-Semitism and Collective Violence," 372.
7 Demina S.M., "Delo vrachei"; Astashkin, "Antisemitskaia reaktsiia sovetskogo obshchestva," 33–37; Speranskaia, "Obshchestvennaia reaktsiia na 'delo vrachei'."
8 Loseva, "Politicheskie kampanii stalinskoi epokhi," 72.
9 Mitin, "Sionistskaia agentura amerikanskogo imperializma," 4.
10 See, e.g., Madievski and Cordes, "1953: La déportation des juifs soviétiques était-elle programmée?"; Kostyrchenko, "Deportatsiia—mistifikatsiia," 92–113; Winston, "Reflections"; Zimin, "Gotovil li Stalin deportatsiiu sovetskikh evreev v 1953 godu?"
11 "French Paper Reports New Version"; Kostyrchenko, "Deportatsiia—mistifikatsiia," 98–99.
12 Soloveichik, "What We Need to Remember," 2
13 Konstantinov, *Evreiskoe naselenie byvshego SSSR*, 112
14 Konstantinov, 217, 225–227.
15 Shipman, "German Experiment."
16 "Information Report: Secret Policy Concerning Jewish Doctors."
17 "The Doctors' Plot," https://www.cia.gov.
18 Kimerling, *Terror na izlete*, 10.
19 Ivanova, "'Companion of Groves,'" 57.
20 "Tesnee splotimsia vokrug partii."
21 Antipina, *Povsednevnaia zhizn' sovetskikh pisatelei*, 406.
22 Ehrenburg, "Velikii zashchitnik mira."
23 "Red Leaders."
24 "Imia Rozy."
25 Gitelman, *Century of Ambivalence*, 156; Dodin, *Izbrannye trudy*, 304; Smolkin, *Kniga zhizni*, 55.

26 Konstantinov, *Evreiskoe naselenie byvshego SSSR*, 248.
27 "Ot litsa vsekh narodnykh mass," 295.
28 Mitsel, *Politika i paranoia*, 54.
29 H. Shapiro, "End of an Era."
30 Feldman, "Reabilitatsiia: arkheologiia poniatiia" (see also Samuel Arthur Casper, "The Bolshevik Afterlife: Posthumous Rehabilitation in the Post-Stalin Soviet Union, 1953–1970," PhD diss., University of Pennsylvania, 2018).
31 Kenig, "A shmues mit Boris Polevoy."
32 Abramovitch, "Mentshn un politik."
33 "Reversal of the Doctors' Plot."
34 "Foreign Policy Implications."
35 *Speech of Nikita Khrushchev*, 43.
36 Kudriashov, *Beriia i sovetskie uchenye v atomnov proekte.*
37 See, e.g., Holloway, "How the Bomb Saved Soviet Physics;" Artemov, "Sovetskii atomnyi proekt."
38 Broad, "A Spy's Path"; Lebedev, "Novye dokumenty po istorii sovetskogo atomnogo proekta."
39 Livne and Goldstein, "'Let My People Go.'"
40 Klein, "Politika SShA i 'delo vrachei'."
41 Rapoport, *Na rubezhe dvukh epokh*, 190.
42 See, e.g., Genina, "'Delo vrachei' v Stalinske," 55–62; Eregina, "Stalinskie ideologicheskie kampanii"; Genina and Kaimashnikova, "A. P. Rozenberg."
43 Movshovich, "Presledovanie evreev Rostova-na-Donu," 323–24.
44 Piklova, *Podorozh mistom i chasom*, 32–34.
45 Mitrokhin, "Etnonatsionalisticheskaia mifologiia."
46 Leibovich, "Intelligentsiia g. Molotova v 1950-e gg.," 190.
47 Mitsel, *Evrei Ukrainy v 1943–1953 gg*, 271.
48 Grüner, "'Russia's Battle against the Foreign,'" 455.
49 Cf. Avrutin, "Racial Categories."
50 See, e.g., Gvozdev, "'Moskva vzbudorazhena, kak pchelinyi ulei"; Astashkin, "Antisemitskaia reaktsiia sovetskogo obshchestva," 32–39.
51 Zubov, *Istoriia Rossii, XX vek*, vol. 2, 289.
52 Blood-libel cases occurred also later in various Soviet locales. See Bemporad, "Empowerment, Defiance, and Demise"; Veidlinger, "Doctors' Plot a Blood Libel?"; Rolnikaite, *I vse eto pravda*, 537–41.
53 Kimerling, *Terror na izlete*, 132.
54 Druskin, *Spasennaia kniga*, 263.
55 Ehrenburg, *Post-War Years*, 320.
56 Pinkus, *Soviet Government and the Jews*, 222.
57 Kostyrchenko, "Kampaniia po bor'be s kosmopolitizmom."
58 Cf. Kostiakova, "Osobennosti bor'by s kosmopolitizmom"; I. A. Nikitina and Takala, "'Karel'skie kosmopolity'."
59 Ehrenburg, "Neobkhodimoe ob'iasnenie."
60 Until the 1950s, when the gene was considered only a hypothetical hereditary

substance, the Soviet detractors of Weismann's genetics denied its existence. Soviet genetics was neglected also in the 1960s.

61 Odesskii and Feldman, "Ideologema 'patriot'."
62 "Postanovlenie orgbiuro TsK VKP(b) 'o zhurnale *Znamia*'."
63 Frezinskii, "Tragediia Emmanuila Kazakevicha."
64 Brodskii and Shpynov, "Osnovateli i zvezdy Gosudarstvennogo Omskogo russkogo narodnogo khora."
65 Olson, *Performing Russia*, 66.
66 "Luchshaia tantseval'naia truppa."
67 See Gel'fond, "Trilogiia Aleksandry Brushtein"; Zorin, *Zelenye tetradi*, 442–43.
68 Fadeev, "Nekotorye voprosy raboty Soiuza pisatelei."
69 "Programma Kommunisticheskoi partii Sovetskogo Soiuza."
70 Grüner, "'Russia's Battle against the Foreign.'"
71 Cousins, "Readers and Writers in Russia," 16. Ehrenburg later argued that his words were misrepresented in that article—see "*A za mnoiu shum pogoni . . .*," 274–75.
72 "Golos moskovskikh pisatelei."
73 O. G. Gerasimova, "Odno leto iz zhizni Mikhailova," 93.
74 Evtushenko, *Volchii passport*, 414.
75 Markwick, *Rewriting History*, 22; Kozlov, *Readers of Novyi Mir*, 4–5.
76 Loewenstein, "Changing Nature of Literary Censorship," 4.
77 "Postanovlenie orgbiuro TsK VKP(b) 'o zhurnale *Znamia*'."
78 H. Smolar, *Oyf der letster pozitsye mit der letster hofenung*, 23.
79 Yanasowicz, *Mit yidishe shrayber in Rusland*, 17–18.
80 Reisin, "Ehrenburg Talks Assimilation."
81 Ehrenburg, "Po povodu odnogo pis'ma."
82 Reisin, "Ehrenburg Talks Assimilation."
83 Cang, "Ehrenburg's Price for Survival."
84 "60-letie I. G. Erenburga."
85 David-Fox, *Crossing Borders*, 164–65.
86 "Ehrenburg Announced as Stalin Prize Winner." Cf. "What Soviet Citizens Talk about the Press Tales of 'Anti-Semitism.'"
87 Berard-Zarzycka, "Ilya Erenburg," 46.
88 Brandenberger, "Stalin's Last Crime?," 194–98.
89 Brogi, *Confronting America*, 135.
90 See, e.g., Barghoorn, *Soviet Cultural Offensive*, 233–34.
91 Magnúsdóttir, *Enemy Number One*, 31–32.
92 "Iz amerikanskikh bibliotek iz'iaty knigi kommunistov."
93 Schwartz, "Ehrenburg Urges Writers' Liberty."
94 Ehrenburg, *Selections from "People, Years, Life"*, xxii.
95 Zubok, *Zhivago's Children*, 231.
96 "Soviet Staff Study."
97 "Ehrenburg Hits Writers."
98 Fejtö, "Literary and Artistic Life."

99 Erlich, "Metamorphoses of Ilya Ehrenburg," 22.
100 S. Kkrushchev, *Memoirs of Nikita Khrushchev*, vol. 2, 557.
101 Fast, "Ehrenburg's 'The Thaw.'"
102 See, e.g., Leneman, *La tragédie des Juifs en U.S.S.R.*, 89–91.
103 Sperber, *Être juif*, 178.
104 L. Shapiro, "Soviet Union" (1964), 276.
105 Rubenstein, *Tangled Loyalties*, 313.
106 Cf. Konstantinov, *Evreiskoe naselenie byvshego SSSR*, 255.
107 "Anti-Semitism Still Exists in Soviet Union."
108 Reisin, "Ehrenburg Talks Assimilation."
109 "Ukaz Prezidiuma Verkhovnogo Soveta."
110 Redlich, "Khrushchev and the Jews," 349.
111 "Statements of Cde. N. S. Khrushchev."
112 Gilburd, "Picasso in Thaw Culture."
113 Dobrenko, "Stalinskaia kul'tura"; Mitrokhin, "Etnonatsionalisticheskaia mifologiia"; Auclert, "'Armed Thaw,'" 121; Abashev, "Iasykom 'kvartirnoi skloki'."
114 Sinel'nikov, "Zhizni vopreki . . ."; Nikolaev, "Salopnitsa pishet roman."
115 Shaginian, "Vsemirnaia vystavka v Brussele."
116 Nekrasov, "Po obe storony okeana."
117 Nurenberg, "Mayn fraynt Mark Shagal."
118 See, e.g., Vergelis, *Shestnadtsat' stran, vkliuchaia Monako*, 215–28.
119 Mak, "Sof'ia Cherniak."
120 Altshuler, Arad, and Krakowski, *Sovetskie evrei pishut Il'e Erenburgu*.
121 Mikhalevich, "Iadro intelligentnosti," 60–61.
122 Kozlov, *Readers of Novyi Mir*, 171–208.

2. REHABILITATION

1 Granin, "Mimoletnoe iavlenie," 9.
2 "Ot litsa vsekh narodnykh mass," 295.
3 Adler, "Life in the 'Big Zone,'" 8.
4 Zemskov, "Situatsiia s zakliuchennymi," 134.
5 Cf. *An Appeal*, 6; Zemskov, "GULAG," 26.
6 Dumitru, "Jewish Social Mobility," 988.
7 Cadiot, "L'affaire Hain."
8 Malkin, "Trudnye gody Liny Shtern."
9 Z. A. Medvedev and R. A. Medvedev, *Izbrannye proizvedeniia*, 565.
10 Delaloye, "Polina Jemtchoujina-Molotov."
11 Artizov et al., *Reabilitatsiia: Kak eto bylo*, 20.
12 "Sovetskaia sotsialisticheskaia zakonnost' neprikosnovenna."
13 "Bust of Mikhoels."
14 Golovkova, "Krainosti ateisticheskoi propagandy," 383.
15 Khort, *Liubov' Orlova*, 113.
16 "Moscow Confirms Police Killed Mikhoels."

17 Kharchenko, "Vspominaia Mironina Semenovicha Vovsi"; Borodulin et al., "Akademik M. S. Vovsi i 'delo vrachei'."
18 Documents from the private archive of Valeriia Gordon.
19 I. I. Kuznetsov, "KGB General Naum Isakovich Eitingon."
20 Kolpakidi and Prokhorov, *Vse o vneshnei razvedke*, 476.
21 McKnight, *Espionage*, 179.
22 Heffernan, "Interrogation of Sándor Radó."
23 Zviagintsev, "Groznyi baloven' sud'by"; Ishchenko, "Lev Sheinin."
24 R. A. Medvedev, *Politicheskie portrety*, 143.
25 Barenberg, "Prisoners without Borders," 518.
26 Geizer, *Leonid Utesov*, 102; Voshchinin, "Dzhaz. Eskiz portreta slushatelia," 243.
27 Kolleritsch, "Jazz in Totalitarian Systems."
28 "Zapiska G. K. Zhukova v TsK KPSS o prisvoenii general'skikh zvanii riadu reabilitirovannykh voennosluzhashchikh."
29 Gorchakov, *Ian Berzin—komandarm GRU*, 165–67.
30 Johnson, "Prophet of Poison Gas."
31 Gilboa, *A Language Silenced*, 222.
32 Demakov, "'Kniga kak ulika'," 75–85; Shchur, "Arkhivy KGB."
33 Martin, *Dissident Histories*, 70.
34 Cothenet, Inkel, and Tinsley, *Imitating Christ*, 52.
35 Shnitman-McMillin, "Stanovlenie pisatelia Georgiia Vladimova."
36 Genina, "Iz istorii repressii v otnoshenii sovetskikh evreev," 351–52.
37 Goldstein, "Aldos guts."
38 D. Fefer, "Moi otets Itsik Fefer."
39 Redlich, "Rehabilitation."
40 E. Markish, *Long Return*, 241–42.
41 Obidina, "Reabilitatsiia zhertv politicheskikh repressii," 247.
42 Khiterer, "Jewish Songs of Leonid Utesov," 32.
43 Reles, *Evreiskie sovetskie pisateli Belorussii*, 165.
44 Estraikh, "Zalman Wendroff," 525.
45 Lavinskaia, "Dokumenty prokuratury o protsesse reabilitatsii zhertv politicheskikh repressii v 1954–1956 gg."
46 Pregeizon, *Dnevnik vospominanii byvshego lagernika*, 275–77.
47 Altshuler, "Itsik Kipnis," 87–88; Kipnis, "Sud'ba Itsika Kipnisa."
48 Libedinskaia, *Zelenaia lampa*, 314.
49 Sloves, *In un arum*, 126.
50 Auerbach, "A dikhter mit a tragishn goyrl," 31–32.
51 "Sekretariu Prezidiuma SP SSSR Surkovy A.A."
52 Ehrenburg, "Evrei."
53 The full text of the letter is published in *Apparat TsK KPSS i kul'tura*, 454–55.
54 Estraikh, *Yiddish in the Cold War*, 18.
55 Stacy, *Russian Literary Criticism*, 209.
56 Hellman, *Fairytales and True Stories*, 392.
57 Shrayer, *Anthology of Jewish-Russian Literature*, 729.

58 "70 let so dnia rozhdeniia L. M. Kvitko"; Chukovskii, *Dni moei zhizni*, 471.
59 J. Gordon, "Soviet Union," 423; Samoilov, *Podennye zapiski*, vol. 1, 366.
60 Greenbaum, "Tradition of the Twenty-Four Soviet Martyrs."
61 H. Smolar, *Oyf der letster pozitsye mit der letster hofenung*, 163–64.
62 For more, see Estraikh, *Yiddish in the Cold War*, 21–37.
63 Estraikh, "Smertel'no opasnoe natsionalnoe edinenie," 343.
64 Ostin, "A briv fun Moskve tsum 'Forverts'."
65 Iakovleva, "Dokumenty vitebskogo obllita," 305–9.
66 Vail and Genis, *60-e. Mir sovetskogo cheloveka*, 298.
67 Krumm, *Isaak Babel*, 178.
68 Iavorskaia, "Gekht Semen Grigor'evich."
69 Khristoforov, "Dokumenty arkhivov bezopasnosti ob Isaake Babele."
70 Rogachevskii, "Babelomania," 98.
71 Estraikh, "Soviet Sholem Aleichem," 73.
72 Shentalinsky, "Babel," 36; Sicher, *Babel' in Context*, 82.
73 "Komissiia po literaturnomu naslediiu I. Babelia."
74 Ehrenburg, "Rech' na vechere, posviashchennom 70-letiiu so dnia rozhdeniia I. E. Babelia," 1.
75 Trekhina, "Posmertnaia kul'turnaia reabilitatsiia Isaaka Babelia."
76 Kozlov, *Readers of Novyi Mir*, 180.
77 Frezinskii, "Babel', Erenburg i drugie," 121.
78 Ehrenburg, "Neobkhodimoe ob'iasnenie," 4.
79 Iudson, "Nisha Livshitsa."
80 "K novym uspekham sovetskoi literatury i iskusstva."
81 Starikov, "Neobkhodimye utochneniia."
82 "Issledovatel'skuiu rabotu—na novyi uroven'."
83 Ehrenburg, "Rech' na vechere, posviashchennom 70-letiiu so dnia rozhdeniia I. E. Babelia," 6.
84 Glenny and Kinsolving, "Soviet Theater," 107.
85 Pirozhkova, *Ia pytaius' vosstanovit' cherty*, 417–18.
86 "Biweekly Propaganda Guidance."
87 Raddatz, "Das denunzierte Wort."
88 Altshuler, *Yahadut Berit-ha-mo'atsot*, 112–13.
89 Anninskii, "V svete Babelia."
90 Dovlatov, *Sobranie sochinenii*, vol. 4, 276.
91 S. Markish, *Babel' i drugie*, 11. To illustrate opposing attitudes toward hyphenated literature: the American writer and translator Edouard Roditi found such notions as German Jewish or Black American literature denigrating and gratuitous; see his "Gibt es eine Neger-Lyrik?," 102.
92 Grinberg, "Reading Between the Lines."
93 Shrayer, *Anthology of Jewish-Russian Literature*, 676.
94 "Missing Jewish Poet."
95 Kim, "Retseptsiia literaturnogo zhurnala 'Prostor'," 19–20; Shuvaeva-Petrosian, "O. E. Mandel'shtam," 154–56.

96 Ahern, "Events on the Road to Immostality."
97 Shifman, You Failed Your Math Test, 158.

3. BIROBIDZHAN

1 See especially Lvavi, *Ha-hityashvut ha-yehudit be-Birobig'an*; Sloves, *Sovetishe yidishe melukheshkayt*; Weinberg, "Purge and Politics"; Kagedan, *Soviet Zion*; Estraikh, "Yiddish Language Conference Aborted"; Weinberg, "Jewish Revival in Birobidzhan"; Kuchenbecker, *Zionismus ohne Zion*; Kotlerman, *In Search of Milk and Honey*.
2 Kostyrchenko, *Tainaia politika Stalina*, vol. 2, 246–48.
3 Pinkhasov, Danilova, and Krikheli, *Evrei bukharski, gorskie, gruzinskie v vodovorote istorii*, 277.
4 Dymshits et al., *Gorskie evrei*, 125–26.
5 Kotlerman, "If There Had Been No Synagogue," 94.
6 Perelman, *Birobidzhan*, 184.
7 Khait, "Storona Birobidzhanskaia."
8 Hill and Gaddy, *Siberian Curse*, 81.
9 Zhuravlev and Brener, *Kniga pamiati zhertv politicheskikh repressii*.
10 Genina, "Iz istorii repressii v otnoshenii sovetskikh evreev," 357–58.
11 Crankshaw, "Russia Abolishes Jewish Province."
12 Friedberg, "New Editions," 78.
13 J. Gordon, "Soviet Union," 272.
14 See, e.g., Held, "Di 'lagernikes' vos boyen Biro-Bidzhan."
15 "Birobidzhan Help Called Diverted."
16 Pinkus, *Soviet Government and the Jews*, 351.
17 Mishchuk, "Retrospektivnyi analiz migratsionnykh protsessov."
18 Prishvin, "Shchedraia zemlia."
19 "Rech' tovarishcha N. S. Khrushcheva."
20 Kapkov, *Oskolki pamiati*, 305.
21 Manoilenko, "Zakonchilas' ego doroga."
22 The Khabarovsk Publishing House produced pamphlets on this campaign in the JAR: Semen S. Eremin, *Opyt vyrashchivaniia kukuruzy v kolkhozakh Evreiskoi avtonomnoi oblasti* (1956); Vladimir I. Sidorenko, *Kak my vyrashchivali kukuruzu na zerno* (1957); Arkadii N. Uzilevskii, *Velikoe iz malogo* (1958).
23 The official title of soldiers who received each of the Order of Glory's three classes. They were accorded the same rights and privileges as those who had received the Hero of the Soviet Union title.
24 S. Gordon, "Tselina."
25 Merker, "Poslednii urozhai Nikity Khrushveva."
26 B. Singer, "State Not Dead, but Is Dying."
27 Salisbury, "Birobidzhan Jews." On Salisbury, see Fainberg, "Portrait of a Journalist."
28 Zhuravleva, "Periodicheskaia pechat' Evreiskoi avtonomnoi oblasti," 89.

29 Shefner, "A nayer un alter grus fun Birobidzhan."
30 "Visit to Khabarovsk and Birobidzhan," 154.
31 Hopkins, "Lenin, Stalin, Khrushchev," 531.
32 Shoshkes, *Tsvishn yidn in vayte lender*, 194
33 In the 1920s only several hundred Cossacks lived in the region: Ryansky, "Jews and Cossacks," 19.
34 Estraikh, "Jews as Cossacks." *Author's personal note*: Around 1960 the film *Seekers of Happiness* once again appeared in Soviet movie theaters. I have a childhood memory of seeing it with my parents in the theater across the street from the apartment building where we lived. As I learned later, there had been a chance of me being born in Birobidzhan because my parents toyed with the idea of moving there. However, by the time of my father's demobilization, the postwar resettlement campaign had come to an end or, more probably, they simply decided to settle in the Ukrainian city of Zaporizhzhia, not far from their prewar home in the Nay-Zlatopol Jewish National District, decimated in the Holocaust and administratively liquidated by the government in 1944. In the mid-1940s some of the district's residents did move to the JAR, though the majority of the survivors migrated to Zaporizhzhia and other cities in the area.
35 Patek, "Jewish Autonomous Oblast," 116.
36 Axebank, "Stalin's 'National Home for Jews.'" Even later, in the 1980s, according to the then head of the JAR's KGB station, propensity to Zionist ideas was "out of character" for the local youth. See Evtushenko, *Est' takaia professiia*, 229–333. Ultimately, however, the Jewish Autonomous Region would give a record emigration to Israel in the 1990s—see Tolts, "Aliya from the Russian Federation," 5–23.
37 Pinkus, *Soviet Government and the Jews*, 379.
38 Salisbury, "Birobidzhan Jews."
39 Kotlerman, "Toska vliublennogo, govoriashchego o svoei vozliublennoi"; Kotlerman, "Ostanovi ruku tvoiu!," 355–59.
40 "Protokol partiinogo sobraniia парторганизации redaktsii," 1.
41 Riant, "Kak ia rabotal v 'Birobidzhaner shtern'."
42 Zhuravleva, "Periodicheskaia pechat' Evreiskoi avtonomnoi oblasti," 58.
43 Kotlerman, *In Search of Milk and Honey*, 245.
44 Maltinsky, *Der moskver mishpet*, 105.
45 Zhuravleva, *Istoriia knizhnogo dela*, 91, 119–20, 158–59; Skvortsova, "Knigi evreiskoi traditsii," 78; Kostyrchenko, *Tainaia politika Khrushcheva*, 181; Kotlerman, *In Search of Milk and Honey*, 218–40.
46 Korolev, "Kampaniia po bor'be s 'burzhuaznym natsionalizmom'."
47 Zhuravlev and Brener, *Kniga pamiati zhertv politicheskikh repressii*, 35, 42, 47, 59, 70, 72, 80, 94.
48 Katsnelson, "Di yidishe kultur-manifestatsye in Moskve."
49 See "New Light on Biro-Bidjan"; "More Red Propaganda"; "In a novine."
50 Zhuravleva, *Istoriia knizhnogo dela v Evreiskoi avtonomnoi oblasti*, 58.
51 Kotlerman, "Ostanovi ruku tvoiu!," 375.

52 Kostyrchenko, *Tainaia politika Khrushcheva*, 181.
53 Zhuravleva, "Periodicheskaia pechat' Evreiskoi avtonomnoi oblasti," 90.
54 Estraikh, *Soviet Yiddish*, 136–40.
55 Vergelis, *Di tsayt*, 411–12.
56 Frankel, "Jewish Birobidzhan."
57 Isaiah 10:19.
58 Kotlerman, "Ostanovi ruku tvoiu!," 378.
59 See, e.g., Sloves, *In un arum*, 145.
60 Shabad, "Surprises Greet Visitor"; Shabad, "Soviet's Only Yiddish Paper."
61 See, e.g., Rabinovich, "Vos dertseylt 'Biro-Bidzhaner shtern'?,"; Rabinovich, "Tipn fun yidn in Biro-Bidzhan."
62 "Paul Novic, David Matis, and Abraham Bick."
63 Gutman, "Soviet Treatment of Jews."
64 See Tulchinsky, "Family Quarrel"; Estraikh, *Yiddish in the Cold War*, 25–26.
65 Estraikh, *Yiddish in the Cold War*, 21.
66 "Khrushchev Airs Analysis on Jews."
67 Norwood, *Antisemitism and the American Left*, 185.
68 In fact, Jews did work in building or metallurgy—see, e.g., Konstantinov, *Evreiskoe naselenie byvshego SSSR*, 220.
69 Pinkus, *Soviet Government and the Jews*, 62.
70 "Beseda tovarishcha N. S. Khrushcheva c korrespondentom frantsuzskoi gazety 'Figaro'."
71 Schwartz, "Stalin Called Himself a Zionist"; "Stalin's Views on Jews Revealed."
72 "The Khrushchev Interview."
73 Ro'i, *Struggle for Soviet Jewish Emigration*, 145–46.
74 Goldman, "Khrushchev and the Soviet Jews."
75 Novick, "Di Birobidzhan 'propagande' in Moskve."
76 Shneiderman, "Tsvey yidn fun Biro-Bidzhan." Also, at least one family was allowed to emigrate directly from the Soviet Union—see Bligh-Grotto, "Birobidjan Refugees."
77 Pinkus, *Soviet Government and the Jews*, 382.
78 See Kotlerman, "'Farbitn di oytsres'."
79 Sherry, *Discourses of Regulation and Resistance*, 89–90.
80 "Stenogramma zasedaniia Pravleniia izdatel'stva Sovetskii pisatel'."
81 Goldberg, *Jewish Problem in the Soviet Union*, 215.
82 Srebrnik, *Dreams of Nationhood*, 204. See also Maksimenkov, *Bol'shaia tsenzura*, 599–606. Although Ambijan was dissolved in 1951, a 1956 secret textbook for students of KGB schools listed it among the existing anti-Soviet Jewish organizations—see Mamaev, Petrov, and Kravchenko, *Antisovetskaia deiatel'nost' evreiskikh natsionalistov i bor'ba s neiu*, 12–13.
83 Klimenko, "Evreiskoi avtonomnoi oblasti 25 let."
84 Database *Cold War in Eastern Europe*, "Extract from Summary Record."
85 Schwartz, "Moscow Depicts Birobidzhan Life."
86 See, in particular, Teller, "Exit of Jews"; Sanua, *Let Us Prove Strong*, 120.

87 *Speech of Nikita Khrushchev*, 10.
88 See, e.g., Teller, "Exit of Jews"; Spiegel, "Jews' Resettling by Soviet."
89 Cf., e.g., Zubkova, *Poslevoennoe sovetskoe obshchestvo*, 220–21; Johnston, *Being Soviet*, xl.
90 Novick, "Di Birobidzhan 'propagande' in Moskve."
91 Aronowicz, "Haim Sloves."
92 Crankshaw, "New Exodus."
93 Database *Cold War in Eastern Europe*, "Reported Renewal of Settlement."
94 Windt, "Rhetoric of Peaceful Coexistence."
95 Greiner, "Soviet View." 212.
96 Troyanovsky, *Cherez gody i rasstoianiia*, 197–98.
97 Mamaev, Petrov, and Kravchenko, *Antisovetskaia deiatel'nost' evreiskikh natsionalistov i bor'ba s neiu*, 12–13.
98 "Mikoyan Bars Jews Visitors"; "Mikoyan Denies Planned Exile."
99 R. A. Medvedev, *Oni okruzhali Stalina*, 179.
100 Estraikh, "Birobidzhan in Khrushchev's Thaw," 66.
101 "Mikoyan on Biro-Bidjan."
102 "Soviet Attitudes."
103 Sirota, "Vospominaniia: Zapiski aktera," 7.
104 Frankel, "Jewish Birobidzhan."
105 Shneiderman, "Tsvey yidn fun Biro-Bidzhan."
106 Lisitsina, "Sozdanie proizvodstvenno-tekhnicheskoi bazy legkoi promyshlennosti"; Mishchuk, "Retrospektivnyi analiz migratsionnykh protsessov," 75.
107 Frankel, "Jewish Birobidzhan." See also Corry, "Economic Geography," 519, 521, 568.
108 B. Katz and Nowak, *The New Localism*, 239.
109 Andrews, "Spatial Paterns," 455.
110 Horodyński, *Syberia inaczej*, 70.
111 Vinokur, "Ugasanie drevnei very."
112 Bederson, "Sholom-Aleikhem i 'vynuzhdennyi evreiskii natsionalizm'," 98–104; Golub', "O meste i znachenii toponimov evreiskogo proiskhozhdeniia."
113 *Evreiskaia avtonomnaia oblast'*, 32.
114 Salisbury, "Birobidzhan Jews."
115 Kostyrchenko, *Tainaia politika Khrushcheva*, 180.
116 See, e.g., Dobrushin, "Di shtot Birobidzhan."
117 S. Gordon, *Birobidzhaner toyshvim*, 70–71.
118 Skoczylas, *Realities of Soviet Anti-Semitism*, 12.
119 Konstantinov, *Evreiskoe naselenie byvshego SSSR*, 20; Manoilenko, "Polveka vzletov i padenii."
120 Horodyński, *Syberia inaczej*, 71.
121 Gen, *A veg in der vayt*, 363–404.
122 Database *Cold War in Eastern Europe*, "Confidential," cwee.fo371.159537.001.pdf.
123 Rabinovich, *Jews in the Soviet Union*, 28–29.

124 A. Jacobs, "Contact and Control," 214–15.
125 Krupnik, "Soviet Cultural and Ethnic Policies," 75–76.
126 A. K. Jacobs, "Many Flavors of Socialism," 129–30.

4. THE "KHRUSHCHEV ALIYAH"

1 See, e.g., Acemoglu, Hassan, and Robinson, "Social Structure and Development."
2 Dobroszycki, *Survivors of the Holocaust in Poland*, 19; Altshuler, *Soviet Jewry since the Second World War*, 3–4; Altshuler, *Soviet Jewry on the Eve of the Holocaust*, 323–26.
3 Actually, this was the last of three agreements. It was preceded by an agreement of 9 September 1944 between the Polish Committee of National Liberation (set up in Moscow in July 1944 and transformed into the Provisional Government in January 1945) and the governments of the Ukrainian and Belorussian republics, and by one of 24 September 1944 with the Lithuanian republic.
4 Ginsburg, "Soviet Union," 345, 350.
5 Chevardin, "Kvoprosu o vospriiatii sovetskoi deistvitel'nosti pol'skimi grazhdanami."
6 Tarasevych, "'Second' Repatriation," 18.
7 Litvak, "Polish-Jewish Refugees," 228–29.
8 For an analysis of Soviet-Polish relations in 1956, see, e.g., Kramer, "Soviet Union"; Machcewicz, *Rebellious Satellite*; and Orekhov, *Sovetskii Soiuz i Pol'sha v gody "ottepeli"*.
9 See, e.g., Engel, "Reconstruction of Jewish Communal Institutions."
10 See, e.g., Gershuni, "Bor'ba khasidov za vyezd iz Sovetskogo Soiuza"; Litvak, "Polish-Jewish Refugees," 227–39; Kaganovitch, "Stalin's Great Power Politics," 68, 82.
11 Gruson, "Poland Slowing Exodus." See also Vialiki, *Belarus'—Pol'sha ŭ XX stahoddzi*, 236.
12 Ablazhei, "Repatriatsiia etnicheskikh spetsposelentsev iz SSSR," 82–84.
13 Kutafin, *Rossiiskoe grazhdanstvo*, 301; Vailiki, *Belarus'—Pol'sha ŭ XX stahoddzi*, 92; Paczkowski and Bukharin, "The Thaw," 396. See also Snapkovskii, *Put' Belarusi v OON*, 2–8.
14 "Sovmestnoe zaiavlenie v sviazi s peregovorami."
15 "Soglashenie mezhdu Pravitel'stvom Soiuza Sovetskikh Sotsialisticheskikh Respublik i Pravitel'stvom Pol'skoi Narodnoi Respubliki"; Pinkus, "Emigration of National Minorities," 15.
16 Skrzypek, "O drugiej repatriacji Polaków z ZSRR," 67.
17 Ruchniewicz, "Tzw. repatriacja ludności polskiej z ZSRR," 175.
18 "Soviet Deporting of Jews Reported"; "Rusn firn yidn keyn Sibir"; L. Shapiro, "Soviet Union" (1957), 315.
19 "Soviet Union," *Jewish Observer*, 5.
20 Carson, "Breaching the Iron Curtain."

21 "Soobshchenie Ispolnitel'nogo komiteta Soiuza obshchestv Krasnogo Kresta i Krasnogo Polumesiatsa SSSR."
22 Towpik, "*Repatriacja Polaków z ZSRR na Ziemię Lubuską w latach*," 143; Szaynok, *Poland-Israel*, 280–81.
23 Stola, "Patterns of the Evolution."
24 "Soviet Jews Going from Poland to Israel."
25 Kichelewski, "Community under Pressure."
26 "Vital Program in Poland."
27 Burgin, *Fun Vilne biz Yisroel*, 209–28.
28 In 1957 emigration from Poland brought to Israel thirty-three thousand Jews accompanied by two thousand Christian spouses. The arrival of numerous mixed families put the openness of Israeli society to the test. The Israeli prime minister, David Ben-Gurion, advocated a Soviet-style approach that gave parents the right to choose their child's nationality. However, he and his supporters faced insurmountable resistance from those who contended that there could be no distinction between a Jew by nationality and a Jew by religion. See Gruson, "Few Polish Jews Back from Israel"; Louvish, "Israel," 235–36; and Herman, *Jewish Identity*, 77.
29 "Report," 13 December 1957.
30 "Report of the Executive Vice-Chairman."
31 Mowshowitz, *A Rabbi's Rovings*, 81–82.
32 "Rabbi Tells of Plight"; Shneiderman, "Tsvey yidn fun Biro-Bidzhan."
33 Kącka-Rytkowska and Stępka, *Repatriacja ludności polskiej z ZSRR*, 117, 121, 128; Margolis, *"Evreiskaia" kamera Lubianki*, 122–27; Vialiki, *Belarus'—Pol'sha ŭ XX stahoddzi*, 156–58; Stravinskienė, "Sovietinis saugumas ir repatriacija iš Lietuvos į Lenkiją," 33–34.
34 Mowshowitz, *A Rabbi's Rovings*, 82.
35 Anash: Hebrew אנ"ש, an abbreviation of *anshé shloménu*, אנשי שלומנו, "the people of our peace."
36 Zaltzman, *Samarkand*, 555–56.
37 Rinskii, "Otvaga, spasshaia zhizn'."
38 Abramovich and Zilberg, *Smuggled in Potato Sacks*, 341–42.
39 Belenkaia and Zinger, *Naperekor*, 74; Stravinskienė, "Sovietinis saugumas ir repatriacija iš Lietuvos į Lenkiją," 33–34. Archival materials do not substantiate allegations of bribes at the Polish consulate in Moscow. See Ruchniewicz, *Repatriacja ludności polskiej z ZSRR w latach*, 167.
40 Ro'i, *Struggle for Soviet Jewish Emigration*, 258. There are even higher estimates of the number of Jewish repatriates who were not Polish citizens before 1939. See, e.g., Stankowski, "How Many Polish Jews Survived the Holocaust?," 216.
41 "Poland to Return Some Repatriates."
42 "Polish Denial on Jews."
43 Gruson, "Poland Slowing Exodus."
44 "Report of Mr. Leavitt."

45 Ruchniewicz, *Repatriacja ludności polskiej z ZSRR w latach*, 230–33; Szaynok, *Poland-Israel*, 291.
46 Ro'i, *Struggle for Soviet Jewish Emigration*, 257.
47 Dickman, "Polish Jewry Today."
48 Friedman, "Will Emigration from Poland Stop?"
49 Gitelman, "Baltic and Non-Baltic Immigrants"; Segal, "Jewish Minorities," 66.
50 Barnai, "Jews in Soviet Lithuania," 441, 451–52.
51 Shmulevitsh, "Hunderter 'farshvundene' yidn fun Vilne"; *Nusekh Vilne byuletin* 3, 24–25.
52 Skrzypek, "O drugiej repatriacji Polaków z ZSRR," 69.
53 Vialiki, *Belarus'—Pol'sha ŭ XX stahoddzi*, 158.
54 Kącka-Rytkowska and Stępka, *Repatriacja ludności polskiej z ZSRR*, 143.
55 Ro'i, "Jewish Emigration," 210–27, and Ro'i, *Struggle for Soviet Jewish Emigration*, 257.
56 Khanin, "Refusenik Community." 76.
57 Kącka-Rytkowska and Stępka, *Repatriacja ludności polskiej z ZSRR*, 117, 121, 128; Stravinskienė, "Sovietinis saugumas ir repatriacija iš Lietuvos į Lenkiją"; Vialiki, *Belarus'—Pol'sha ŭ XX stahoddzi*, 159–180.
58 Peretz, *Let My People Go*, 70.
59 Govrin, *Israeli-Soviet Relations*, 142–43.
60 Sfard, *Mit zikh un mit andere*, 219–20.
61 Weiner, *Making Sense of War*, 200.
62 See the analysis in Machcewicz, "Antisemitism in Poland in 1956."
63 Blit, "New Poland."
64 Blit, "Poland and the Jewish Remnant," 218–19. See also Finsber, "Ale yidn fun Poyln raysn zikh aroystsuforn."
65 Schneiderman, "Vos yidn in Poyln tuen far di tsurikgekumene fun Rusland." For more on the "luxury goods" brought by Jewish repatriates, see Towpik, "*Repatriacja Polaków z ZSRR na Ziemię Lubuską*," 146–47.
66 Vialiki, *Belarus'—Pol'sha ŭ XX stahoddzi*, 115–17, 270.
67 Kaplan, "United States Aid to Poland."
68 Estraikh, "ORT in Post-Holocaust Poland," 203–6.
69 Estraikh, "ORT in Post-Holocaust Poland," 207. See also Schneiderman, "'ORT' in Poyln lernt fakhn."
70 Friedman, "Arabs Ask Reds."
71 Schneiderman, "Vos yidn in Poyln tuen far di tsurikgekumene fun Rusland"; Korinski, *Dr. Shmuel Aleksander Libo*.
72 "Report," 6 October 1959.
73 Czerniakiewicz, *Przemieszczenia ludności polskiej z ZSRR*, 68; Szaynok, *Poland-Israel*, 291–92. See also Stankowski, "How Many Polish Jews Survived the Holocaust?," 216.
74 See, e.g., Kitaev, "'Kriminalisticheskii ekstrasens' Vol'f Messing."
75 Gessen, *Belostok—Moskva*, 92.
76 B. Smolar, "Communism, Pensions and Inter-Marriage."

77 "Report on Poland," 10–18 January 1962.
78 Ponizova, "Lishenie grazhdanstva v sovetskii period."
79 Cohen, "Renewed Association."
80 Jockusch and Lewinsky, "Paradise Lost?," 392; Nesselrodt, "'I Bled Like You'"; Estraikh, "Missing Years."
81 Berger, "Toyznter poylishe yidn zaynen in 1956 geforn bazukhn kroyvim in sovetn-farband"; Podemski, "Polish Tourist Abroad"; Stola, "Opening a Non-Exit State," 106.
82 Khersonskii, *50th Anniversary*, 17.
83 Turkow Kaminska, *Don't Want to Be Brave*, 77, 78, 245; Pickhan, *Von Hitler vertrieben*, 85. Ida Kamińska headed the Yiddish State Theater established in Lviv in December 1939. See Stepanchikova, "L'vivs'kyi evreis'kyi derzhavnyi teatr."
84 Sfard, *Mit zikh un mit andere*, 157–58.
85 "Briv fun Moyshe Broderzon," 4.
86 Shamovich, "Kontserty Anny Guzik."
87 "Moishe Broderzon, Yiddish Dramatist"; S-M. Broderzon, *Mayn laydns-veg mit Moyshe Broderzon*, 170–71.
88 H. Smolar, *Oyf der letster pozitsye mit der letster hofenung*, 244–45.
89 Mark, "Evreiskaia literatura v Pol'she," 861.
90 Emiot, *In mitele yorn*, 39.
91 Vergelis, "Literaturnye otshchepentsy." For more on Polish Yiddish writers who lived in the Soviet Union, see Estraikh, "Missing Years."
92 Morevski, *There and Back*, 28.
93 See, e.g., Rakowski, "Derinerungen vegn Maksim Gorkin"; Shmulevitsh, "Di benkshaft fun Mark Rakovski."
94 Weingartner, "Michael C. Astour."
95 Cummy, "*Tsevorfene bleter*," 179; Gevisser, *Lost and Found in Johannesburg*, 57–61.
96 Auerbach, "Fate of a Yiddish Poet," 246–50; Lancman, "Literary Estate."

5. JEWS IN SOVIET SOCIETY

1 Rozenblat and Elenskaia, "Dinamika chislennosti i rasseleniia belorusskikh evreev v XX veke."
2 Database *Cold War in Eastern Europe*, "Extract from Summary Record."
3 Kushkova, *Navigating the Planned Economy*, 60–61.
4 See, e.g., Kupovetskii and Krupnik, "Lakhlukhi"; Marmyl', "Krymchaki"; Katunina and Katunin, "Prichiny likvidatsii obshchin karaimov."
5 Tul'tseva, "Evolution of Old Russian Sectarianism"; L'vov, "Russkie iudeistvuiushchie kak tekstual'noe soobshchestvo."
6 Zaslavsky and Luryi, "Passport System"; Karklins, "Determinants of Ethnic Identification."
7 Gitelman, "Evolution of Jewish Culture," 4–5.
8 Kahan, *Jewish Social and Economic History*, 189.

9 Wiesel, *Jews of Silence*, 65–66.
10 Sarnov, *Nash sovetskii novoiaz*, 288.
11 Melikhov, *Ispoved' evreia*, 14.
12 Kushkova, "Jewish Ethnic Economy," 97; Arkhipova, Kirziuk, and Iugai, "Skryt' opasnoe imia."
13 Voinovich, *Povesti i rasskazy*, 632.
14 Leder, *My Life in Stalinist Russia*, 96.
15 Cohn, *High Title of a Communist*, 87.
16 See, e.g., Chlenov, "Who Are These 'Mountain Jews'?"; Ramazanova, "Dagestan v sostave SSSR," vol. 1, 304.
17 Tolts, "Demograficheskii portret evreev Azerbaidzhana."
18 Kostyrchenko, *Gosudarstvennyi antisemitizm v SSSR ot nachala do kul'minatsii*, 6.
19 See, e.g., Sommer and Kopiński, "Execute the Poles"; Viola, "Antisemitism in the 'Jewish NKVD.'"
20 Yekelchyk, *Stalin's Empire of Memory*, 4.
21 Kostyrchenko, *Gosudarstvennyi antisemitizm v SSSR ot nachala do kul'minatsii*, 7.
22 Romm, "Question of the National Question," 219.
23 Grossman, *Life and Fate*, 94, 577.
24 Mitrokhin, "Elita 'zakrytogo obshchestva'."
25 E. M. Jacobs, "Jewish Representation in Local Soviets"; Masiukova, "Evrei i natsional'naia politika v SSSR," 304.
26 Kononenko and Danylenko, "Regional Features," 251.
27 Konstantinov, *Evreiskoe naselenie byvshego SSSR*, 213, 217; Kononenko, *Evreis'ke naselennia Podillia*, 195.
28 Gerovich, "Matematicheskii rai."
29 Bystriakov, "Khronika zhizni evreev Ekaterinoslava." Importantly, those who graduated in 1953 usually had not faced restrictions in 1948, the year of their admission.
30 *Apparat TsK KPSS i kul'tura*, 30–33.
31 Database *Cold War in Eastern Europe*, "Confidential, British Embassy, Moscow, 20 June 1960."
32 Tomoff, *Creative Union*, 168.
33 Database *Cold War in Eastern Europe*, "Confidential, British Embassy, Moscow, 16 April 1962."
34 "Otpor provokatoram."
35 Zaslavsky and Luryi, "Passport System," 149.
36 Tolts, "Mixed Marriage," 96.
37 Kantserova and Shabalina, "Dinamika brachnosti evreiskogo naseleniia v Srednem Povolzh'e," 155.
38 Altshuler, *Soviet Jewry since the Second World War*, 27; Chlenov, "Who Are These 'Mountain Jews'?"; Emel'iachenko, "Bukharskie evrei v sotsiokul'turnom prostranstve Srednei Azii"; Tolts, "Jews in Georgia," 111.

39 Miasnikov, "O nekotorykh osobennostiakh podbora i verbovki agentov," 111.
40 Tokarev, *Etnografiia narodov SSSR*, 210.
41 Gorokhova, "Diskussii 1990-kh gg.," 108.
42 Kazakevich, *Slushaia vremia*, 218–19.
43 Rzehak, "Linguistic Challenge," 49.
44 Lomtadze, "Rusizmy v rechi gruzinskikh evreev."
45 Melikhov, *Ispoved' evreia*, 14.
46 Cf. Ionova, "Na perekrestke kul'tur."
47 Cf. Safran, "Isaak Babel's El'ia Isaakovich," 269.
48 Konstantinov, *Evreiskoe naselenie byvshego SSSR*, 21, 25, 38.
49 Zhukova, "Evrei gorskie (taty)."
50 Cf. Zelenin, "Agrarnaia politika N.S. Khrushcheva i sel'skoe khoziaistvo," 403–4.
51 Shilovskii, M. B., "Obshchestvenno-politicheskaia situatsiia v Novosibirskom gosudarstvennom universitete," 105.
52 V. A. Gerasimova and Kliueva, "Antisemitizm v pozdnem SSSR v predstavlenii sibirskikh evreev."
53 Bunin, "Sergei Vladimirovich Obraztsov i ego teatr."
54 Tolts, "Demographic Trends," 149.
55 Lestschinsky, "Ken Biro-Bidzhan farbesern di lage fun di yidn in sovet-Rusland?," 9, 11.
56 Konstantinov, *Evreiskoe naselenie byvshego SSSR*, 167, 204–5, 217–18.
57 Pinkus, *Soviet Government and the Jews*, 447.
58 Konstantinov, *Evreiskoe naselenie byvshego SSSR*, 98–101, 106, 108.
59 Checinski, "Soviet Jews and Higher Education," 10–11.
60 Stein, "Soviet Intelligentsia."
61 Haimson, "Three Generations," 235.
62 Tromly, *Making the Soviet Intelligentsia*, 100–101.
63 Florin, "Many Ways of Being Soviet," 153.
64 Bertelsen, "Crossing Ethnic Barriers," 15.
65 Shayduk-Immerman, "Feeling Alive," 81.
66 Kononenko, *Evreis'ke naselennia Podillia*, 245–46.
67 Estraikh, *Yiddish in the Cold War*, 96–97.
68 Abramov, *Gorskie evrei Kuby*, 162–63.
69 Fitzpatrick, "Social Parasites"; Lastovka, "Tuneiadstvo v SSSR."
70 Cohn, "Paradox," 23.
71 Burford, "Getting the Bugs Out"; Losev, "Tuneiadets Iosif Brodsky."
72 See, e.g., Stiazhkina, "Sated People."
73 Mars and Altman, "Cultural Bases," 550.
74 "Information Report: Black Market Operations,"
75 Blusiewicz, "Illegal, Anti-Socialist,"
76 Khakkarainen, "'Evreiskie den'gi' v epokhu transformatsii."
77 Cheikhetov, "Private Entrepreneurship," 212–16.
78 Stončius, "Vil'niusskoe delo valiutchikov."

79 "New Charges Enter Soviet Trial of Priests."
80 Litvinoff, "Nazi Slave Labour Camp."
81 Kline, "Soviet Recourse to the Death Penalty," 56–57, 68; Florin, "Many Ways of Being Soviet," 166.
82 "Vovche kublo."
83 "Soviet Dooms Head of Currency Ring."
84 L. Shapiro, "Russia's New Pogrom."
85 Shabad, "Soviet to Execute 6 as Speculators."
86 Feofanov and Barry, *Politics and Justice in Russia*, 22.
87 Simkin, "Death Sentence."
88 See, e.g., Zellweger, "Principle of Socialist Legality."
89 Pass and Ryzhii, "Ogosudarstvlenie promyslovoi kooperatsii v SSSR vo vtoroi polovine 1950-kh gg."; Kostyrchenko, *Tainaia politika Khrushcheva*, 419.
90 Heinzen, "Soviet Entrepreneurs,"
91 Database *Cold War in Eastern Europe*, "Confidential," 31 July 1962.
92 Florin, "Many Ways of Being Soviet," 165–68; Kostyrchenko, *Tainaia politika Khrushcheva*, 419–20.
93 Amar, *Yom Kippur in Lviv*, 102; Mitsel, *Polityka i paranoia*, 101–4.
94 Kushkova, *Navigating the Planned Economy*, 324–25.
95 Cf. Cheikhetov, "Chastnye predprinimateli," 531.
96 Redlich, "Khrushchev and the Jews," 345.
97 L. Shapiro, "Russia's New Pogrom."
98 Kaser, "Pace of Soviet Industrial Reform"; Liberman, "Are We Flirting with Capitalism?"; Lisovitskii, "Evsei Liberman—ideolog 'kosyginskoi' khoziaistvennoi reform."
99 Boldyrev and Düppe, "Programming the USSR"; Medovar, "Velikii Botvinnik."
100 "Final zlachynstva—lava padsudnykh."
101 C. A. Schwartz, "Economic Crime," 294–95; Tishkov, Alaberdeev, and Latov, "Istoriia bor'by v SSSR s khishcheniiami sotsialisticheskoi sobstvennosti."

6. A STIFLED TRADITION

1 Decter, "Status of the Jews"; Taylor, "Sectarians in Soviet Courts," 286–87.
2 Amar, "Yom Kippur in Lviv."
3 Altshuler, *Religion and Jewish Identity*, 148.
4 Shabad, "Soviet Dooms 3 for Speculations."
5 Altshuler, *Religion and Jewish Identity*, 97, 110.
6 Goldberg, *Jewish Problem in the Soviet Union*, 127.
7 Smilovitsky, "Byelorussian Jewry and the 'Doctors' Plot," 51–52.
8 Zibert, "Polozhenie iudeiskoi obshchiny Omska."
9 Barnai, "Jews in Soviet Lithuania," 452.
10 "British Communists in the Soviet Union," 21.
11 Altshuler, *Religion and Jewish Identity*, 154
12 Corley, "Judaism in the Former Soviet Union," 74–75.

13 Kononenko, *Evreis'ke naselennia Podillia*, 280.
14 Rogoff, "Religye oyf der yidisher gas."
15 Kaspina, "Folk Judaism," 67.
16 "Some Soviet Jews Free to Worship."
17 L. Shapiro, "Soviet Union" (1958), 318. *Author's note*: Rabbi Levin's brother lived in my home city of Zaporizhzhia. My parents knew him and his family. I remember the rabbi's niece, who was a younger colleague of my father, also a teacher. She would share with my parents—in Yiddish and Russian—news about her uncle: that he received a nice apartment in Moscow, was visited by foreign guests, and so on. The information would come from her brother, who lived in Leningrad but was in contact with his Moscow uncle. All this was kept secret from the rabbi's brother, who could never forgive his clerical sibling for marring his Soviet reputation. In particular, being the brother of a rabbi hindered his attempts to become a member of the Party.
18 Yodfat, "Jewish Religious Communities," 66.
19 "[Perepiska] s raznymi upravleniiami," 12.
20 Pilipenko, "Repressivnaia politika gosudarstva v otnoshenii tserkvi," 134.
21 Charnyi, "Problemy izdaniia iudaistskoi religioznoi literatury."
22 Altshuler, *Religion and Jewish Identity*, 158–60.
23 Wiesel and Abrahamson, *Against Silence*, 97.
24 Deutch Kornblatt, "Jewish Converts to Orthodoxy," 216.
25 Deutsch Kornblatt, *Doubly Chosen*, 52–83.
26 Barkane, "Rukovoditeli evreiskikh religioznykh obshchin i gosudarstvennaia vlast' v Latviiskoi SSR," 191.
27 "Dolady, otchety, informatsii i spravki o religioznoi obstanovke v oblasti."
28 S. Z. Schulman, "*Undzer Rebenyu*," 219–36.
29 Wiesel, *Jews of Silence*, 30.
30 J. Anderson, *Religion, State and Politics*, 16.
31 Gachechiladze, "Historical Geography."
32 Corley, "Judaism in the Former Soviet Union," 76–77; Pinkus, *Soviet Government and the Jews*, 443.
33 Pinkus, *Soviet Government and the Jews*, 329.
34 Belenky, *Akoste, Shpinoze, Maymon*, 3–4.
35 Belenky, "O sovremennom iudaizme v SShA i Izraile," 106.
36 Shakhnovich, "Pravda o sovremennom iudaizme."
37 Belenky, *Iudaizm*, 130.
38 Belenky, 9.
39 Belenky, 94, 222.
40 Belenky, 237–38.
41 Grushevoi, "K istorii izucheniia v Rossii Talmuda i perioda ego sozdaniia," 95.
42 Altshuler, *Religion and Jewish Identity*, 104–5.
43 Lokshin, "Iudaizm v otsenke ekspertov KGB."
44 A. Ivanov and Kupovetsky, *Dokumenty po istorii i kul'ture evreev v arkhivakh Sankt-Peterburga*, 379.

45 Pinkus, *Soviet Government and the Jews*, 337.

46 Estraikh, *Yiddish in the Cold War*, 113.

47 Pinkus, *Soviet Government and the Jews*, 339.

48 Estraikh, *Yiddish in the Cold War*, 114.

49 Gen, *Undzere tsaytn*, 22.

50 Skrebneva, "Muzhskoi imennik viteblian 2-oi poloviny XX veka."

51 Cf. Beider, "Discontinuity of Jewish Naming Traditions"; Amosova and Nikolaeva, "Praktiki peremeny imen."

52 Altshuler, *Religion and Jewish Identity*, 161.

53 Brandon, "State's Pot and the Soldier's Spoon," 110–11.

54 This meaning is different from the one the word acquired in American Jewish slang (namely, a "big deal," a large production with much ado).

55 See, e.g., Kaminskii, *Organizatsiia i tekhnika sovetskoi torgovli*, 503.

56 Fedotov, *Tovarovedenie gastronomicheskikh tovarov*, 61.

57 E. Markish, *Long Return*, 137.

58 Druskin, *Spasennaia kniga*, 292.

59 Nakhimovsky, "Russian Jews Reclaim Their Foodways," 67.

60 Khanin, *Documents*, 32.

61 See, e.g., Zelenin, "Agrarnaia politika N.S. Khrushcheva i sel'skoe khoziaistvo"; Lebina, "Khleb—imia prilagatel'noe."

62 Mitsel, "Moskovskaia khoral'naia sinagoga, vlast' i zarubezhnye kontakry."

63 *Status of the Jews*, 21.

64 Altshuler, *Religion and Jewish Identity*, 181.

65 Brener, *Lekhaim, Birobidzhan!*, 126.

66 "Some Soviet Jews Free to Worship."

67 Iarkov, *Evrei v Kyrgyzstane*, 128.

68 Ro'i, "Religious Life," 67–69. *Author's note*: My pious grandfather, with whom we lived in the same apartment, unofficially practiced as a religious butcher. His father, my great-grandfather, was a rabbi, who published two books, in Hebrew, discussing various issues of kosher slaughtering. The revolution interrupted the family tradition of piety. My mother and all her seven siblings were completely secular. In general, only many years later, when I already lived in Moscow, did I meet several seriously observant Jews who belonged to the generation of my parents, born in the first two decades of the twentieth century.

As long as my grandfather lived with us, that is, the first ten years of my life, we ate kosher-slaughtered chickens as well as, from time to time, ducks, geese, and turkeys. The fowl would be bought alive at the market. Sometimes my mother would keep a goose on our balcony, force-feeding it for a while before asking her father to take the bird to the bathroom, which functioned also as his slaughterhouse. The aim of force-feeding was to get better *grivenes* (or *gribenes*), cracklings, and schmaltz, or fat, rather than foie gras (nobody in our surroundings had ever heard of it). *Grivenes*, or *shkvarki* in Russian, with mashed potatoes was a popular dish in our family. My mother also cooked an excellent *heldzl*—chicken-neck skin stuffed with flour, schmaltz, onion, and some other ingredients. On our menu there was a virtual item: *martsepanes*, or marzipan. If I did not want to eat something cooked by my mother, she would react by asking the same rhetorical question: "Do you prefer to eat marzipan?" It is worth mentioning that my mother never saw real marzipan, and I learned its taste many years later, outside the Soviet Union.

69 Shternshis, "Salo on Challah," 15.
70 Kaspina, "Folk Judaism," 75–76.
71 Ro'i, *Islam in the Soviet Union*, 463–64.
72 Nakhimovsky, "Public and Private in the Kitchen," 153.
73 Hoffman, *Red Shtetl*, 117.
74 Tulviste, "History Taught at School," 122–23.
75 P. Ivanov, "Ob odnoi oshibochnoi kontseptsii."
76 Artamonov's 1962 book was also criticized by some historians—see, e.g., I. A. Fedorov's review in *Voprosy istorii* 3 (1963): 146–50.
77 Golden, "Khazar Studies," 34; Klejn, *Soviet Archeology*, 304.
78 Ikhilov, *Narodnosti lezginskoi gruppy*, 149–52.
79 "Voprosy drevnei istorii i filologii."
80 Solodukho, *Soviet Views of Talmudic Judaism*, ix.
81 Gluskina, "Life and Work of Joseph Amussin"; Vasil'kov, Grishina, and Perchenok, "Repressirovannoe vostokovedenie," 116.
82 B. Smolar, "Russia Today."
83 Fedosik, Prokhorov, and Khodin, *Giler Markovich Livshits*.
84 Andreev, "Rukopisi mertvogo moria."
85 *K. Marx and F. Engels on Religion*, 321.
86 Pospielovsky, *Soviet Antireligious Campaigns*, 6–7; Metel', "Sovetskaia istoriografiia pervonachal'nogo khristianstva."
87 Kapera, "Bibliography of J. D. Amussin."
88 Shraga, "Soviet Jew."
89 "Orientalists Begin Meeting"; Kapera, "Qumran Commentaries."

7. THE CULTURAL LANDSCAPE

1 See, e.g., Estraikh, *Yiddish in the Cold War*, 23–26.
2 Database *Cold War in Eastern Europe*, "Confidental, 25 May 1956."
3 "Yiddish Theatre to Reopen."
4 Ro'i, *Struggle for Soviet Jewish Emigration*, 59–60.
5 Bezarov, "Do pytannia pro prychyny zakryttia Evreiskoho teatru."
6 Tal, "Mne 47 let."
7 Frenkel, "'Sonim af tsulokhes'—'vragam nazlo'," 200.
8 Vaisman, "Sidi Tal' i evreiskaia kul'tura v Chernovtsakh."
9 Ro'i, *Struggle for Soviet Jewish Emigration*, 58.
10 Frenkel, "'Sonim af tsulokhes'—'vragam nazlo'," 197–98.
11 Feodor Chaliapin (1873–1938) was a highly acclaimed Russian opera singer.
12 Frenkel, "'Sonim af tsulokhes'—'vragam nazlo'," 201.

13 Frenkel, "Did Mikhail Epelbaum Study at Warsaw Conservatoire?"
14 Sirotin, "Emil' Gorovets—pasynok svoego vermeni."
15 Estraikh, *Yiddish in the Cold War*, 60–64.
16 H. Schwartz, "Jews of Minsk Cling to Yiddish Speech."
17 Gronow, "Ethnic Music," 95–97; "Katalog sovetskikh plastinok."
18 Pertsovski, "Nayer program fun Leningrader yidishn muzik-ansambl."
19 Frenkel, "Iz istorii evreiskoi kul'tury v SSSR epokhi 'ottepeli'," 315–16; Gammer, "Aktery umiraiut na podmostkakh"; A. Ivanov, "Yiddish Music and Musicology," 150–51.
20 Frenkel, "Iz istorii evreiskoi kul'tury v SSSR epokhi 'ottepeli'," 318–22.
21 Miasnikov, "O nekotorykh osobennostiakh podbora i verbovki agentov," 111.
22 Shabad, "Moscow Revives Yiddish Theater"; Kotliarova, *Plecho Mikhoelsa*, 110.
23 Braudo, *Kulisn un hinterkulisn*, 197–229.
24 See, e.g., Sutzkever, "Encounters with Russian Jewish Writers."
25 D. Garber, "Choir and Drama in Riga," 44.
26 Levin, "Short-Lived Revival," 243.
27 Khersonskii, "Sozdanie evreiskikh khudozhestvennykh kollektivov v Litve," 286–87.
28 Novick, *Jews in the Soviet Union*, 15.
29 Beilinson, "O Tallinnskom Evreiskom teatre."
30 Manzhukh, "Boris Landau i Genia Lev."
31 D. Garber, "Choir and Drama in Riga," 42–43.
32 Shraga, "Some Yiddish Spoken Again in Russia."
33 Yakub, "Der yidisher dramatisher kolektiv in Dvinsk."
34 "Pasport Birobidzhanskogo narodnogo teatra."
35 Tukhovskaia, "Kishinevskii evreiskii narodnyi teatr"; Golidovsky, "Defiance and Death."
36 Sullivan, "Our Visit to Moscow"; Nelson, "Living in Harmony"; Abel'skaia, "'Odesskii aktsent' v pesniakh V. Vysotskogo," 243; Shternshis, "White Piano in a Shtetl," 117, 119.
37 Dashicheva, "Nadezhdy opravdannye i utrachennye."
38 Mikhailova, *Samorodki Dagestana*, 8–10, 20.
39 Wachsmann, *Der sowjetische Heine*, 2.
40 S. Markish, "Officially Published Russian Literature," 227–28.
41 Ash, *Liudi i bogi*, 66.
42 Estraikh, *Evreiskaia literaturnaia zhizn' Moskvy*, 134–35.
43 Estraikh, *Yiddish in the Cold War*, 29–31; "'Ekh, Govard! . . .'"
44 Hirsh Lekert, a worker from Vilna who was executed for attempting to assassinate Governor General Victor von Wahl in revenge for the humiliation of Jewish workers who had been arrested, became a symbol of Jewish heroism. In the early Soviet Union, schools, streets, and enterprises carried his name.
45 Brushtein, "Puteshestvie v stranu Vchera"; Estraikh, "Missing Years," 178.
46 Shraga, "Soviet Jewish Writers' Memoirs."

47 Ehrenburg, "Kiev."
48 S. Markish, *Babel' i drugie*, 223–32.
49 Shraga, "Soviet Jewish Writers' Memoirs."
50 Tanny, *City of Rogues and Schnorrers*, 311.
51 Klige, "As the Reader Pleases," 94–95; Lovell, *Russian Reading Revolution*, 56.
52 I. B. Singer, "Sholem Aleichem."
53 Estraikh, "Soviet Sholem Aleichem," 74.
54 Estraikh, "Soviet Sholem Aleichem," 74.
55 Katsnelson, "Di yidishe kultur-manifestatsye in Moskve."
56 "Vecher, posviashchennyi Sholom-Aleikhemu."
57 Maydansky, "Tsu vayterdiker farfulkumung," 149.
58 Remenik, *Sholom-Aleikhem*, 3.
59 L. Shapiro, "Soviet Union" (1960), 261–62. In 1959 stamps bearing a portrait of Sholem Aleichem were issued also in Israel and Romania. Bernard Isaacs, the translator of *The Bewitched Tailor*, came to the Soviet Union from England. He was imprisoned in the Gulag twice for a total of about eight years; see Durham, "Russians Wrong about Briton."
60 Sandler, *Stupeni k chudu*, 3–8.
61 See Eduard Flink's letter in the Moscow journal *Lechaim* 2 (2001) (https://lechaim.ru). His collection of stories, *Metronom*, came out in Dnipropetrovsk in 1989.
62 Aleksandrovich, *Ia pomniu . . .*, 212–14.
63 Ro'i, "Nehama Lifshitz," 173.
64 Vergelis, "Esli by zhil Sholom-Aleikhem."
65 Spiegel, "Mikoyan Denies Exiling of Jews"; "Mikoyan Says Reds Plan No Jewish Colony"; Sanua, *Let Us Prove Strong*, 120.
66 "Soviet Plan to Begin Publishing"; Novick, "Volume of Sholom Aleichem's Works"; "Sholom Aleichem Centenary," 24.
67 "Soviet Concessions."
68 Reznik, *Vmeste ili vroz'?*, 516.
69 Cang, "Meeting a Yiddish Writer," 11.

8. SOVIET HOMELAND

1 Reles, *Evreiskie sovetskie pisateli Belorussii*, 154.
2 E. M. Katz, "Literary Development of Yekhiel Shraybman," 290.
3 R. Zaslavskii, "Drugoi zhizni u nee ne bylo."
4 E. M. Katz, "Literary Development of Yekhiel Shraybman," 291.
5 "Stenogramma zasedaniia Pravleniia izdatel'stva Sovetskii pisatel'," 50.
6 Fray, "Otvet neproshennym 'zashchitnikam'."
7 Shmeruk, "Yiddish Publications in the U.S.S.R.," 106–8.
8 L. Shapiro, "Soviet Union" 59 (1958), 320.
9 H. Smolar, *Oyf der letster pozitsye mit der letster hofenung*, 204–5.
10 See, e.g., Altshuler, *Briv fun yidishe sovetishe shraybers*, 433.

11 See Estraikh, "Zalman Wendroff," 521.
12 Lerner, "Tsendliker yorn mit mayn fraynd dem dikhter Meir Kharats," 172–78; Olaru, "'Ia povazhaiu vsikh liudei, iaki liubliat' svoiu movu . . .'"
13 Suller, "Jewish Culture."
14 H. Smolar, *Oyf der letster pozitsye mit der letster hofenung*, 256–57.
15 Ro'i, *Struggle for Soviet Jewish Emigration*, 278–79. A former Moscow Jewish activist would get *Folks-Shtime* from an Israeli diplomat—see Podolskii, *Besedy ob ivrite i o mnogom drugom*, 220. *Author's note*: In 1970 we had a visitor at our tiny apartment in the Ukrainian city of Zaporizhzhia. His name was Comrade Gostinsky. Later my parents realized that they did not remember his first name insofar as colleagues addressed each other as "Comrade Such-and-Such" according to the Soviet Yiddish etiquette of the time. Gostinsky had illegally emigrated from Poland, studied in Moscow at the Yiddish Department of the Communist University of the National Minorities of the West, and come to the Jewish National District, in the Zaporizhzhia region, at the same time as my father. Both worked as teachers at Yiddish schools. In 1937 Gostinsky was arrested, allegedly as a Polish spy, and spent the next sixteen years in the Gulag. He came to Zaporizhzhia from the Siberian city of Novosibirsk, where he had settled after his liberation, to visit friends and colleagues. It was the first and last time I saw him, though I would feel his presence for years to come. Gostinsky's old friends had arranged for him subscriptions to *Folks-Shtime* and the Parisian *Naye Prese*, which he, after perusing them, would send on to my father. I also became an avid reader of the out-of-date issues. Given the dearth of information on Jewish-related topics, each of the Warsaw and Paris newspapers was a window, even if a narrow one, into the Jewish world.
16 Lirik, "Vos es dertsyeln tsurikgekumene fun festival in Moskve."
17 Suller, "Jewish Culture in the Soviet Union."
18 Cf. Frenkel, "Zapreshchalas' li 'Krovavaia shutka' v SSSR?," 449.
19 Lirik, "Vos es dertsyeln tsurikgekumene fun festival in Moskve"; "USSR Yiddish Culture"; Kwaterko, "Vikhtiker tsuzamentref mit yidishe sovetishe shrayber in Moskve."
20 Kwaterko, "In Moskve mit blumen."
21 Vergelis, "Ekzotishe tayge."
22 Goldberg, *Jewish Problem in the Soviet Union*, 219.
23 "Redaktor fun Kanader Vokhnblat brengt frishn grus fun sovetnfarband."
24 Sloves, *A shlikhes keyn Moskve*, 89–91. See also Goldberg, *Jewish Problem in the Soviet Union*, 211–12.
25 Estraikh, "Soviet Yiddish Cultural Diplomacy."
26 Barghoorn, *Soviet Cultural Offensive*, 79.
27 S-M. Broderzon, *Mayn laydns-veg mit Moyshe Broderzon*, 65, 146.
28 Estraikh, "Soviet Yiddish Cultural Diplomacy."
29 Lokshin, "Iz istorii literatury 'samogo slabogo zvena'."
30 See, e.g., Neuweld, "Latest Soviet Census."
31 Kostyrchenko, *Tainaia politika Khrushcheva*, 194–95.

32 "Protokol no. 4 zasedaniia Sekretariata Pravleniia Soiuza pisatelei SSSR ot 11 fevralia 1961."
33 Shmeruk, "Yidishe kultur in ratn-farband," 144–45.
34 Tsanin, "Tsen yor 'Sovetish heymland'."
35 See Sloves, "Sovetish heymland," 162–65.
36 Moskovich, "Postwar Soviet Theories," 105–9; Vergelis, "Undzer replik."
37 See Estraikh, "Era of *Sovetish Heymland*."
38 Cf. Wechsler, "Rationale for Restriction"; Halperin, "Jewish Problem in U.S. Medical Education."
39 Zaslavsky and Brym, *Soviet-Jewish Emigration*, 19.
40 Fedchenko, *Povsednevnaia zhizn' sovetskogo cheloveka*, 45.
41 Peretz, *Let My People Go*, 95.
42 "Russians Boycott Cleveland Group"; Harrison, *Passover Revisited*, 23–28; Ferziger, "'Outside the Shul'"; Kelner, "People-to-People," 204.
43 Orbach, *American Movement to Aid Soviet Jews*, 19–35.
44 Fineberg, Transcript of interview. Fineberg had an abiding interest in Soviet Jewish problems; see his "Defrauding Minority Groups."
45 See, e.g., Smirnov, "Zaokeanskaia chernaia sotnia."
46 See, e.g., "Chikagskaia 'Tribiun' zashchishchaet ubiitsu."
47 Kazakevich, *Slushaia vremia*, 178.
48 Naumov, *Nepravednyi sud*; Estraikh, "Aron Vergelis"; Kupovetsky, "Aron Vergelis"; Estraikh, "Odinochestvo evreiskogo redaktora."
49 "Gekirtster protokol," 64–65; H. Smolar, *Oyf der letster pozitsye mit der letster hofenung*, 261–62.
50 H. Smolar, "Zikhroynes fun gevezene redaktorn fun yidish tsaytungen in Poyln," 37.
51 "Stenogramma zasedaniia sekretariata." See also Estraikh, *Evreiskaia literaturnaia zhisn' Moskvy*, 286–89.
52 Estraikh, "'Jewish Street' or Jewish Cul-de-Sac?," 30.
53 Estraikh, *Evreiskaia literaturnaia zhisn' Moskvy*, 289–90.
54 *Kremlevskii kinoteatr*, 819.
55 Sutyrin, "Dokladnaia zapiska v Sekretariat Pravleniia Soiuza pisatelei SSSR."
56 Vergelis, "Di goldene keyt fun der yidisher literature," 103, 105–6, 108.
57 Rosenfeld, "Soviet Arrest of Professor."
58 "Memorial to the Unknown Jewish Martyr"; "Jewish Communists Rap Soviet Policy"; Shulman, "Sovetish-yidisher general zogt foroys untergang fun rusishe yidn"; Carr, "Dragunski."
59 Epshteyn, "Ven Arn Vergelis hot zikh geshlogn kegn di natsis."
60 "Vergelis zogt, az er fartret nisht dos sovetishe yidntum."
61 "Jewish Editor in Russian Mission."
62 Vergelis, *Rayzes*, 11.
63 Vergelis, *Rayzes*, 7–8; Vergelis, *On the Jewish Street*, 7–8. See also Barghoorn, *Soviet Cultural Offensive*, 72.
64 Garthoff, *Journey through the Cold War*, 164.

65 Schappes, "Vergelis Visit," 5.
66 J. Brumberg and A. Brumberg, *Sovyetish Heymland*, 8.
67 Burnham, "Soviet Defended on State of Jews."
68 "Russians Boycott Cleveland Group."
69 See, e.g., "Warns American Jewry."
70 Wiesel, *Jews of Silence*, 8.
71 Wiesel and Abrahamson, *Against Silence*, 234. Vergelis appeared in Brussels to defend Moscow at a public meeting; see Orbach, *American Movement to Aid Soviet Jews*, 72.
72 Wiesel, *The Testament*, 259.
73 Fishbein, "What Are We Afraid Of?" See also Vergelis, *Rayzes*, 50.
74 Glatstein, "Khrushtshov-veter."
75 Schappes, "Vergelis Visit," 7. For the blood-libel cases, see Bemporad, "Empowerment, Defiance, and Demise," 358–59.
76 "Intervyu mit Dr. N. Goldmann."
77 Letter of Zachariah Shuster to Maximo Yagupsky.
78 Novick, "Getseylte teg mit Arn Vergelis."
79 Schappes, "Vergelis Visit," 6–7.
80 See, e.g., "Dragunski."
81 Vergelis, "Jews in the Soviet Union."
82 Novick, "A Journal Which Destroyed Hope."
83 Rosenfeld, "Soviet Arrest of Professor."
84 Vergelis, *Rayzes*, 62.
85 See, e.g., Bergman, "New Commissar of Yiddish Literature."
86 It came out in book form in 1979, 1982, 1985, and 1990. Evgeniia Kataeva, Vergelis's wife and daughter of the Soviet Russian literary celebrity Valentin Kataev, is listed as the translator though she did not know any Yiddish. At best she could have helped Vergelis edit his own translation.
87 Kostyrchenko, *Tainaia politika Khrushcheva*, 318.
88 "Moscow Will Admit Parcels of Matzoh." Reiner played an outsized role in Soviet-American cultural diplomacy. In 1958 he briefed State Department officers about his private meeting with Khrushchev and Mikoyan at the Kremlin. Both men personally assured him that "they would welcome greater numbers of Americans to visit the Soviet Union," political tensions between the two superpowers notwithstanding, because "this program of cultural exchange is good for both sides." See Metsner, "Grassroots Diplomacy," 30–31.
89 "Noted French Jews Attend Vergelis Fete."
90 Rutland, "Leadership of Accommodation or Protest?," 281.
91 Estraikh, *Yiddish in the Cold War*, 77–78.
92 Belenkaia and Zinger, *Naperekor*, 177.
93 Pinkus, *Soviet Government and the Jews*, 72–74.
94 "Soviet Anti-Semitism." See also E. Schulman, "Sovetish Heimland."
95 Sloves, "Sovetish heymland," 163.
96 E. Schulman, *Di sovetish-yidishe literatur*, 155.

97 "Soviet Jewish Culture," 38–40.
98 Chertok, "New Magazine in Yiddish," 178.
99 Eliasberg, "... *Odin iz prezhnego Peterburga*", 146.
100 Glibitskaia, "Osnovatel' khar'kovskoi universitetskoi shkoly bibliografov."
101 Remenik, "Evreiskaia literatura v SSSR," 858.
102 Remenik, "Notitsn vegn undzer proze," 146.
103 Morozov, *Documents on Soviet Jewish Emigration*, 57–58.
104 See, e.g., Shneer, "A Study in Red"; Melamed, "Fate of the Archives."
105 Shevelev, "Iz istorii evreiskikh akademicheskikh podrazdelenii v Belorusskoi Sovetskoi Sotsialisticheskoi Respublike," 78–79.
106 Fishman, *Book Smugglers*, 234–35.
107 Axelrod-Rubin, "Jewish Contribution," 287–88.
108 Altshuler, "Georgian Jewish Culture," 32–37.
109 Braun, "Jews in Soviet Music," 85.
110 A. Brumberg, "'Sovyetish Heymland'," 29, 31.
111 Hence the drive, in the 1980s, to train young Yiddish literati; see Estraikh, *Yiddish in the Cold War*, 132–44.
112 Quoted in Estraikh, *Soviet Yiddish*, 108–9.
113 Estraikh, "Soviet Yiddish Orthography."
114 Moskovich, "Important Event"; Moscovich, "Russian-Yiddish Dictionary."

9. MEMORY OF WAR

1 Grubyan, "In a friling-tog a klorn."
2 Bloshtein, "A por bamerkungen vegn dem zhurnal 'Yidishe shriftn'."
3 Sfard, "Vegn dem hoypt-forvurf fun khaver H. Bloshtein."
4 Pomerantz, *Di sovetishe haruge-malkhes*, 97.
5 Z. Garber and Zukerman, "Why Do We Call the Holocaust 'The Holocaust'?," 202. In fact, the word "holocaust" did appear in Soviet English-language publications, notably the weekly *Moscow News*, but only as a stronger generic synonym for "catastrophe," e.g., "nuclear holocaust."
6 Grossman, *The Road*, 99.
7 Tec and Weiss, "Heroine of Minsk."
8 Zemskov, "Liudskie poteri SSR v Velikoi Otechestvennoi voine."
9 Rubenstein, "Il'ia Ehrenburg and the Holocaust," 54.
10 Rubenstein, "Il'ia Ehrenburg and the Holocaust," 50–51.
11 Daniel, "Moscow Line Shifts."
12 Johnston, "Peace or Pacifism?," 278.
13 "Pauk svastiki vypolzaet iz nory"; "Pravda ob Oberlendere."
14 See, e.g., Mandelstam Balzer, *Religion and Politics in Russia*, 160.
15 Tomilin, "Pepel stuchit v serdtse"; "Imenem soten tysiach."
16 Krivosheev, "Izverg zhivet v gorode Tselle."
17 "Kar'era Fridrikha Vialona." See also Arbuzov, "Kak byl razoblachen gitlerovskii 'doktor' Vialon."

18 Bazyler, *Holocaust, Genocide, and the Law*, 112, 119, 121; Astashkin, "'Delo Ervina Shiule'."
19 Ginzburg, "Pravo na trevogu."
20 See, e.g., Linets, "Sudebnyi protsess 1966 goda v Mineral'nykh vodakh."
21 Hirszowicz, "Holocaust in the Soviet Mirror," 43.
22 Peidi, "Kalevi-Liiva obviniaet."
23 Schiessl, *Alleged Nazi Collaborators*, 109.
24 Laht, "Liudi, pomnite!"
25 Kovács, *Communism's Jewish Question*, 126.
26 Schiessl, *Alleged Nazi Collaborators*, 109.
27 "Chikagskaia 'Tribiun' zashchishchaet ubiitsu."
28 I. Fefer, *Izbrannoe*; Halkin, *Stikhi. Ballady. Dramy.*
29 Slavin, "Varshavskaia noch'," 17.
30 D. U. "Zloveshchaia amnistiia."
31 Blinov, "Gorod, vstavshii iz ruin."
32 Zhitomirskii, "U pol'skikh druzei."
33 H. Smolar, *Oyf der letster pozitsye mit der letster hofenung*, 303.
34 Panfilov, "Pepel stuchit s serdtse," 2.
35 Remenik, "Der ufshtand in Varshever geto in der yidisher sovetisher literature," 150.
36 Charnyi, "Sovetskii gosudarstvennyi antisemitizm." Ber (Bernard) Mark, from 1949 director of the Jewish Historical Institute in Warsaw, wrote about the Warsaw Ghetto until the end of his life in 1966. His early historical narrative took shape as a seventy-page pamphlet *Powstanie w ghetcie warszawskiem* (Warsaw Ghetto Uprising), published in Moscow in 1944 under the auspices of the Soviet-sponsored Union of Polish Patriots. In 1947 the Moscow publishing house Der Emes brought out his book *Der ufshtand fun Varshever geto* (The Warsaw Ghetto Uprising).
37 "25-ia godovshchina vosstaniia v Varshavskom getto."
38 Yevseev, "Flunky at Their Beck and Call." Cf. Almog, "Alfred Nossig."
39 Vergelis, *Rayzes*, 404.
40 Weinreich, *College Yiddish*, 45.
41 Leff, "When the Facts Didn't Speak for Themselves."
42 Izakov, "V teatrakh i kino SShA." For Izakov's experience during the anticosmopolitan campaign, see Kostyrchenko, *Tainaia politika Stalina*, vol. 2, 331, 333, 335.
43 Tiurina, "Chto novogo na Brodvee."
44 See, e.g., Duban, "Generalization of Holocaust Denial"; Duban, "Honest to One's Self."
45 Sashenkov, "'Dnevnik Anny Frank' na nemetskoi stsene." See also Olsen, "Anne Frank Speaks to the Germans."
46 Smith, *The Russians*, 480.
47 V. Z., "Proshloe, ne stavshee istoriei."
48 D. Markish, "Viktor Lui."

49 "Moscow Not Producing 'Diary of Anne Frank.'"
50 L. Shapiro, "Soviet Union" (1963), 354; Tsepliovich, *Razgovor s samim soboi*, 101.
51 Vladykina, "Theatre at Moscow University"; Costanso, "Emergence of Alternative Culture," 86–88.
52 Dmitrievskii, *Zhizn' v epizodakh*, 246; "Teatr dramy i komedii."
53 Bezirganova, *Russkii teatr v Gruzii*, 124–28, 370, 390, 427, 466, 467, 651.
54 Beilinson, "O Tallinnskom Evreiskom teatre."
55 "Otovsiudu."
56 "'Diary of Anne Frank' Sole American Entry"; "Anne Frank Diary Chosen"; "'Diary' a Hit at Moscow Festival"; Zorkaia and Khaiutin, "Shestnadtsat' chasov v sutki"; Kozovoi, "Foot in the Door," 27–28.
57 "Skouras Hammers at Yanks." Some people apparently decided that it was the Soviet side's decision to remove the film from the competition—Barnouw and Ringold, *Phenomenon of Anne Frank*, 54, 81.
58 Thayer, "Cultural Diplomacy."
59 "Pat Answer to Soviet Lag."
60 Sullivan, "Our Visit to Moscow"; Nelson, "Living in Harmony"; Abel'skaia, "'Odesskii aktsent' v pesniakh V. Vysotskogo," 243; Shternshis, "White Piano in a Shtetl," 117, 119.
61 "Soviet Ban Lifted"; "Menedzher fun der Amerikaner oysshtelung in Moskve shildert erfolg fun yidishe bikher."
62 Kushner, "Exhibiting Art," 23.
63 Lazarev, "Melkoe i krupnoe."
64 "Podvodia itogi . . ."
65 Bondarchuk, "Zhdem vas snova v Moskve!"
66 Reni, "Bol'shaia tema Moskovskogo kinofestivalia."
67 Vagarshian, *Kinopanorama mira*, 74.
68 Kirschnick, *Anne Frank und die DDR*, 83–98; Shneer, "Yiddish Music in East Germany," 172–74.
69 "Zakonchilas' pervaia nedelia festivalia."
70 Semenko, "Smuggling the Other," 65.
71 Missinne and Michajlova, "Anne Frank in de DDR en Rusland."
72 Missinne and Michajlova, "Anne Frank in de DDR en Rusland."
73 These words appeared as quotes in numerous books by Jewish authors. See, e.g., Shakhnovich, *Reaktsionnaia sushchnost' iudaizma*, 17; Belenky, *Chto takoe Talmud*, 140; Remenik, *Sholom-Aleikhem*, 188.
74 Ehrenburg, "Introduction to 'The Diary of Anne Frank,'" 60.
75 See, e.g., Heydemann, "Deutschlandpolitische Neuansätze der 60er Jahre," 19; Rogers, "Restoring a German Career."
76 Slomovitz, "Purely Commentary."
77 "Obvinitel'noe zakliuchenie po delu Globke."
78 Vl. Kuznetsov, "Palach na skam'e podsudimykh."
79 Kostyrchenko, *Tainaia politika Khrushcheva*, 294.

80 Gavrilov, "Piat' uchenicheskikh tetradei."
81 Evans, "From 'Truth' to 'Time,'" 38.
82 Ginszurg, *Tsena pepla*, 90–95.
83 Teif, "Di balade vegn Ane Frank."
84 Teif, *Rukopozhatie*.
85 "Ves'ma tipichnaia sovetskaia intelligentka."
86 Avgustevich, "Tri stikhotvoreniia Moiseia Teifa na muzyku Aleksandra Vustina."
87 Dvuzhil'naia, "Grigorii Frid. Monoopera 'Dnevnik Anny Frank'."
88 "Jews in Moscow Hail 'Annefrank.'"
89 Ganevskii, "Tri spektaklia ital'anskoi truppy."
90 Lednev, "Ubiitsa priznaet sebia vinovnym"; Bai, "Prizraki proshlogo: Palach reabilitirovan."
91 Lediakh, *Natsistskie prestupniki i sudebnaia praktika v FRG*, 154.
92 Rolnikaite, *I vse eto pravda*, 523; Rolnikaite, *Doroga domoi*, 173–77.
93 Asher, "Black Book and the Holocaust"; Altman and Karasik, "Istoriia i sud'ba 'Chernoi knigi'."
94 Rivosh, "Tsvishn lebn un toyt." The Russian text, "Mezhdu zhizn'iu i smert'iu," came out in the journal's annual *God za godom* 3 (1987).
95 Lev, *Literarishe portretn*, 268–77.
96 Stončius, "Anti-Semitism in Soviet Lithuania," 26; Barnai, "Jews in Soviet Lithuania," 449.
97 Davoliūtė, "Cold War Cinema," 62.
98 Levin, "Participation"; "Hirsh Rolnik."
99 Rolnikaite, *I vse eto pravda*, 517.
100 Rolnikaitė, *Turiu papasakoti*; Polin-Galay, "Lithuanian Jews Remember Perpetrators," 509, 528.
101 Feferman, *Soviet Jewish Stepchild*, 51.
102 See, e.g., Monson, "West German Statute"; Sharples, "In Pursuit of Justice."
103 "Bonn Stand on Nazi Trials."
104 *Prestupleniia nemetsko-fashistskikh okkupantov v Belorussii*.
105 Toleikis and Belcher, "Repress, Reassess, Remember," 281.
106 Gershenson, *Phantom Holocaust*, 66–68.
107 Solzhenitsyn, *Bodalsia telenok s dubom*, 74.
108 Timoshkina, "Representations of the Holocaust," 126.
109 Zigmonte, "Pamiat'—oruzhie."
110 Rolnikaite, *I vse eto pravda*, 557; Zeltser, *Unwelcome Memory*, 144.
111 H. Smolar, *Oyf der letster pozitsye mit der letster hofenung*, 350.
112 Cf. Reshetnikov, "Russkie emigranty-soprotivlentsy protiv vostochnykh batal'onov vermakhta vo Frantsii."
113 Rolnikaite, *I vse eto pravda*, 508–23.
114 Zeltser, *Unwelcome Memory*, 265.
115 "Druzhba narodov SSSR i nasha velikaia pobeda."
116 Rolnikaite, *I eto vse pravda*, 526–27. See also Tippner, "Writings of a Soviet Anne Frank?," 73–77.

117 Goldsmith, "Another 'Diary.'"
118 Dawidowicz, *Holocaust and the Historians*, 84–85.
119 Cf. Walke, "'To Speak for Those Who Cannot,'" 216.
120 Gershenson, *Phantom Holocaust*, 115.
121 Tippner, "The Writings of a Soviet Anne Frank?," 64.
122 Gitelman, "History, Memory and Politics," 30.
123 See, e.g., Goldhagen, "Der Holocaust in der Sowjetischen Propaganda und Geschichtsschreibung," 502–3; Goldhagen, "Soviet Treatment of the Holocaust," 305. An uncensored text, entitled *Ia dolzhna rasskazat': Khroniki Vil'niusskogo getto* (I Must Tell: Chronicles of the Vilnius Ghetto), came out in Yekaterinburg as late as 2003. For an insightful analysis of Rolnikaite's successful strategy for dealing with ideological restrictions, see Tippner, "Conflicting Memories."
124 "Govorit Moskva."
125 "Russ Press Agency's Full-Length Docufilm."
126 Tippner, "Conflicting Memories," 375.

10. "BABI YAR"

1 See, e.g., Zubok, *Zhivago's Children*, 162, 396.
2 See Sidorova, "Massovaia literatura i chitatel'skie predpochteniia 1960-kh godov—nachala 1980-kh gg."
3 Piłnik, "Representation of Babi Yar," 86.
4 Maiofis, "Dvukhpartiinaia organizatsiia i dvukhpartiinaia literature."
5 Voznesensky, *Prozhilki prozy*, 243.
6 "Soviet Party Rift Hinted."
7 Crankshaw, "Host of Young Men."
8 Kogan, *O vremeni i o sebe*, 81.
9 Sheldon, "Transformation of Babi Yar," 138.
10 Chebotareva, "'Vy—khudozhnik, ne remeslennik'," 274.
11 Rudy, "Soviet Russian Literary Scene," 253.
12 Blium, *Evreiskii vopros pod sovetskoi tsenzuroi*, 126.
13 "Amerikanskoe kladbishche na Kube."
14 Cantorovich, "Soviet Reactions."
15 Evtushenko, *Selected Poems*, 82.
16 Mankoff, "Babi Yar," 399.
17 Nekrasov, "Pochemu eto ne sdelano?"
18 "Pamiatnik pogibshim v Bab'em Iaru."
19 "Palacham latyshskogo naroda ne uiti ot kary!"
20 Gitelman, "Soviet Reactions to the Holocaust, " 3.
21 Ayzenshtadt, "A denkmol in Babi Yar."
22 See Zeltser, *Unwelcome Memory*, 25–26.
23 "Za dal'neishii rastsvet ukrainskogo sovetskogo muzykal'nogo iskusstva."
24 Nekrasov, "Pochemu eto ne sdelano?"

25 G. A., "Babii iar."
26 "Eto neobkhodimo sdelat'."
27 Krupyna, "Zhertv bahato, a v hazetakh nichoho ne pishut' . . ."
28 Evtushenko, *Selected Poems*, 82.
29 Pinkus, *Soviet Government and the Jews*, 116.
30 Evtushenko, *Selected Poems*, 83.
31 Evtushenko, 81, 91.
32 Evtushenko, "Tovatishch redaktor." See also Volkov, *Dialogi s Evgeniem Evtushenko*, 224–25.
33 Ogryzko, *Okhraniteli i liberaly*, vol. 2, 51.
34 Toker, "Holocaust in Russian Literature," 123.
35 Bezymenski, *Kniga satiry*, 384.
36 Vail and Genis, *60-e: Mir sovetskogo cheloveka*, 33.
37 *Pochta Il'i Erenburga*, 471.
38 Ogryzko, *Okhraniteli i liberaly*, vol. 1, 243. The Black Hundreds were reactionary, antirevolutionary, and anti-Semitic groups in Russia in the early twentieth century.
39 Dobrenko, "Stalinskaia kul'tura," 52.
40 Pinkus, *Soviet Government and the Jews*, 120.
41 Evtushenko, "Plach po tsenzure," 15.
42 Surovtseva, "'Dorogoi Nikita Sergeevich'."
43 Kostyrchenko, *Tainaia politika Khrushcheva*, 352.
44 Mankoff, "Babi Yar and the Struggle for Memory," 402–3.
45 Kostyrchenko, *Tainaia politika Khrushcheva*, 352.
46 "Rech' deputata A. E. Korneichuka"; "Murder of Jews Retold in Soviet"; "Nazi Mass-Murder of Jews Mentioned"; "Sovet-shrayber dermont tsum ershtn mol yidn zaynen geven natsishe hoypt karbobes."
47 "Za vysokuiu ideinost' i khudozhestvennoe masterstvo sovetskoi literatury."
48 Pavlychko, "I trud, i talant—delu kommunizma."
49 Conquest, "Sad Case of Yevgeny Yevtushenko."
50 Margolin, "Tel' Avivskii bloknot"; Drubetskaia, "Vokrug Bab'ego Iara."
51 Kostyrchenko, *Tainaia politika Khrushcheva*, 364.
52 N. S. Khrushchev, *Vysokaia ideinost' i khudozhestvennoe masterstvo*, 58–61.
53 Redlich, "Khrushchev and the Jews," 346–47.
54 "Rech' tov. N. S. Khrushcheva." See also Budnitskii, "Kto vzial v plen Pauliusa."
55 Chuprinin, *Ottepel', 1960–1962*, 485.
56 Estraikh, "Yevgeny Yevtushenko's 'Babi Yar,'" 354.
57 Adzhubei, *Te desiat' let*, 347.
58 See, e.g., L. Shapiro, "Soviet Jewry since the Death of Stalin," 95–96; Feofanov and Barry, *Politics and Justice in Russia*, 22–32.
59 Sarnov, *Sluchai Erenburga*, 407.
60 Evtushenko, *Volchii passport*, 649. See Khrushchev's reply to Bertrand Russell in Pinkus, *Soviet Government and the Jews*, 72–74.
61 "Dorogoi Nikita Sergeevich, Vasha rech' sbila menia s tolku . . ."

62 "[Perepiska] s raznymi upravleniiami," 41.
63 "[Perepiska] s raznymi upravleniiami," 41.
64 Estraikh, "Yevgeny Yevtushenko's 'Babi Yar.'"
65 Estraikh, "Yevgeny Yevtushenko's 'Babi Yar,'" 357–58. See Lenin, *Polnoe sobranie sochinenii*, 211, and Isakovskii, *O poeticheskom masterstve*, 64–65.
66 "Protiv ideologicheskikh izvrashchenii v literature"; "Za printsipial'nuiu literaturnuiu kritiku"; Yekelchyk, *Stalin's Empire of Memory*, 129, 159.
67 Estraikh, "Yevgeny Yevtushenko's 'Babi Yar,'" 358; Zeltser, "Tema 'Evrei v Bab'em Iaru' v Sovetskom Soiuze," 97.
68 Izmozik, "Pis'ma vo vlast' i reaktsiia vlasti."
69 Estraikh, "Yevgeny Yevtushenko's 'Babi Yar,'" 359.
70 See Grüner, "Anti-Semitism and Collective Violence"; Leibovich, "Antisemitskie nastroeniia v sovetskom tylu"; Marley, *To the Tashkent Station*, 112–13, 231–32, 264.
71 Estraikh, "Yevgeny Yevtushenko's 'Babi Yar,'" 359.
72 Estraikh, "Yevgeny Yevtushenko's 'Babi Yar,'" 363.
73 Gitelman, "History, Memory and Politics," 27.
74 See, e.g., Petrov, "Trinadtsataia simfoniia."
75 "Moscow Jews Told to Keep Mum."
76 Drubetskaia, "Vokrug Bab'ego Iara," 197.
77 Shepard, "TV: Soviet Poet Heard."
78 "Yevtushenko Thanked for Poem."
79 Drubetskaia, "Vokrug Bab'ego Iara," 200; Blium, *Evreiskii vopros pod sovetskoi tsenzuroi*, 133.
80 See, in particular, Pilnik, "Representation of Babi Yar."
81 "Informatsionnoe soobshchenie KGB USSR."
82 Sheldon, "Neither Yevtushenko nor Shostakovich."
83 Salisbury, "Soviet Poet Is Published Here."
84 "Russian Art and Anti-Semitism," 433.
85 Wasserstein, "Oxford's Poetry Revolution."
86 Tsvibel', *Ot Stantsii Zima k Bab'emu Iaru*, 25.
87 See Estraikh, *Yiddish in the Cold War*, 97–98.

11. FIGHTING ZIONISM

1 Heller, *Arab-Israeli Conflict*, 92–93.
2 Kostyrchenko, *Tainaia politika ot Brezhneva do Gorbacheva*, 468.
3 Ro'i, *Struggle for Soviet Jewish Emigration*, 236–43.
4 See Tannenbaum and Haim, "Journeys to a New Homeland," 276.
5 "1962, Moskve, ivrit-rusish verterbukh"; Prestina-Shapiro, *Slovar' zapreshchennogo iazyka*, 18, 20–22, 175; Kostenko, "Prepodavanie ivrita c MGIMO."
6 Aikhenvald, *Sovremennyi ivrit*, 8–9.
7 "Head of Russian Palestine Society Visits Hechal Shlomo."
8 "Israeli Scientists Will Attend Red Parley."

9 Agranovskaia, *Evrei v Rossii*, 173.
10 G. S. Nikitina, "Izrail' i amerikanskii inperializm."
11 G. S. Nikitina, "Ekspansiia Izrailia v Afriku i neokolonializm."
12 Bol'shakov, "Kritika sionizma v sovetskoi istoriografii."
13 Knott, "Israel: A Russian Interpretation," 166.
14 Epstein and Kozheurov, *Rossiia i Izrail'*, 29–33.
15 Estraikh, *Yiddish in the Cold War*, 74.
16 Estraikh, *Yiddish in the Cold War*, 78–79.
17 Govrin, *Israeli-Soviet Relations*, 117.
18 Kriukov, "Russkaia Palestina," 62–63.
19 Svet, "Kontsert Valentiny Levko."
20 Ermishina, "K voprosu o kul'turnom vzaimodeistvii SSSR i Israilia," 309.
21 Ro'i, *Struggle for Soviet Jewish Emigration*, 323–25.
22 "Soviet Jewish Culture," 40.
23 "Novye nobelevskie laureaty"; Vergelis, "Vstrecha s Agnonom"; Frukhtman, "I, Agnon i Shestidnevnaia voina."
24 See Grinberg, *The Commissar*.
25 Friedgut, "The Zionist Family," 251.
26 Beizer, "'I Don't Know Whom to Thank.'"
27 "Department of State Position Paper."
28 Mamaev, Petrov, and Kravchenko, *Antisovetskaia deiatel'nost' evreiskikh natsionalistov i bor'ba s neiu*, 21–22.
29 Salisbury, "Fear Grows among Soviet Jews"; Livne and Goldstein, "'Let My People Go.'"
30 Smirnov, "Provokatsionnaia vydumka amerikanskoi propagandy"; "Oproverzhenie TASS."
31 Pinkus, *Soviet Government and the Jews*, 63.
32 Pinkus, *Soviet Government and the Jews*, 71.
33 Ro'i, *Struggle for Soviet Jewish Emigration*, 79–80; Pinkus, "Emigration of National Minorities," 11–13.
34 "Six Aged Soviet Jews Arrive in Israel"; Database *Cold War in Eastern Europe*, 14 December 1954.
35 See Kostyrchenko, "Sestra otvetila za brata."
36 Memorandum from the Assistant Secretary of State for Near Eastern, South Asian, and African Affairs.
37 Ro'i, "Soviet Policy towards Jewish Emigration," 47.
38 Ro'i, *Struggle for Soviet Jewish Emigration*, 258.
39 D. Zaslavskii, "Diplomat s ulitsy Lilienblum."
40 "Soviet Kidnapping Stirs Israel"; Sherman, "Jewish Solidarity"; "Moscow Rejects Israeli Protest"; Zorza, "Russia Denies Israeli Diplomatist's Story."
41 Sheinin, "Tragediia obmanutykh."
42 Lokshin, "Zabytyi 1957-i."
43 Silber, "'Immigrants from Poland Want to Go Home,'" 204.
44 Young, "To Russia with 'Spain,'" 395–419, 414–17.

45 K. Ivanov and Sheinis, *Gorsudarstvo Izrael'*, 143–44.
46 "Begstvo iz 'raia'."
47 Iyul'skii, "Ad v izrail'skom 'raiu'."
48 Bendor, "Russian Tourists in Israel."
49 Morozov, *Documents on Soviet Jewish Emigration*, 31.
50 "Soviet Tourists Attack Israel." Plotkin's book was published in Ukrainian (*Poïzdka do Izraïliu: Podorozhni notatky* [Kiev, 1959]) and in a Russian translation (*Poezdka v Izrail: Putevye zametki* [Moscow, 1959]).
51 See Plotkin, "Promised Land."
52 "Prodazha dushi."
53 Aleksandrov, "Sud ili fars?"
54 Cantorovich, "Soviet Reactions," 104.
55 Shayduk-Immerman, "Feeling Alive," 91–92. In 1979, when the author of this book applied for emigration, he had five invitations: one of them came from his second cousin, who had emigrated in the early 1970s from Leningrad, and four invitations carried names of absolutely unknown people.
56 Ro'i, *Struggle for Soviet Jewish Emigration*, 228–29.
57 Database *Cold War in Eastern Europe*, "Confidentially," 20 November 1961.
58 L. Shapiro, "Soviet Union" (1968), 497–98.
59 Margulis, *"Evreiskaia" kamera Lubianki*, 149–62.
60 Redlich, "Jewish Appeals in the USSR," 25–26.
61 Zand, "Reply to Mr. Davies."
62 "Zhit' v mire, razvivat' sotrudnichestvo."
63 Ro'i, *Struggle for Soviet Jewish Emigration*, 328.
64 "Paris Pledge," 18–19.
65 Masiukova, "Zakonodatel'noe regulirovanie evreiskoi emigratsii iz SSSR," 236–37.
66 Florsheim, "Demographic Significance of Jewish Emigration," 12.
67 Konstantinov, *Evreiskoe naselenie byvshego SSSR*, 248.

BIBLIOGRAPHY

"1962, Moskve, ivrit-rusish verterbukh." *Sovetish Heymland* 5 (1962): 104.

"60-letie I. G. Erenburga." *Literaturnaia gazeta*, 30 January 1951, 2.

"70 let so dnia rozhdeniia L. M. Kvitko." *Literaturnaia gazeta*, 17 November 1960, 2.

Abashev, Vladimir V. "Iasykom 'kvartirnoi skloki': Desakralizatsiia sovetskogo iskusstva v romane Ivana Shevtsova 'Tlia' (1964 g.)." *Vestnik Permskogo universiteta* 3 (2017): 89–97.

Abel'skaia, Raisa Sh. "'Odesskii aktsent' v pesniakh V. Vysotskogo." *Nauchno-tekhnicheskie vedomosti SPbGPU: Gumanitarnye i obshchestvennye nauki* 2 (2011): 242–47.

Ablazhei, Natalia N., "Repatriatsiia etnicheskikh spetsposelentsev iz SSSR v 'strany narodnoi demokratii' v 1955 godu." *Vestnik Novosibirskogo gosudarstvennogo universiteta* (Series: History and Philosophy) 10, no. 10 (2011): 81–85.

Abramov, Khananil. *Gorskie evrei Kuby (Azerbaidzhan)*. Haifa: n.p., 2003.

Abramovich, Solomon, and Yakov Zilberg, eds. *Smuggled in Potato Sacks: Fifty Stories of the Hidden Children of the Kaunas Ghetto*. London: Vallentine Mitchell, 2011.

Abramovitch, Raphael, "Mentshn un politik: Berias mapole—farlust far der velt." *Forverts*, 14 July 1953, 4–5.

Acemoglu, Daron, Tarek A. Hassan, and James A. Robinson. "Social Structure and Development: A Legacy of the Holocaust in Russia." *Quarterly Journal of Economics* 126, no. 2 (2011): 895–946.Adler, Nanci. "Life in the 'Big Zone': The Fate of Returnees in the Aftermath of Stalinist Repression." *Europe-Asia Studies* 51, no. 1 (1999): 5–19.

Adzhubei, Aleksei I. *Te desiat' let*. Moscow: Sovetskaia Rossiia, 1989.

Afanas'ev, E. S. et al., eds. *Apparat TsK KPSS i kul'tura. 1953–1957: Dokumenty*. Moscow: ROSSPEN, 2001.

Afiani, V. Iu., and N. G. Tomilina, eds. *"A za mnoiu shum pogoni . . ." Boris Pasternak i vlast': Dokumenty, 1956–1972*. Moscow: ROSSPEN, 2001.

Agranovskaia, Marina. *Evrei v Rossii: Istoricheskie ocherki*. Moscow: Jewish University, 1994.

Ahern, Kathleen. "Events on the Road to Immortality: An Evening of Mandelstam at Moscow State University, 1965." *Symposium* 62, no. 4 (2009): 219–34.

Aikhenvald, Aleksandra I. *Sovremennyi ivrit*. Moscow: Nauka, 1990.

Aleksandrov, I. "Sud ili fars?" *Pravda*, 28 April 1961, 6.

Aleksandrovich, Mikhail. *Ia pomniu . . . .* Moscow: Progress, 1992.

Almog, Shmuel. "Alfred Nossig: A Reappraisal." *Studies in Zionism* 4, no. 1 (1983): 1–29.

Altman, Ilya, and Karasik, Olga. "Istoriia i sud'ba 'Chernoi knigi': Pisateli i dokumenty epokhi." *Filologiia i kultura* 3 (2018): 133–38.

Altshuler, Mordechai. *Briv fun yidishe sovetishe shraybers.* Jerusalem: Hebrew University, 1979.

———. "Georgian Jewish Culture under the Soviet Regime." *Soviet Jewish Affairs* 5, no. 2 (1975): 21–39.

———. *Religion and Jewish Identity in the Soviet Union, 1941–1964.* Waltham, MA: Brandeis University Press, 2012.

———. *Soviet Jewry on the Eve of the Holocaust: A Social and Demographic Profile.* Jerusalem: Hebrew University, 1998.

———. *Soviet Jewry since the Second World War: Population and Social Structure.* New York: Greenwood, 1987.

———. *Yahadut Berit-ha-mo'atsot ba-aspaḳlaryah shel 'itonut yidish be-Polin: Bibliyografyah 1945–1970.* Jerusalem: Hebrew University, 1975.

Altshuler, Mordechai, Yitzhak Arad, and Shmuel Krakowski, eds. *Sovetskie evrei pishut Il'e Erenburgu: 1953–1966.* Jerusalem: Yad Vashem, 1993.

Amar, Tarik Cyril. "Yom Kippur in Lviv." *East European Jewish Affairs* 35, no. 1 (2005): 91–110.

"Amerikanskoe kladbishche na Kube." *Pravda Ukrainy*, 22 August 1961, 4.

Amosova, Svetlana, and Svetlana Nikolaeva. "Praktiki peremeny imen u evreev Podolii i Bukoviny v sovetskii period." In *Dialog pokolenii v slavianskoi i evreiskoi kul'turmoi traditsii*, edited by Olga Belova et al., 259–80. Moscow: Sefer, 2010.

Anderson, John. *Religion, State and Politics in the Soviet Union and Successor States.* Cambridge: Cambridge University Press, 1994.

Anderson, Kirill M., ed. *Kremlevskii kinoteatr: 1928–1953, dokumenty.* Moscow: ROSSPEN, 2005.

Andreev, M. "Rukopisi mertvogo moria." *V mire knig* 3 (1961): 6.

Andrews, A. "Spatial Patterns of Higher Education in the Soviet Union." *Soviet Geography* 19, no. 7 (1978): 443–57.

"Anne Frank Diary Chosen for Exhibition." *Bnai Brith Messenger*, 28 August 1959, 8.

Anninskii, Lev. "V svete Babelia." *Sovetskaia kultura*, 27 October 1990, 16.Antipina, Valentina A. *Povsednevnaia zhizn' sovetskikh pisatelei: 1930–1950 gody.* Moscow: Molodaia gvardiia, 2005.

"Anti-Semitism Still Exists in Soviet Union, Ilya Ehrenburg Reports." *The Sentinel*, 21 May 1959, 3.

An Appeal to the Conscience of Mankind: Memorializing the United Nations for an Inquiry into and the Redress of the Cultural and Spiritual Genocide Systematically Pursued against the Jewish People by the Soviet Union. New York: Jewish Labor Committee, 1951.

Arbuzov, V. G. "Kak byl razoblachen gitlerovskii 'doktor' Vialon." *Voprosy arkhivovedeniia* 4 (1963): 103–4.

Arkhipova, A., A. Kirziuk, and E. Iugai. "Skryt' opasnoe imia: Poetika politicheskoi formuly." *Vestnik RGGU: Fol'kloristika* 12 (2017): 102–19.

Aronowicz, Annette. "Haim Sloves, the Jewish People, and a Jewish Communist's Allegiances." *Jewish Social Studies* 9, no. 1 (2002): 95–142.

Artizov, A. et al., eds. *Reabilitatsiia: Kak eto bylo*. Moscow: MFD, 2000.

Ash, Sholom [Asch, Sholem]. *Liudi i bogi: Izbrannye proizvedeniia*. Moscow: Khudozhestvennaia literatura, 1966.

Asher, Havey. "The Black Book and the Holocaust." *Journal of Genocide Research* 1, no. 3 (1999): 401–16.

Astashkin, Dmitrii Iu. "Antisemitskaia reaktsiia sovetskogo obshchestva na 'delo vrachei' (po materialam novgorodskogo upravleniia MGB)." *Kaspiiskii region: Politika, ekonomika, kul'tura* 1 (2015): 32–39.

———. "'Delo Ervina Shiule' i voennye prestupleniia na okkupirovannoi territorii Novgorodskoi oblasti." *Novgorodskii istoricheskii sbornik* 12 (2015): 331–49.

Auclert, Raphaelle. "The 'Armed Thaw': Cultural War under Peaceful Coexistence: A Comparative Study between the 1950s and Today." *Journal of Russian American Studies* 2, no. 2 (2018): 114–34.

Auerbach, Karen. "The Fate of a Yiddish Poet in Communist Eastern Europe: Naftali Herts Kon in Poland, 1959–1965." *Polin: Studies in Polish Jewry* 21 (2009): 243–64.

Avgustevich, Semen. "Tri stikhotvoreniia Moiseia Teifa na muzyku Aleksandra Vustina." *Korni* 22 (2004): 120–28.

Avrutin, Eugene M. "Racial Categories and the Politics of (Jewish) Difference in Late Imperial Russia." *Kritika: Explorations in Russian and Eurasian History* 8, no. 1 (2007): 13–40.

Axebank, Albert. "Inside Stalin's 'National Home for Jews.'" *The Observer*, 27 June 1976, 10.

Axelrod-Rubin, Inessa. "The Jewish Contribution to the Development of Oriental Studies in the USSR." In *Jews in Soviet Culture*, edited by Jack Miller, 247–315. London: Transaction Books, 1984.

Ayzenshtadt, Miriam. "A denkmol in Babi Yar." *Eynikayt*, 7 July 1945, 2.

Bai, Vladimir. "Prizraki proshlogo: Palach reabilitirovan." *Izvestiia*, 9 February 1965, 2.

Barenberg, Alan. "Prisoners without Borders: Zazonniki and the Transformation of Vorkuta after Stalin." *Jahrbücher für Geschichte Osteuropas* 57, no. 4 (2009): 513–34.

Barghoorn, Frederick C. *The Soviet Cultural Offensive: The Role of Cultural Diplomacy in Soviet Foreign Policy*. Princeton, NJ: Princeton University Press, 2015.Barkane, Karina. "Rukovoditeli evreiskikh religioznykh obshchin i gosudarstvennaia vlast' v Latviiskoi SSR (1944–1964)." *Trudy po evreiskoi istorii i kul'ture* 50 (2014): 190–99.

Barnai, Samuel. "Jews in Soviet Lithuania: The Revival after the Holocaust." In *The History of Jews in Lithuania: From the Middle Ages to the 1990s*, edited by Vladas Sirutavičius, Darius Staliūnas, and Jurgita Šiaučiūnaitė-Verbickien, 429–54. Paderborn, Germany: Ferdinand Schöningh, Brill Deutschland GmbH, 2020.

Barnouw, David, and Jeannette K. Ringold. *The Phenomenon of Anne Frank*. Bloomington: Indiana University Press, 2018.

Baron, Salo W. *The Russian Jew under Tsars and Soviets*. New York: Macmillan, 1976.

Bazyler, Michael J. *Holocaust, Genocide, and the Law: A Quest for Justice in a Post-Holocaust World*. New York: Oxford University Press, 2016.

Bederson, Vsevolod D. "Sholom-Aleikhem i 'vynuzhdennyi evreiskii natsionalizm' v identichnosti Evreiskoi avtonomnoi oblasti." *Vestnik Permskogo universiteta: Psikhologiia* 2 (2013): 98–104.

"Begstvo iz 'raia'." *Evrei i evreiskii narod* 3, no. 9 (1963): 204–5.

Beider, Alexander. "Discontinuity of Jewish Naming Traditions." *Avotaynu* 28, no. 2 (2012): 43–53.

Beilinson, Isak. "O Tallinnskom Evreiskom teatre." 28 January 2004. https://muuseum.jewish.ee/Culture/Beilinson.html .

Beizer, Michael. "'I Don't Know Whom to Thank': The American Jewish Joint Distribution Committee's Secret Aid to Soviet Jewry." *Jewish Social Studies* 15, no. 2 (2009): 111–36.

Belenkaia, Liliia, and Boris Zinger. *Naperekor: Evreiskoe natsional'noe dvizhenie v SSSR i ego ideologiia (1945–1976 gg.)*. Minsk: MET, 2004.

Belenky, Moyshe [Belenkii, Moisei]. *Akoste, Shpinoze, Maymon*. Moscow: Emes, 1941.

———. *Chto takoe Talmud*. Moscow: Nauka, 1963.

———. *Iudaizm*. Moscow: Political Literature, 1966.

———. "O sovremennom iudaizme v SShA i Izraile." *Voprosy istorii religii i ateizma* 7 (1959): 106–15.Beluga, Zoia I. et al., eds. *Prestupleniia nemetsko-fashistskikh okkupantov v Belorussii, 1941–1944*. Minsk: Belarus', 1965.Bemporad, Elissa. "Empowerment, Defiance, and Demise: Jews and the Blood Libel Specter under Stalinism." *Jewish History* 26, no. 3–4 (2012): 343–61.

Bendor, Ephraim. "Russian Tourists in Israel." *Jewish Advocate*, 7 August 1958, 6.

Berard-Zarzycka, Ewa. "Ilya Erenburg in Stalin's Post-War Russia." *Soviet Jewish Affairs* 17, no. 1 (1987): 31–48.

Berger, Y. "Toyznter poylishe yidn zaynen in 1956 geforn bazukhn kroyvim in sovetn-farband." *Morgn-Frayhayt*, 4 February 1957, 5.

Bergman, Maius. "New Commissar of Yiddish Literature." *The New Leader*, 5 March 1962, 19–21.

Bertelsen, Olga. "Crossing Ethnic Barriers Enforced by the KGB: Kharkiv Writers' Lives in the 1960s–70s." *East/West: Journal of Ukrainian Studies* 7, no. 1 (2020): 7–54.

"Beseda tovarishcha N. S. Khrushcheva c korrespondentom frantsuzskoi gazety 'Figaro'." *Izvestiia*, 27 March 1917, 1–2.

Bezarov, Oleksandr. "Do pytannia pro prychyny zakryttia Evreiskoho teatru imeni Sholom-Aleikhema v Chernivtsiakh." *Aktual'ni pytannia suspil'nykh nauk ta istorii medytsyny* 4 (2018): 72–78.

Bezirganova, Inna. *Russkii teatr v Gruzii*. Tbilisi: Russkii klub, 2015.

Bezymenski, Aleksandr. *Kniga satiry*. Moscow: Sovetskii pisatel, 1961.

"Birobidzhan Help Called Diverted." *New York Times*, 23 September 1954, 5.

"Biweekly Propaganda Guidance." 19 August 1964, CIA Archive, document no. CIA-RDP78-03061A000200080006-7. Approved for release in April 2014.

Bligh-Grotto, Miriam. "Birobidjan Refugees." *Bnai Brit Messenger*, 12 April 1957, 23–24.

Blinov, V. "Gorod, vstavshii iz ruin." *Gudok*, 14 September 1955, 4.

Blit, Lucjan. "The New Poland: Living Dangerously." *The Observer*, 13 January 1957, 8.

———. "Poland and the Jewish Remnant." *Commentary*, March 1957, 215–21.Blium, Arlen V. *Evreiskii vopros pod sovetskoi tsenzuroi, 1917–1991*. Saint Petersburg: Petersburg Jewish University, 1996.

Bloshtein, Hirsh. "A por bamerkungen vegn dem zhurnal 'Yidishe shriftn'." *Folks-Shtime*, 31 December 1956, 4.

Blusiewicz, Tomasz. "Illegal, Anti-Socialist and Petty Bourgeois: How Maritime Smuggling in the Baltic Undermined the Soviet Economy." *Zeitschrift für Ostmitteleuropa-Forschung* 68, no. 4 (2019): 551–75.

Bol'shakov, Vladimir V. "Kritika sionizma v sovetskoi istoriografii." *Voprosy istorii* 9 (1973): 78–88.

Bondarchuk, Sergei. "Zhdem vas snova v Moskve!" *Sovetskaia kul'tura*, 19 August 1959, 1.

"Bonn Stand on Nazi Trials Irks Soviets." *American Jewish World*, 1 January 1965, 2.

Borodulin, V. I. et al. "Akademik M. S. Vovsi i 'delo vrachei'." *Acta medico-historica Rigensia* 10 (2016): 190–207.

Brandenberger, David. "Stalin's Last Crime? Recent Scholarship on Postwar Soviet Antisemitism and the Doctor's Plot." *Kritika: Explorations in Russian and Eurasian History* 6, no. 1 (2005): 187–204.

Braudo, Meir. *Kulisn un hinterkulisn*. Tel Aviv: Ha-Menorah, 1971.

Braun, Joachim. "Jews in Soviet Music." In *Jews in Soviet Culture*, edited by Jack Miller, 65–106. London: Transaction Books, 1984.

Brener, Iosif. *Lekhaim, Birobidzhan!* Krasnoyarsk: Krasnoiarskii pisatel, 2007.

"British Communists in the Soviet Union: Jews in the Soviet Union." *World News* 4, no. 2 (12 January 1957): 20–23.

"Briv fun Moyshe Broderzon." *Yidishe Shriftn* 12 (1956): 4.

Broad, William J. "A Spy's Path: Iowa to A-Bomb to Kremlin Honor." *New York Times*, 12 November 2007, 1.

Broderson, Sheyne-Miriam. *Mayn laydns-veg mit Moyshe Broderzon: Di milkhome hot gedoyert far undz zibetsn yor*. Buenos Aires: Tsentral-farband fun Poylishe Yidn in Argenține, 1960.

Brodskii, Il'ia E., and Stanislav N. Shpynov. "Osnovateli i zvezdy Gosudarstvennogo Omskogo russkogo narodnogo khora." *Natsional'nye prioritety* 3 (2015): 44–60.

Brogi, Alessandro. *Confronting America: The Cold War between the United States and the Communists in France and Italy*. Chapel Hill: University of North Carolina Press, 2011.Brumberg, Abraham. "'Sovyetish Heymland' and the Dilemmas of Jewish Life in the USSR." *Soviet Jewish Affairs* 2, no. 1 (1972): 27–41.

Brumberg, Joseph, and Abraham Brumberg. *Sovyetish Heymland: An Analysis*. New York: Anti-Defamation League of B'nai B'rith, 1965.
Brushtein, Aleksandra. "Puteshestvie v stranu Vchera." *Sovetskoe iskusstvo*, 24 September 1939, 6.
Budnitskii, Oleg. "Kto vzial v plen Pauliusa." *Ogonek*, 5 February 2018, 38–41.
Bunin, Leonid. "Sergei Vladimirovich Obraztsov i ego teatr." *Zhurnal Vestnik Online*. 15 (274), 17 June 2001. http://www.vestnik.com/issues/2001/0717/win/bunin.htm.
Burford, Russel E., Jr. "Getting the Bugs out of Socialist Legality: The Case of Joseph Brodsky and a Decade of Soviet Anti-Parasite Legislation." *American Journal of Comparative Law* 22, no. 3 (1974): 465–508.
Burgin, Yechiel. *Fun Vilne biz Yisroel: Bletlekh fun a lebn*. Tel Aviv: n.p., 1988.
Burnham, Alexander. "Soviet Defended on State of Jews." *New York Times*, 22 November 1963, 23.
Burton, Christopher. "Soviet Medical Attestation and the Problem of Professionalisation under Late Stalinism, 1945–1953." *Europe-Asia Studies* 57, no. 8 (2005): 1211–29.
"Bust of Mikhoels, Killed under Stalin, Unveiled in Moscow." *The Sentinel*, 3 December 1959, 3.
Bystriakov, Aleksandr. "Khronika zhizni evreev Ekaterinoslava." *Evreiskaia starina: Setevoi zhurnal* 2, no. 85 (2015). https://berkovich-zametki.com/2015/Starina/Nomer2/Bystrjakov1.php.
Cadiot, Juliette. "L'affaire Hain: Kyiv, hiver 1952." *Cahiers du monde russe* 2–3 (2018): 255–88.
Cang, Joel. "Ehrenburg's Price for Survival." *Jewish Advocate*, 1 February 1962, 3.
———. "Meeting a Yiddish Writer in Russia." *Jewish Advocate*, 29 October 1959, 1, 11.
Cantorovich, Nati. "Soviet Reactions to the Eichmann Trial: A Preliminary Investigation 1960–1965." *Yad Vashem Studies* 35 (2007): 103–41.
Carr, Maurice. "Dragunski: Soviet Jewry Will Disappear by Assimilation." *Jerusalem Post*, 26 November 1961, 2.
Carson, Saul. "Breaching the Iron Curtain." *Jewish Advocate*, 25 April 1957, 1.
Cassedy, Steven. *To the Other Shore: The Russian Jewish Intellectuals Who Came to America*. Princeton, NJ: Princeton University Press, 1997.
Chebotareva, Tatyana. "'Vy—khudozhnik, ne remeslennik': Perepiska Korneia Chukovskogo i Mirry Ginsburg." *Arkhiv evreiskoi istorii* 4 (2007): 248–318.
Checinski, Michael. "Soviet Jews and Higher Education." *East European Jewish Affairs* 3, no. 2 (1973): 3–16.
Cheikhetov, Serguei B. "Chastnye predprinimateli." In *Marginaly v sovetskom sotsiume: 1930-e—seredina 1950-kh godov*, edited by S. A. Krasil'nikov and A. A. Shadt, 417–531. Moscow: Politicheskaia entsiklopediia, 2017.
———. "Private Entrepreneurship in the Soviet Union: 1920s–1980s." PhD diss., University of California, Santa Cruz, 2002.
Chertok, Semyon. "A New Magazine in Yiddish." *Soviet Literature* 1 (1962): 176–81.

Chevardin, Aleksei V. "K voprosu o vospriiatii sovetskoi deistvitel'nosti pol'skimi grazhdanami v period Vtoroi mirovoi voiny." In *Sovetskii sotsiokulturnyi proekt: Istoricheskii shans ili global'naia antiutopiia*, edited by Evgeni I. Rabinovich, 326–32. Yekaterinburg: University of the Humanities, 2015.

"Chikagskaia 'Tribiun' zashchishchaet ubiitsu." *Izvestiia*, 3 March 1961, 4.

Chlenov, Mikhail A. "Who Are These 'Mountain Jews'?" *Anthropology & Archeology of Eurasia* 48, no. 1 (2009): 29–38.

Chukovskii, Kornei I. *Dni moei zhizni*. Moscow: Boslen, 2009.

Chuprinin, Sergei I. *Ottepel', 1960–1962: Stranitsy russkoi sovetskoi literatury*. Moscow: Moskovskii rabochii, 1990.

Cohen, Nathan. "The Renewed Association of Jewish Writers and Journalists in Poland, 1944–1948." In *Yiddish after the Holocaust*, edited by Joseph Sherman, 15–36. Oxford: Boulevard Books, 2004.

Cohn, Edward. *The High Tide of a Communist: Postwar Party Discipline and the Values of the Soviet Regime*. DeKalb: Northern Illinois University Press, 2015.

———. "The Paradox of Party Discipline in the Khrushchev-Era Communist Party." In *Communist Parties Revisited: Sociocultural Approaches to Party Rule in the Soviet Bloc, 1956–1991*, edited by Rüdiger Bergien and Jens Gieseke, 23–45. New York: Berghahn, 2018.

Conquest, Robert. "The Sad Case of Yevgeny Yevtushenko: The Politics of Poetry." *New York Times*, 30 September 1973, 16.

Corley, Felix. "Judaism in the Former Soviet Union: Three Snapshots." *East European Jewish Affairs* 25, no. 1 (1995): 73–79.

Corry, Martha Lucille. "The Economic Geography of the Soviet Far East." Phd diss., State University of Iowa, 1953.

Costanso, Susan E. "The Emergence of Alternative Culture: Amateur Studio-Theaters in Moscow and Leningrad 1957–1984." Phd diss., Northwestern University, 1994.

Cothenet, Edouard, Simone Inkel, and Lucy Tinsley. *Imitating Christ*. Wheathampstead, UK: A. Clarke, 1974.

Cousins, Norman. "Readers and Writers in Russia: A Conversation with Ilya Ehrenburg in Moscow." *Saturday Review*, 3 October 1959, 15–17.

Crankshaw, Edward. "Host of Young Men." *The Observer*, 10 January 1960, 6.

———. "A New Exodus in the Air." *The Observer*, 11 January 1959, 10.

———. "Russia Abolishes Jewish Province." *The Observer*, 20 May 1951, 3.

Cummy, Justin. "*Tsevorfene bleter*: The Emergence of Yung Vilne." *Polin: Studies in Polish Jewry* 14 (2001): 170–91.

Czerniakiewicz, Jan. *Przemieszczenia ludności polskiej z ZSRR, 1944–1959*. Warsaw: Wydawnictwo Naukowe PWN, 2004.

D. U. "Zloveshchaya amnistiia." *Literaturnaya gazeta*, 11 September 1954, 4.

Daniel, Clifton. "Moscow Line Shifts to Bonn Arms Peril." *New York Times*, 19 December 1954, 1.

Dashicheva, A. "Nadezhdy opravdannye i utrachennye." *Sovetskaia kultura*, 12 August 1967, 3.

The Database *Cold War in Eastern Europe* (Taylor & Francis). Files from the Political Departments of the UK Foreign Office.

———. "Confidential." cwee.fo371.159537.001.pdf.

———. "Confidential, British Embassy, Moscow, 16 April 1962." cwee.fo371.166268 .001.pdf.

———. "Confidential, British Embassy, Moscow, 20 June 1960." cwee.fo371.152030 .00.pdf.

———. "Confidential." 31 July 1962. cwee.fo371.166266.001.pdf.

———."Confidental, 25 May 1956." cwee.fo371.122938.001.pdf.

———. "Extract from Summary Record of Conversation between the Prime Minister [Harold Macmillan] and Mr. Khrushchev at Dinner on 23 February [1959]." cwee.fo371.152020.001.pdf.

———. 14 December 1954. swee.fo371.111753.001.pdf.

———. Patrick F. Hancock [ambassador to Israel 1959–62], "Confidentially." 20 November 1961.

———. "Reported Renewal of Settlement of Soviet Jews in Birobidjan." 14 January 1959. cwee.fo371.143517.001.pdf.

David-Fox, Michael. *Crossing Borders: Modernity, Ideology, and Culture in Russia and the Soviet Union*. Pittsburgh: University of Pittsburgh Press, 2015.

Davoliūtė, Violeta. "Cold War Cinema and the Traumatic Turn in Europe: *Fact* (1980) as a Soviet Mirror of the Holocaust Film." *Studies in Russian and Soviet Cinema* 14, no. 1 (2020): 57–71.

Dawidowicz, Lucy S. *The Holocaust and the Historians*. Cambridge, MA: Harvard University Press, 1981.

Decter, Moshe. "The Status of the Jews in the Soviet Union." *Foreign Aflairs* 41, no. 2 (1963): 426–28.

Delaloye, Magali. "Polina Jemtchoujina-Molotov et les femmes du Kremlin." *Vingtième Siècle: Revue d'histoire* 2 (2015): 61–72.

Demakov, I. N. "'Kniga kak ulika': Pechatnye izdaniia iz dokumentov arkhivno-sledstvennykh del GAAOSO." In *Vos'mye Chupinskie kraevedcheskie chteniia*. Yekaterinburg: n.p., 2019, 75–85.

Demina, S. M. "Delo vrachei: Regional'nyi uroven'." In *Istoriia Altaiskogo kraia, XVII–XX vv*. Barnaul, Russia: Altai State Pedagogical University, 2005, 352–58.

"Department of State Position Paper." 5 May 1953, Washington, 611.80/5–953. https://history.state.gov.

Deutsch Kornblatt, Judith. *Doubly Chosen: Jewish Identity, the Soviet Intelligentsia, and the Russian Orthodox Church*. Madison: University of Wisconsin Press, 2004.

———. "Jewish Converts to Orthodoxy in Russia in Recent Decades." In *Jewish Life after the USSR*, edited by Zvi Y. Gitelman, Musya Glants, and Marshall I. Goldman, 209–223. Bloomington: Indiana University Press, 2003.

"'Diary' a Hit at Moscow Festival." *Chicago Daily Tribune*, 7 August 1959, 3.

"'Diary of Anne Frank' Sole American Entry at Moscow Film Show." *The Sentinel*, 23 July 1959, 3.

Dickman, Irving R. "Polish Jewry Today." 23 January 1958, JDC Archive, NY55-64_CR_029_1101, item ID846205.

Dmitrievskii, Vitalii N. *Zhizn' v epizodakh*. Saint Petersburg: Kompozitor, 2011.

Dobrenko, Evgeny. "Stalinskaia kul'tura: Skromnoe oboianie antisemitizma." *Novoe literaturnoe obozrenie* 101 (2010): 52–83.

Dobroszycki, Lucjan. *Survivors of the Holocaust in Poland: A Portrait Based on Jewish Community Records, 1944–1947*. Armonk, NY: M. E. Sharpe, 1994.

Dobrushin, Iekhezkel. "Di shtot Birobidzhan." *Literarishe bleter*, 1 February 1935, 71.

"The Doctors' Plot." 15 July 1953. https://www.cia.gov.

Dodin, Abram L. *Izbrannye trudy, vospominaniia*. Saint Petersburg: VSEGEI, 2007.

"Dolady, otchety, informatsii i spravki o religioznoi obstanovke v oblasti." State Archives of Zhytomyr Oblast, year 1963: R-4994, op. 4, d. 7, 108; year 1964: R-4994, op. 4, d. 8.

"Dorogoi Nikita Sergeevich, Vasha rech' sbila menia s tolku. . . ." *Literaturnaia gazeta*, 4 June 1997, 14.

Dovlatov, Sergei. *Sobranie sochinenii*, 4 vols. Saint Petersburg: Azbuka, 1999.

"Dragunski: Soviet Jewry Will Disappear by Assimilation." *Jerusalem Post*, 26 November 1961, 2.

Drubetskaia, Tatiana B. "Vokrug Bab'ego Iara: K istorii russko-izrail'skikh literaturnykh sviazei." In *XX vek: dve Rossii—odna kultura*, edited by Inga A. Shomrakova, 197–200.

Saint Petersburg: St. Petersburg State University of Culture and Arts, 2006.

Druskin, Lev. *Spasennaia kniga: Vospominaniia leningradskogo poeta*. London: Overseas Publications Interchange, 1984.

"Druzhba narodov SSSR i nasha velikaia pobeda." *Pravda*, 6 May 1965, 2.

Duban, James. "The Generalization of Holocaust Denial: Meyer Levin, William James, and the Broadway Production of *The Diary of Anne Frank*." *Philosophy and Literature* 39, no. 1A (2015): A234–A48.

———. "Honest to One's Self: Censorship and Variants in American Editions of Meyer Levin's *In Search*." *Shofar* 33, no. 2 (2015): 27–52.

Dubnow, Simon. *History of the Jews in Russia and Poland: From the Death of Alexander I, until the Death of Alexander III*. Philadelphia: Jewish Publication Society of America, 1918.

Dumitru, Diana. "Jewish Social Mobility under Late Stalinism: A View from the Newly Sovietizing Periphery." *Slavic Review* 78, no. 4 (2019): 986–1008.

Durham, Michael. "Russians Wrong about Briton Who 'Died in Stalin Camp.'" 6 September 1992. www.independent.co.uk.

Dvuzhil'naia, Inessa F. "Grigorii Frid. Monoopera 'Dnevnik Anny Frank': Teatr odnoi aktrisy." *Nauchnye trudy Belorusskoi gosudarstvennoi akademii muzyki* 14 (2015): 68–83.

Dymshits, Valerii A. et al. *Gorskie evrei: Istoriia͡, ėtnografiia͡, kul'tura*. Moscow: Daat, 1999.

"Ehrenburg Announced as Stalin Prize Winner." *Christian Science Monitor*, 28 January 1953, 3.

"Ehrenburg Hits Writers." *New York Times*, 28 July 1950, 6.

Ehrenburg, Ilya. "Evrei." *Krasnaia zvezda*, 1 November 1942, 3.

———. "Introduction to 'The Diary of Anne Frank.'" *Soviet Review* 1, no. 5 (1960): 56–61.

———. "Kiev." *Literaturnaia gazeta*, 27 September 1960, 4.

———. "Neobkhodimoe ob'iasnenie." *Literaturnaia gazeta*, 9 February 1957, 3–4.

———. "Po povodu odnogo pis'ma." *Pravda*, 21 September 1948, 3.

———. *Post-War Years, 1945–1954*. Cleveland: World, 1967.

———. "Rech' na vechere, posviashchennom 70-letiiu so dnia rozhdeniia I. E. Babelia." 11 November 1964, Yad Vashem Archives, record group P.21, file 4.

———. *Selections from "People, Years, Life"*. Oxford: Pergamon, 1972.

———. "Velikii zashchitnik mira." *Pravda*, 11 March 1953, 3.Eliasberg, Galina, *". . . Odin iz prezhnego Peterburga": S. L. Tsinberg-istorik evreiskoi literatury, kritik i publitsist*. Moscow: Russian State University for the Humanities, 2005.

Emel'iachenko, Tat'iana G. "Bukharskie evrei v sotsiokul'turnom prostranstve Srednei Azii." *Vostok. Afro-Aziatskie obshchestva: Istoriia i sovremennost'* 3 (2012): 39–47.

Emiot, Israel. *In mitele yorn*. Rochester, NY: Jewish Community Council, 1963.

Engel, David. "The Reconstruction of Jewish Communal Institutions in Postwar Poland: The Origins of the Central Committee of Polish Jews, 1944–45." *East European Politics and Societies* 10, no. 1 (1996): 85–107.

Epshtein, Alek D., and Stanislav A. Kozheurov. *Rossiia i Izrail': Trudnyi put' navstrechu*. Jerusalem: Gesharim/Mosty kul'tury, 2011.

Epshteyn, Shakhno. "Ven Arn Vergelis hot zikh geshlogn kegn di natsis." *Morgn-Frayhayt*, 19 November 1963, 3.

Eregina, Natialia T. "Stalinskie ideologicheskie kampanii i vysshaia meditsinskaia shkola (1946–1953)." *Novyi istoricheskii vestnik* 4, no. 22 (2009): 48–57.

Erlich, Victor. "The Metamorphoses of Ilya Ehrenburg." *Problems of Communism*, July–August 1965, 15–24.

Ermishina, Kseniia V. "K voprosu o kul'turnom vzaimodeistvii SSSR i Israilia nakanune Shestidnevnoi voiny." *Trudy po iudaike* (2019): 308–14.

Estraikh, Gennady. "Anti-Nazi Rebellion in Peretz Markish's Drama and Prose." In *A Captive of the Down: The Life and Work of Peretz Markish*, edited by Joseph Sherman et al., 172–85. Oxford: Legenda, 2011.

———. "Birobidzhan in Khrushchev's Thaw: The Soviet and the Western Outlook." *Journal of Modern Jewish Studies* 18, no. 1 (2019): 56-74.

———. "David Bergelson in and on America." In *David Bergelson: From Modernism to Socialist Realism*, edited by Joseph Sherman and Gennady Estraikh, 205–21. Oxford: Legenda, 2007.

———. "The Era of *Sovetish Heymland*: Readership of the Yiddish Press in the Former Soviet Union." *East European Jewish Affairs* 25, no. 1 (1995): 17–22.

———. *Evreiskaia literaturnaia zhisn' Moskvy, 1917–1991*. Saint Petersburg: European University, 2015.

———. "Hersh Smolar: A Polish Personage in the Soviet Jewish Cultural Scene,

1940s–1960s." In *Polish Jews in the Soviet Union (1939–1959): History and Memory of Deportation, Exile, and Survival*, edited by Katharina Friedla and Markus Nesselrodt, 175–98. Boston: Academic Studies Press, 2021.

———. "'Jewish Street' or Jewish Cul-de-Sac? From *Sovetish Heymland* to *Di Yidishe Gas*." *East European Jewish Affairs* 26, no. 1 (1996): 25–33.

———. "The Missing Years: Yiddish Writers in Soviet Bialystok, 1939–41." *East European Jewish Affairs* 46, no. 2 (2016): 176–91.

———. "Odinochestvo evreiskogo redaktora: K 100-letiiu so dnia rozhdeniia Arona Vergelisa." *Narod knigi v mire knig* 133 (April 2018): 7–9.

———. "ORT in Post-Holocaust Poland." In *Educating for Life: New Chapters in the History of ORT*, edited by Rachel Bracha, Adi Drori-Avraham, and Geoffrey Yantian, 196–220. London: World ORT, 2010.

———. "Soviet Sholem Aleichem." In *Translating Sholem Aleichem: History, Politics and Art*, edited by Gennady Estraikh et al., 62–82. Oxford: Legenda, 2012.

———. "Soviet Yiddish Cultural Diplomacy in the Post-Stalinist 1950s." In *Jewish Lives under Communism: New Perspectives*, edited by Katerina Caprová and Kamil Kijek, 174–94. New Brunswick, NJ: Rutgers University Press, 2022.

———. *Soviet Yiddish: Language Planning and Linguistic Development*. Oxford: Oxford University Press, 1999.

———. "Soviet Yiddish Orthography: An Iron Logic or Coincidence?" *Shvut* 1–2 (1995): 218–41.

———. "Yevgeny Yevtushenko's 'Babi Yar': A Russian Poet's Page in Post-Holocaust History." In *Distrust, Animosity, and Solidarity: Jews and Non-Jews during the Holocaust in the USSR*, edited by Christoph Dieckmann and Arkadi Zeltser, 331–69. Jerusalem: Yad Vashem, 2021.

———. *Yiddish in the Cold War*. Oxford: Legenda, 2008.

———. "Yiddish Language Conference Aborted." *East European Jewish Affairs* 25, no. 2 (1995): 91–96.

———. "Zalman Wendroff: The *Forverts* Man in Moscow." *Leket: Yiddish Studies Today* 1 (2012): 509–28.

Etinger, Iakov. "The Doctors' Plot: Stalin's Solution to the Jewish Question." In *Jews and Jewish Life in Russia and the Soviet Union*, edited by Yaakov Ro'i, 103–24. Ilford, UK: Frank Cass, 1995.

"Eto neobkhodimo sdelat'." *Literaturnaia gazeta*, 22 December 1958, 2.

Evans, Christine E. "From 'Truth' to 'Time': Soviet Central Television, 1957–1985." PhD diss., University of California, Berkeley, 2010.

Evreiskaia avtonomnaia oblast'. Khabarovsk, Russia: Khabarovsk, 1959.

Evtushenko, Evgeni [Yevtushenko, Yevgeni], "Plach po tsenzure." *Ogonek*, 2–9 February 1991, 14–16.

———. *Selected Poems*. Baltimore: Penguin, 1962.

———. "Tovatishch redaktor." *Literaturnaia gazeta*, 9 June 2019, 12.

———. *Volchii passport*. Moscow: Vagrius, 1998.

Fadeev, Aleksandr. "Nekotorye voprosy raboty Soiuza pisatelei." *Literaturnaia gazeta*, 28 March 1953, 3.

Fainberg, Dina. "A Portrait of a Journalist as a Cold War Expert: Harrison Salisbury." *Journalism History* 41, no. 3 (2015): 153–64.

Fast, Howard. "Ehrenburg's 'The Thaw.'" *Daily Worker*, 12 January 1957, 6.

Fedchenko, Mikhail N. *Povsednevnaia zhizn' sovetskogo cheloveka (1945–1991 gg.).* Kurgan, Russia: Kurgan State University, 2009.

Fedosik, V. A., A. A. Prokhorov, and S. N. Khodin, eds. *Giler Markovich Livshits: K 100-letiiu so dnia rozhdeniia.* Minsk: Belorussian State University, 2009.

Fedotov, Vasilii A. *Tovarovedenie gastronomicheskikh tovarov.* Moscow: Gostorgizdat, 1955.

Fefer, Dora. "Moi otets Itsik Fefer." *Zarkhiviv VUChK—GPU—KGB* 3–4 (1998): 382–85.

Fefer, Itsik. *Izbrannoe.* Moscow: Sovetskii pisatel, 1957.

Feferman, Kiril. *Soviet Jewish Stepchild: The Holocaust in the Soviet Mindset, 1941–1964.* Saarbrücken, Germany: VDM Verlag Dr. Müller, 2009.

Fejtö, François. "Literary and Artistic Life in the U.S.S.R." *The World Today* 16, no. 4 (1960): 167–75.

Feofanov, Yuri, and Donald D. Barry. *Politics and Justice in Russia: Major Trials of the Post-Stalin Era.* Armonk, NY: M. E. Sharpe, 1996.

Ferziger, Adam S. "'Outside the Shul': The American Soviet Jewry Movement and the Rise of Solidarity Orthodoxy, 1964–1986." *Religion and American Culture: A Journal of Interpretation* 22, no. 1 (2012): 83–130.

"Final zlachynstva—lava padsudnykh." *Evrei i evreiskii narod* 4, no. 1 (1965): 36.

Fineberg, [Solomon] Andhil. "Defrauding Minority Groups." In *Soviet Total War: "Historic Mission" of Violence and Deceit*, vol. 1, 52–57. Washington, DC: U.S. Government Printing Office, 1956.

———. Transcript of interview. William E. Wiener Oral History Library of the American Jewish Committee. New York Public Library Oral Histories, box 24, no. 1 (1974), 5-208, 5-210.

Finsber, V. "Ale yidn fun Poyln raysn zikh aroystsuforn." *Forverts*, 13 December 1956, 2.

Fishbein, J. I. "What Are We Afraid Of?" *The Sentinel*, 14 November 1963, 7.

Fishman, David F. *The Book Smugglers: Partisans, Poets, and the Race to Save Jewish Treasures from the Nazis.* Lebanon, NH: University Press of New England, 2017.

Fitzpatrick, Sheila. "Social Parasites: How Tramps, Idle Youth, and Busy Entrepreneurs Impeded the Soviet March to Communism." *Cahiers du monde russe* 47, no. 1–2 (2006): 377–408.Florin, Moritz. "The Many Ways of Being Soviet: Urban Elites, People's Friendship, and Ethnic Diversity in Postwar Soviet Frunze." *Ab Imperio* 4 (2018): 147–70.

Florsheim, Yoel. "Demographic Significance of Jewish Emigration from the USSR." *Soviet Jewish Affairs* 10, no. 1 (1980): 5–22.

"Foreign Policy Implications of Stalin's Death and the Doctors' Plot." 18 June 1953, CIA, Freedom of Information Act Electronic Reading Room, document CIA-RDP80-00810A001500150002-7.Frankel, Max. "Jewish Birobidzhan Is Found Quiet Corner in Brisk Siberia." *New York Times*, 1 May 1959, 1.

Fray, Sof'ia. "Otvet neproshennym 'zashchitnikam'." *Trud*, 21 July 1959, 3.

"French Paper Reports New Version of How Stalin Died in Rage over Jews." *Washington Post and Times Herald*, 8 June 1957, 4.

Frenkel, Alexander. "Did Mikhail Epelbaum Study at Warsaw Conservatoire? The Early Years of an Eminent Yiddish Singer." In *Three Cities of Yiddish: St. Petersburg, Warsaw and Moscow*, edited by Gennady Estraikh and Mikhail Krutikov, 104–23. Oxford: Legenda, 2017.

———. "Iz istorii evreiskoi kul'tury v SSSR epokhi 'ottepeli': Leningradskii evreiskii muzykal'no-dramaticheskii ansambl'." In *Idish: Iazyk i kul'tura v Sovetskom Soiuze*, edited by Leonid Katsis, Mariia Kaspina, and David Fishman, 312–26. Moscow: Russian State University for the Humanities, 2009.

———. "'Sonim af tsulokhes'—'vragam nazlo': Evreiskaia estrada v Leningrade epokhi ottepeli." *Iz istorii evreiskoi muzyki v Rossii* 3 (2015): 191–242.Frezinskii, Boris. "Babel', Erenburg i drugie." *Zvezda* 6 (2014): 121–40.

———. "Il'ia Erenburg i dnevnik Mashi Rol'nikaite." *Narod knigi v mire knig* 82 (October 2009): 1–6.

———. *Pochta Il'I Erenburga: Ia slyshu vse, 1916–1967*. Moscow: Agraf, 2006.

———. "Tragediia Emmanuila Kazakevicha." *Narod knigi v mire knig* 102 (February 2013): 1–9.

Friedberg, Maurice. "New Editions of Soviet Belles-Lettres: A Study in Politics and Palimpsests." *American Slavic and East European Review* 13, no. 1 (1954): 72–88.

Friedgut, Theodore H. "The Zionist Family." In *The Jewish Movement in the Soviet Union*, edited by Yaacov Ro'i, 250–72. Baltimore: Johns Hopkins University Press, 2012.

Friedman, Milton. "Arabs Ask Reds to Stop Polish Jews from Emigrating." *The Sentinel*, 21 November 1957, 9.

———. "Will Emigration from Poland Stop?" *Jewish Advocate*, 21 November 1957, 2.

Frukhtman, Lev. "I, Agnon i Shestidnevnaia voina." *ISRAGEO*, 10 December 2016. http://www.isrageo.com/2016/12/10/agnonobel50/.

G. A. "Babii iar." *Novoe russkoe slovo*, 20 October 1961, 8.

Gammer, Efim. "Aktery umiraiut na podmostkakh." *Mishpokha* 22 (2012): 116–19.

Ganevskii, V. "Tri spektaklia ital'anskoi truppy. *Teatr* 8 (1963): 129–34.

Garber, David. "Choir and Drama in Riga. *East European Jewish Affairs* 4, no. 1 (1974): 39–44.

Garber, Zev, and Bruce Zukerman. "Why Do We Call the Holocaust 'The Holocaust'? An Inquiry into the Psychology of Labels. *Modern Judaism* 9, no. 2 (1989): 197–211.

Garthoff, Raymond L. *A Journey through the Cold War: A Memoir of Containment and Coexistence*. Washington, DC: Brookings Institution, 2002.

Gavrilov, Iu. "Piat' uchenicheskikh tetradei. *Literaturnaia gazeta*, 31 May 1960, 4.

Geizer, Matvei. *Leonid Utesov*. Moscow: Molodaia gvardiia, 2008.

"Gekirtster protokol fun dem tsuzamentref mitn hoypt-redaktor fun der Varshever tsaytung 'Folks-shtime' Hersh Smolyar. *Di yidishe gas* 4 (1995): 62–71.

Gelatelly, Robert. *Lenin, Stalin, and Hitler: The Age of Social Catastrophe*. New York: Alfred A. Knopf, 2007.

Gel'fond, Maria M. "Trilogiia Aleksandry Brushtein 'Doroga ukhodit vdal' . . .': Istoriia, zamysel, voploshchenie." *Detskie chteniia* 6, no. 2 (2014): 269–85.

Gen, Tevie. *A veg in der vayt*. Moscow: Sovetskii pisatel, 1977.

Genina, Elena S. "'Delo vrachei' v Stalinske (1953 g.)." *Izvestiia Altaiskogo gosudarstvennogo universiteta* 4, no. 1 (2009): 55–62.

———. "Iz istorii repressii v otnoshenii sovetskikh evreev v 1953 g. (po materialam Sibiri i Dal'nego Vostoka)." In *Nauchnye trudy po iudaike*. 2:350–62. Moscow: Sefer, 2011.

Genina, Elena S., and Elena B. Kaimashnikova. "A. P. Rozenberg: 'Delo vrachei' v Stalinskom gosudarstvennom institute dlia usovershenstvovaniia vrachei (1953 g.)." *Vestnik Kemerovskogo gosudarstvennogo universiteta* 4 (2019): 915–23.

Gerasimova, Olga G. "Odno leto iz zhizni Mikhailova: Sovetskaia deistvitel'nost' glazami iugoslavskogo intelligenta." *Intelligentsia i mir* 3 (2012): 87–102.

Gerasimova, V. A., and V. P. Kliueva. "Antisemitizm v pozdnem SSSR v predstavlenii sibirskikh evreev: Predvaritel'nye nabliudeniia." *Vestnik Tomskogo gosudarstvennogo universiteta: Istoriia* 65 (2020): 165–70.

Gerovich, Viacheslav. "'Matematicheskii rai': Parallel'naia sotsial'naia infrastruktura poslevoennoi sovetskoi matematiki." *Logos* 30, no. 2 (2020): 93–128.

Gershenson, Olga. *The Phantom Holocaust: Soviet Cinema and Jewish Catastrophe*. New Brunswick, NJ: Rutgers University Press, 2013.

Gershuni, Aharon Eliahu. "Bor'ba khasidov za vyezd iz Sovetskogo Soiuza." *Alef*, 4 September 1989, 46–55; 11 September 1989, 42–47; 18 September 1989, 52–56; 25 September 1989, 42–47.

Gessen, Esther. *Belostok—Moskva*. Moscow: AST, 2014.

Gevisser, Mark. *Lost and Found in Johannesburg*. Johannesburg: Jonathan Ball, 2014.

Gilboa, Yehoshua A. *A Language Silenced: The Suppression of Hebrew Literature and Culture in the Soviet Union*. Rutherford, NJ: Fairleigh Dickinson University Press, 1982.

Gilburd, Eleonory. "Picasso in Thaw Culture." *Cahiers du monde russe* 47, no. 1–2 (2006): 65–108.

Ginsburg, George. "The Soviet Union and the Problem of Refugees and Displaced Persons, 1917–1956." *American Journal of International Law* 51, no. 2 (1957): 325–61.

Ginzburg, Lev. "Pravo na trevogu." *Literaturnaia gazeta*, 16 December 1961, 4.

———. *Tsena pepla*. Moscow: Sovetskii pisatel, 1962.

Gitelman, Zvi. "Baltic and Non-Baltic Immigrants in Israel: Political and Social Attitudes and Behavior," *Studies in Comparative Communism* 12, no. 1 (1979): 75–78.

———. *A Century of Ambivalence*. Bloomington: Indiana University Press, 2001.

———. "The Evolution of Jewish Culture and Identity in the Soviet Union." In *Jewish Culture and Identity in the Soviet Union*, edited by Yaacov Ro'i and Avi Beker, 3–24. New York New York University Press, 1991.

———. "History, Memory and Politics: The Holocaust in the Soviet Union." *Holocaust and Genocide Studies* 5, no. 1 (1990): 23–37.

———. "Soviet Reactions to the Holocaust, 1945–1991." In *The Holocaust in the Soviet Union: Studies and Sources on the Destruction of the Jews in the Nazi-Occupied Territories of the USSR, 1941–1945*, edited by Lucjan Dobroszycki and Jeffrey S. Guroch, 3–28. Armonk, NY: M. E. Sharpe, 1993. Goldhagen, Erich. "Der Holocaust in der Sowjetischen Propaganda und Geschichtsschreibung." *Viertel-jahrshefte für Zeitgeschichte* 28, no. 4 (1980): 502–7.

———. "The Soviet Treatment of the Holocaust." In *The Nazi Holocaust: Historical Articles on the Destruction of European Jews*. Vol. 1. *Perspectives on the Holocaust*, edited by Michael R. Marrus, 304–10. Westport, CT: Meckler, 1989.

Goldmann, Nahum. "Khrushchev and the Soviet Jews." *New York Herald Tribune*, 7 May 1958, 18.

Goldsmith, S. J. "Another 'Diary.'" *The Sentinel*, 27 January 1966, 11.

Goldstein, Joseph Simon. "Aldos guts." *Forverts*, 29 September 1954, 4.

Golidovsky, Yuri. "Defiance and Death in Kishinev: Remembering the Yiddish Actor Ruvim Levin." *Pakn Treger*, Winter 2017/5778. https://www.yiddishbook center.org.

"Golos moskovskikh pisatelei." *Literaturnaia gazeta*, 1 November 1958, 3.

Golovkova, Lidiia A. "Krainosti ateisticheskoi propagandy v strane Sovetov." *Ezhe-godnaia bogoslovskaia konferentsiia Pravoslavnogo Sviato-Tikhonovskogo gumanitar-nogo universiteta* 21 (2011): 378–84.

Golub', Boris M. "O meste i znachenii toponimov evreiskogo proiskhozhdeniia na territorii Evreiskoi avtonomnoi oblasti." *Vestnik Priamurskogo gosudarstvennogo universiteta im. Sholem-Aleikhema* 3 (2014): 37–47.

Goluboff, Sascha L. *Jewish Russians: Upheavals in a Moscow Synagogue*. Philadelphia: University of Pennsylvania Press, 2003.

Gorchakov, Ovidii A. *Ian Berzin—komandarm GRU*. Saint Petersburg: Neva, 2004.

Gordon, Joseph. "Soviet Union." *American Jewish Year Book* 55 (1954): 271–82.

———. "Soviet Union." *American Jewish Year Book* 57 (1956): 416–34.

Gordon, Shmuel. *Birobidzhaner toyshvim*. Moscow: Emes, 1948.

———. "Tselina." *Sovetish Heymland* 3 (1961): 3–18.Gorokhova, Evgeniia Iu. "Diskussii 1990-kh gg. ob ukazanii natsional'noi prinadlezhnosti grazhdan SSSR i Rossii v ofitsial'nykh dokumentakh." *Vestnik Moskovskogo universiteta* 4 (2017): 105–28.

"Govorit Moskva." *Gudok*, 19 May 1967, 4.

Govrin, Yosef. *Israeli-Soviet Relations, 1953–1967: From Confrontation to Disruption*. London: Frank Cass, 1998.

Granin, Daniil. "Mimoletnoe iavlenie." *Ogonek* 6 (1988): 9–11.

Greenbaum, Avraham. "A Note on the Tradition of the Twenty-Four Soviet Martyrs." *Soviet Jewish Affairs* 17, no. 1 (1987): 49–52.

Greiner, Bernd. "The Soviet View: An Interview with Sergo Mikoyan." *Diplomatic History* 14, no. 2 (1990): 205–21.

Grinberg, Marat. *The Commissar: Aleksandr Askoldov*. Bristol, UK: Intellect, 2006.

———. "Reading between the Lines: The Soviet Jewish Bookshelf and Post-Holocaust Soviet Jewish Identity." *East European Jewish Affairs* 48, no. 3 (2018):

401–6.Haimson, Leopold H. "Three Generations of the Soviet Intelligentsia." *Foreign Affairs*, January 1959, 235–46.

Halkin [Galkin], Samuel [Samuil]. *Stikhi. Ballady. Dram.* Moscow: Goslitizdat, 1958.

Halperin, Edward C. "The Jewish Problem in U.S. Medical Education, 1920–1955." *Journal of the History of Medicine and Allied Sciences* 56, no. 2 (2001): 140–67.

Harrison, Andrew. *Passover Revisited: Philadelphia's Efforts to Aid Soviet Jews 1963–1998*. Madison, NJ: Fairleigh Dickinson University Press, 2001.

"Head of Russian Palestine Society Visits Hechal Shlomo." *Jerusalem Post*, 5 January 1962, 3.

Heffernan, Michael. "The Interrogation of Sándor Radó: Geography, Communism and Espionage between World War Two and the Cold War." *Journal of Historical Geography* 47 (2015): 74–88.

Heinzen, James. "Soviet Entrepreneurs in the Late Socialist Shadow Economy: The Case of the Kyrgyz Affair." *Slavic Review* 79, no. 3 (2020): 544–65.

Held, Adolph. "Di 'lagernikes' vos boyen Biro-Bidzhan." *Forverts*, 20 September 1936, section 2, 1.

Heller, Joseph. *The United States, the Soviet Union and the Arab-Israeli Conflict, 1948–67: Superpower Rivalry*. Manchester: Manchester University Press, 2016.

Hellman, Ben. *The Fairytales and True Stories: The History of Russian Literature for Children and Young People, 1574–2010*. Leiden: Brill, 2013.

Herman, Simon N. *Jewish Identity: A Social Psychological Perspective*. Beverly Hills, CA: Sage, 1977.

Heydemann, Günther. "Deutschlandpolitische Neuansätze der 60er Jahre." *Historisch-Politische Mitteilungen* 1 (1994): 15–32.

Hill, Fiona, and Clifford G. Gaddy. *The Siberian Curse: How Communist Planners Left Russia Out in the Cold*. Washington, DC: Brookings Institution, 2003.

"Hirsh Rolnik." Yad Vashem: Jews in the Red Army, 1941–1945. https://www.yadvashem.org.

Hirszowicz, Lukasz. "The Holocaust in the Soviet Mirror." *East European Jewish Affairs* 22, no. 1 (1992): 39–50.

Hoffman, Charles E. *Red Shtetl: The Survival of a Jewish Town under Soviet Communism*. New York: American Jewish Joint Distribution Committee, 2002.

Hopkins, Mark W. "Lenin, Stalin, Khrushchev: Three Concepts of the Press." *Journalism Quarterly* 42, no. 4 (1965): 523–31.

Horodyński, Dominik. *Syberia inaczej*. Warsaw: Wydawnictwo Ministerstwa Obrony Narodowej, 1959.

Iakovleva, Galina N. "Dokumenty vitebskogo obllita kak istochnik po istorii kul'turno-prosvetitel'skikh uchrezhdenii na Vitebshchine v period 'ottepeli'." In *Aktual'nye problem istochnikobedenii*, edited by A. N. Dulov et al., 305–9. Vitebsk, Belarus: Vitebsk State Univetsity, 2013.

Iarkov, Aleksandr P. *Evrei v. Kyrgyzstane*. Bishkek, Kyrgyzstan: Menora, 2000.

Iavorskaia, Alena. "Gekht Semen Grigor'evich (1900–1964)". In *Oni ostavili sled v istorii Odessy*. http://odessa-memory.info/index.php?id=187.

Ikhilov, Mikhail M. *Narodnosti lezginskoi gruppy*. Makhachkala, Dagestan: Dagestan Branch of the Academy of Sciences, 1967.

"Imenem soten tysiach." *Pravda*, 31 January 1963, 4.

"Imia Rozy." *Booknik*, 27 Match 2014. http://booknik.ru.

"In a novine—oyfgedekt a farloymdung vegn Biro-Bidzhan." *Morgn-Frayhayt*, 1 January 1956, 5.

"Information Report: Black Market Operations in the Lithuanian SSR." 7 July 1953, CIA-RDP82-00457R012600250002-7.

"Information Report: Secret Policy Concerning Jewish Doctors." 9 March 1953, CIA, Freedom of Information Act Electronic Reading Room. https://www.cia.gov.

"Informatsionnoe soobshchenie KGB USSR o pochtovoi rozsylke stikhov i dokimentov v adres lits evreiskoi natsional'nosti ot 29.09.1969 goda." In *Elektronnyi arkhiv ukraïns'koho vyzvol'noho rukhu*. https://avr.org.ua/viewDoc/24869.

"Intervyu mit Dr. N. Goldman." *Tog-Morgn-Zhurnal*, 13 December 1963, 1, 10.

Ionova, Irina A. "Na perekrestke kul'tur: zametki o kishinevskom prostorechii." *Slavianskie chteniia: Teoreticheskii zhurnal* 3, no. 9 (2014): 5–16.

Isakovskii, Mikhail. *O poeticheskom masterstve*. Moscow: Sovetskii pisatel, 1960.

Ishchenko, P. P. "Lev Sheinin—chelovek s neobychnoi biografiei i sud'boi." *Vestnik Universiteta imeni O. E. Kutafina* 8 (2019): 157–59.

Iskateli zhemchuga; novelly izrail'skikh pisatelei. Moscow: Nauka, 1966.

"Israeli Scientists Will Attend Red Parley." *The Sentinel*, 28 June 1962, 8.

"Issledovatel'skuiu rabotu—na novyi uroven'." *Voprosy literatury* 9 (1961): 58–97.

Iudson, Mikhail. "Nisha Livshitsa." *Zametki po evreiskoi istorii* 5, 20 May 2013. http://litbook.ru/article/3764/.

Ivanov, Alexander. "Yiddish Music and Musicology in Petrograd/Leningrad/St. Petersburg through the Prism of the City Archives." In *Three Cities of Yiddish: St. Petersburg, Warsaw and Moscow*, 141–57. Oxford: Legenda.

Ivanov, Alexander, and Mark Kupovetsky. *Dokumenty po istorii i kul'ture evreev v arkhivakh Sankt-Peterburga*. Saint Petersburg: Mir, 2013.

Ivanov, Konstantin, and Zinovii Sheinis. *Gorsudarstvo Izrail', ego polozhenie i politika*. Moscow: Politizdat, 1959.

Ivanov, P. "Novyi zhurnal dlia molodezhi." *Gudok*, 25 September 1956, 4.

———. "Ob odnoi oshibochnoi kontseptsii." *Pravda*, 25 December 1951, 3.

Ivanova, Natal'ia. "The 'Companion of Groves' and the Leader: A Certain Assonance." *Russian Studies in Literature* 39, no. 1 (2002): 33–59.

Iyul'skii, Rostislav. "Ad v izrail'skom 'raiu'." *Sovetskaia kultura*, 25 March 1958, 4.

"Iz amerikanskikh bibliotek iz'iaty knigi kommunistov." *Novoe russkoe slovo*, 12 June 1953, 5.

Izakov, Boris. "V teatrakh i kino SShA." *Sovetskaia kultura*, 10 March 1956, 4.

Izmozik, Vlanlen S. "Pis'ma vo vlast' i reaktsiia vlasti, 1945–1947 gg." *Noveishaia istoriia Rossii* 18 (2017): 225–44.

Jacobs, A. "Contact and Control: Americans Visit the Soviet Union, 1956-1985." PhD diss., Indiana University, 2019.

Jacobs, Adrianne Kathleen. "The Many Flavors of Socialism: Modernity and Tradition in Late Soviet Food Culture, 1965–1985." PhD diss., University of North Carolina, 2015.

Jacobs, Everett M. "Jewish Representation in Local Soviets, 1959–1973." *East European Jewish Affairs* 6, no. 1 (1976): 18–26.

"Jewish Communists Rap Soviet Policy on Jews." *The Sentinel*, 26 June 1958, 3.

"Jewish Editor in Russian Mission." *New York Times*, 12 November 1963, 20.

"Jews in Moscow Hail 'Annefrank.'" *New York Times*, 12 April 1963, 28.

Jockusch, Laura, and Tamar Lewinsky. "Paradise Lost? Postwar Memory of Polish Jewish Survival in the Soviet Union." *Holocaust and Genocide Studies* 24, no. 3 (2010): 373–99.

Johnson, Ian. "Prophet of Poison Gas: Yakov Fishman and the Soviet Chemical Weapons Program, 1924–1937." *Vulcan* 6 (2018): 16–36.

Johnston, Timothy. *Being Soviet: Identity, Rumour, and Everyday Life under Stalin, 1939–1953*. Oxford: Oxford University Press, 2011.

———. "Peace or Pacifism? The Soviet 'Struggle for Peace in All the World,' 1948–54." *Slavonic and East European Review* 86, no. 2 (2008): 259–81.

K. Marx and F. Engels on Religion. Moscow: Foreign Languages, 1957.

"K novym uspekham sovetskoi literatury i iskusstva." *Sovetskaia kultura*, 28 November 1957, 1.

Kącka-Rutkowska, Bożena, and Stanisław Stępka. *Repatriacja ludności polskiej z ZSRR, 1955–1959: Wybór dokumentów*. Warsaw: Wydawnictwo SGGW, 1994.

Kaganovitch, Albert. "Stalin's Great Power Politics, the Return of Jewish Refugees to Poland, and Continued Migration to Palestine, 1944–1946." *Holocaust and Genocide Studies* 26, no. 1 (2012): 59–94.

Kagedan, Allan L. *Soviet Zion: The Quest for a Russian Homeland*. New York: St. Martin's, 1994.

Kahan, Arkadius. *Essays in Jewish Social and Economic History*. Chicago: University of Chicago Press, 1986.

Kalb, Marvin L. "Now Russia's 'Angry Young Poets.'" *New York Times*, 31 December 1961, SM12.

Kaminskii, Iakov A. *Organizatsiia i tekhnika sovetskoi torgovli*. Moscow: Gostorgizdat, 1954.

Kantserova, I. E., and L. P. Shabalina. "Dinamika brachnosti evreiskogo naseleniia v Srednem Povolzh'e (na primere g. Ul'ianovska)." *Vestnik Volgogradskogo gosudarstvennogo universiteta*, series 7, no. 1 (2010): 154–58.

Kapera, Zdzisław J. "A Bibliography of J. D. Amussin: Concerning the Dead Sea Scrolls." *Revue de Qumrân* 14, no. 1 (1989): 121–26.

———. "The Qumran Commentaries and Their Significance for the History of the Qumran Community by Joseph Amusin." *Revue de Qumrân* 6, no. 4 (1969): 590–92.

Kapkov, Iurii. *Oskolki pamiati*. Saint Petersburg: n.p., 2004.

Kaplan, Stephen S. "United States Aid to Poland, 1957–1964: Concerns, Objectives and Obstacles." *Western Political Quarterly* 28, no. 1 (1975): 147–66.

"Kar'era Fridrikha Vialona: Voennyi prestupnik na vysokom postu v Berline." *Izvestiia*, 2 February 1963, 6.

Karklins, Rasma. "Determinants of Ethnic Identification in the USSR: The Soviet Jewish Case." *Ethnic and Racial Studies* 10, no. 2 (1987): 27–47.

Kaser, Michael. "Kosygin, Liberman, and the Pace of Soviet Industrial Reform." *The World Today* 21, no. 9 (1965): 375–88.

Kaspina, Maria. "Folk Judaism: Variations of Religious Practices among the Jews of Ukraine and Moldova." *State, Religion and Church* 3, no. 1 (2016): 63–81.

"Katalog sovetskikh plastinok." https://records.su.

Katsnelson, Yitshok. "Di yidishe kultur-manifestatsye in Moskve." *Folks-Shtime*, 29 May 1956, 3.

Katunina, E.V., and Iu. A. Katunin. "Prichiny likvidatsii obshchin karaimov v 40–60-e g.g. XX v." *Kul'tura narodov Prichernomor'ia* 62 (2005): 74–81.

Katz, Bruce, and Jeremy Nowak. *The New Localism: How Cities Can Thrive in the Age of Populism*. Washington, DC: Brookings Institution, 2018.

Katz, Elena M. "The Literary Development of Yekhiel Shraybman: A Jewish Writer in Soviet Clothing." *East European Jewish Affairs* 38, no. 3 (2008): 281–301.

Kazakevich, Emmanuil. *Slushaia vremia*. Moscow: Sovetskii pisatel, 1990.

Kelner, Saul. "People-to-People: Cleveland's Jewish Community and Exodus of Soviet Jews." In *Cleveland Jews and the Making of a Midwestern Community*, edited by Sean Martin and John J. Grabowski, 203–22. New Brunswick, NJ: Rutgers University Press, 2020.

Kenig, G. "A shmues mit Boris Polevoy." *Morgn-Frayhayt*, 26 October 1956, 3.

Khait, David. "Storona Birobidzhanskaia." *Bezbozhnik* 6 (1936): 8–9.

Khakkarainen, Marina. "'Evreiskie den'gi' v epokhu transformatsii: Obshchestvo, vlast', etnichnost' v vospominaniiakh o sovetskom vremeni." *Antropologicheskii forum* 18 (2013): 243–66.

Khanin, Vladimir (Ze'ev). *Documents on Ukrainian-Jewish Identity and Emigration, 1944–1990*. London: Frank Cass, 2003.

———. "The Refusenik Community in Moscow: Social Networks and Models of Identification." *East European Jewish Affairs* 41, no. 1–2 (2011): 75–88.

Kharchenko, Iu. A. "Vspominaia Mirona Semenovicha Vovsi." *Medicus* 4 (2015): 35–39.

Khersonskii [Chersonskij], Milan. "Cozdanie evreiskikh khudozhestvennykh kollektivov v Litve." In *Idish: Iazyk i kul'tura v Sovetskom Soiuze*, edited by Leonid Katsis, Mariia Kaspina, and David Fishman, 282–300. Moscow: Russian State University for the Humanities, 2009.

———. *50th Anniversary of Jewish Amateur Art Collective*. Vilnius: Lietuvos žydų bendruomenė, 2006.

Khiterer, Victoria. "The Jewish Songs of Leonid Utesov." *On the Jewish Street* 2, no. 1 (2012): 1–48.

Khort, Aleksandr. *Liubov' Orlova*. Moscow: Molodaia gvardiia, 2007.

"Khrushchev Airs Analysis on Jews." *New York Times*, 11 April 1958, 7.

"The Khrushchev Interview." *Morgn-Frayhayt*, 20 April 1958, English page.

Khrushchev, Nikita S. *Vysokaia ideinost' i khudozhestvennoe masterstvo—velikaia sila sovetskoi literatury i iskusstva*. Moscow: Gospolitizdat, 1963.

Khrushchev, Sergei, ed. *Memoirs of Nikita Khrushchev*. Vol. 2. *The Reformer, 1945–1964*. University Park: Pennsylvania State University Press, 2006.

Kichelewski, Audrey. "A Community under Pressure: Jews in Poland, 1957–1967." *Polin: Studies in Polish Jewry* 21 (2008): 159–86.

———. "Imagining 'the Jew' in Stalinist Poland: Nationalists or Cosmopolites." *European Review of History— Revue européenne d'histoire* 17, no. 3 (2010): 505–22.

Kim, Sergei. "Retseptsiia literaturnogo zhurnala 'Prostor' v gody redaktorstva I. P. Shukhova–1963–1979 gg." Master's thesis, University of Tartu, 2019.

Kimerling, Anna S. *Terror na izlete: "Delo vrachei" v ural'skoi provintsii*. Perm, Russia: Perm State Institute of Art and Culture, 2011.

Kipnis, Bella. "Sud'ba Itsika Kipnisa." *Materialy IX mizhnarodnoï naukovoï konferentsiï "Dolia evreis'koï dukhovnoï ta material'noï spadshchyby v XX stolitti."* Kyiv: Institut iudaïky, 2001. https://judaica.kiev.ua/old/Conference/Conf28.htm.

Kirschnick, Sylke. *Anne Frank und die DDR: Politische Deutungen und persönliche Lesarten des berühmten Tagebuchs*. Berlin: Ch. Links, 2009.

Kitaev, N. N. "'Kriminalisticheskii ekstrasens' Vol'f Messing: Pravda i vymysel." *V zashchitu nauki* 4 (2008): 102–43.

Klein, B. S. "Politika SShA i 'delo vrachei'." *Voprosy istorii* 6 (2006): 35–47.

Klejn, Leo S. *Soviet Archeology: Trends, Schools, and History*. Oxford: Oxford University Press, 2012.

Klige, S. A. "As the Reader Pleases." *Soviet Sociology* 29, no. 2 (1990): 93–110.

Klimenko, Filipp. "Evreiskoi avtonomnoi oblasti 25 let." *Dal'nii Vostok* 3 (1959): 139–43.

Kline, George L. "The Soviet Recourse to the Death Penalty for Crimes against Socialist Property (1961–1986)." *Sofia Philosophical Review* 3 (2009): 45–74.

Knott, Charlotte A. "Israel: A Russian Interpretation." *Journal of Palestine Studies* 5, no. 1–2 (1976): 163–67.

Kogan, Moisei. *O vremeni i o sebe*. Saint Petersburg: Petropolis, 1998.

Kolleritsch, Elisabeth. "Jazz in Totalitarian Systems (Nazi Germany and Former USSR): The Life of the Trumpet Player Eddie Rosner." *European Scientific Journal* 2 (2015): 256–63.

Kolpakidi, A. I., and Dmitrii Prokhorov. *Vse o vneshnei razvedke*. Moscow: AST, 2002.

"Komissiia po literaturnomu naslediiu I. Babelia." *Literaturnaia gazeta*, 28 April 1956, 2.

Kononenko, Valerii. *Evreis'ke naselennia Podillia*. Vinnytsia, Ukraine: Nilan-LTD, 2017.

Kononenko, Valerii, and Oleksandr Danylenko. "Regional Features and the Socio-Demographic Development of the Jews of Podilia." *East European Jewish Affairs* 49, no. 3 (2019): 230–60.

Konstantinov, Viacheslav. *Evreiskoe naselenie byvshego SSSR v XX veke*. Jerusalem: n.p., 2007.

Korinski, Leybl, ed. *Dr. Shmuel Aleksander Libo.* Tel Aviv: Farband fun Vilner in Yisroel, 1972.

Korolev, D. V. "Kampaniia po bor'be s 'burzhuaznym natsionalizmom' v srede birobidzhanskikh pisatelei v 1948 g." In *Evrei v Sibiri i na Dal'nem Vostoke: Istoriia i sovremennost'*, edited by Iakov M. Kofman, 143–55. Krasnoyarsk, Russia: Kranoiarskii pisatel, 2007.

Kostenko, Iurii. "Prepodavanie ivrita c MGIMO." In *Iazyk ivrit: Issledovanie i prepodavanie*, 102–4. Moscow: Sefer, 2012.

Kostiakova, Iuliia B. "Osobennosti bor'by s kosmopolitizmom v natsional'nov regione (po materialam pressy Khakasii)." *Istoricheskie, filosofskie, politicheskie i iuridicheskie nauki, kul'turologiia i iskusstvovedenie* 7, no. 2 (2011): 124–30.

Kostyrchenko, Gennadii V. "Deportatsiia—mistifikatsiia: Proshchanie s mifom stalinskoi epokhi." *Otechestvennaia istoriia* 1 (2003): 92–113.

———. "'Ekh, Govard! . . .': Literaturnaia istoriia razryva G. Fasta s SSSR." In *Materialy Shestnadtsatoi Ezhegodnoi Mezhdunarodnoi Mazhdistsiplinarnoi konferentsii po iudaike*, vol. 3, edited by Konstantin Burmistrov et al., 370–83. Moscow: Sefer, 2009.

———. *Gosudarstvennyi antisemitizm v SSSR ot nachala do kul'minatsii, 1938–1953.* Moscow: Materik, 2005.

———. "Kampaniia po bor'be s kosmopolitizmom v SSSR." *Voprosy istorii* 8 (1994): 47–60.

———. "Sestra otvetila za brata: 'Delo' Marii Veitsman 1953 goda." *Archiv evreiskoi istorii* 1 (2004): 389–92.

———. *Tainaia politika Khrushcheva: Vlast', intelligentsia, evreiskii vopros.* Moscow: Mezhdunarodnye otnosheniia, 2012.

———. *Tainaia politika ot Brezhneva do Gorbacheva.* Vol. 1. *Vlast'—ecreiskii vopros—intelligentsia.* Moscow: Mezhdunarodnye otnosheniia, 2019.

———. *Tainaia politika Stalina: Novaia versiia, 2 vols.* Moscow: Mezhdunarodnye otnosheniia, 2015.

Kotlerman, Ber Boris. "'Farbitn di oytsres': Buzi Miler un di internatsionalizatsye fun dem yidishn 'burzhuazn natsionalizm'." In *Mizrekh: Jewish Studies in the Far East*, edited by Ber Boris Kotlerman, 248–58. Frankfurt: Peter Lang, 2009.

———. "If There Had Been No Synagogue There, They Would Have Had to Invent It: The Case of the Birobidzhan 'Religious Community of the Judaic Creed' on the Threshold of Perestroika." *East European Jewish Affairs* 42, no. 2 (2012): 87–97.

———. *In Search of Milk and Honey: The Theater of Soviet Jewish Statehood (1934–49).* Bloomington, IN: Slavica, 2009.

———. "'Ostanovi ruku tvoiu!': Pis'ma na ivrite iz Birobidzhana, god 1958-oi." In *Sovetskaia geniza: Novye arkhivnye razyskaniia po istorii evreev v SSSR*, edited by Gennady Estraikh and Alexander Frenkel, 351–433. Boston and Saint Petersburg: Academic Studies Press, 2020.

———. "Toska vliublennogo, govoriashchego o svoei vozliublennoi." *Knigi v mire knig* 128 (1928): 1–6.

Kotliarova, Mariia. *Plecho Mikhoelsa: Vospominaniia aktrisy GOSETa*. Moscow: Tarbut, 2003.

Kovács, András, ed. *Communism's Jewish Question: Jewish Issues in Communist Archives*. Berlin: Walter de Gruyter, 2017.

Kozlov, Denis. *The Readers of "Novyi Mir": Coming to Terms with the Stalinist Past*. Cambridge, MA: Harvard University Press, 2013.

Kozovoi, Andrei. "A Foot in the Door: The Lacy-Zarubin Agreement and Soviet-American Film Diplomacy during the Khrushchev Era, 1953–1963." *Historical Journal of Film, Radio and Television* 36, no. 1 (2016): 21–39.

Kramer, Mark. "The Soviet Union and the 1956 Crises in Hungary and Poland: Reassessments and New Findings." *Journal of Contemporary History* 33, no. 2 (1998): 163–214.

Kriukov, Aleksandr A. "Russkaia Palestina: Istoriia i sovremennost'." *Aziia i Afrika segodnia* 9 (2010): 62–63.

Krivosheev, Vadim. "Izverg zhivet v gorode Tselle." *Izvestiia*, 7 August 1963, 4.

Krumm, Reinhard. *Isaak Babel: Biografiia*. Moscow: ROSSPEN, 2008.

Krupnik, Igor. "Soviet Cultural and Ethnic Policies towards Jews: A Legacy Reassessed." In *Jews and Jewish Life in Russia and the Soviet Union*, edited by Yaakov Ro'i, 67–86. Ilford, UK: Frank Cass, 1995.

Krupyna, Viktor O. "Zhertv bahato, a v hazetakh nichoho ne pishut' . . . ." *Ukraïns'kii istorychnyi zhurnal* 4 (2012): 140–53.

Kuchenbecker, Antje. *Zionismus ohne Zion: Birobidžan: Idee und Geschichte eines jüdischen Staates in Sowjet-Fernost*. Berlin: Metropol, 2000.

Kudriashov, N. A. *Beriia i sovetskie uchenye v atomnov proekte*. Moscow: NIIaU MIFI, 2013.

Kupovetskii, Mark, and Igor Krupnik. "'Lakhlukhi'—kurdistanskoe evrei v SSSR." *Sovetskaia etnografiia* 2 (1982): 107–11.

Kupovetsky, Mark. "Aron Vergelis: Survivor of the Destruction of Soviet Yiddish Culture, 1949–1953." *Jews in Russia and Eastern Europe* 1 (2007): 40–94.

Kushkova, Anna. "An Essay on the Jewish Ethnic Economy: The Case of Belz, Moldova." *East European Jewish Affairs* 43, no. 1 (2013): 77–100.

———. *Navigating the Planned Economy: Accommodation and Survival in Moscow's Post-War "Soviet Jewish Pale."* Chapel Hill: University of North Carolina Press, 2017.

Kushner, Marilyn S. "Exhibiting Art at the American National Exhibition in Moscow, 1959: Domestic Politics and Cultural Diplomacy." *Journal of Cold War Studies* 4, no. 1 (2002): 6–26.

Kutafin, Oleg E. *Rossiiskoe grazhdanstvo*. Moscow: Iurist, 2004.

Kuznetsov, Ilya I. "KGB General Naum Isakovich Eitingon (1899–1981)." *Journal of Slavic Military Studies* 14, no. 1 (2001): 37–52.

Kuznetsov, Vl. "Palach na skam'e podsudimykh." *Pravda*, 9 July 1963, 4.

Kwaterko, Abraham. "In Moskve mit blumen fun Poylishe yidn." *Folks-Shtime*, 11 September 1957, 3.

———. "Vikhtiker tsuzamentref mit yidishe sovetishe shrayber in Moskve." *Folks-Shtime*, 27 August 1957, 3.

Laht, Uno. "Liudi, pomnite!" *Literaturnaia gazeta*, 11 March 1961, 4.

Lancman, Ina. "Literary Estate as Mirror of Persecution: The Papers of Naftali Hertz Kon." *Gazeta* 24, no. 2 (2017): 9–13.

Lastovka, Tat'iana. "Tuneiadstvo v SSSR (1961–1991): Iuridicheskaia teoriia i sotsial'naia praktika." *Antropologicheskii forum* 11 (2011): 212–29.

Lavinskaia, Olga B. "Dokumenty prokuratury o protsesse reabilitatsii zhertv politicheskikh repressii v 1954–1956 gg." *Otechestvennye arkhivy* 3 (2007): 38–47.

Lazarev, Lazar. "Melkoe i krupnoe." *Literaturnaia gazeta*, 8 August 1959, 3.

Lebedev, Iuri A. "Novye dokumenty po istorii sovetskogo atomnogo proekta iz semeinogo arkhiva Geroia Rossii Zh. A. Kovalia." *Voprosy istorii estestvoznaniia i tekhniki* 37, no. 4 (2016): 702–35.

Lebina, Nataliia B. "Khleb—imia prilagatel'noe." *Noveishaia istoriia Rossii* 2 (2011): 210–20.

Leder, Mary M. *My Life in Stalinist Russia: An American Woman Looks Back*. Bloomington: Indiana University Press, 2001.

Lediakh, Irina A. *Natsistskie prestupniki i sudebnaia praktika v FRG*. Moscow: Iuridicheskaia literatura, 1973.

Lednev, Valerii. "Ubiitsa priznaet sebia vinovnym." *Izvestiia*, 27 December 1963, 2.

Leff, Laurel. "When the Facts Didn't Speak for Themselves: The Holocaust in the *New York Times*, 1939–1945." *International Journal of Press/Politics* 2 (2000): 52–72.

Leibovich, Oleg L. "Antisemitskie nastroeniia v sovetskom tylu." In *SSSR vo Vtoroi Mirovoi voine: Okkupatsiia, kholokost, stalinizm*, edited by Oleg Budnitskii, 280–96. Moscow: ROSSPEN, 2014.

———. "Intelligentsiia g. Molotova v 1950-e gg.: Tendentsiia k samoopredeleniiu." *Intelligent v provintsii*, edited by M. E. Glavatskii et al., 187–91. Yekaterinburg, Russia: Ural State University, 1997.

Leneman, Leon. "Dos vort 'yevrey' (yid) in sovetishe pasportn mit royte tint." *Forverts*, 16 November 1963, 8.

———. *La tragédie des Juifs en U.S.S.R.* Paris: Desclée de Brouwer, 1959.

Lenin, Vladimir. *On Literature and Art*. Rochville, MD: Wildside, 2008.

———. *Polnoe sobranie sochinenii*. Vol. 19. Moscow: Politizdat, 1968.

Lerner, Yosl. "Tsendliker yorn mit mayn fraynd dem dikhter Meir Kharats." In Meir Kharats, *Nokhn sakhakl, fir*, 172–78. Jerusalem: Eygns, 1993.

Lestschinsky, Jacob. "Ken Biro-Bidzhan farbesern di lage fun di yidn in sovet-Rusland?" *Forverts*, 23 February 1935, 9, 11.

Letter of Zachariah Shuster to Maximo Yagupsky, 15 December 1964. Records of the American Jewish Committee, Paris Office. YIVO Archives, RG347.7.41, box 50, file 478.

Lev, Misha. *Literarishe portretn: Shraybers un kinstlers fun mayn dor*. Tel Aviv: H. Leivick, 2007.

Levin, Dov. "Participation of the Lithuanian Jews in the Second World War." *Journal of Baltic Studies* 6, no. 4 (1975): 300–310.

———. "The Short-Lived Revival of Yiddish Culture in Postwar Soviet Lithuanina (1953–1971) or the Story of an Odd Communist." In *Under the Red Banner: Yiddish Culture in Communist Countries in the Postwar Era*, edited by Elvira Grözinger and Magdalena Ruta, 239–46. Wiesbaden: Harrassowitz Verlag, 2008.

Libedinskaia, Lidiia. *Zelenaia lampa*. Moscow: Ast, 2013.

Liberman, Evsei G. "Are We Flirting with Capitalism? Profits and 'Profits.'" *Problems in Economics* 8, no. 4 (1965): 36–41.

Linets, Sergei I. "Sudebnyi protsess 1966 goda v Mineral'nykh vodakh po delu posobnikov nemetskikh okkupantov." *Gumanitarnye i iuridicheskie issledovaniia* 1 (2018): 75–85.

Lirik, A. S. "Vos es dertsyeln tsurikgekumene fun festival in Moskve." *Forverts*, 8 September 1957, section 2, 2.

Lisitsina, Liudmila S. "Sozdanie proizvodstvenno-tekhnicheskoi bazy legkoi promyshlennosti v 1954–1964 gg. v Dal'nevostochnov regione." *Izvestiia Altaiskogo gocudarstvennogo universiteta* 4, no. 3 (2007): 116–21.

Lisovitskii, Vladimir N. "Evsei Liberman—ideolog 'kosyginskoi' khoziaistvennoi reform." *Istoriko-ekonomicheskie issledovania* 17, no. 3 (2016): 433–52.

Litvak, Yosef. "Polish-Jewish Refugees Repatriated from the Soviet Union at the End of the Second World War and Afterwards." In *Jews in Eastern Poland and the USSR, 1939–46*, edited by Norman Davies and Antony Polonsky, 227–39. New York: St. Martin's, 1991.

Litvinoff, Emanuel. "From Nazi Slave Labour Camp to Soviet Death Cell." *The Guardian*, 5 October 1962, 19.

Livne, Yacov, and Yossi Goldstein. "'Let My People Go': The Beginnings of Israel's Operation to Open Soviet Immigration Gates." *Soviet and Post-Soviet Review* 47, no. 3 (2020): 1–21.

Loewenstein, Karl E. "The Changing Nature of Literary Censorship, 1961–1965." *Soviet and Post-Soviet Review* 39, no. 1 (2012): 3–21.

Lokshin, Aleksandr. "Iudaizm v otsenke ekspertov KGB." *Vostochnyi arkhiv* 2 (2020): 84–88.

———. "Iz istorii literatury 'samogo slabogo zvena': Popytka vozrozhdeniia." *Lekhaim* 4 (2004): 35–43.

———. "Zabytyi 1957-i: Rasskazyvaiut pis'ma." *Lekhaim* 7 (2003): 22–27.

Lomtadze, T. R. "Rusizmy v rechi gruzinskikh evreev." In *Iasyki. Kul'tury. Perevod*, 329–35. Moscow: Moscow State University, 2018.

Losev, Lev. "Tuneiadets Iosif Brodsky." *Rodina* 9 (2006): 82–86.

Loseva, Irina V. "Politicheskie kampanii stalinskoi epokhi v rossiiskoi provintsii: 'Delo vrachei' v Gor'kovskoi oblasti." *Izvestiia Rossiiskogo gosudarstvennogo pedagogicheskogo universiteta* 12 (2008): 70–73.

Louvish, Misha. "Israel." *American Jewish Year Book* 60 (1959): 231–47.

Lovell, Stephen. *The Russian Reading Revolution: Print Culture in the Soviet and Post-Soviet Eras*. New York: St. Martin's, 2000.

"Luchshaia tantseval'naia truppa." *Sovetskaia kultura*, 13 February 1964, 1.Lvavi, Jacob. *Ha-hityashvut ha-yehudit be-Birobig'an*. Jerusalem: Hebrew University, 1965.

L'vov, Aleksandr L. "Russkie iudeistvuiushchie kak tekstual'noe soobshchestvo: O granitsakh primenimosti etnokonfessional'nykh kategorii." *Etnograficheskoe obozrenie* 6 (2009): 120–33.

Machcewicz, Paweł. "Antisemitism in Poland in 1956." *Polin: Studies in Polish Jewry* 9 (1996): 170–83.

———. *Rebellious Satellite: Poland, 1956*. Washington, DC: Woodrow Wilson Center, 2009.

Madievski, Samson, and Françoise Cordes. "1953: La déportation des juifs soviétiques était-elle programmée?" *Cahiers du Monde russe* 41, no. 4 (2000): 561–68.

Magnúsdóttir, Rósa. *Enemy Number One: The United States of America in Soviet Ideology and Propaganda, 1945–1959*. New York: Oxford University Press, 2019.

Maiofis, Mariia. "Dvukhpartiinaia organizatsiia i dvukhpartiinaia literatura? Politicheskoe voobrazhenie sovetskikh pisatelei i stanovlenie pozdnesovetskoi kul'turnoi paradigmy (konets 1956–nachalo 1957 gg.)." *Ab Imperio* 3 (1926): 267–309.

Mak, Irina. "Sof'ia Cherniak: 'Evreiskie khudozhniki ponimaiut, chto takoe kvech.'" 7 September 2017. https://lechaim.ru.

Maksimenkov, L. B., ed. *Bol'shaia tsenzura: Pisateli i zhurnalisty v strane sovetov, 1917–1956*. Moscow: Materik, 2005.

Malkin, V. B. "Trudnye gody Liny Shtern." In *Tragicheskie sud'by: Repressirovannye uchenye Akademii nauk SSSR*, 156–81. Moscow: Nauka, 1995.

Maltinsky, Khaim. *Der moskver mishpet iber di birobidzhaner*. Tel Aviv: Nay-lebn, 1981.

Mamaev, L. A., N. G. Petrov, and V. F. Kravchenko. *Antisovetskaia deiatel'nost' evreiskikh natsionalistov i bor'ba s neiu organov gosuderstvennoi bezopasnosti*. Moscow: KGB, 1956.

Mandelstam Balzer, Marjorie. *Religion and Politics in Russia: A Reader*. London: Routledge, 2015.

Mankoff, Jeff. "Babi Yar and the Struggle for Memory, 1944–2004." *Ab Imperio* 2 (2004): 393–415.

Manoilenko, Irina. "Polveka vzletov i padenii." *Birobidzhaner Shtern*, 13 March 2013. www.gazetaeao.ru.

———. "Zakonchilas' ego doroga." *Birobidzhaner Shtern*, 8 February 2012. www.gazetaeao.ru.

Manzhukh, Ilja. "Boris Landau i Genia Lev." https://ilman.simdif.com.

Margolin, Iu. "Tel' Avivskii bloknot." *Novoe russkoe slovo*, 6 February 1962, 8.

Margolis, Mikhael D. *"Evreiskaia" kamera Lubianki*. Jerusalem: Gesharim, 1996.

Mark, Ber. "Evreiskaia literatura v Pol'she." In *Kratkaia literaturnaia entsiklopediia*, vol. 2. Moscow: Sovetskaia entsiklopedia, 1964.

Markish, David. "Viktor Lui: Voprosy bez otvetov." *Lechaim* 9 (2002). https://lechaim.ru.

Markish, Esther. *The Long Return*. New York: Ballantine Books, 1978.

Markish, Shimon. *Babel' i drugie*. Moscow: Gesharim, 1997.

———. "The Role of Officially Published Russian Literature in the Reawakening of Jewish National Consciousness (1953–1970)." In *Jewish Culture and Identity in the Soviet Union*, edited by Yaacov Ro'i and Avi Beker. New York: New York University Press, 1991, 208–31.

Markwick, R. *Rewriting History in Soviet Russia: The Politics of Revisionist Historiography, 1956–1974*. New York: Palgrave Macmillan, 2001.

Marley, Rebecca. *To the Tashkent Station: Evacuation and Survival in the Soviet Union at War*. Ithaca, NY: Cornell University Press, 2009.

Marmyl', Olga G. "Krymchaki: Istoriia i real'nost'." *Kul'tura narodov Prichernomor'ia* 6 (1999): 167–70.

Mars, Gerald, and Yochanan Altman. "The Cultural Bases of Soviet Georgia's Second Economy." *Soviet Studies* 35, no. 4 (1983): 546–60.

Martin, Barbara. *Dissident Histories in the Soviet Union: From De-Stalinization to Perestroika*. London: Bloomsbury Academic, 2019.

Masliukova, Irina V. "Evrei i natsional'naia politika v SSSR: Teoriia i praktika (v 1950-kh–1960-kh gg.)." In *Evrei Rossii, Evropy i Blizhnego Vostoka*, 302–14. Saint Petersburg: Petersburg Institute of Judaica, 2019.

———. "Zakonodatel'noe regulirovanie evreiskoi emigratsii iz SSSR (1960–1990 gg.)." In *Evrei v mirovoi istorii, culture i politike*, 235–42. Saint Petersburg: Petersburg Institute of Judaica, 2020.

Maydansky, Moyshe. "Tsu vayterdiker farfulkumung." *Sovetish Heymland* 11 (1968): 149.

McKnight, David. *Espionage and the Roots of the Cold War: The Conspiratorial Heritage*. London: Cass, 2002.

Medvedev, Roi A. *Oni okruzhali Stalina*. Moscow: Vremia, 2012.

———. *Politicheskie portrety*. Moscow: AST, 2008.

Medvedev, Zhorez A., and Roi A. Medvedev. *Izbrannye proizvedeniia*. Moscow: Prava cheloveka, 2005.

Melamed, Efim. "The Fate of the Archives of the Kiev Institute of Jewish Proletarian Culture: Puzzles and Discoveries." *East European Jewish Affairs* 42, no. 2 (2012): 99–110.

Melikhov, Aleksandr. *Ispoved' evreia*. Saint Petersburg: Novyi Gelikon, 1994.

Memorandum from the Assistant Secretary of State for Near Eastern, South Asian, and African Affairs (Rountree) to the Acting Secretary of State. 13 March 1957, Washington. https://history.state.gov.

"Memorial to the Unknown Jewish Martyr." *Jewish Quarterly* 4, no. 3 (1956): 29–30.

Mendes, Philip. "A Convergence of Political Interests: Isi Leibler, the Communist Party of Australia and Soviet Anti-Semitism, 1964–66." *Australian Journal of Politics and History* 55, no. 2 (2009): 157–69.

"Menedzher fun der Amerikaner oysshtelung in Moskve shildert erfolg fun yidishe bikher." *Forverts*, 13 September 1959, 12.

Merker, Aleksandr. "Poslednii urozhai Nikity Khrushveva." 13 August 2019. http://krasnoturinsk.info.

Metel', Olga V. "Sovetskaia istoriografiia pervonachal'nogo khristianstva v kontse 50–60-kh gg. XX v." *Vestnik Omskogo universiteta* 4 (2007): 107–11.

Metsner, Michael. "Grassroots Diplomacy: American Cold War Travelers and the Making of a Popular Détente, 1958–1972." PhD diss., Case Western Reserve University, 2018.

Miasnikov, Fedor A. "O nekotorykh osobennostiakh podbora i verbovki agentov iz chisla lits evreiskoi natsional'nosti." *Trudy Vysshei shkoly* [KGB] 8 (1974): 109–14.

Mikhailova, Irina. *Samorodki Dagestana*. Makhachkala, Dagestan: Nauka-Dagestan, 2014.

Mikhalevich, Aleksandr. "Iadro intelligentnosti." *Molodoi kommunist* 10 (1966): 60–61.

"Mikoyan Bars Jews Visitors." *Jewish Advocate*, 15 January 1959, 1.

"Mikoyan Denies Planned Exile of Jews to Siberia." *American Israelite*, 22 January 1959, 1.

"Mikoyan on Biro-Bidjan." *Jewish Chronicle*, 23 January 1959, 13.

"Mikoyan Says Reds Plan No Jewish Colony." *Chicago Daily Tribune*, 16 January 1959, 3.

Mishchuk, Svetlana N. "Retrospektivnyi analiz migratsionnykh protsessov v Evreiskoi avtonomnoi oblasti." *Regional'nye problemy* 18, no. 3 (2015): 74–81.

"Missing Jewish Poet Has Died in Siberia, Ehrenburg Relates." *New York Times*, 12 February 1961, 4.

Missinne, Lut, and Irina Michajlova. "Anne Frank in de DDR en Rusland." *Internationale Neerlandistiek* 57, no. 1 (2019): 11–34.

Mitin, Mark. "Sionistskaia agentura amerikanskogo imperializma." *Gudok*, 26 February 1953, 4.

Mitrokhin, Nikolai A. "Elita 'zakrytogo obshchestva': MGIMO, mezhdunarodnye otdely apparata TsK KPSS i prosopografiia ikh sotrudnikov." *Ab imperio* 4 (2013): 145–86.

———. "Etnonatsionalisticheskaia mifologiia v sovetskom partiino-gosudarstvennom apparate." *Otechestvennye zapiski* 3 (2002): 281–98.

———. *Russkaia partiia: Dvizhenie russkikh natsionalistov v SSSR: 1953–1985 gody*. Moscow: Novoe literaturnoe obozrenie, 2003.

Mitsel, Mikhail. *Evrei Ukrainy v 1943–1953 gg.: Ocherki dokumentirovannoi istori*. Kyiv: Dukh i litera, 2004.

———. "Moskovskaia khoral'naia sinagoga, vlast' i zarubezhnye kontakry: Period pozdnei 'ottepeli' i perekhoda k 'kollektivnomu rukovodstvu' (1960–1965)." In *100 let: Moskovskaia khoral'naiasinagoga*, edited by Alexander Lokshin, 215–17. Moscow: Dom evreiskoi knigi, 2006.

———. *Polytika i paranoia: KPU v borot'bi proty "mizhnarodnoho sionizmu" (1953–1986)*. Kyiv: Dukh i Litera, 2021.

"Moishe Broderzon, Yiddish Dramatist." *New York Times*, 21 August 1956, 29.

Molotov, Viachslav M. "Doklad na XVIII s'ezde VKP(B)." *Pravda*, 16 March 1939, 5.

Monson, Robert A. "The West German Statute of Limitations on Murder: A Political, Legal, and Historical Exposition." *American Journal of Comparative Law* 30, no. 4 (1982): 605–25.

"More Red Propaganda." *Jewish Advocate*, 15 December 1955, A2.

Morevski, Abraham. *There and Back: Memories and Thoughts of a Jewish Actor*. Translated by Joseph Leftwich. London: J. Clarke, 1967.

Morozov, Boris, ed. *Documents on Soviet Jewish Emigration*. Hoboken, NJ: Taylor & Francis, 2013.

"Moscow Confirms Police Killed Mikhoels, Yiddish Actor, in '48." *New York Times*, 17 January 1963, 5.

"Moscow Jews Told to Keep Mum." *The Sentinel*, 1 March 1962, 3.

"Moscow Not Producing 'Diary of Anne Frank'; Play Translated in Russian." *Daily News Bulletin of the Jewish Telegraphic Agency*, 27 August 1958, 4.

"Moscow Rejects Israeli Protest." *New York Times*, 22 September 1957, 5.

"Moscow Will Admit Parcels of Matzoh." *New York Times*, 17 January 1964, 2.

Moskovich, Wolf. "An Important Event in Soviet Yiddish Cultural Life: The New Russian-Yiddish Dictionary." *Soviet Jewish Affairs* 14, no. 3 (1984): 31–49.

———. "Postwar Soviet Theories on the Origin of Yiddish." In *Origins of the Yiddish Language*, edited by Dovid Katz, 105–9. Oxford: Pergamon, 1987.

———, "The Russian-Yiddish Dictionary of 1984 and the Problems of the Maintenance of Soviet Yiddish after the Second World War." In *Under the Red Banner: Yiddish Culture in the Communist Countries in the Postwar Era*, edited by E. Grözinger and M. Ruta, 231–38. Wiesbaden: Harrassowitz Verlag, 2008.

Movshovich, Evgeni. "Presledovanie evreev Rostova-na-Donu pri Sovetskoi vlasti." In *Materialy Odinnadtsatoi ezhegodnoi mezhdunarodnoi mezhdistsiplinarnoi konferentsii po iudaizmu*, edited by Rashid M. Kaplanov and Vikrotiia V. Mochalova, 305–28. Moscow: Institute of Slavic Studies, 2004.

Mowshowitz, Israel. *A Rabbi's Rovings*. Hoboken, NJ: Ktav, 1985.

"Murder of Jews Retold in Soviet." *New York Times*, 26 April 1962, 11.

Nakhimovsky, Alice S. "Public and Private in the Kitchen: Eating Jewish in the Soviet State." In *Food and Judaism*, edited by Leonard J. Greenspoon, Ronald A. Simkins, and Gerald Shapiro, 149–68. Omaha, NE: Creighton University Press, 2005.

———. "You Are What They Ate: Russian Jews Reclaim Their Foodways." *Shofar: An Interdisciplinary Journal of Jewish Studies* 25, no. 1 (2006): 63–77.

Naumov, Vladimir P., ed. *Nepravednyi sud: Poslednii stalinskii rasstrel*. Moscow: Nauka, 1994.

"Nazi Mass-Murder of Jews Mentioned in Soviet Parliament for First Time." *Daily News Bulletin* of the Jewish Telegraphic Agency, 27 April 1962, 2.

Nekrasov, Viktor. "Po obe storony okeana." *Novyi Mir* 12 (1960): 110–52.

———. "Pochemu eto ne sdelano?" *Literaturnaia gazeta*, 10 October 1958, 2.

Nelson, Don. "Living in Harmony." *Sunday News*, 13 September 1960, 4.

Nesselrodt, Markus, "'I Bled Like You, Brother, although I Was a Thousand Miles Away': Postwar Yiddish Sources on the Experiences of Polish Jews in Soviet Exile during World War II." *East European Jewish Affairs* 46, no. 1 (2016): 47–67.

Neuweld, Mark. "The Latest Soviet Census and the Jews." *Commentary*, May 1960, 426–29.
"New Charges Enter Soviet Trial of Priests." *Christian Science Monitor*, 17 January 1962, 6.
"New Light on Biro-Bidjan." *Jewish Advocate*, 1 December 1955, A2.
Nikitina, Galina S. "Ekspansiia Izrailia v Afriku i neokolonializm." *Narody Azii i Afriki* 3 (1963): 36–44.
———. "Izrail' i amerikanskii inperializm." *Sovetskoe vostokovedenie* 5 (1958): 71–79.
Nikitina, Irina A., and Irina P. Takala. "'Karel'skie kosmopolity': Finskii dramaticheskii teatr v 1946–1953 godakh." *Trudy Kare'skogo nauchnogo tsentra RAN* 3 (2014): 125–33.
Nikolaev, Nik. "Salopnitsa pishet roman." *Ogonek* 48 (1964): 30.
Norwood, Stephen H. *Antisemitism and the American Left*. Cambridge: Cambridge University Press, 2013.
"Noted French Jews Attend Vergelis Fete." *Morgn-Frayhayt*, 22 December 1963, English page.
Novick, Paul. *Assimilation and the Jewish People*. New York: Morning Freiheit, 1964.
———. "Di Birobidzhan 'propagande' in Moskve." *Morgn-Frayhayt*, 20 February 1959, 5.
———. "Getseylte teg mit Arn Vergelis." *Yidishe Kultur* 10 (1963): 41–43.
———. *Jews in the Soviet Union: Impressions of a Two Months' Visit to the USSR, November–December 1964*. New York: Morning Freiheit, 1965.
———. "A Journal Which Destroyed Hope." *Morgn-Frayhayt*, 9 November 1986, 4.
——— "Theory of 'the Melting Pot'—and the Test of Reality." *Morgn-Frayhayt*, 20 October 1963, 15.
———. "Volume of Sholom Aleichem's Works in Yiddish Is to Appear in Moscow Soon." *Morgn-Frayhayt*, 23 February 1959, 15.
"Novye nobelevskie laureaty." *Literaturnaia gazeta*, 5 December 1966, 4.
Nurenberg, Amshei. "Mayn fraynt Mark Shagal." *Sovetish Heymland* 12 (1967): 122–27.
Nusekh Vilne byuletin 3 (New York, February 1958).
"Obvinitel'noe zakliuchenie po delu Globke." *Pravda*, 20 June 1963, 7.
Odesskii, Mikhail P., and David M. Feldman. "Ideologema 'patriot' v russkoi, sovetskoi i postsovetskoi kul'ture: Lozung i rugatel'stvo." *Obshchestvennye nauki i sovremennost'* 1 (2008): 109–23.
Ogryzko, Viacheslav. *Okhraniteli i liberaly: V zatianuvshemsia poiske kompromissa*, 2 vols. Moscow: Literaturnaia Rossiia, 2015.
Olaru, Dragoş. "'Ia povazhaiu vsikh liudei, iaki liubliat' svoiu movu . . .': Meir Kharats u Chernivtsiakh." *Jews and Slavs* 26 (2018): 174–84.
Olsen, Arthur J. "Anne Frank Speaks to the Germans." *New York Times*, 17 February 1957, 18.
Olson, Laura J. *Performing Russia: Folk Revival and Russian Identity*. London and New York: RoutledgeCurzon, 2004
"Oproverzhenie TASS." *Pravda*, 2 March 1959, 3.

Orbach, William W. *The American Movement to Aid Soviet Jews*. Amherst: University of Massachusetts Press, 1979.

Orekhov, Aleksandr. *Sovetskii Soiuz i Pol'sha v gody "ottepeli": Iz istorii sovetsko-pol'skikh otnoshenii*. Moscow: Indrik, 2005.

"Orientalists Begin Meeting in Michigan." *New York Times*. 14 August 1967, 6.

Ostin, N. "A briv fun Moskve tsum 'Forverts'." *Forverts*, 27 January 1954, 4.

"Ot litsa vsekh narodnykh mass vyrazhaem Vam glubokii vozmutitel'nyi protest." *Otechestvennye zapiski* 1 (2012): 294–310.

"Otovsiudu." *Iskusstvo kino*, 31 January 1959, 146.

"Otpor provokatoram: Na press-konferentsii v Dome druzhby," Pravda, 6 March 1970, 1.

Paczkowski, Andrzej, and Nikolai I. Bukharin. "The Thaw: The Twentieth Congress of the Soviet Communist Party, the Polish October, and the Struggle for Autonomy." In *White Spots—Black Spots: Difficult Matters in Polish-Russian Relations*, edited by Adam Daniel Rotfeld and Anatoly V. Tolkunov, 371–400. Pittsburgh: University of Pittsburgh Press, 2015.

"Palacham latyshskogo naroda ne uiti ot kary!" *Pravda*, 5 April 1945, 1.

"Pamiatnik pogibshim v Bab'em Iaru." *Pravda*, 4 April 1945, 3.

"The Paris Pledge: Kosygin on Reunification of Families." *Jews in Eastern Europe* 3, no. 6 (1967): 14–25.

Pass, Andrei A., and Pavel A. Ryzhii. "Ogosudarstvlenie promyslovoi kooperatsii v SSSR vo vtoroi polovine 1950-kh gg.: Prichiny i posledstviia." *Sotsium i vlast'* 5 (2012): 114–22.

"Passport Birobidzhanskogo narodnogo teatra Khabarovskogo kraia." Russian State Archive of Literature and Art, f. 970, op. 22, ed. khr. 1596.

Patek, Artur. "The Jewish Autonomous Oblast in the USSR in the Documents of the British Foreign Office (1952–1958)." *Scripta Judaica Cracoviensia* 17 (2019): 105–20.

"Pauk svastiki vypolzaet iz nory." *Izvestiia*, 3 February 1960, 4.

"Paul Novic[k], David Matis, and Abraham Bick." CIA-RDP91-00965R000500120021-0, approved for release 7 March 2001.

Pavlychko, Dmytro V. "I trud, i talant—delu kommunizma." *Pravda Ukrainy*, 9 April 1963, 3.

Peidi, Ilmar. "Kalevi-Liiva obviniaet." *Pravda*, 27 February 1961, 4.

Perelman, Osher. *Birobidzhan: Shilderungen fun a rayze in yuli-oygust 1934*. Warsaw: Groshn-bibliotek, 1934.

"[Perepiska] s raznymi upravleniiami KGB." The SBU Archives (Kyiv), f. 16, op. 5, ed. khr. 10.

Peretz, Pauline. *Let My People Go: The Transnational Politics of Soviet Jewish Emigration during the Cold War*. New Brunswick, NJ: Transaction, 2015.

Pertsovski, Joseph. "Nayer program fun Leningrader yidishn muzik-ansambl." *Folks-Shtime*, 24 April 1958, 4.

Petrov, Vladislav O. "Trinadtsataia simfoniia: Novaia duel' Shostakovicha s vlast'iu." *Actualscience* 1, no. 2 (2015): 77–80.

Pickhan, Gertrud. *Von Hitler vertrieben, von Stalin verfolgt: Der Jazzmusiker Eddie Rosner*. Berlin: Be.bra-Wiss.-Verlag, 2010.

Piklova, Liudmyla. *Podorozh mistom i chasom*. Khmelnytskyi, Ukraine: Khesed Besht, 2009.

Pilnik, Shay Arie. "The Representation of Babi Yar in Soviet Russian and Yiddish Literature." PhD diss., Jewish Theological Seminary of America, 2013.

Pinkhasov, Robert, Svetlana Danilova, and Semen Krikheli. *Evrei bukharskie, gorskie, gruzinskie v vodovorote istorii*. New York: n.p., 2017.

Pinkus, Benjamin. "The Emigration of National Minorities from the USSR in the Post-Stalin Era." *Soviet Jewish Affairs* 13, no. 1 (1983): 5–35.

———. *The Soviet Government and the Jews: 1948–1967: A Documented Study*. Cambridge: Cambridge University Press, 1986.

Pirozhkova, Antonina. *Ia pytaius' vosstanovit' cherty: Vospominaniia*. Moscow: AKT, 2013.

Plotkin, Grigorii. "The Promised Land." *Jews and the Jewish People* 1, no. 1 (1960): 93.

Podemski, Krzysztof. "The Polish Tourist Abroad: From Stalinism to Schengen and Wizz Air." *Folia Turistica* 25, no. 1 (2011): 211–30.

Podolskii, Barukh. *Besedy ob ivrite i o mnogom drugom*. Tel Aviv: Sefer Israel, 2004.

"Podvodia itogi . . ." *Literaturnaia gazeta*, 18 August 1959, 1.

"Poland to Return Some Repatriates." *New York Times*, 1 April 1957, 10.

Polin-Galay, Hannah. "Naming the Criminals: Lithuanian Jews Remember Perpetrators." *Holocaust and Genocide Studies* 30, no. 3 (2016): 506–31.

"Polish Denial on Jews." *New York Times*, 20 April 1957.

Pomerantz, Alexander. *Di sovetishe haruge-malkhes: Tsu zeyer tsentn yortsayt*. Buenos Aires: Yidisher visnshaftlekher institute, 1962.

Ponizova, Elena V. "Lishenie grazhdanstva v sovetskii period." *Trudy Instituta gosudarstva i prava Rossiiskoi akademii nauk* 6 (2013): 120–29.

Pospielovsky, Dmitry V. *Soviet Antireligious Campaigns and Persecutions*. Basingstoke, UK: Macmillan, 1988.

"Postanovlenie orgbiuro TsK VKP(b) 'o zhurnale *Znamia*'." Fond Aleksandra N. Iakovleva. 27 December 1948. https://www.alexanderyakovlev.org/fond/issues-doc/69490.

"Pravda ob Oberlendere." *Izvestiia*, 6 April 1960, 4.

Pregeizon, Tzi. *Dnevnik vospominanii byvshego lagernika (1949–1955)*. Moscow: Gesharim, 2005.

Prestina-Shapiro, Liia F. *Slovar' zapreshchennogo iazyka*. Minsk: MET, 2005.

Prishvin, Andrei. "Shchedraia zemlia." *Pravda*, 25 March 1956, 3.

Proch, Franciszek. "Poland in 1956: Chronicle of Events, July 1, 1956–December 31, 1956." *Polish Review* 2, no. 1 (1957): 104–19.

"Prodazha dushi." *Izvestiia*, 30 August 1959, 5.

"Programma Kommunisticheskoi partii Sovetskogo Soiuza." *Pravda*, 2 November 1961, 1–8.

Prokof'ev, Aleksandr A. "Proslavliat', vospevat', vospityvat' geroizm." *Pravda*, 27 March 1963, 4.

"Protiv ideologicheskikh izvrashchenii v literature." *Pravda*, 2 July 1951, 2, and *Literaturnaia gazeta*, 3 July 1951, 2.

"Protokol no. 4 zasedaniia Sekretariata Pravleniia Soiuza pisatelei SSSR ot 11 fevralia 1961." Russian State Archive of Literature and Art, f. 631, op. 30, ed. kh. 874.

"Protokol partiinogo sobraniia partorganizatsii redaktsii gazety 'Birobidzhaner shtern'." 26 November 1954, State Archive of the JAR, f. 362, op. 1, ed. kh. 2.

"Rabbi Tells of Plight of Polish Jews." *Jewish Advocate*, 10 April 1958, 1.

Rabinovich, Solomon [Shloyme; Semen]. *Jews in the Soviet Union*. Moscow: Novosti Press Agency, 1965.

———. "Tipn fun yidn in Biro-Bidzhan." *Morgn-Frayhayt*, 15 January 1957, 5.

———. "Vos dertseylt 'Biro-Bidzhaner shtern'?" *Morgn-Frayhayt*, 3 January 1957, 5.

Raddatz, Fritz J. "Das denunzierte Wort. Verbot, Verrat, Verfolgung: Wie Mach und Ideologie das Schreiben vergifteten." *Die Zeit*, 14 October 1999, 18–21.

Rakowski, Mark. "Derinerungen vegn Maksim Gorkin." *Morgn-Frayhayt*, 18 June 1957, 3.

Ramazanova, Dil'shad Sh. "Dagestan v sostave SSSR: Administrativno-politicheskii status territorii i aktual'nye problem natsional'noi politiki (1921–2017)." 2 vols. PhD diss., Dagestan State University, 2019.

Rapoport, Iakov L. *Na rubezhe dvukh epoch: Delo vrachei 1953 goda*. Moscow: Kniga, 1983.

"Ratifikatsiia sovetsko-pol'skogo Soglasheniia o srokakh i poriadke dal'neishei repatriatsii iz SSSR lits pol'skoi natsional'nosti." *Pravda*, 6 June 1956, 4.

"Rech' deputata A. E. Korneichuka." *Izvestiia*, 26 April 1962, 4.

"Rech' tov. N. S. Khrushcheva." *Pravda*, 10 March 1963, 4.

"Rech' tovarishcha N. S. Khrushcheva." *Pravda*, 22 January 1956, 2.

"Red Leaders." *Life*, 29 March 1943, 40.

"Redaktor fun Kanader Vokhnblat brengt frishn grus fun sovetnfarband." *Morgn-Frayhayt*, 1 December 1956, 4.

Redlich, Shimon. "Jewish Appeals in the USSR: An Expression of National Revival." *East European Jewish Affairs* 4, no. 2 (1974): 24–37.

———. "Khrushchev and the Jews." *Jewish Social Studies* 34, no. 4 (1972): 343–53.

———. "Rehabilitation of the Jewish Anti-Fascist Committee: Report No. 7." *Soviet Jewish Affairs* 20, no. 2–3 (1990): 85–98.

Reisin, Saul. "Ehrenburg Talks Assimilation." *Jewish Advocate*, 6 August 1959, 1.

Reles, Girsh [Hirsh]. *Evreiskie sovetskie pisateli Belorussii: Vospominaniia*. Minsk: Dmitrii Kolas, 2006.

Remenik, Grigory [Hersh]. "Evreiskaia literatura v SSSR." In *Kratkaia literaturnaia entsiklopediia*, vol. 2, 856–58. Moscow: Soviet Encyclopedia, 1964.

———. "Notitsn vegn undzer proze." *Sovetish Heymland* 1 (1965): 146.

———. *Sholom-Aleikhem: Kritiko-biograficheskii ocherk*. Moscow: Goslitizdat, 1963.

Reni, Peter. "Bol'shaia tema Moskovskogo kinofestivalia." *Pravda*, 12 August 1959, 6.

"Report of the Executive Vice-Chairman to the Executive Committee Meeting," 1957, 1, NY56–64_CR_030_0249, JDC Archive. "Report of Mr. Leavitt," August

1957, NY55–64_CR_031_0608, item ID847083, JDC Archive. "Report on Poland" (n.d.), 10–18 January 1962, NY55–64_CR_30_0435, JDC Archive.
"Report" (n.d.), 6 October 1959, NY55–64_CR_030_0238, JDC Archive.
"Report" (n.d.), 13 December 1957, NY55–64_CR_029_1116, JDC Archive (English translation of Smolar, Boris, "JDC's New Plans of Aid in Poland," *Forverts*, 13 December 1957).
Reshetnikov, Stepan. "Russkie emigranty-soprotivlentsy protiv vostochnykh batal'onov vermakhta vo Frantsii (1943–1944 gg.)." *Zhurnal istoricheskikh issledovanii* 1 (2019): 105–22.
"The Reversal of the Doctors' Plot and Its Immediate Aftermath." 17 May 1953, CIA, Freedom of Information Act Electronic Reading Room, document CIA-RDP91T01172R000200160001-3.
Reznik, Semen. *Vmeste ili vroz'?: Sud'ba evreev v SSSR*. Moscow: Zakharov, 2005.
Riant, Maks. "Kak ia rabotal v 'Birobidzhaner shtern'." *Birobidzhaner Shtern*, 6 June 2018. www.gazetaeao.ru.
Rinskii, Mikhail. "Otvaga, spasshaia zhizn'." ISRAGEO. 13 October 2019. http://www.isrageo.com/2019/10/13/otvagaskopasa/.
Rivosh, Elmar. "Mezhdu zhizn'iu i smert'iu." *God za godom* 3 (1987): 141–216.
———. "Tsvishn lebn un toyt." *Sovetish Heymland* 5 (1962): 38–62 and 6 (1962): 54–85.
Roditi, Edouard. "Gibt es eine Neger-Lyrik?" *Der Monat* 2 (1948): 102–7.
Rogachevskii, Andrei. "Babelomania: Recent Russian-Language Studies on the Life and Work of Isaac Babel." *East European Jewish Affairs* 27, no. 1 (1997): 97–104.
Rogers, Daniel E. "Restoring a German Career, 1945–1950: The Ambiguity of Being Hans Globke." *German Studies Review* 31, no. 2 (2008): 303–24.
Rogoff, Hillel. "Religye oyf der yidisher gas." *Forverts*, 24 November 1956, 6.
Ro'i, Yaacov. *Islam in the Soviet Union: From the Second World War to Gorbachev*. New York: Columbia University Press, 2000.
———. "Jewish Emigration and Soviet-Arab Relations, 1954–67." In *Zionism and Arabism in Palestine and Israel*, edited by Elie Kedourie and Sylvia Kedourie, London: Frank Cass, 1982.
———. "Nehama Lifshitz: Symbol of the Jewish National Awakening." In *Jewish Culture and Identity in the Soviet Union*, edited by Yaakov Ro'i and Avi Beker, 168–90. New York: New York University Press, 1991.
———. "The Religious Life of the Bukharan Jewish Community in Soviet Central Asia after World War II." In *Bukharan Jews in the Twentieth Century: History, Experience and Narration*, edited by Ingeborg Baldauf, Moshe Gammer, and Thomas Loy, 57–75. Wiesbaden: Reichert Verlag, 2008.
———. "Soviet Policy towards Jewish Emigration: An Overview." In *Russian Jews on Three Continents: Migration and Resettlement*, edited by Noah Lewin-Epstein, Yaacov Ro'i, and Paul Ritterband, 45–67. London: Routledge, 1997.
———. *The Struggle for Soviet Jewish Emigration 1948–1967*. Cambridge: Cambridge University Press, 1991.
Rolnikaite, Mariia [Masha; Maša]. *Doroga domoi*. Moscow: Knizhnik, 2016.

Rolnikaite, Mariia. *I vse eto Pravda.* Saint Petersburg: Zolotoi vek, 2002.

———. *Turiu papasakoti.* Vilnius: Valstybine politines ir mokslines literaturos leidykla, 1963.

Romm, Mikhail. "The Question of the National Question, or a Rally for a Genuinely Russian Cinema." In *Soviet Jews in World War II: Fighting, Witnessing, Remembering,* edited by Harriet Murav and Gennady Estraikh, 219–29. Boston: Academic Studies Press, 2014.

Rosenfeld, Stephen S. "Soviet Arrest of Professor Sours Red Visit." *Washington Post,* 16 November 1963, 7.

Rozenblat, Evgeni, and Irina Elenskaia. "Dinamika chislennosti i rasseleniia belorusskikh evreev v XX veke." *Diaspory* 4 (2002): 27–52.

Rubenstein, Joshua. "Il'ia Ehrenburg and the Holocaust in the Soviet Press." In *Soviet Jews in World War II: Fighting, Witnessing, Remembering,* edited by Harriet Murav and Gennady Estraikh, 36–56. Boston: Academic Studies Press, 2014.

Rubenstein, Joshua, and V. P. Naumov, eds. *Stalin's Secret Pogrom: The Postwar Inquisition of the Jewish Anti-Fascist Committee.* New Haven, CT: Yale University Press in association with the United States Holocaust Memorial Museum, 2005.

———. *Tangled Loyalties: The Life and Times of Ilya Ehrenburg.* New York: Basic Books, 1996.

Ruchniewicz, Małgorzata. *Repatriacja ludności polskiej z ZSRR w latach, 1955–59.* Warsaw: Volumen, 2000.

———. "Tzw. repatriacja ludności polskiej z ZSRR w latach 1955–1959." *Dzieje Najnowsze* 3, no. 2 (1999): 159–77.

Rudy, Peter. "The Soviet Russian Literary Scene in 1961: A Mild Permafrost Thaw." *Modern Language Journal* 46, no. 6 (1962): 245–54.

Runin, Boris. "Uroki odnoi poeticheskoi biografiii (Zametki o lirike Evg. Evtushenko)." *Voprosy literatury* 2 (1963): 17–45.

"Rusn firn yidn keyn Sibir." *Forverts,* 10 November 1956, 1, 9.

"Russ Press Agency's Full-Length Docufilm about Jews in Soviet." *Variety,* 8 November 1967, 1, 20.

"Russian Art and Anti-Semitism: Two Documents: Yevtushenko vs. Khrushchev." *Commentary,* June 1963, 433–37.

"Russians Boycott Cleveland Group on USSR Anti-Semitism." *The Sentinel,* 12 December 1963, 4.

Rutland, Suzanne D. "Leadership of Accommodation or Protest? Nahum Goldmann and the Struggle of Soviet Jewry." In *Nahum Goldmann: A Statesman without a State,* edited by Mark A. Raider, 273–96. Albany: State University of New York Press, 2009.

Ryansky, Feliz. "Jews and Cossacks in the Jewish Autonomous Region." *Refuge* 12, no. 4 (1992): 19–21.

Rzehak, Lutz. "The Linguistic Challenge: Bukharan Jews and Soviet Language Policy." In *Bukharan Jews in the 20th Century: History, Experience and Narration,* edited by Ingeborg Baldauf, Moshe Gammer, and Thomas Loy, 37–83. Wiesbaden: Reichert-Verlag, 2008.

Safran, Gabriella. "Isaak Babel's El'ia Isaakovich as a New Jewish Type." *Slavic Review* 61, no. 2 (2002): 253–72.

Salisbury, Harrison E. "Birobidzhan Jews Drop Yiddish, Prefer Russian, Visitor Is Told." *New York Times*, 22 June 1954, 6.

———. "Fear Grows among Soviet Jews at Resurgence of Anti-Semitism." *New York Times*, 8 February 1962, 1.

———. "Soviet Poet Is Published Here." *New York Times*, 27 September 1962, 34.

Samoilov, David. *Podennye zapiski*, 2 vols. Moscow: Vremia, 2002.

Sandler, Boris. *Stupeni k chudu*. Moscow: Sovetskii pisatel, 1988.

Sanua, Marianne Rachel. *Let Us Prove Strong: The American Jewish Committee*. Waltham, MA: Brandeis University Press, 2007.

Sarnov, Benedict. *Nash sovetskii novoiaz: Malen'kaia entsiklopediia real'nogo sotsializma*. Moscow: EKSMO, 2005.

———. *Sluchai Erenburga*. Moscow: EKSMO, 2006.

Sashenkov, E. "'Dnevnik Anny Frank' na nemetskoi stsene." *Sovetskaia kultura*, 2 February 1957, 4.

Schappes, Morris U. "The Vergelis Visit: What the Soviet Yiddish Poet and Editor Told Us—and Learned Here." *Jewish Currents* 18, no. 1 (1964): 4–7.

Schechter, Brandon. "The State's Pot and the Soldier's Spoon: Rations (*Paëk*) in the Red Army." In *Hunger and War: Food Provisioning in the Soviet Union during World War II*, edited by Wendy Z. Goldman and Donald Filtzer. Bloomington: Indiana University Press, 2015.

Schiessl, Christoph. *Alleged Nazi Collaborators in the United States after World War II*. Lanham, MD: Lexington Books, 2016.

Schneiderman, Samuel Loeb. "'ORT' in Poyln lernt fakhn tsvey toyznt tsurikgekumene yidn." *Forverts*, 15 January 1960, 4.

———. "Tsvey yidn fun Biro-Bidzhan dertseyln zeyere iberlebungen." *Forverts*, 10 December 1959, 2.

———. "Vos yidn in Poyln tuen far di tsurikgekumene fun Rusland." *Forverts*, 27 January 1958, 2.

Schulman, Elias. *Di sovetish-yidishe literature*. New York: Tsiko, 1971.

———. "Sovetish Heimland: Lone Voices, Stiffed Creators." *Judaism* 14, no. 1 (1965): 64–65.

Schulman, Sebastian Z. "*Undzer Rebenyu*: Religion, Memory, and Identity in Postwar Moldova." In *Going to the People: Jews and the Ethnographic Impulse*, edited by Jeffrey Veidlinger, 219–36. Bloomington: Indiana University Press, 2016.

Schwartz, Charles A. "Economic Crime in the U. S. S. R.: A Comparison of the Khrushchev and Brezhnev Eras." *International and Comparative Law Quarterly* 30, no. 2 (1981): 281–96.

Schwartz, Harry. "Ehrenburg Urges Writers' Liberty." *New York Times*, 25 December 1953, 3.

———. "Jews of Minsk Cling to Yiddish Speech." *New York Times*, 3 October 1955, 8.

———. "Moscow Depicts Birobidzhan Life." *New York Times*, 31 August 1958, 23.

Schwartz, Harry. "Stalin Called Himself a Zionist but Cited Soviet Jewish 'Problem.'" *New York Times*, 17 March 1955, 79.

Segal, Zvi. "Jewish Minorities in the Baltic Republics in the Postwar Years." *Journal of Baltic Studies* 19, no. 1 (1988): 60–66.

"Sekretariu Prezidiuma SP SSSR Surkovy A.A." Russian State Archive of Literature and Art, *f.* 631, *op.* 43, *ed. khr.* 128.

Semenko, Aleksei. "Smuggling the Other: Rita Rait-Kovaleva's Translation of J. D. Salinger's *The Catcher in the Rye*." *Translation and Interpreting Studies* 11, no. 1 (2016): 61–88.

Sfard, David. *Mit zikh un mit andere: Oytobiografye un literarishe eseyen.* Jerusalem: Yerusholaimer almanakh, 1984.

———. "Vegn dem hoypt-forvurf fun khaver H. Bloshtein tsu di 'Yidishe Shriftn'." *Folks-Shtime*, 5 January 1957, 3.

Shabad, Theodore. "Moscow Revives Yiddish Theater: First Professional Jewish Play in 15 Years Is Put On." *New York Times*, 14 February 1963, 4.

———. "Soviet Dooms 3 for Speculations." *New York Times*, 31 August 1963, 3.

———. "Soviet to Execute 6 as Speculators: 9 Others Get Prison Terms." *New York Times*, 24 October 1962, 7.

———. "Soviet's Only Yiddish Paper Expands Circulation 12-Fold." *New York Times*, 22 January 1967, 17.

———. "Surprises Greet Visitor to Vilna: Yiddish Paper on Newsstand—Shops Are Attractive." *New York Times*, 26 June 1965, 6.

Shaginian, Marietta. "Vsemirnaia vystavka v Brussele." *Izvestiia*, 3 September 1958, 6.

Shakhnovich, Mikhail I. "Pravda o sovremennom iudaizme." *Agitator* 23 (1963): 52–54.

———. *Reaktsionnaia sushchnost' iudaizma.* Moscow: Nauka, 1960.

Shamovich, Evgeniia. "Kontserty Anny Guzik." *Teatr* 8 (1956): 183.

Shapiro, Henry. "End of an Era: Case of Nine Doctors." *Christian Science Monitor*, 23 January 1954, 5.

Shapiro, Leon. "Soviet Jewry since the Death of Stalin: A Twenty-Five Year Perspective." *American Jewish Year Book* 79 (1979): 77–103.

———. "Soviet Union." *American Jewish Year Book* 58 (1957): 309–17.

———. "Soviet Union." *American Jewish Year Book* 59 (1958): 316–24.

———. "Soviet Union." *American Jewish Year Book* 60 (1959): 208–14.

———. "Soviet Union." *American Jewish Year Book* 61 (1960): 257–64.

———. "Soviet Union." *American Jewish Year Book* 64 (1963): 350–58.

———. "Soviet Union." *American Jewish Year Book* 65 (1964): 266–77.

———. "Soviet Union." *American Jewish Year Book* 69 (1968): 491–503.

Shapiro, Leonard. "Russia's New Pogrom." *Sunday Times*, 15 April 1962, 6.

Sharples, Caroline. "In Pursuit of Justice: Debating the Statute of Limitations of Justice for Nazi Crimes in Britain and West Germany during the 1960s." *Holocaust Studies* 20, no. 3 (2015): 81–108.

Shayduk-Immerman, Olesya. "Feeling Alive: Unofficial Jewish Practices in the USSR in the 1970s and 1980s." PhD diss., University of California, Berkeley, 2019.

Shchur, Iurii. "Arkhivy KGB: Kak zaporozhskie 'chekisty' na 'sionistskuiu' poemu okhotilis'." 9 April 2018. https://zp.depo.ua.Shefner, Borekh. "A nayer un alter grus fun Birobidzhan." *Forverts*, 1 June 1954, 25.

Sheinin, Lev. "Tragediia obmanutykh." *Literaturnaia gazeta*, 29 October 1957, 4.

Sheldon, Richard. "Neither Yevtushenko nor Shostakovich Should Be Blamed." *New York Times*, 25 August 1985, 20.

———. "The Transformation of Babi Yar." In *Soviet Society and Culture: Essays in Honor of Vera S. Dunham*, edited by Terry L. Thompson and Richard Sheldon, 124–61. Boulder, CO: Westview, 1988.

Shentalinsky, Vitaly. "Babel: Lies, Confessions and Denials." *Index on Censorship* 8 (1991): 32–37.

Shepard, Richard F. "TV: Soviet Poet Heard: Yevtushenko, on Channel 4, Discusses 'Babi Yar,' Work on Anti-Semitism." *New York Times*, 12 May 1962, 51.

Sherman, George. "Jewish Solidarity a Shock for Russians." *The Observer*, 22 September 1957, 4.

Sherry, Samantha. *Discourses of Regulation and Resistance: Censoring Translation in the Stalin and Khrushchev Era Soviet Union*. Edinburgh: Edinburgh University Press, 2015.

Shevelev, Dmitrii. "Iz istorii evreiskikh akademicheskikh podrazdelenii v Belorusskoi Sovetskoi Sotsialisticheskoi Respublike v 1920-kh—nachale 1940-kh gg." In *Sovetskaia iudaika: Istoriia, problematika, personalii*, edited by M. Kupovetsky, 72–81. Jerusalem/Moscow: Gesharim/Mosty kul'tury, 2017.Shilovskii, M. B. "Obshchestvenno-politicheskaia situatsiia v Novosibirskom gosudarstvennom universitete v 1960–1967 gg." *Vestnik NGU: Istoriia, filologiia* 6, no. 1 (2007): 105–7.

Shifman, Mikhail A., ed. You Failed Your Math Test, Comrade Einstein. Singapore: World Scientific Publishing, 2005.

Shipman, Alexa R. "The German Experiment: Health Care without Female or Jewish Doctors." *International Journal of Women's Dermatology* 3, no. 1, supplement (2017): 518–20.

Shmeruk, Khone. "Yiddish Publications in the U.S.S.R.: From the Late Thirties to 1948." *Yad Vashem Studies on the European Jewish Catastrophe and Resistance* 4 (1960): 99–133.

———. "Yidishe kultur in ratn-farband: Geshikhte un perspektivn." *Di goldene keyt* 76 (1972): 144–45.

Shmulevitsh, Yitshak. "Di benkshaft fun Mark Rakovski." *Forverts*, 27 February 1959, 8.

———. "Hunderter 'farshvundene' yidn fun Vilne hobn zikh itst plutsling opgezukht." *Forverts*, 31 August 1957, 3.

Shneer, David. "Eberhard Rebling, Lin Jaldati, and Yiddish Music in East Germany, 1949–1962." In *Dislocated Memories: Jews, Music, and Postwar German Culture*, edited by Lily E. Hirsch and Tina Frühauf, 161–86. Oxford: Oxford University Press, 2014.

———. "A Study in Red: Jewish Scholarship in the 1920s Soviet Union." *Science in Context* 20, no. 2 (2007): 197–213.

Shnitman-McMillin, Svetlana. "Stanovlenie pisatelia Georgiia Vladimova, ili istoriia o tom, kak Zhora Volocevich na sebia donosy pisal." *Znamia* 1 (2019): 135–42.

"The Sholom Aleichem Centenary." *Jews in Eastern Europe* 1 (1959): 24.

Shoshkes, Khaim [Henry]. *Tsvishn yidn in vayte lender.* Tel Aviv: Ha-Menorah, 1964.

Shraga, N. "Some Yiddish Spoken Again in Russia." *Jerusalem Post*, 22 May 1959, 1.

———. "Soviet Jew Gets Ph.D. for Thesis on Jewish Subjects." *Jerusalem Post*, 22 June 1965, 3.

———. "Soviet Jewish Writers' Memoirs." *Jerusalem Post*, 21 October 1960, 11.

Shrayer, Maxim. *An Anthology of Jewish-Russian Literature: Two Centuries of Dual Identity in Prose and Poetry*. New York: Routledge, 2015.

Shternshis, Anna. "Salo on Challah: Soviet Jews' Experience of Food in the 1920s–1950s." In *Jews and Their Foodways*, edited by Anat Helman, 10–27. New York: Oxford University Press, 2015.

———. "White Piano in a Shtetl: Material Culture and Ethnic Identity in the Post–Soviet Jewish Urban Community." *Jewish Social Studies* 16, no. 2 (2010): 111–26.

Shulman, Abraham. "Sovetish-yidisher general zogt foroys untergang fun rusishe yidn." *Forverts*, 25 December 1959, 2.

Shuvaeva-Petrosian, Elena. "O. E. Mandel'shtam: Armianskii tekst." In *Istoriia i politika*, 151–59. Stepanakert, Azerbaijan: Dzhizak Plius, 2020.

Sicher, Efraim. *Babel' in Context: A Study in Cultural Identity*. Boston: Academic Studies Press, 2012.

Sidorova, Galina P. "Massovaia literatura i chitatel'skie predpochteniia 1960-kh godov—nachala 1980-kh gg." *Sotsiologicheskie issledovaniia* 2 (2011): 128–36.

Silber, Marcos. "'Immigrants from Poland Want to Go Home': The Politics of Return Migration and Nation Building in 1950s Israel." *Journal of Israeli History* 27, no. 2 (2008): 201–19.

Simkin, Lev. "Death Sentence despite the Law: A Secret 1962 Crimes-against-Humanity Trial in Kiev." *Holocaust and Genocide Studies* 27, no. 2 (2013): 299–312.

Sinel'nikov, Mikhail. "Zhizni vopreki. . . ." *Literaturnaia gazeta*, 12 November 1964, 3.

Singer, Bernard. "State Not Dead, but Is Dying." *Jewish Advocate*, 10 May 1951, 22.

Singer, Isaac Bashevis. "Sholem Aleichem: Spokesman for People." *New York Times*, 20 September 1964, 11.

Sirota, Motl. "Vospominaniia: Zapiski aktera." *Lekhaim* 7 (2008): 37.

Sirotin, Aleksandr. "Emil' Gorovets—pasynok svoego vermeni." https://www.chayka.org.

"Six Aged Soviet Jews Arrive in Israel." *Daily News Bulletin of the Jewish Telegraphic Agency*, 9 December 1954, 2.

Skoczylas, Elehie. *The Realities of Soviet Anti-Semitism*. Philadelphia: Foreign Policy Research Institute, University of Pennsylvania, 1965.

"Skouras Hammers at Yanks for Frigid Stance on Moscow Festival; Calls It Serious Error in Judgement." *Variety*, 26 August 1959, 4, 13.

Skrebneva, T. V. "Muzhskoi imennik viteblian 2-oi poloviny XX veka: Dinamicheskii aspekt." In *Belaruskaia mova i literatura u slavianskim etnakul'turnym kantekstse*, 120–22. Vitebsk, Belarus: Vitebsk State University, 2010.

Skrzypek, Andrzej. "O drugiej repatriacji Polaków z ZSRR (1954–1959)." *Kwartalnik Historyczny* 98, no. 4 (1991): 63–74.

Skvortsova, S. I. "Knigi evreiskoi traditsii kontsa XIX—nachala XX vekov v fondakh muzeia." In *Birobidzhanskii proekt: Opyt mezhnatsional'nogo vzaimodeistviia*, edited by Valerii S. Gurevich et al., 78–83. Birobidzhan, Russia: Government of the Jewish Autonomous Region, 2008.

Slomovitz, Philip. "Purely Commentary: Are Nazis Being Whitewashed? . . . False Philanthropy." *Detroit Jewish News*, 25 March 1960, 2.

Sloves, Khaim. *A shlikhes keyn Moskve*. New York: IKUF, 89–91.

———. *In un arum*. New York: IKUF, 1970.

———. "Sovetish heymland." In *Yidishe dialogn: Asifes fun yidishn velt-kongres*, edited by Moyshe Livni, 162–65. Paris: Cultural Department of World Jewish Congress, 1968.

———. *Sovetishe yidishe melukheshkayt*. Paris: H. Sloves, 1979.

Smilovitsky, Leonid. "Byelorussian Jewry and the 'Doctors' Plot." *East European Jewish Affairs* 27, no. 2 (1997): 39–52.

Smirnov, K. "Provokatsionnaia vydumka amerikanskoi propagandy." *Izvestiia*, 21 February 1959, 4.

———. "Zaokeanskaia chernaia sotnia: Razgul antisemitizma v SShA." *Izvestiia*, 18 May 1963, 5.

Smith, Hedrick. *The Russians*. New York: Times Books, 1983.

Smolar, Boris. "Communism, Pensions and Inter-Marriage Keep Jews in Poland." *The Sentinel*, 13 December 1962, 13.

———. "Russia Today." *Jewish Advocate*, 2 January 1969, 7.

Smolar, Hersh. *Oyf der letster pozitsye mit der letster hofenung*. Tel Aviv: I. L. Peretz Farlag, 1982.

———. "Zikhroynes fun gevezene redaktorn fun yidish tsaytungen in Poyln." In *Yahadut Berit-ha-mo'atsot ba-aspaklaryah shel 'itonut yidish be-Polin*, edited by Mordechai Altshuler, 33–39. Jerusalem: Hebrew University, 1975.

Smolkin, Rafail. *Kniga zhizni*. Montreal: Accent Graphics Communications, 2016.

Snapkovskii, Vladimir E. *Put' Belarusi v OON, 1944–1945 gg*. Minsk: Navuka i tekhnika, 1994.

"Soglashenie mezhdu Pravitel'stvom Soiuza Sovetskikh Sotsialisticheskikh Respublik i Pravitel'stvom Pol'skoi Narodnoi Respubliki o srokakh i poriadke dal'neishei repatriatsii iz SSSR lits pol'skoi natsional'nosti." *Pravda*, 20 March 1956, 3.

Solodukho, Iuli [Iudel]. *Soviet Views of Talmudic Judaism*. Edited by J. Neusner. Leiden: Brill, 1973.

Soloveichik, Meir Y. "What We Need to Remember." *Commentary*, April 2020, 11–12.

Solzhenitsyn, Alexander. *Bodalsia telenok s dubom: Ocherki literaturnoi zhizni*. Moscow: Soglasie, 1996.

"Some Soviet Jews Free to Worship." *New York Times*, 8 August 1956, 2.

"Soobshchenie Ispolnitel'nogo komiteta Soiuza obshchestv Krasnogo Kresta i Krasnogo Polumesiatsa SSSR." *Izvestiia*, 14 July 1957, 6.

"Sovet-shrayber dermont tsum ershtn mol yidn zaynen geven natsishe hoypt karbobes." *Forverts*, 27 April 1962, 8.

"Sovetskaia sotsialisticheskaia zakonnost' neprikosnovenna." *Izvestiia*, 7 April 1953, 1.

"Sovetsko-pol'skoe soglashenie o repatriatsii iz SSSR lits pol'skoi natsional'nosti vstupilo v silu." *Pravda*, 11 July 1957, 4.

"Soviet Anti-Semitism: An Exchange." *Commentary*, January 1965, 35–37.

"Soviet Attitudes." *Jewish Chronicle*, 23 January 1959, 16.

"Soviet Ban Lifted on Two Jewish Books." *American Jewish Week*, 14 August 1959, 16.

"Soviet Concessions." *Jewish Chronicle*, 6 March 1959, 36.

"Soviet Deporting of Jews Reported." *New York Times*, 9 November 1956, 18.

"Soviet Dooms Head of Currency Ring." *New York Times*, 13 December 1961, 47.

"Soviet Jewish Culture." *Jews in Eastern Europe* 3, no. 6 (1967): 38–40.

"Soviet Jews Going from Poland to Israel." *Morgn-Frayhayt*, 11 August 1957, 15.

"Soviet Kidnapping Stirs Israel." *Jewish Advocate*, 19 September 1957, 1.

"Soviet Party Rift Hinted in Conflict over Poet Ouster." *Christian Science Monitor*, 11 May 1957, 15.

"Soviet Plan to Begin Publishing Yiddish Writers after Ten Years." *The Sentinel*, 26 February 1959, 3.

"Soviet Staff Study: The Soviet Writer and Soviet Cultural Policy." 15 September 1959, CIA Archive, document no. 5077054e993247d4d82b6ac0, approved for release June 2007.

"Soviet Tourists Attack Israel." *Jewish Advocate*, 21 August 1958, 5.

"Soviet Union." *Jewish Observer: A Periodical Survey of Events Affecting Jews in the Soviet Bloc* 4 (March 1959): 5.

"Sovmestnoe zaiavlenie v sviazi s peregovorami mezhdu Delegatsiei TsK KPSS i Pravitel'stva Sovetskogo Soiuza i Delegatsiei TsK PORP i Pravitel'stva Pol'skoi Narodnoi Respubliki." *Pravda*, 19 November 1956, 1.

Speranskaia, A. N. "Obshchestvennaia reaktsiia na 'delo vrachei' (na materialakh Cheliabinskoi oblasti)." *Vestnik IuUrGU: Sotsial'no-gumanitarnye nauki* 19, no. 2 (2019): 68–72.

Sperber, Manès. *Être juif.* Paris: Odole Jacob, 1994.

Speech of Nikita Khrushchev before a Closed Session of the XXth Congress of the Communist Party of the Soviet Union on February 25, 1956. Washington, DC: U.S. Government Printing Office, 1957.

Spiegel, Irving. "Jews' Resettling by Soviet Is Seen: U.S. Group Says Moscow May Develop Birobidzhan under 7-Year Plan." *New York Times*, 11 January 1959, 2.

———. "Mikoyan Denies Exiling of Jews." *New York Times*, 16 January 1959, 1.

Srebrnik, Henry F. *Dreams of Nationhood: American Jewish Communists and the Soviet Birobidzhan Project, 1924–1951.* Boston: Academic Studies Press, 2010.

Stacy, Robert H. *Russian Literary Criticism: A Short History.* Syracuse, NY: Syracuse University Press, 1974.

"Stalin's Views on Jews Revealed in Records of Yalta Conference." *Daily News Bulletin of the Jewish Telegraphic Agency*, 18 March 1955, 4.

Stankowski, Albert. "How Many Polish Jews Survived the Holocaust?" In *Jewish*

Presence in Absence: The Aftermath of the Holocaust in Poland, 1944–2010, edited by Feliks Tych *et al.* Jerusalem: Yad Vashem, 2014.

Starikov, Dmitri. "Neobkhodimye utochneniia." *Literaturnaia gazeta*, 10 April 1958, 2.

"Statements of Cde. N. S. Khrushchev at a CPSU CC Presidium Meeting, 25 April 1963." 25 April 1963, Wilson Center, Digital Archive: International History Declassified. http://digitalarchive.wilsoncenter.org.

The Status of the Jews behind the Iron Curtain: What the Delegation of the Rabbinical Council of America Found in Its Survey inside Russia and the Satellite Nations. New York: New York Journal American, n.d.

Stein, Jay W. "The Soviet Intelligentsia." *Russian Review* 10, no. 4 (1951): 283–92.

"Stenogramma zasedaniia Pravleniia izdatel'stva Sovetskii pisatel'." 6 July 1963, Russian State Archive of Literature and Art, f. 1234, op. 19, ed. khr. 60.

"Stenogramma zasedaniia sekretariata." 29 November 1962, Russian State Archive of Literature and Art, *f.* 631, *op.* 30, *ed. khr.* 952.

Stepanchikova, Tetiana. "L'vivs'kyi evreis'kyi derzhavnyi teatr (1939–1941)." *Visnyk L'vivs'koho universitetu* 3 (2003): 35–51.

Stiazhkina, Olena. "Sated People: Gendered Modes of Acquiring and Consuming Prestigious Soviet Foods." In *Seasoned Socialism: Gender and Food in Late Soviet Everyday Life*, edited by Anastasia Lakhtikova, Angela Brintlinger, and Irina Glushchenko, 132–64. Bloomington: Indiana University Press, 2019.

Stola, Dariusz. "Opening a Non-Exit State: The Passport Policy of Communist Poland, 1949–1980." *East European Politics and Societies and Cultures* 29, no. 1 (2015): 96–119.

———. "Patterns of the Evolution of the Communist Regime: The Case of International Mobility from Poland." *Divinatio* 42–43 (2016): 121–85.

Stončius, Justas. "Anti-Semitism in Soviet Lithuania in the Period 1944–1990: Summary of Doctoral Dissertation." Klaipeda University, 2018.

———. "Vil'niusskoe Delo Valiutchikov. 1962 g.: Antisemitizm v Sovetskoi Litve." *Tirosh: Studies in Judaica* 17 (2018): 186–97.

Stravinskienė, Vitalija. "Sovietinis saugumas ir repatriacija iš Lietuvos į Lenkiją (1956–1959)." *Lituanistica* 55, no. 1–2 (2009): 26–37.

Stupples, Peter. "Il'ya Erenburg and the Jewish Anti-Fascist Committee." *New Zealand Slavonic Journal* 2 (1933): 13–28.

Suller, Chaim. "Eyewitness Report on Jewish Culture in the Soviet Union." *Daily Worker*, 31 August 1956, 6.

———. "Jewish Culture in the USSR Today: Another Look One Year Later." *The New Leader*, 14 September 1959, 12.

Sullivan, Ed. "Our Visit to Moscow." *Daily News*, 10 August 1959, 37.

Surovtseva, Ekaterina V. "'Dorogoi Nikita Sergeevich': Pis'ma I. G. Erenburga N. S. Khrushchevu." In *Nauka i obrazovanie: Sokhraniaia proshloe, cozdaem budushchee*, edited by German Iu. Guliaev, 81–86. Penza, Russia: Nauka i prosveshchenie, 2018.

Sutyrin, Vladimir A. "Dokladnaia zapiska v Sekretariat Pravleniia Soiuza pisatelei

SSSR o zhurnale 'Sovetish geimland'." Russian State Archive of Literature and Art, *f.* 3107, *op.* 1, *ed. khr.* 244.

Sutzkever, Abraham. "Encounters with Russian Jewish Writers." *Jewish Advocate*, 11 September 1958, 11C.

Svet, Gershon. "Kontsert Valentiny Levko." *Novoe russkoe slovo*, 28 April 1966. 3.

Szaynok, Bożena. *Poland-Israel, 1944–1968: In the Shadow of the Past and of the Soviet Union*. Warsaw: Institute of National Remembrance Commission for the Prosecution of Crimes against the Polish Nation, 2012.

Tal, Sidi. "Mne 47 let: Zhin', rabota, gastroli, roli." 8 September 1959. http://sidi-tal.blogspot.com/p/blog-page_16.html.

Tannenbaum, Michal, and Orly Haim. "Journeys to a New Homeland: Language and Identity in the Poetry of Alexander Penn and Nathan Alterman." *Journal of Modern Jewish Studies* 3 (2007): 273–87.

Tanny, Jarrod. City of Rogues and Schnorrers: Russia's Jews and the Myth of Old Odessa. Bloomington: Indiana University Press, 2011.

Tarasevych, Roman. "The 'Second' Repatriation of the Poles in Stanislav Region (1956–1959)." Skhid 4 (2020): 15-20.

Taylor, Pauline B. "Sectarians in Soviet Courts." *Russian Review* 24, no. 3 (1965): 278–88.

"Teatr dramy i komedii." *Entsiklopediia Sankt-Peterburga*. https://my-dict.ru.

Teif, Moyshe [Moisei]. "Di balade vegn Ane Frank." *Folks-Shtime*, 24 December 1960, 4.

———. *Rukopozhatie*. Moscow: Sovetskii pisatel, 1964.

Teller, Judd L. "Exit of Jews to Siberia Hinted." *Christian Science Monitor*, 5 January 1959, 4.

"Tesnee splotimsia vokrug partii." *Literaturnaia gazeta*, 7 March 1953, 8.

Thayer, Robert H. "Cultural Diplomacy: Seeing Is Believing." *Vital Speeches of the Day* 25, no. 24 (1959): 740–44.

Timoshkina, Alisa. "Representations of the Holocaust in Soviet Cinema." PhD diss., King's College London, 2014.

Tippner, Anja. "Conflicting Memories, Conflicting Stories: Masha Rol'nikaite's Novel and the Soviet Culture of Holocaust Remembrance." *East European Jewish Affairs* 48, no. 3 (2018): 372–90.

———. "The Writings of a Soviet Anne Frank? Masha Rol'nikaite's Holocaust Memoir *I Have to Tell* and Its Place in Soviet Literature." *Search and Research: Lectures and Series* 19 (2013): 59–80.

Tishkov, S. V., R. R. Alaberdeev, and Iu. V. Latov. "Istoriia bor'by v SSSR s khishcheniiami sotsialisticheskoi sobstvennosti." *Istoriko-ekonomicheskie issledovaniia* 8, no. 1 (2007): 51–80.

Tiurina, L. "Chto novogo na Brodvee." *Ogonek*, 20 May 1956, 20.

Tokarev, Sergei A. *Etnografiia narodov SSSR: Istoricheskie osnovy byta i kul'tury*. Moscow: Moscow State University Press, 1958.

Toker, Leona. "The Holocaust in Russian Literature." In *The Literature of the Holocaust*, edited by Alan Rosen, 118–30. Cambridge: Cambridge University Press, 2013.

Toleikis, Vytautas, and Mark Belcher. "Repress, Reassess, Remember: Jewish Heritage in Lithuania." *Osteuropa* 58, no. 8/10 (2008): 279–87.

Tolts, Mark. "Aliya from the Russian Federation: An Analysis of Recent Data." Jews in Eastern Europe 1-2. (2002): 5-23.

———. "Demograficheskii portret evreev Azerbaidzhana." *Diaspory* 1 (2013): 131–57.

———. "Demographic Trends among the Jews in the Three Slavic Republics of the Former USSR: A Comparative Analysis." In *Papers in Jewish Demography 1993*, edited by Sergio DellaPergola and Judith Even, 147–75. Jerusalem: Hebrew University, 1997.

———. "The Jews in Georgia in the Late Soviet Period: A Demographic Profile." In *Studies in Caucasian, Georgian, and Bukharan Jewry: Historical, Sociological and Cultural Aspects*, edited by Golda Akhiezer, Reuven Enoch, and Sergei Weinstein, 102–16.

Ariel, Israel: Ariel University, 2013.

———. "Mixed Marriage and Post-Soviet Aliyah." In *Jewish Intermarriage around the World*, edited by Shulamit Reinharz and Sergio DellaPergola, 89–104. New Brunswick, NJ: Transaction, 2009.

Tomilin, V. "Pepel stuchit v serdtse." *Izvestiia*, 30 January 1963, 4.

Tomoff, Kiril. *Creative Union: The Professional Organization of Soviet Composers, 1939–1953*. Ithaca, NY: Cornell University Press, 2018.

Towpik, Witold. "Repatriacja Polaków z ZSRR na Ziemię Lubuską w latach, 1955–1959—kategorie repatriantów." *Rocznik Lubuski* 31, no. 2 (2005): 137–53.

Trekhina, Maria. "Posmertnaia kul'turnaia reabilitatsiia Isaaka Babelia: Zachem pisateliu novyi obraz?" In *Literatura i władza Związki na gruncie rosyjskim w XVIII-XXI wieku*, edited by Magdalena Dąbrowska, Piotr Głuszkowski, and Katarzyna Roman-Rawska, 113–28.

Warsaw: Instytut Rusycystyki Uniwersytetu Warszawskiego, 2017.

Tromly, Benjamin. *Making the Soviet Intelligentsia: Universities and Intellectual Life under Stalin and Khrushchev*. Cambridge: Cambridge University Press, 2015.

Troyanovsky, Oleg A. *Cherez gody i rasstoianiia: istoriia odnoi sem'i*. Moscow: Tsentrpoligraf, 2017.

Tsanin, Mordechai. "Tsen yor 'Sovetish heymland'." *Di Letste Nayes*, 24 September 1971, 3.

Tsepliovich, Grigorii. *Razgovor s samim soboi*. Israel, 1991.

Tsvibel', Dmitrii. *Ot Stantsii Zima k Bab'emu Iaru: Evreiskie obertony tvorchestva Evtushenko*. Petrozavodsk, Russia: PIN, 2008.

Tukhovskaia, Olga. "Kishinevskii evreiskii narodnyi teatr (1966–1971) v kul'turnoi zhizni polietnichnogo goroda." *Ava*, 8 September 2011. https://ava.md.

Tulchinsky, Gerald. "Family Quarrel: Joe Salsberg, the 'Jewish' Question, and Canadian Communism." *Labour/Le Travail* 56 (2005): 149–73.

Tul'tseva, L. A. "The Evolution of Old Russian Sectarianism (on Data from Voronezh Oblast)." *Soviet Sociology* 16, 1 (1977): 20–48.

Tulviste, Peeter. "History Taught at School versus History Discovered at Home: The

Case of Estonia." *European Journal of Psychology of Education* 9, no. 2 (1994): 121–26.

Turkow Kaminska, Ruth. *I Don't Want to Be Brave Anymore.* Washington, DC: New Republic Books, 1978. "Ukaz Prezidiuma Verkhovnogo Soveta o nagrazhdenii pisatelia Erenburga I. G. ordenom Lenina." *Izvestiia*, 25 January 1961, 1.

"USSR Yiddish Culture." *Jewish Advocate*, 19 September 1957, 2.

Vagarshian, Laert. *Kinopanorama mira.* Yerevan: Aipetrat, 1961.

Vail, Petr, and Aleksander Genis. *60-e: Mir sovetskogo cheloveka.* Moscow: Novoe literaturnoe obozrenie, 1998.

Vaisman, Asia. "Sidi Tal' i evreiskaia kul'tura v Chenovtsakh 1940–1980 godov." In *Idish: Iazyk i kul'tura v Sovetskom Soiuze*, edited by Leonid Katsis, Mariia Kaspina, and David Fishman, 301–11. Moscow: Russian State University for the Humanities, 2009.

Vasil'kov, V., A. M. Grishina, and F. F. Perchenok. "Repressirovannoe vostokovedenie: Vostokovedy, podvergshiesia repressiiam v 20–50-e gody." *Narody Azii i Afriki* 4 (1990): 113–24.

"Vecher, posviashchennyi Sholom-Aleikhemu." *Literaturnaia gazeta*, 15 May 1956, 3.

Veidlinger, Jeffrey. "The Pen and the Sword: The Wartime Plays of Peretz Markish." In *A Captive of the Down: The Life and Work of Peretz Markish*, edited by Joseph Sherman et al., 157–71. Oxford: Legenda, 2011.

———. "Was the Doctors' Plot a Blood Libel?" In *Ritual Murder in Russia, Eastern Europe, and Beyond: New Histories of an Old Accusation*, edited by Eugene M. Avrutin, Jonathan Dekel-Chen, and Robert Weinberg, 238–52. Bloomington: Indiana University Press, 2017.Vergelis, Aron. "Di goldene keyt fun der yidisher literature." *Sovetish Heymland* 4 (1963): 101–12.

———. *Di tsayt.* Moscow: Sovetskii pisatel, 1981.

———. "Ekzotishe tayge." *Birobidzhaner Shtern*, 11 September 1960, 4.

———. "Esli by zhil Sholom-Aleikhem." *Literaturnaia gazeta*, 14 January 1960, 4.

———. "Jews in the Soviet Union." *Soviet Weekly*, 13 April 1961, 8.

———. "Literaturnye otshchepentsy." *Literaturnaia gazeta*, 9 August 1959, 4.

———. *On the Jewish Street: Travel Notes.* Moscow: Novosti Press Agency, 1971.

———. *Rayzes.* Moscow: Sovetskii pisatel, 1976.

———. *Shestnadtsat' stran, vkliuchaia Monako: Putevye zametki.* Moscow: Sovetskii pisatel, 1990.

———. "Undzer replik." *Sovetish Heymland* 4 (1987): 128–30.

———. "V partiinoe biuro SSP." *Nash sovremennik* 1 (1999): 209–11.

———. "Vstrecha s Agnonom." *Literaturnaia gazeta*, 19 April 1967, 15.

"Vergelis Was Here." *Bnai Brith Messanger*, 6 December 1963, 36.

"Vergelis zogt, az er fartret nisht dos sovetishe yidntum." *Tog-Morgn-Zhurnal*, 15 November 1963, 1.

"Ves'ma tipichnaia sovetskaia intelligentka." https://zina-korzina.livejournal.com.

Vialiki, Anatol F. *Belarus'—Pol'sha ŭ XX stahoddzi: Neviadomaia repatryiatsyia, 1955–1959 hh.* Minsk: BDPU, 2007.

Vinokur, A. "Ugasanie drevnei very." *Nauka i religiia* 1 (1967): 41–43.

Viola, Lynne. "Antisemitism in the 'Jewish NKVD' in Soviet Ukraine on the Eve of World War II." *Holocaust and Genocide Studies* 34, no. 3 (2020): 393–408.

"The Visit to Khabarovsk and Birobidzhan of Israeli Ambassador to Moscow Yosef Avidar and His Wife, Yemima Tchernovitz (1956): Excerpt from Yemima's Diary," introduced and annotated by Yaacov Ro'i. In *Mizrekh: Jewish Studies in the Far East*, edited by Ber Boris Kotlerman, 141–70. Frankfurt: Peter Lang, 2009.

"Visitor We Must Suspect." *Jewish Advocate*, 14 November 1963, 8.

"Vital Program in Poland." *Jewish Advocate*, 18 April 1957, 6.

Vladykina, Valeriia. "The Theatre at Moscow University." *Moscow News*, 6 January 1968, 24.

Voinovich, Vladimir. *Povesti i rasskazy*. Moscow: Fabula, 1993.

Volkov, Solomon. *Dialogi s Evgeniem Evtushenko*. Moscow: ACT, 2018.

Voshchinin, Igor S. "Dzhaz. Eskiz portreta slushatelia." In *Natsional'noe kul'turnoe nasledie Rossii: regional'nyi aspekt*, edited by S. V. Solov'eva, 237–48. Samara, Russia: Samara State Institute of Culture, 2019.

"Vovche kublo." *Evrei i evreiskii narod* 3, no. 4 (1963): 37.

Voznesensky, Andrei. *Prozhilki prozy*. Moscow: PROZAiK, 2011.

V. Z. "Proshloe, ne stavshee istoriei." *Literaturnaia gazeta*, 9 March 1957, 4.

Wachsmann, Constanze. *Der sowjetische Heine: Die Heinrich Heine-Rezeption in den russischsprachigen Rezeptionstexten der Sowjetunion (1917–1953)*. Berlin: Weißensee Verlag, 2001.

Walke, Anika. "'To Speak for Those Who Cannot': Masha Rol'nikaite on the Holocaust and Sexual Violence in German-Occupied Soviet Territories." *Jewish History* 33, no. 1–2 (2020): 215–44.

"Warns American Jewry Not to Fall into Trap of Visiting Russian Jew." *The Sentinel*, 14 November 1963, 8.

Wasserstein, Bernard. "Oxford's Poetry Revolution." *Prospect* 142 (January 2008): 54–57.

Wechsler, Harold S. "The Rationale for Restriction: Ethnicity and College Admission in America, 1910–1980." *American Quartely* 36, no. 5 (1984): 643–47.

Weinberg, Robert. "Jewish Revival in Birobidzhan in the Mirror of *Birobidzhanskaya zvezda*, 1946–49." *East European Jewish Affairs* 26, no. 1 (1996): 35–53.

———. "Purge and Politics in the Periphery: Birobidzhan in 1937." *Slavic Review* 52, no. 1 (1993): 13–27.

Weiner, Amir. *Making Sense of War: The Second World War and the Fate of the Bolshevik Revolution*. Princeton, NJ: Princeton University Press, 2002.

Weingartner, James J. "Michael C. Astour: A Biographical Essay." 21 May 2015, SIUE Faculty Research, Scholarship, and Creative Activity, 2. http://spark.siue.edu.Weinreich, Uriel. *College Yiddish: An Introduction to the Yiddish Language and to Jewish Life and Culture*. New York: YIVO, 1984.

"What Soviet Citizens Talk about the Press Tales of 'Anti-Semitism.'" *Daily Worker*, 19 January 1953, 3.

Wiesel, Elie. *The Jews of Silence*. Philadelphia: Jewish Publication Society of America, 1966.

Wiesel, Elie. *The Testament*. New York: Schocken Books, 1981.
Wiesel, Elie, and Irving Abrahamson. Against Silence: The Voice and Vision of Elie Wiesel. New York: Holocaust Library, 1985.
Windt, Theodore Otto Jr. "The Rhetoric of Peaceful Coexistence: Khrushchev in America, 1959." *Quarterly Journal of Speech* 57, no. 1 (1971): 11–22.
Winston, Victor H. "Reflections on the Anticipated Mass Deportation of Soviet Jews." *Post-Soviet Affairs* 31, no. 6 (2015): 471–90.
"World Reaction—Soviet Confusion: Western Communists Join in Protests." *Jews in Eastern Europe: A Periodical Survey of Events Affecting Jews in the Soviet Bloc* 2, no. 5 (1964): 24–34.
Yakub, Z. "Der yidisher dramatisher kolektiv in Dvinsk." *Folks-Shtime*, 20 December 1956, 3.
Yanasowicz, Itzhak. *Mit yidishe shrayber in Rusland*. Buenos Aires: Kiem, 1959.
Yekelchyk, Serhy. *Stalin's Empire of Memory: Russian-Ukrainian Relations in the Soviet Historical Imagination*. Toronto: Toronto University Press, 2014.
"Yevtushenko Thanked for Poem." *Jewish Advocate*, 27 September 1962, 18.
"Yiddish Theatre to Reopen in Moscow in '57." *Daily Worker*, 19 September 1956, 7.
Yodfat, Aryeh. "Jewish Religious Communities in the USSR." *East European Jewish Affairs* 1, no. 2 (1971): 61–67.
Young, Glennys. "To Russia with 'Spain': Spanish Exiles in the USSR and the Longue Dureé of Soviet History." *Kritika: Explorations in Russian and Eurasian History* 15, no. 2 (2014): 395–419.
"Za dal'neishii rastsvet ukrainskogo sovetskogo muzykal'nogo iskusstva: Na sobranii kompozitorov Kieva." *Pravda Ukrainy*, 19 March 1949, 2.
"Za dal'neishii rastsvet ukrainskoi sovetskoi muzykal'noi kul'tury." *Pravda Ukrainy*, 24 April 1950, 4.
"Za printsipial'nuiu literaturnuiu kritiku." *Literaturnaia gazeta*, 7 July 1951, 3.
"Za vysokuiu ideinost' i khudozhestvennoe masterstvo sovetskoi literatury." *Izvestiia*, 29 March 1963, 3.
"Zakonchilas' pervaia nedelia festivalia." *Sovetskaia kultura*, 11 August 1959, 4.
Zaltzman, Hillel. *Samarkand: The Underground with a Far-Reaching Impact*. New York: Chamah, 2015.
Zand, Michael. "A Reply to Mr. Davies." *New York Times*, 6 December 1971, 39.
"Zapiska G. K. Zhukova v TsK KPSS o prisvoenii general'skikh zvanii riadu reabilitirovannykh voennosluzhashchikh." 29 April 1955, Fond Aleksandra N. Iakovleva. https://www.alexanderyakovlev.org.
Zaslavskii, David. "Diplomat s ulitsy Lilienblum." *Pravda*, 22 September 1957, 3.
Zaslavskii, Ritalii. "Drugoi zhizni u nee ne bylo: Iz vospominanii o Rive Baliasnoi." *Egupets* 3 (1997): 92–99.
Zaslavsky, Victor, and Robert Brym. *Soviet-Jewish Emigration and Soviet Nationality Policy*. London: Macmillan, 1983.
Zaslavsky, Victor, and Yuri Luryi. "The Passport System in the USSR and Changes in Soviet Society." *Soviet Union* 6 (1979): 137–53.

Zelenin, Il'ia E. "Agrarnaia politika N.S. Khrushcheva i sel'skoe khoziaistvo." *Trudy Instituta rossiiskoi istorii RAN* 2 (2000): 394–425.

Zelenina, Galina S. "'Otravlennaia vata' i 'privitaia gipertoniia': Istochniki i funktsii slukhov vokrug 'dela vrachei'." *Antropologicheskii forum* 31 (2016): 119–54.

Zellweger, Edouard. "The Principle of Socialist Legality." *Journal of the International Commission of Jurists* 5, no. 2 (1964): 163–202.

Zeltser, Arkadi. "Tema 'Evrei v Bab'em Iaru' v Sovetskom Soiuze v 1941–1945 godakh." In *Babyn Iar: Masove ubyvstvo i pam'iat' pro n'oho,* edited by Vitalii Nakhmanovich, 83–100. Kyiv: FOP Moskalenko O.M., 2012.

———. *Unwelcome Memory: Holocaust Monuments in the Soviet Union.* Jerusalem: Yad Vashem, 2019.

Zemskov, Viktor N. "GULAG: Istoriko-sotsiologicheskii aspect." *Sotsiologicheskie issledovaniia* 6 (1991): 10–27.

———. "Liudskie poteri SSR v Velikoi Otechestvennoi voine." *Bereginia.777.Sova* 2 (2015): 187–201.

———. "Situatsiia s zakliuchennymi v pervye poslestalinskie gody." *Izvestiia Samarskogo nauchnogo tsentra Rossiiskoi akademii nauk* 16, no. 3 (2014): 130–36.

"Zhit' v mire, razvivat' sotrudnichestvo." *Pravda,* 5 December 1966, 4.

Zhitomirskii, Aleksandr. "U pol'skikh druzei." Soviet Union, 25 October 1958, 4.

Zhukova, Liudmila. "Evrei gorskie (taty)." In *Etnicheskii atlas Uzbekistana,* edited by Alisher Ilkhamov and Liudmila Zhukova, 82. Tashkent: Open Society Institute and Assistance Foundation, 2002.

Zhuravlev, Vladimir N., and Iosif S. Brener. *Kniga pamiati zhertv politicheskikh repressii na territorii Evreiskoi avtonomnoi oblasti.* Birobidzhan, Russia: Birobidzhan, 2011.

Zhuravleva, Olga P. *Istoriia knizhnogo dela v Evreiskoi avtonomnoi oblasti.* Khabarovsk, Russia: Far Eastern Scientific Library, 2008.

———. "Periodicheskaia pechat' Evreiskoi avtonomnoi oblasti (1928–1960gg.)." In *Birobidzhanskii proekt: Opyt mezhnatsional'nogo vzaimodeistviia,* edited by Valerii S. Gurevich et al., 84–91. Birobidzhan, Russia: Government of the JAR, 2008.

Zibert, Natal'ia P. "Polozhenie iudeiskoi obshchiny Omska v kontekste religioznoi politiki gosudarstva vo vtoroi polovine 1940-kh–1960-e gg." *Izvestiia Altaiskogo gosudarstvennogo universiteta: Istoricheskie nauki i arkheologiia* 2 (2020): 34–39.

Zigmonte, Dagnia. "Pamiat'—oruzhie." *Literaturnaia gazeta,* 27 May 1965, 3.

Zimin, Il'ia A. "Gotovil li Stalin deportatsiiu sovetskikh evreev v 1953 godu?" *Istoriia gosudarstva i prava* 15 (2017): 15–17.

Zorin, Leonid G. *Zelenye tetradi.* Moscow: Novoe literaturnoe obozrenie, 1999.

Zorkaia, N., and Iu. Khaiutin. "Shestnadtsat' chasov v sutki." *Literaturnaia gazeta,* 8 August 1959, 1.

Zorza, Victor. "Russia Denies Israeli Diplomatist's Story." *Manchester Guardian,* 23 September 1957, 5.

Zubkova, Elena Iu. *Poslevoennoe sovetskoe obshchestvo: Politika i povsednevnost' 1945–1953.* Moscow: ROSSPEN, 2000.

Zubok, Vladislav. *Zhivago's Children: The Last Russian Intelligentsia*. Cambridge, MA: Harvard University Press, 2009.

Zubov, Andrei B. *Istoriia Rossii, XX vek*. Moscow: ACT, 2009.

Zviagintsev, Aleksandr G. "Groznyi baloven' sud'by, ili po zakonam svoego vremeni." *Soiuz kriminalistov I kriminologov* 3–4 (2014): 383–90.

INDEX

ABOUT THE AUTHOR

GENNADY ESTRAIKH is Professor at New York University. He received his doctorate from the University of Oxford. His fields of expertise are Soviet Jewish history, Jewish intellectual history, and Yiddish language and literature. His most recent monograph is *Transatlantic Russian Jewishness* (2020). He is the recipient of the National Jewish Book Award (2014) for coediting *1929: Mapping the Jewish World.*